Praise for *Boys, A Rescue Plan*

Michael Gurian's new book, *Boys, A Rescue Plan*, written with Sean Kullman, Director of the Global Initiative for Boys and Men, captures the crisis we see among many of our boys and provides solutions proven to work over the last three decades. As a neuroscientist and psychiatrist, I highly recommend this book from the mental health side of the aisle and the parenting and educating sides. This rescue plan is packed with practical neuroscience-based strategies everyone can use immediately.

–Daniel Amen, M.D., *New York Times* Bestselling Author of *Change Your Brain, Change Your Life* and Founder of Amen Clinics.

In my book *The War Against Boys*, published nearly 25 years ago, I showed how boys were languishing academically and socially. Since then, their situation has worsened. I am heartened by this wonderful new book by Kullman and Gurian. *Boys, A Rescue Plan* moves past the politics of masculinity and provides practical, research-based, boy-friendly solutions. The authors speak unabashedly about the male brain, and offer a no-nonsense guide to helping our sons thrive.

–Christina Hoff Sommers, Ph.D., *New York Times* Bestselling Author of *The War Against Boys* and *Freedom Feminism*.

I always look forward to the excellent resources that Dr. Gurian creates and the pages of this book, co-written with Sean Kullman, are filled with an abundance of ideas and practical tools we will be sure to use here at The Center, A Place of Hope. As you read, you will have many moments of insights and find yourself saying, "That is just what I needed!" With two sons of my own, I am passionate about reaching and saving our boys and this is the tool to do just that.

–Dr. Gregory Jantz, Bestselling Author of *The Anxiety Reset*, Co-Author of *Raising Boys by Design*, and Founder of The Center, A Place of Hope.

I have been a supporter of Michael Gurian and the Gurian Institute's work for the better part of twenty years, and I have served with Sean Kullman on the Advisory Board of The Boys Initiative. In *Boys, A Rescue Plan*, the authors have come together to create a rare combination of political call-to-action and practical guide to raising boys in a complex age. As the founding principal of a Christian school for boys, an educator of more than fifty years, and a former member of the Maryland State Board of Education, I highly recommend this book to anyone concerned with the health and welfare of our sons.

–Vermelle Greene, Ph.D., Educational Consultant and Author of *Please Teach Me Like I'm a Boy!*

Michael Gurian has done it again! His new book with Sean Kullman, *Boys, A Rescue Plan*, provides us with a solid template for considering the nature of boys and young men today. Each chapter in the book identifies the target audience, but I would encourage every teacher and every school counselor to keep this treasure of a book at hand. This book makes short work of the negative stereotypes and returns the reader to an awareness and respect for the true nature of boys and men.

–Patricia McGann, Bestselling Author of Steadfast Parenting

I believe *Boys, A Rescue Plan* is **the** book for our times. The research is clear – males are suffering from deaths of despair at rates higher than females. This is not only a tragedy for boys and men, but also for girls and women. Gurian and Kullman bring good science and practical data to help improve the lives of all. This book can help end the battle of the sexes now and forever. Male and female health are different sides of the same coin. As a father of six, grandfather of seventeen, and great grandfather of four, I believe this is a book everyone should read."

–Jed Diamond, Ph.D., Bestselling Author of
The Irritable Male Syndrome and Male Menopause.

One of my favorite boy champions, Michael Gurian, has partnered with Sean Kullman, Director of the Global Initiative for Boys and Men to write a book the world needs: *Boys, A Rescue Plan*. The authors take a deep dive into research, neuroscience, educational statistics, true stories and the blatant loss of boys and men's lives to show why we cannot continue to ignore our boy crisis in the Western world. Michael and Sean don't just explore the why, they offer practical solutions that will improve the health and well-being of future generations and will not diminish the health and well-being of girls. This book has the potential of changing our world for the better, and we sure need it.

–Maggie Dent, Bestselling Author of
Mothering Our Boys and From Boys to Men

Boys, A Rescue Plan emphasizes the unique needs of boys in an environment where their male difference is grossly underappreciated, suppressed, and ignored. Sean Kullman and Michael Gurian address this hole in our culture by focusing on the negative outcomes of boys which have too often and facilely been attributed to their socialization in the patriarchy and toxic masculinity. After showing us how the outcomes show up in families, schools, and other social institutions and in male mental health, the authors describe ways to help boys, emphasizing how their uniqueness can be used to raise them to nurture their health and wholeness for contributing to society.

–Paul Golding, Ph.D., Founder, Santa Fe Boys Educational Foundation

In *Boys, A Rescue Plan,* Sean Kullman and Michael Gurian explore the myriad challenges facing today's boys while offering practical strategies to address them. Informed by neuroscience, clinical methodology, and good educational practice, the authors expose the flaws of politically driven ideologies that erroneously downplay sex differences, acknowledge issues affecting males disproportionately, and offer workable solutions for parents, educators, and policymakers. Predicated upon compelling, data-driven evidence, *Boys, A Rescue Plan* counters cultural narratives that too often – whether naively or willfully – ignore the stark reality that boys and men are in crisis

–Paul Cumbo, Author of *A Path to Manhood* and
Principal/Co-Founder of the Camino Institute.

Boys, A Rescue Plan could not have come at a more significant time in our history. Filling this book with science-based research, wisdom, compassion, and real-life stories, Kullman and Gurian peel back the confusion over masculinity and the current state of boyhood to offer a new vision for helping boys thrive. Read this book and discover hope for the boys you love.

–Tim Wright, Lutheran Pastor and Bestselling Author of
the *Adventures of Toby Baxter* series of young adult books.

Why do many boys and men fail to thrive in America? In their fascinating new book, *Boys, A Rescue Plan,* Michael Gurian and Sean Kullman help readers understand the crisis, its complex causes, and practical strategies for solving the problem. As a man, a father, and a soon-to-be grandfather of a boy, I found myself on a surprising journey of self-awareness as I turned each page. By the time I finished the book, I had tucked away a cache of tools, information, numerous resources (some for my son) and, most of all, hope for our boys.

–J. E. Tobin, Ph.D., author of *When We Were Wolves*
and *Triple Divide*

Boys, A Rescue Plan is an important work detailing the boy/male crisis with well-researched information in key areas of concern. The emphasis on science and brain sex differences is particularly compelling. Most importantly, the authors offer concrete solutions emphasizing steps that can be taken that have proven successful results.

–Philip W. Cook, Author of *Abused Men* and former broadcast journalist.

Having lost a son to suicide, I understand the urgency of addressing the current crisis affecting our boys. *Boys, A Rescue Plan* offers essential guidance and hope for those striving to protect our young men.

–Kimber Erickson, co-founder of The Kellen Cares Foundation.

Boys, A Rescue Plan is a tremendously important book in helping us better understand how we can help raise our boys while recognizing the key differences between the sexes and what specific needs boys have. Encouraging the reader to become a "citizen scientist," authors Gurian and Kullman envision a culture of true understanding beyond the politicization that has encumbered our support of boys in recent decades. *Boys, A Rescue Plan* is a must-read for anyone involved in education, raising of boys, and policy.

–Mark W. Sutton, author of *How Democrats Can Win Back Men*

Boys, A Rescue Plan is a captivating look at dimensions of male nature and nurture, illuminating endemic cultural bias, promulgated through public policy and funding choices, starkly highlighting reasons for many of the outcomes we see today. As a lawmaker working with colleagues to create a commission for boys and men, I have experienced the challenges our boys are facing in school and the devastating outcomes parents and grandparents are seeing in the addiction, overdose, and suicide deaths of our sons. Sean Kullman and Michael Gurian address male and female differences with compelling data points, beautifully written stories from their experiences in teaching and counseling, and practical solutions to help our boys in school and life. I highly recommend *Boys, A Rescue Plan* for any parent and policymaker who wants to help our communities heal, grow, and thrive.

–Representative Mary Dye, Washington State sponsor of

The Washington Commission on the Status of Boys and Men Bill

I have worked with Michael Gurian and the Gurian Institute for seven years to provide professional development and consulting on sex/gender and racial sensitivity. As I became an Administrative Coordinator of Instruction (ACI) for the Black Student Achievement Plan in the Los Angeles Unified School District, this work became even more relevant. Now it continues with increased vigor since I retired from the District. In developing and providing GI Equity training, I have found the work in *Boys, A Rescue Plan* crucial to issues facing children of color. GI isn't just talking about boys in education but doing something to help all boys. As race, ethnicity, and socioeconomic factors are layered with sex and gender, our interventions can meet the full diversity of children where they are. I highly recommend this book and its fresh approach not just for general readers but also for people involved in the equity field.

–Glynetta Fletcher, Ed.D., Retired Principal and ACI,

Los Angeles Unified School District.

BOYS, A RESCUE PLAN

PREVIOUS BOOKS BY MICHAEL GURIAN

Child Development and Parenting
The Minds of Girls
Saving Our Sons
The Purpose of Boys
Nurture the Nature
The Wonder of Girls
The Wonder of Boys
Raising Boys by Design (with Gregory Jantz, Ph.D.)
The Wonder of Children (previously published as *The Soul of the Child*)
A Fine Young Man
The Good Son
What Stories Does My Son Need? (with Terry Trueman)
It's a Baby Boy! It's a Baby Girl!
(by the Gurian Institute, with Adrian Goldberg, DSW, Stacie Bering, MD)

Education
The Minds of Boys (with Kathy Stevens)
Boys and Girls Learn Differently! (with Kathy Stevens, Patricia Henley, Terry Trueman)
The Boys and Girls Learn Differently Action Guide for Teachers (with Arlette C. Ballew)
Strategies for Teaching Boys and Girls—Elementary and Secondary Level (with Kathy Stevens, Kelley King)
Successful Single-Sex Classrooms (with Kathy Stevens, Peggy Daniels)

Psychology
Lessons of Lifelong Intimacy
The Wonder of Aging
How Do I Help Him?
What Could He Be Thinking?
Love's Journey
The Invisible Presence (previously published as *Mothers, Sons and Lovers*)
The Prince and the King

Business-Corporate
Leadership and the Sexes (with Barbara Annis)

For Young Adult Readers
Understanding Guys
From Boys to Men

Memoir, Fiction, Poetry
The Storm in My Mother's Eyes (michaelgurian.substack.com/)
The Stone Boys
Ancient Wisdom, Modern Words
The Sabbath
The Miracle
The Blind Woman and Other Stories
An American Mystic
The Odyssey of Telemachus

Boys, A Rescue Plan

Moving Beyond the Politics of Masculinity
to Healthy Male Development

by

Sean Kullman

President of the Global Initiative for Boys and Men

and

Michael Gurian

New York Times Bestselling Author of
The Wonder of Boys and *Saving Our Sons*

Published by Gurian Institute Press
The Gurian Institute, LLC

Email Michael Gurian at michaelgurian@comcast.net or through: www.michaelgurian.com.
Email Sean Kullman at seanjameskullman@gmail.com or seank@airr.pro.

Readers should be aware that Internet websites offered as citations and/or sources for further information may have changed or disappeared between the time this was written and when it was read. Readers should be aware that some of the anecdotes in this book, including some gathered from media reports, are composites of two or more comments or stories that needed to be shortened for narrative flow. In no cases have meanings been changed, nor changes of statistics. In case studies, names have been changed, and details that might invade the confidentiality of a person or family.

Limit of Liability/Disclaimer of Warranty: The advice and strategies contained herein may not be suitable for your situation. This publication is sold with the understanding that the author and publisher are not engaged in rendering medical, health, or any other kind of personal professional services in the book. The reader should consult his or her medical, health, or other competent professional before adopting any of the suggestions in this book or drawing inferences from it. The author and publisher specifically disclaim all responsibility for any liability, loss or risk, personal or otherwise, which is incurred as a consequence, directly or indirectly, of the use and application of any of the contents of this book.

Books and other materials by Michael Gurian and the Gurian Institute can be accessed through most brick-and-mortar stores, most online outlets, and the websites: www.michaelgurian.com and www.gurianinstitute.com.

Print ISBN: 979-8-9921599-0-5
eBook ISBN: 979-8-9921599-1-2

Dedication

By Sean:
For my incredible wife Theresa
and our boys Michael and Nicholas
whose love has inspired every word.

By Michael:
For my beloved Gail (1957–2023)
and our children, Gabrielle and Davita,
their spouses, Jack and Ben,
and grandchildren, Lev and Effy.

Contents

Foreword.. ix
Introduction.. xi

Part I: The Male Mental Health Crisis
Chapter 1: The Three Causes of the Male Mental Health Crisis.................. 3
Chapter 2: Diseases of Despair Among Our Males..................................... 15
Chapter 3: Diagnosing and Treating Male-Type Depression..................... 21
Chapter 4: We Can't Save Lives if We Won't Admit the Problem.............. 35
Chapter 5: What Was The American Psychological Association
           Thinking? 47
Chapter 6: False Allegations, Suicide, Opioid Deaths, and the
           Self-Medication of Boys.. 55
Chapter 7: Understanding and Uplifting the Science of Male Fragility 63

Part II: Boys, Sexual Dimorphism, and the Culture of the Exception
Introduction.. 75
Chapter 8: Why I Do Not Generally Use "Cisgender" 77
Chapter 9: When a Student Is Suspended for Using the
           "Wrong" Pronoun 93
Chapter 10: Not Breast-Feeding but Chest-Feeding? A Culture
            of the Exception 109
Chapter 11: I Am a Boy, Hear Me Roar 125

Part III: Big Three Politics That Keep Us from Helping Boys
Introduction.. 135
Chapter 12: The Danger of Feminaphobia 137
Chapter 13: The Silent Killer, Males Left Out of National,
            State, or Local Budgets 149
Chapter 14: When America Embraced Wonder Woman
            and Forgot G.I. Joe.. 157
Chapter 15: Digging Deeper into Our Spiritual Sickness
            Regarding Males 173

Chapter 16: The Death of 17-Year-Old Jack and the Story
that Followed.. 183
Chapter 17: Does the Child Have Brain Sex Dysphoria or
Gender Dysphoria? 191

Part IV: The Seven Point Plan to Rescue Our Boys

Introduction.. 215
Chapter 18: Raise Our Boys to Thrive in a Three Family System 217
Chapter 19: Provide Seven Nurturing Elements to Boys
Who Are in Trouble.. 231
Chapter 20: Train All Schools in Boy-Friendly Practices 239
Chapter 21: Complete Your Own Classroom Citizen Science................. 247
Chapter 22: Compel School Boards to Include Sex Differences
in Annual Reports 255
Chapter 23: Decrease the Male-Gender Gap in College Education 265
Chapter 24: Build and Support Community Programs That
Help Boys Thrive.. 275

Notes and Resources.. 293
Bibliography.. 321
Appendix... 327
About the Authors... 330
About The Gurian Institute 332
The Global Initiative for Boys and Men............................ 333
Index... 334

Foreword

Scientists are rarely advocates and advocates are rarely scientists. And those who raise children and grandchildren, even as they have a long and deeply loving marriage, rarely have the time to have an international impact and create an infrastructure that will outlast them. Their accomplishments are rarely infused with the balance and wisdom that emanates from raising children and loving the children's mother.

In the thirty-five years that I have known Michael Gurian, I have witnessed him be all that. Through his books, speaking, workshops, and the Gurian Institute, Michael has done more to help educators understand the difference between the way boys and girls learn than any other human. He has accomplished this by educating educators about the science behind boys' and girls' brain differences that create different ways of optimal learning. Yet unlike many other social thinkers who see these differences, Michael understands the importance of LGBTQIA+ and gender fluidity, as well.

Fortunately, in *Boys, A Rescue Plan*, we are also blessed with Sean Kullman. Sean is a younger generation's version of Michael Gurian (except for the grandchildren!) Sean is also a data-driven advocate with whom I have worked for more than a decade on the Coalition for a White House Council on Boys and Men. Like Michael, he has formed an organization, the Global Initiative for Boys and Men, as a platform by which his data can be used by executives and legislators to advocate for Commissions on Boys in Men in numerous states, the White House, and Congress

As a result of these two multi-dimensional authors, *Boys, A Rescue Plan* is a multi-dimensional book that integrates both science and politics, powerful dilemmas and equally powerful solutions. The book addresses the price a nation pays when young men commit suicide four times as often as young women yet there are eight federal offices of women's health and no federal offices of men's health. This book also provides solutions for families, schools, communities, and government that incorporate cultural and scientific considerations and fascinate us in the process.

While the focus of *Boys, A Rescue Plan* is on boys because boys have recently been neglected, both authors care deeply about our daughters. Both Kullman and Gurian are guided by the philosophy that we are all in the same family boat: when only one sex wins, both sexes lose.

Happily, *Boys, A Rescue Plan* avoids pitfalls of many other analyses of boys and men. The authors do not argue that we need to return to the "man-up" type of male who represses his feelings and fears, the provider-protector whom some will consider an aggressive dominator. Nor do they argue that we need to develop a boy who constantly expresses his feelings and fears but lacks resilience, the nurturer/connector some people will consider a loser. In other words, the authors understand that while every boy and parent need to understand the difference between heroic intelligence and health intelligence, all young males need not follow any one masculine or non-masculine path. Regarding contemporary arguments over masculinity, *Boys, A Rescue Plan* understands that every virtue taken to its extreme becomes a vice. For that reason, they focus on *male* development rather than culture arguments over what is the right masculinity.

Boys, A Rescue Plan is a huge step toward creating a more loving, caring and yet resilient and productive next generation.

Warren Farrell, Ph.D.
Author, *The Boy Crisis* and *Role Mate to Soul Mate*
November 2, 2024

Introduction

Authors' Note: *Boys, A Rescue Plan* is published just as a new U.S. President, Donald Trump, begins his new term. We publish in a time when sex and gender were hot button topics for both the Republican and Democratic parties during their 2024 campaigns. Our book broadens the necessary conversation and offers solutions that address root causes. We hope President Trump will fund a White House Council on Boys and Men early in his term and we hope he will work with the new Congress to address the crisis our boys are facing in pre-K through 12 education, physical and mental health, and male social growth.

BETWEEN THEM, MICHAEL GURIAN AND SEAN KULLMAN have worked for more than sixty years in the field of boys' development on both the diagnostic and the solution sides. Both of us have been academics, and both have moved into the public, educational, and policy spheres. Our work has focused on what children need to thrive, with an emphasis on how boys thrive in homes, schools, and social-emotional development, and what our culture needs to do if we are to focus on boys' needs in public policy.

Michael is a social philosopher and mental health counselor in private practice, President of the Gurian Institute, author of 36 books as well as the MichaelGurian.Substack.com, and co-host of the *Wonder of Parenting Podcast*. Many of his books have inspired national debate on issues related to sex, gender, educational achievement, psychology, parenting, and social policy. *The Wonder of Boys* (1996), his third book on male development, was credited by national media as "the impetus for the boys' movement."

Sean taught middle school, high school, and college English and was actively involved in boys and girls sports programs as a coach and director. In 2019, he became President of the Global Initiative for Boys and Men. Sean writes a weekly substack (InHisWords.us), and has educated policymakers on the outcomes of boys and men. He is the founder of the American Institute for Responsible Research, which provides research services in education, mental and physical health, and other seminal areas.

Sean and Michael began to collaborate on this book during a series of conversations with one another and with others who work in what Michael calls "The Big Three" (academics, government, and media). In these conversations Michael and Sean noticed the hyper-use of *masculine norms theory* or *the politics of masculinity* to explain why boys have struggled for more than three decades. According to the politics of masculinity, our boys and men abandon natural love, empathy, care for others and self, moral conduct, accomplishment, success, and the values of equality and diversity because they are forced by our culture to accept masculine social roles (often called "the Man Box") in which they are trained to be:

- Emotionally suppressed. To project strength always, don't cry or show sad feelings, only show anger.
- Self-sufficient. Don't talk about feelings with others, solve any issues you have on your own.
- Superior. Be dominant and violent including using, abusing, and controlling women and girls.
- Heteronormative. Avoid close relationships with other men and boys so that you will not be called gay.
- Economically and socially limited. Be the sole breadwinner, make your family obey you, don't wear pink, be manly.

According to the proponents of this theory, most boys who don't adhere to these masculine norms pay a significant price by being ostracized from society for their disloyalty to the norms. Other boys who do adhere to masculine social norms have it no better because they will be destroyed from within as 1) the masculine roles limit the psyche of the boy and 2) toxic masculine norms (toxic masculinity) make them do immoral things that require punishment. Overall, we are told, boys harm people, become violent, fail in school, abuse substances and porn, and reject women's equality because of masculine norms, roles, and stereotypes. Even suicide is connected to the politics of masculinity in this theory as masculine norms and roles make boys not cry or talk about their feelings, which compels them to end their own lives.

Assessing and Replacing Masculine Norms Theory

A recent example of masculine norms theory used in the media is "Why Do Some Teen Boys Turn Aggressive? The Surprising Role of Masculinity," reported by *SciTechDaily* on July 15, 2024. "A new study by a team of psychology researchers shows that adolescent boys may also respond aggressively when they believe their masculinity is under threat—especially boys growing up in environments with rigid, stereotypical gender norms. The findings, reported today in the Journal, *Developmental Science,* underscore the effects of social pressure that many boys face to be stereotypically masculine . . . beyond just aggression, manhood threats are associated with a wide variety of negative, antisocial behaviors, such as sexism, homophobia, political bigotry, and even anti-environmentalism. Our findings call for actively challenging the restrictive norms and social pressure that boys face to be stereotypically masculine, particularly during puberty and coming from their parents and peers."

Because stereotype threat is a real phenomenon, accounting for it in society can be helpful. Girls who are told that they are not good at math are more likely to feel inadequate in their math-reasoning than girls who are told that they are good at math. Programs to help girls in science, technology, engineering, and math (STEM) assist girls in avoiding these negative stereotypes. Similarly, boys and men who are told that they must live in the Man Box can be assisted to step out of social stereotypes and limited social roles as part of their maturation. A successful Nurturing Fathers program in Phoenix, AZ does just that. M.A.N.C.A.V.E. (Men All Need to Be Caring, Actively Engaged, Vested, and Encouraged) was founded by City of Phoenix Head Start Program Coordinator Marion Hill to help dads, parents, grandparents, and male role models to enhance their child-raising in families and communities. One of the tools used in this program is the Man Box.

Marion Hill told Michael Gurian recently, "Look, we know that masculine stereotypes don't *cause* boys' and men's problems, but the Man Box model can help us, especially with boys and young men who have hardened themselves for survival." Michael asked Marion to say more about what does *cause* male problems, and Marion provided a history of his program's development.

"The first step for us was to understand males–not just masculinity– but *males*. We want to know who they are, what makes them tick, *their nature*. Gurian Institute's (GI) *nature-based theory* and work in male/female brain difference helped us look at how men father naturally using paternal nurturance, and how to enhance that male nurturance with children and families. By dealing with their biology, we are working with the men rather than against them.

"Personally, when I discovered evolutionary biology and the science around these things in 2016 at your workshop, I realized these were the missing pieces in both our preschool classrooms and in our parent outreach. We began to work with GI in our schools at that time, and within two years, this led to the creation of M.A.N.C.A.V.E. Now we use brain science and *bi-strategic parenting* (valuing both female and male leadership in families) as our base theory. We added the Man Box model to our program because it reaches some of the dads—but our lane is definitely the brain science and the bi-strategic parenting that we know to be natural to women and men."

Marion's assessment of what is needed by males, and the program he founded, mirrors the vision of this book. *Boys, A Rescue Plan* works with a Nature Imperative much more than a Culture Imperative. By this we mean: boy-friendly families, schools, and politics do their best to raise and educate healthy boys and men when they begin with nature (the science of male development); bring in healthy nurture (family, schools, other institutions that raise and educate boys); and look at culture ("masculinity") models when needed but not as a starting point. We favor what Michael calls the *Nurture the Nature* approach. (He published a book with that title in 2007.) The nature-based theory Marion mentioned is an example of nurture-the-nature: parents and others nurture the child's core personality by knowing who the child is and understanding the child's nature as their baseline for human development. Because the neuroscience of sex and gender has grown over the last thirty years, our society can ground social programming like M.A.N.C.A.V.E.'s in who boys and men *are* rather than mainly in the politics of masculinity and social norms theories that may or may not have much to do with who boys and men really are.

Moving Beyond Limited Social Theory to Rescue Our Sons

Natural male development is universal across cultures and racial groups because the science of male development applies to *all males* no matter where they are being raised and educated and includes males on the gender spectrum and males with chromosomal abnormalities. Because masculine norms theory and the politics of masculinity only apply to certain boys, we find these culture tools inadequate to fully work for boys across racial groups and throughout the socio-economic continuum. The Big Three mainly or only use masculine norms theory to the exclusion of exploring male nature to try to dictate agendas for boys and men. Sean and Michael agree that sometimes The Big Three are right about the Man Box, but more often they are wrong. Perhaps equally worrisome, they often use masculinity conversations to attack males as inherently defective and thus unneeded by nature, nurture, or culture. Our culture has had forty years of the politics of masculinity and people all around us still don't know how to help *our males*. Boys and men remain under-nurtured and under-developed, many of them purposeless, whether masculine or not. This book is about changing this trajectory.

You Can Be a Citizen Scientist

Thirty years ago, in *The Wonder of Boys*, Michael asked our culture to emphasize expansive manhood development in our democratic society rather than emphasizing masculinity study and politics. In the ensuing decades, he has continued to call for our first emphasis on male and female development inclusive of gender interests and themes but not bound by social construct theories. In *Boys, A Rescue Plan*, Michael's final book in sex and gender development, he is joined by Sean Kullman, who agrees with this social position, and brings new facts that make the argument even more important today.

Meanwhile, because Michael and Sean are (perhaps like many of you) suspicious of the overuse of the politics in sex and gender, we ask you to become a citizen scientist to test out the theory and practice of this book and any similar book or media. Don't just believe one or two experts (or opinion makers). Use this book to do your own research. Take your yellow pad or computer or smartphone into the world and take notes as you study the boys around you. Watch them live, emote, love, laugh, challenge, aggress, regress, develop, struggle, and grow. Study their hardiness and their sensitivities. Note everything about human nature and male nature that you see in a collective science.

When you see masculine stereotypes being taught to your sons, of course you can talk about that with them. Meanwhile, as you study boys and men from a *nature-based perspective*, you will likely find that most boys around you are not dominant; most wear pink and other pastels at some point in life; most if not all the boys you know have friends with whom they are intimate in their own natural boyish way; most boys talk about feelings with trusted others like peers or mentors (though perhaps not as much as girls do or as much as parents of teen boys especially would like); some boy might be violent or abusive to girls and women, but most boys are not; most boys and men enjoy their mother's, sister's, and female partner's equality, though they don't mind some healthy competition for resources, too. Most boys are trying to be both strong and sensitive in their own ways.

When Sean and Michael understand and work with the *nature of boys*, we do so as both experts and citizen scientists like you, who have studied boys and men for decades. We have found that the civilization-wide struggles our males are having right now, in real time, need social attention to the very nature of who it is to be male.

Here is a snapshot of the struggle our boys are experiencing today.

Notice how stark these numbers are when compared to girls' lives.

We thank colleagues Mark Perry of the University of Michigan and Thomas Mortenson of the Pell Institute for Higher Education for their "For Every 100 Girls" research.

For Every 100 Girls/Women......	There Are This Many Boys/Men....
Who earn an associate's degree	61
25 to 29 years who have a master's degree	61
Who earn a master's degree	65
Who are college-bound seniors with an A or A+ grade point average	65
Enrolled in US graduate schools	68
Who earn a bachelor's degree	73
Who are enrolled in US colleges	75
In High School who took an AP course in 2020	76
Who are in the top 10% of their high school class	79
Who take AP/Honors courses in Natural Sciences	79
25 to 29 years who have a first professional or doctor's degree	80
Who take high school AP/Honors courses in math	82
Who earn a doctor's degree	85
25 to 29 years whose highest level of education is a bachelor's degree	88
Whose entry into kindergarten is delayed	139
In public schools (K-12) classified as having mental retardation	140
In K-12 and classified as having a specific learning disability	144
Who repeat kindergarten	145
Ages 3-17 years diagnosed with communication disorders	168
Who abuse illicit drugs and alcohol	180
Who are suspended from school	195
Expelled from public schools	223
25 to 34 years old who die	227
Who die by opioid overdose	227
Who are homeless and unsheltered	234
In public schools classified as having an emotional disturbance	255
15 to 24 years who die	270
Ages 15 to 19 who commit suicide	293
Murdered in 2020	344
Ages 25 to 29 who commit suicide	418
Incarcerated in local jails	614
Ages 20-24 who die of homicide	717
Who die on the job	1,118
Incarcerated in state and federal prisons	1,225
Incarcerated in federal prisons	1,331
Who died in combat in Afghanistan and Iraq	4,102
Who have been wounded in action in Afghanistan and Iraq	5,026

Studying the Boy Crisis

As a citizen scientist, you may end up doing some of what we do for a living–study the boy crisis. Michael first used the term in 2005 (*The Minds of Boys*) then returned to the theme in *The Purpose of Boys (2008), How Do I Help Him? (2011)* and *Saving Our Sons (2017)* to try to capture the difficulties that boys are having today. The term "boy crisis" was used for a cover story in Newsweek in 2006 that featured *The Minds of Boys*. In 2019, the powerful book *The Boy Crisis* was published by Warren Farrell and John Gray to explore important aspects of the crisis, including what Dr. Farrell calls *dad deprivation*. In 2022, Richard Reeves' *On Boys and Men,* provided further research on the boy crisis, noting its specific escalation in this last decade. Christina Hoff Sommers, Lisa Britton, Ruth Whippman, Michael Thompson, Bill Pollack, Leonard Sax and others have explored the boy crisis via a variety of important lenses. Dr. Sommers called our post-modern approach to males "a war on boys," and Dr. Sax, in *Boys Adrift*, has shown just how adrift many of our young males are.

In Part I of *Boys, A Rescue Plan,* Sean and Michael provide further evidence of the crisis, especially focusing on the male mental health decline in the last two decades. This is not a crisis of "masculinity" as the culture-based approach proposes, but a crisis of male brains under-nurtured, unprotected, and medically and psychologically neglected across boyhood and well into adulthood. Millions of boys and men struggle with brain disorders, childhood and adolescent trauma, dad deprivation, severe educational decline, increased unemployment, homelessness, sexual abuse, child abuse, sex trafficking, criminal activity, suicide, addiction behavior, overdose deaths, increased self-loathing, and male loneliness, which is a highly dangerous form of social withdrawal that can intersect with the illness of violence as we will explore in Part I. Loneliness and male depression are not caused by "codes of masculinity." To solve the male health crisis, we must look at the place where mental health resides–*the brain of the male who is presently under-nurtured.* This book does that.

Boys and men want to become loving, wise, and successful male adults (good men). They are born to be of service to others. They want to be ready to sacrifice themselves for the health and well-being of children and families. They enter our world hoping to take risks and find their balance, challenge others and empathize, love and be loved. They are *males* who want to live with various and beautiful goals. They need our help as *males* to become adult men via a brain-healthy and boy-friendly developmental arc of maturation, service, and purpose.

The Four Sections of the Book

Sean and Michael will ask you to reassess the politics of our culture while providing insight and solutions to male issues in your home, school, neighborhood, and city.

We include actionable strategies in all four parts of the book.

- **Protecting the Mental Health of Boys.** We will explore social-emotional issues males face today, provide analysis of the real causes of increased male mental illness in America and the Western World, and provide solutions you can use to meet the mental health needs of boys and young men in your family, school, and community.
- **Understanding the Neuroscience of the Male Brain.** Michael will provide in depth discussion of male and female brains so that you can become a citizen science of nature, nurture, and culture aligned rather than at odds. This research will help you understand your daughters, too, and everyone on the gender spectrum.
- **Adjusting Social Politics to Be Boy-Friendly.** Sean's work with state and federal legislatures will be especially featured in this section. Sean helps legislators and stakeholders on a federal and state by state basis to address male health and wellness gaps and to develop male-friendly social and political investment.
- **Instituting the Rescue Plan.** In the chapters of Part IV, we will provide dozens of solution-based programs, including M.A.N.C.A.V.E., with which the Gurian Institute and the Global Initiative for Boys and Men have worked over the decades. These programs specifically solve the boy crisis one location at a time.

In providing these four sections, we will be arguing that the core problem facing boys today is our society-wide abandonment of *natural male development*.

A Comparison of Research Methods

Because our approach to boyhood is based in neuropsychology, neuro-anthropology, and evolutionary biology, we employ our *male development theory* that is replicable worldwide; we do not solely focus on theories about masculinity that only apply to limited groups of males who may live under stereotype threat. Our data base is mainly brain scans that show male/female differences across cultures and races (wherever XX and XY chromosomes express themselves); thus, our research pool is in the millions.

We believe that our colleagues in the Big Three who focus only or mainly on masculinity theories do so because their sample sizes are small. As you read this book and study boys around you, we hope you will become wary of researchers who avoid brain science and, in its place, speak with a few boys and men (usually 100 to 300) via surveys, questionnaires, and personal interviews. In these surveys, you may notice that the questions asked often or mainly regard social conditioning via definitions of masculinity. For instance, an author or researcher might ask college students and/or the boys in the neighborhood how much boys cry. Adolescent boys will generally agree that they do not cry a lot, though they might not know that there are biological reasons for this, which we will explore in Part II.

The boys and young men may also be asked whether they talk about feelings as much as girls. They generally do not and self-report this gap accurately even though most of them don't know the male neurobiology behind this gap.

They may also be asked whether masculine stereotypes are harmful to them. Adolescent males will generally say that they are harmful because those social norms and stereotypes are what they have studied in their high school, college, or in social media.

This kind of small sample research and the loaded questions fall into *confirmation bias*. A small population confirms a bias already held by the researcher. Then a book is published in which the author argues that the boy crisis is caused by masculine norms based on the limited and biased data. While no actual proof is offered for causation except other articles and books that also use small sample sociological questionnaires and confirmation bias, this sociological research bypasses maleness and, thus, does not address the real drama of male nature. No doubt the author is trying to help boys and men, but flawed research ends up allowing a culture to pretend it is solving the troubles that boys have, but instead, it is increasing its abandonment of who males are, what they need, and how a boy becomes a productive and beloved man.

The abandonment of male development is dangerous to a civilization. Abandoned and neglected males find silos, groups, and gangs, on the street or online, to support them in their battle against the neglect. They want to belong somewhere in some place and time with some people who understand the nature they feel in families, schools, communities, and public policy. They struggle to survive in a competitive world. They struggle to find meaningful relationships at home and in the neighborhood. They often cannot discover purpose in school and life, to be employed and motivated, to lead and follow. Abandoned and neglected, some of them may join groups that use masculine norms to help them to survive. The masculine norms did not cause abandonment or trauma, but they sometimes provide succor. Meanwhile, most boys who are neglected will themselves practice neglect. Abandoned, they will abandon. Under-nurtured, they grow up withdrawn from life and then in turn under-nurture others.

As the programs in Part IV will reveal, we can join one another right now to deal with the very real drama of neglect in The Big Three playing out in our culture via programs already developed and programs you can further develop with your own insights and resources. Working to rescue one young male at a time, you could include masculinity conversations. Meanwhile, we hope you will also help the boys around you–and their families, schools, and communities–to focus on their own particular and shared natural development.

This is where they need you, us, and everyone to meet them–male development is where they are.

A Note on Format

Because Sean and Michael have researched and written separate articles on all of these topics, we decided to shape this book into a hybrid essay/ chapter format that allows you to use one chapter/essay at a time in family discussion, in a high school class or university course, in a book study group or professional learning community, and in a policy meeting or policy forum. As you use each chapter, don't be surprised if some people around you roll their eyes, people who argue that male and female don't exist anymore. In Part II especially, where Michael outlines the male brain and male nature, he will arm you with responses to that fallacious argument.

One term he will use is "the culture of the exception." Like "The Big Three" "the boy crisis," and "male nature," the culture of the exception is a through line regarding our culture's tendency to uplift the lives of a few people by trying to deny or sacrifice the lives of the majority. LGBTQIA+ advocacy today, which is needed and important, provides an example of the culture of the exception as some advocates try to erase male/female (sex) to pretend that gender fluidity (gender) is the final story about humanity. In reality, gender fluidity applies to a few people statistically while male/female (sex) applies to all people. Erasing the whole to assist a part is bad science and it is not needed to protect LGBTQIA+ people, as Michael will show in Part II. Sean and Michael use the essay/chapter format to provide practical advice for dealing with all males, including gender exceptions, so that in helping you advocate for parts and the whole at once, this book does not exclude anyone.

You will find elements of repetition in some of chapters of this book. While we are writing for general readers, one of our core themes is that boy rescue depends on high school, college, university, and graduate school classes studying the male brain and male needs. We have written each chapter to be part of the flow of a book for everyone, but we've also repeated certain themes in some chapters so that each chapter can exist as a stand-alone essay for classroom reading.

This tack will be helpful for book groups, as well, we believe. Your home or school adult reading group, like a dynamic classroom, can choose chapters to discuss even if all your members have not finished the whole book. The Essential Questions boxes at the end of most of the chapters provide a short Discussion Guide for each chapter we hope will be useful to your book groups and for high school and university classrooms.

By understanding nature and science for all, we will raise boys to become the good, loving, wise, and successful men we need them to be—not just some boys but all boys. In nurturing the nature of boys, we can solve a lot of our social crises today—which are about the drama of maleness abandoned to its own devices in an era that actually needs good men as much or more than it ever has.

Thank you for reading and using this book.

Please write to us to share your own citizen science around sex, gender, and the development of boys.

Write: seanjameskullman@gmail.com or seank@airr.pro.

Write: gurianmichael@gmail.com.

Part I: The Male Mental Health Crisis

"When a boy drives down the serpentine road of mental health, feeling depressed and isolated because he feels no one who knows the real him loves him, no one needs him, and there's no hope of that changing, he may one day find a cliff and drive off."

–Warren Farrell and John Gray, The Boy Crisis

Chapter 1

The Three Causes of the Male Mental Health Crisis

(While this essay is useful for general readers and parents, it is also particularly useful to educators, policymakers, media, and professionals involved in the mental health field.)

IN ONE MONTH, mass shootings took dozens of lives in Dayton, Ohio and El Paso, Texas. The month before, the month later, last year, this year, and for more than two decades, American mass shootings, perpetrated mainly by young to middle life males, have shocked us. Everyone has a theory as to why these shootings happen. Politicians give their different viewpoints. Advocacy groups choose their theme for advocacy. Mental health professionals like myself (Michael) have weighed in since the 1990s when the school shootings began. Yet no matter the points of view and no matter our collective spurts of passion to solve the crisis after each shooting, the boy crisis continues. As names of schools or names of cities become part of our national lexicon (Sandy Hook, Virginia Tech, Littleton, Jonesboro, Las Vegas, Springfield) we also see male suicide rates in the tens of thousands per year (something Sean will explore further in the next chapter) and even more body counts from male-driven tragedies in inner cities where, statistically, the bulk of killing goes on, gang to gang, male to male.

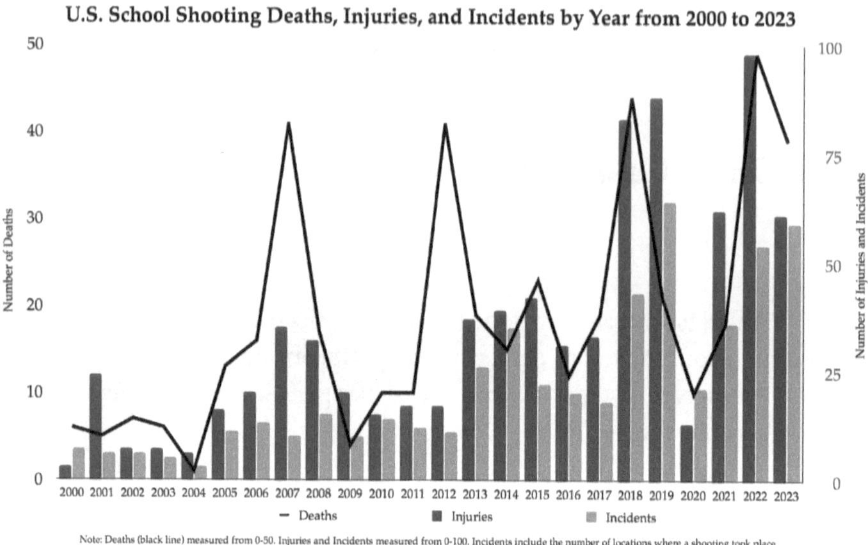

Note: Deaths (black line) measured from 0-50. Injuries and Incidents measured from 0-100. Incidents include the number of locations where a shooting took place.

News stories about these tragedies generally repeat three themes: "extremist rhetoric," "get rid of guns," and "toxic masculinity." While lawmakers must indeed better legislate and enforce laws that protect our society from AR-15s, excessive gun use, and mentally ill males accessing these weapons, and while we must all watch out for extremist groups and remain vigilant against social toxicity, the three common themes are not enough explanation for what is going on. The three themes hide a deeper social ill: we have tacitly decided that helping boys thrive *as boys* is anathema to our modern feminist goals, and we are paying the price. As millions of boys grow up on the *depression spectrum,* the Big Three uses culture-terms like "toxic masculinity" and "patriarchal gender norms" to pretend we have things all figured out, but boys do what they do for brain-related reasons, not masculine stereotypes.

Elizabeth Bruenig, a Washington Post reporter, wrote on February 16, 2018, just days after the Parkland shooting, "Nothing symbolizes the foreclosure of the future like the slaughter of a nation's young. And it's so routine now—an average of one shooting every 60 hours—that attention will quickly fade, as it does with subjects one doesn't intend to do anything about. Another word for that bitter fatalism is defeat." These almost bitter words ring true, don't they? Americans are becoming numb to these crimes even as we mourn the victims. Our schools are generally safe places to be, and most boys are not violent or unsafe, but how can we not fully see the mental health dangers our boys are experiencing and bringing to our schools without our hearts breaking?

Our Boy Crisis

When I travel to communities to speak and lead trainings, people are often surprised to learn just how deep the boy crisis goes. It goes far beyond male violence, though we can and must address that violence, as we will do in this chapter.

Did You Know?
Boy Crisis Statistics

*America has the highest rate of male incarceration per capita of any country in the world. Among males 17 or younger, the boy-to-girl ratio in correctional institutions is 9:1. Among 18-21 year olds, the ratio grows to 14:1. Boys of color are systematically moved from neighborhoods to schools to prisons; meanwhile, prisons are populated mainly by white males, so this is an issue that includes race but goes beyond race, too—it goes to the heart of under-nurtured maleness in America.

- Suicide kills over 38,000 American boys and men per year, and males kill themselves at four times the rate of girls. Males of color are increasingly turning to suicide as a way out of despair, especially among returning veterans, and suicide among our males is now the second leading cause of death in America. But, again, minority status and race are not the only factor in male distress: according to the National Academy of Sciences, more white males have died of suicide in the last three decades than of AIDS.
- Boys are twice as likely as girls to be victims of violence in America, but in certain age groups, the ratio is 6:1. For instance, among adolescent children, six males die from violence for every one female. Boys of color in the inner city are considered "highly likely" to die from violent causes by or about age 25—the end of male adolescence.
- Boys receive two-thirds of the D's and F's in our schools but less than 40 percent of the A's. Some boys, of course, test very well and are doing quite well, but overall, in every racial or ethnic group, we find girls doing better than boys in overall markers. The well-known female gap

in math/science is now a 2-point gap while the male gap in literacy is a 10-point gap, leaving males 1 and 1/2 years behind females in literacy skills, and skewing aggregate scores toward much higher female and much lower male performance in school.

- Boys are twice as likely as girls to be labeled "emotionally disturbed" and twice as likely to be diagnosed with a behavioral or learning disorder. The Centers for Disease Control and Prevention report that 20% of children 3 to 17 "have, in any given year, a mental or emotional illness," and depression among children and teens is worsening.

- One in eleven Americans, most of them males, are diagnosed with ADD/ADHD. Our Gurian Institute research in more than 1,000 schools shows us one-third of schoolboys misdiagnosed with ADD/ADHD. While some boys do need medication, millions of males are being medicated unnecessarily, with severe consequences for motivation and growth. Given that 80 percent of the world's Ritalin is used in the U.S., we have a particularly American problem.

- Boys are four times as likely as girls to be suspended or expelled from early childhood and K–12 learning environments. Our Gurian Institute research shows America's schools, from Pre-K through college, struggling in large part because teachers and staff have not received training in male/female learning and behavior difference. Graduate schools of education don't teach a *Boys and Girls Learn Differently*® class to future teachers, often because they don't think it politically correct. But without this training, our hard-working teachers are often unable to manage and grow male energy and acumen most effectively.

The latest PISA study (Programme for International Student Assessment) from the Organization of Economic Cooperation and Development (OECD) shows boys behind girls in most developmental, behavioral, academic, and social markers in *all industrialized countries*. Weekly and sometimes daily, I receive an email from a parent or professional in Korea, China, Japan, Qatar,

Nigeria, Brazil, Vietnam, Australia, and many other countries asking, "What can we do to help our failing boys?" The boy crisis is a worldwide problem.

In various years, the World Health Organization has published its Global Burden of Disease Study (GBDS) led by the Institute for Health Metrics and Evaluation. This study corroborates the OECD's PISA study on learning and education then goes even further into health markers. In the last decade, the GBDS has concluded that even when female depression, eating disorders, and violence-against-females are included in data, males are doing statistically worse in numerous mental health markers in a number of countries. Perhaps most surprising to people is the study's wide reach: the health and wellness gender gap favoring females exists in countries like China or Oman that we have tended to believe are 'patriarchal,' and thus should be more stressful for females than males.

The WHO studies in total ask us to see much more clearly our millions of invisible boys. In various parts of the world, health outcomes among boys and men continue to be substantially worse than among girls and women, yet this gender-based disparity in mental health has received little national, regional or global attention in the Big Three, nor has it led to deeper sympathy for boys that translates into action on their behalf. Why?

Paralysis in the Big Three

When I do media interviews on male violence, I hear, "It's the patriarchal male role, isn't it?" When I go to universities to speak, I hear, "It's privileged white males not wanting to give up dominance and power." When I go to nonprofits and government agencies, I hear, "It's because boys are being told they have to be stoic, right? Boys are told not to share feelings and hurts, and they are taught to dominate, and when they can't take it anymore, they hurt people, right?" In the *USA Today* article (February 15, 2018) after the Parkland shooting, I read, "Not only do traditional notions of masculinity prevent men from seeking counseling or other forms of help they need, help which may prevent these mass shootings, but violence is also inculcated as a more masculine alternative than help-seeking." The sociologists and the reporter continue, "Men are forced to be tough and unemotional. It's an example of toxic masculinity, the stereotypical and historically harmful definition of what it means to be a man….as women have gained greater power and opportunity in the last century, men have lost some of what they were taught made them 'real men,' including, in many cases, being the breadwinner. Men who think they're falling short of traditional gender norms are more likely to engage in 'stereotypically masculine behaviors,' like violence."

Violence, a disease that depressed and mentally ill males suffer from disproportionately, is not caused by "traditional gender norms." The culture-based approach to male violence in The Big Three is part of our national paralysis as we miss that the American Medical Association has treated violence as a disease for almost forty years, and that males who become psychotic, sociopathic, and/or violently depressed do not do so because they are masculine/not masculine. Many of the men who kill and hurt others are breadwinners and traditionally focused, making the "lost male role" not a *cause* of violence. Similarly, the "not talking about feelings *causes* violence" argument is, as Harvard's Steven Pinker has put it, "a myth." Some people talk about their feelings, others don't; some men are stoic, others gush. Most stoic people are never violent while emotionally expressive men can be quite violent. While some men repress too much of what they feel—every mental health counselor, including myself, tries to help them open up their hearts– men and boys do not kill people because they don't discuss their feelings.

Boys and men become violent because their brain chemistry experiences the disease of violence on *the male depression spectrum.* Millions of American males, starting quite young, are chronically stressed by factors we will explore in this book, and so stressed, they live in *male-type depression* that manifests at its mildest in under-motivation and anhedonia and at its most severe in despair that becomes psychosis, rage, and violence. Often, the violence is a way of self-medicating via dopamine-spiking in the mentally ill male brain. To save our children and adults, we must track the actual causes of male chronic stress and the male depression spectrum.

The Provable Causes of Male Violence

Psychologist Gregory Jantz, author of *Raising Boys by Design,* and Founding Director of the mental health agency, The Center, A Place of Hope in Edmonds, Washington, discussed the disease of violence this way on our *Wonder of Parenting* podcast. "Violent boys and men are deeply wounded and depressed. They have experienced significant trauma and loss; they have been betrayed and they feel betrayed. Their lives feel meaningless to them and so the lives of others become meaningless. Gradually, they focus their internal struggle on plotting and planning revenge and when they feel well prepared, they commence the violent taking of others' lives and/or their own. The wounded-ness in these males–their despair, their depression, and their violence–become most of what they are. This is a disease of our culture we must treat as a male disease."

Dr. Jantz has captured violent boys well. My research corroborates his findings.

Here are the *three provable primary causes* for male depression and, in some boys on that depression spectrum, their violence.

First Cause: *Environmental neurotoxins attacking a boy's genes and development.* Neurotoxins in polluted air, in lead and aluminum in homes, in BPH in plastics, in artificial sweeteners, red dye, and monosodium glutamate in food, in endocrine disruptors in fertilizer and pesticides negatively affect gene expression toward male depression and violence. This cause of mental illness, depression, and violence remains under-studied in the Big Three yet wreaks havoc on our society by attacking genes at a cellular level. Two males may experience the same trauma in their lives but one of them grows up to kill or injure people and the other does not. Why? Specific gene damage from environmental toxins collaborate as one reason.

Second Cause: *Trauma received and experienced by boys between birth and young adulthood.* Traumas include physical and sexual abuse, poverty, repeatedly witnessing violence, repetitive and dangerous bullying, head injury and repeated concussions, substance abuse, and other continuing negative stressors in social-emotional growth. To become violent, our males will most likely experience significant and repeated trauma to brain development at some point in their first decade and a half of life (please google the ACE's model–Adverse Childhood Experiences–on the Center for Disease Control's website for more on how trauma affects the human brain). As we will discuss later, the male brain has internal fragilities and vulnerabilities that make it more prone to violence after trauma than the female brain.

Third Cause: *Under-nurturance in the essential components of male development by nuclear, extended, and communal families.* Our society began breaking down neuro-developmentally essential scaffolding for male development around fifty years ago. This breakdown included depleting father-attachment, attacking males as dangerous, and removing healthy male development systems from social institutions. A continuing and multifaceted crippling of male maturity and psychological health in families and child-supportive institutions dramatically under-nurtures males across our society, contributing to negative mental health outcomes.

Just one of these three may be enough to cause a male to become violent–to develop and express the wounded-ness Dr. Jantz described. Two or more, or all three at once, will significantly increase the likelihood that he will try to destroy what he can when he can. These three causes of male violence are attacks on his cellular structure, his gene expression, and his brain's blood flow and synapses.

A Potential Correlation: *Cultural stereotypes and gender norms.* While there is conclusive scientific evidence across disciplines for the three causes I've just noted, there is only opinion-as-evidence that "gender stereotypes" and "gender norms of masculinity" (patriarchal norms, not crying enough, not talking about feelings, and stoicism) cause violent depression in males. At best, a correlation exists in masculine masking after or while male-type depression sets in. (I will explore how to know if a boy or man has male-type depression in greater detail later in this book). What do we mean? Here's a famous example.

The hero of the Marvel movie, *Black Panther*, the uncle and king, traumatizes his nephew, who then goes on to do bad things. The hero of the movie, played by the late Chadwick Boseman, says this about his masculine brother, "We created him, we created our own monster." Similarly, we create monsters in a society via the three causes and some of those monsters will wear the mask of correlation—of masculine armor and guns blazing; of a buff soldier who shows no empathy; and of dominance as a game to get back at bullies who have traumatized him. This mask is not masculinity *per se*, as masculinity teaches moral values that disallow this kind of behavior, but the mask correlates with stereotypes of masculinity the Big Three has used over the last fifty years: pride of gun ownership, lack of empathy for prey, masculinized video games, and armoring a self to survive and thrive.

But as we all try to ascertain why boys become violent, let's honestly ask: Did the armor *cause* the bad guy in Black Panther to kill people? Did the school shooters in our neighborhood kill children because they also played *Assassin's Creed*? Do our depressed and mentally ill boys and men really become violent because they are "privileged" or "patriarchal?" From a science-based standpoint, our answer will have to be No. It will have to be No in schools, families, universities, media, government, and throughout the culture. We will keep discussing the mask and armor to discuss the surface of things, but once No makes sense across the society, we will be able to dig deeper into the real causes of male violence. Realizing the "No," we can begin to come out of our cultural paralysis and our distracting correlations to deal with boys' root causes.

We will see that the problem is not whether codes of masculinity are or are not taught to boys. While guns allow higher numbers of people to die from violence than knives or fists, and while armoring a male self to face suffering can lead to violent self-protection, masculinity is not an illness, thus it does not cause mental and physical disease. Neglect of healthy male development, however, can and will cause distress in males as neural and cellular damage, significant trauma to male development, and lack of healthy attachment and nurturance of the boy etiologically create a perfect storm to cause male depression, chronic stress, and in some males, the disease of violence.

Abandoned Boys and Men

Masks of masculinity exist, but they are not the monster's origin story. Rather, the problem is that our post-modern society *has abandoned healthy male development.* What would healthy male development look like?

Did You Know?
Essentials for Healthy Male Development

For strong mental health, we must provide our males with these human practices.
1. Nurturing and motivational mothering.
2. Father attachment and paternal nurturance.
3. Three to five significant mentors in boyhood and through adolescence.
4. Boy-specific educational pedagogy and boy-friendly counseling interventions.
5. Resilience training as a parenting baseline and empathic resilience-nurturing after trauma.
6. Work-ethic training (contribution to household, service to school and others) from the pre-K years forward.
7. Protection while *in utero* and throughout life from gene-distorting neurotoxins in food, fertilizer, plastics, and pollution.
8. Real human relationships without significant mediation of screens/excessive screen time.
9. Personal spiritual development (humility training, internal self-development), including various, significant and healthy Rites of Passage throughout adolescence.

> 10. Male role modeling and identity development, in all
> their complexities, equal to female role development,
> including purpose and motivation training from the
> pre-K years forward.

In all ten of these developmental needs, discussion of the politics of masculinity is often a distraction from what is most needed now: that we build structures into a changing society to develop male health from birth onward. If we won't see past potential for masculinity-correlation to the real causes of violence and male mental illness, we will continue putting all our social capital into "boys and men have it all except when they won't give up old social norms" or "boys kill people because of toxic masculinity," which invests our culture in an argument between people who believe masculinity's traditional form is our salvation and those who blame it for every modern heartache. This allows The Big Three to use "masculinity" as the word that should encompass the strivings of our boys and men when it is only a small piece of the light cast into the world by male evolution and maturation. Pursuing that piece of light, we leave millions of boys and men abandoned to under-nurturance, trauma, and shame, and miss how depressed these sons become. We feel satisfied that we have explained the masks of masculinity repeatedly as if that explanation will solve the boy crisis, but the crisis increases not decreases in our paralysis.

If you work in or near the social services world, you may have noticed evidence of our society's abandonment of healthy male development as Joy Moses, a policy analyst for the Center for American Progress, discovered in her research. "Funding for both government and nonprofit programs to help males has been scarce. A recent survey shows the top two ways that nonprofit service providers connect with males is through parole and child support enforcement programs. As a low-income man, you have to get in trouble to get help." Her research on lack of Big Three help for males was confirmed by Jacquelyn Boggess, co-director of the Center for Family Policy and Practice, a Wisconsin-based think tank, who wrote in *The Atlantic*, "The majority of United States anti-poverty programs almost exclusively serve women and children." While our assistance to women and children is sacred, our lack of support for male development is tragic. Community by community, our sons need *male-specific nurturing and help.*

I believe, and Sean agrees, that most people in the grass roots, like you, and like us, sense something wrong in our society's approach to males. To us, the "something wrong" is rooted in the Big Three's war between the Nature

Imperative (who boys and men are by nature) and the Culture Imperative (positing masculine culture constructs and stereotypes as the culprit in male distress). Sean and I come down on the side of nature more than culture. It is difficult to pinpoint when the culture war began, but perhaps the Billy Joel song, "Captain Jack," is worth a listen fifty years later. If you find it wherever you get music, see if you hear what I hear: a song that chronicles a depressed boy then a depressed young man who is abandoned by his family and society. Any natural attempt in him at a healthy hunt or at self-motivation is replaced by seeking dopamine rewards from drugs, alcohol, and bare love, each of which furthers his lack of purpose, his lack of healthy male development, and his immaturity unintended by family and society but obvious and tragic. Unlike the monster in Black Panther, this boy does not use violence as a form of self-medication to increase his own dopamine and his brain's reward chemistry; instead, he withdraws from life, family, and success to become a chronically depressed man.

Social Avoidance of Real Causation and Male Development

Throughout this book Sean and I will bring evidence and insight to bear on the male crisis, its causes, and male development needs. We will fill in more and more science of male development for you so that you can use it in your world. I have been personally moved where I go to speak and train when people say, "Why aren't the ten male developmental needs taught to everyone? If masculinity is just a small part of the puzzle, why don't we get the whole puzzle?" When I lay out the science of male violence for audiences, for instance, they realize its importance at an inchoate level. One teacher told me, "We just leave behind our boys more and more by using the feminist language about masculinity. The actual male development stuff should be taught everywhere feminism is taught."

Audiences, even feminist moms, get that something is wrong. Many of these people are, like I am, parents of daughters. They know girls get depressed, anxious, suffer mental declines, and have a number of issues in our society. They also know: girls rarely shoot up schools. Even feminist moms feel a gut sense that males and females are different. When boys become depressed and lonely, experiencing diseases of despair, they often hurt themselves and others because their mental disease mixes with male dopamine release to include physical violence. The feminist moms know that if we abandon our girls socially, there will be negative consequences, but those consequences will not be as violent as occurs when we abandon our boys. In the grass roots, even if not much in the Big Three, the root causes of male depression and violence are beginning to emerge as important topics.

An example appears in three decades of popular fatherhood research in which a direct link in more than 80 percent of violent males is made to under-nurturance by fathers and male role models. When a child's father and male role model attachment is depleted for boys and girls, there are some similar and some different consequences. In *The Boy Crisis,* Dr. Warren Farrell goes deeply into this research, noting that girls are harmed by lack of a father, but tend to bounce back more quickly than boys. In other words, both girls and boys can become depressed by the lack of fathering and paternal nurturance, but a boy without a father or surrogate father is often the depressed boy who can become violent.

Tim Wright, author of *Searching for Tom Sawyer,* put fathering this way: "The father pours maleness into his son so that the son can grow up whole. If the father is gone, the boy may not fully develop and mature into the man we want him to be." Father attachment is one of the ten essentials for healthy male development because fathering is a unique *male* blend of love, challenge, risk-taking, empathy, impulse-control, self-regulation, and character and social-emotional development that helps all children, but because it is *male nurturance* it affects young males distinctly–making males more successful, better at self-regulation, more loving and empathic, and better able to grow up and mature.

Modern society is a new world in which we have replaced old ideas about feminine and masculine to our credit. But our rising sputters, even fails, when we forget that human beings are male and female (including the gender spectrum to be discussed in Part II). Putting all our eggs in the "masculine social norms" basket neglects who we each are and what we each need. It allows us to under-nurture our males in our mis-read of "the masculine." We miss developing boys into loving, wise, and successful men and thus we increase male violence. Meanwhile, we think we are being highly moral as a civilization. We embolden social paradigms into primacy in our social debate but forget to deal with human nature. We don't want our boys to hurt or kill us, but we avoid both the disease—impact of neglect on male nature—and the cure—assets that already exist in that nature if we will nurture those assets to fruition.

<h1 style="text-align:center">Chapter 2</h1>

<h1 style="text-align:center">Diseases of Despair Among Our Males</h1>

> "Each act unfailingly begets an act, that act begets another, and so on to the end, and the seer can look forward down the line and see just when each act is to have birth, from cradle to grave."
>
> –Mark Twain

(This essay is useful for general readers and parents, and particularly for legislators, staffers, therapists, social workers, college students in various disciplines, and those involved in suicide and drug-addiction prevention.)

HUMAN DEATH IS AN UNFORTUNATE POINT of understanding regarding the male mental health crisis. In all age groups, males are dying of overdoses at rates considerably higher than their female counterparts in the same age group. In many instances, the frequency also crosses age groups. For instance, males 20-24, 25-29, and 30-34 are dying at rates higher than *all* female groups.

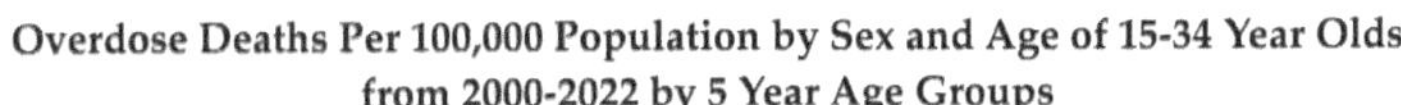

Overdose Deaths Per 100,000 Population by Sex and Age of 15-34 Year Olds from 2000-2022 by 5 Year Age Groups

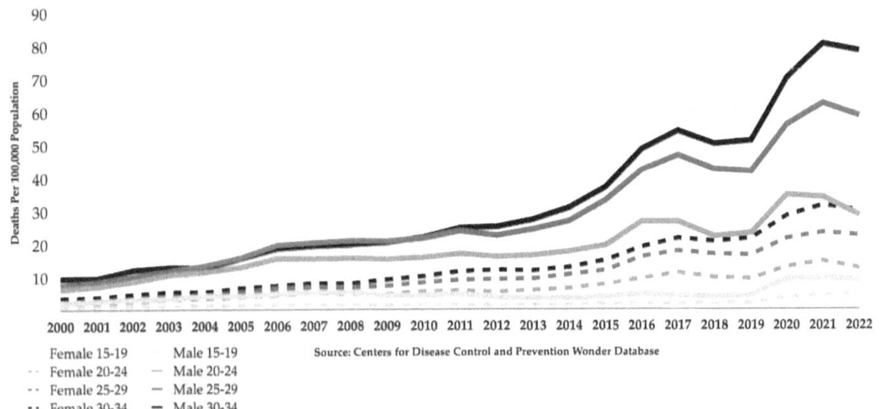

When we combine rates of overdose and suicide deaths per 100,000, we see an even greater disparity. As Michael noted, our girls and women suffer from mental disease and experience suffering and despair, but there is a troubling reality in our Western world especially: male despair leads to more loss of life. Comparing the graph above (overdose death/100,000) to the graph here (combined overdose and suicide deaths/100,000) I (Sean) hope you can also see how much wider the gap expands across all age groups.

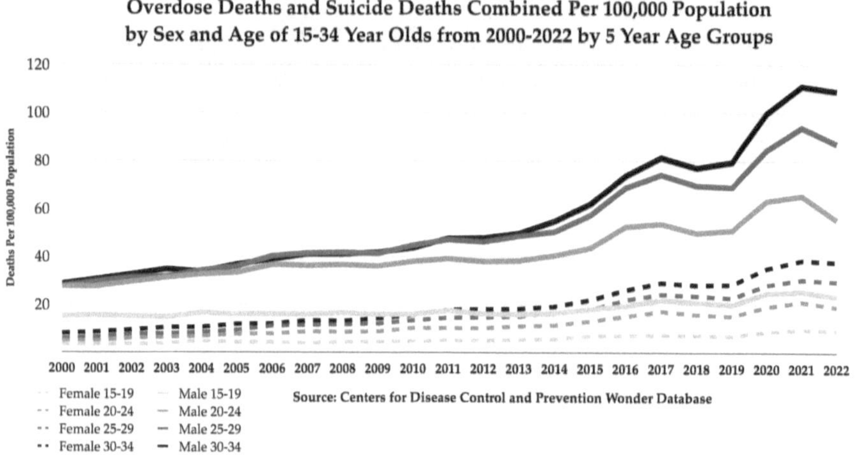

Male loneliness and deaths of despair are a significant mental health issue, not just for males themselves but for everyone around them—which means, for our society as a whole. While we focus culturally on women's mental health, especially on increases in overt depression and anxiety among our girls in the Post-Covid era, our society must also notice that 72% of overdose deaths and 75% of suicide deaths are male. A worthy mental exercise is to think about our culture's commitment to solving breast cancer in which 1% of deaths are male and 99% of deaths are female. Take a look at this article from Johns Hopkins Medicine. *Male Breast Cancer: A Rare, Increasing Trend. The color pink isn't exclusive to women, and neither is the disease that it often represents: breast cancer. While breast cancer is more than 100 times more common in women than men, men are much less likely to detect breast cancer early on.* The article is useful on its face because most of us do not know that males have a "25 percent higher mortality rate of male breast cancer compared to female breast cancer." As with so many human diseases, males are more likely to die of the disease, but I want to use this article to make another point: breast cancer is much more likely to impact women. We all know this. If the title and content of the article focused on males having a 25% higher mortality rate of breast cancer without acknowledging the wide differences between the sexes in mortality from the disease, the title and content would be deceptive.

I feel the same way when reading articles about deaths of despair among males. Throughout the media, articles discuss how much more likely girls are to attempt suicide than boys. These articles point out something important but are also deceptive because they don't acknowledge that boys are four times more likely to succeed at suicide–to die. Similarly, articles in the Big Three discuss the increase of female overdose and suicide deaths in the last ten years. Again, these are important articles, but they specifically avoid the male problem, which is far more severe than the female problem on this topic. There are few articles in the Big Three that focus specifically on male mortality from overdose deaths and suicide, especially compared to the number on female.

Let's change that by using the table below to specifically notice how females and males 15-19-years-of-age showed a 163% and 63% increase in combined overdose-suicide deaths respectively over two decades. Just pointing this out, however, does not acknowledge that 75-80 percent of those deaths are male.

Average Overdose & Suicide Deaths Combined 2000 to 2022
Per 100,000 People by Selected Age Groups and Years

Sex and Age	2000 to 2003	2004 to 2007	2008 to 2011	2012 to 2015	2016 to 2019	2020 to 2022	Increased Rate/100,000 from 2000-03 to 2020-22
Female 15-19	3.5	4.4	4.7	5.8	7.1	9.2	5.7
Male 15-19	15.1	16.1	16.5	16.7	20.6	24.6	9.6
Female 20-24	5.5	7.8	9.6	11.5	16.0	19.9	14.3
Male 20-24	28.9	34.7	37.5	40.1	51.8	61.3	32.4
Female 25-29	7.0	10.2	13.0	16.1	23.3	29.5	22.5
Male 25-29	30.0	37.9	43.7	50.7	70.5	88.6	58.6
Female 30-34	9.1	12.0	15.3	19.5	28.1	37.2	28.1
Male 30-34	31.6	37.6	43.6	53.6	78.1	106.7	75.2
Total Female	25.2	34.4	42.5	52.9	74.4	95.8	70.7
Total Male	105.6	126.3	141.3	161.0	221.0	281.3	175.7
Percent of Male Deaths	80.7%	78.6%	76.9%	75.3%	74.8%	74.6%	

It's About the Brain

In Part III, I will delve even more deeply into the Big Three's political approach of abandonment regarding male distress and privation but for now, I'm hopeful that the graph helps you see how desperate our male situation has become regarding increased negative male mental health outcomes. Michael and I will use this book to point out various angles on how male mental health mainly rests on looking at the male brain interacting with genetics and environment rather than pretending that masculine norms are causal of male mental illness. As Michael did in Chapter 1, we will look at mechanisms of neuroscience in male behaviors, decisions, and reactions, especially how our culture's under-nurturance of the male brain's assets and difficulties have harmed boys and men, and all of us for decades.

In our present political climate around sex and gender, the Big Three focuses mainly on culture-theory as causal, but some studies do get at the brain science, like this one in the *Proceedings of the National Academy of Sciences*, *PNAS*, (Srikanth Ryali, Yuan Zhang, Carlo de los Angeles, Kaustubh Supekar, and Vinod Menon), "Deep learning models reveal replicable, generalizable, and behaviorally relevant sex differences in human functional brain organization." The authors know the difficulty politically with dealing in brain science and hint at it early: "Sex plays a crucial role in human brain development, aging, and the manifestation of psychiatric and neurological disorders. However, our understanding of sex differences in human functional brain organization and their behavioral consequences has been hindered by inconsistent findings and a lack of replication." Rather than noting four decades of replication, the study's authors begin by avoiding those decades of knowledge, a tact politically useful in our present climate in which admitting male/female brain difference at the outset can be problematic or worthy of cancellation. Fortunately, the study's authors press forward, detailing their method.

"We address these challenges using a spatiotemporal deep neural network (stDNN) model to uncover latent functional brain dynamics that distinguish male and female brains. Our stDNN model accurately differentiated male and female brains, demonstrating consistently high cross-validation accuracy (>90%), replicability, and generalizability across multi-session data from the same individuals and three independent cohorts (N ~ 1,500 young adults aged 20 to 35). Explainable AI (XAI) analysis revealed that brain features associated with the default mode network, striatum, and limbic network consistently exhibited significant sex differences (effect sizes > 1.5) across sessions and independent cohorts.

"Furthermore, XAI-derived brain features accurately predicted sex-specific cognitive profiles, a finding that was also independently replicated. *Our results demonstrate that sex differences in functional brain dynamics are not only highly replicable and generalizable but also behaviorally relevant, challenging the notion of a continuum in male-female brain organization.* **Our findings underscore the crucial role of sex as a biological determinant in human brain organization, have significant implications for developing personalized sex-specific biomarkers in psychiatric and neurological disorders, and provide innovative AI-based computational tools for future research**" (my emphasis).

To talk about male mental health is to talk about the male brain. To talk about the male brain we need to admit there is such a thing. Fortunately, for decades, some scientists have done so (you'll keep meeting them in this book), like the scientists in this study. Another word for male/female brain difference is *sexual dimorphism.* This sexual dimorphism has been confirmed for forty years worldwide by neuroscientists and can help us look at deaths of despair. We can see much higher numbers for males than females because the sexually dimorphic male brain is affected. Similarly, when we look at mental diseases that females experience more than males (e.g. anorexia or bulimia), we are not looking at "femininity," but at the female brain. "Masculinity" is not dying in the tens of thousands from the disease of despair, male brains are. (Michael will deepen your knowledge of sexual dimorphism and male/female difference, and thus, also, the brains of girls and women in comparison in the next chapter and in Part II).

Fear of discussing sexual dimorphism, avoidance of male, and overuse of masculinity go hand in hand. When the media and the Big Three overall avoid powerful outcome data disaggregated by sex for *males*, how can policies and practices get built that will save boys and men? If we avoid the issues that male brain grapple with alone right now and mainly without resources, we are abandoning our boys and men to significant challenges and complexities at a neural level.

A Time for Reason and Compassion

An example of male-avoidance occurred in Washington State recently. Blair Daly, President of the Washington Initiative for Boys and Men, myself, and others lobbied the state legislature to establish a commission on the status of boys and men, which would have been the first in the country. Unfortunately, the Commission was <u>cavalierly dismissed</u> by the Chair of the Committee (who needed to bring it up for a vote in the legislature) despite that <u>78% of suicide</u> and <u>70% of overdose deaths</u> in Washington are male; that the bill had bi-partisan support in both houses; that a <u>thorough report</u> by the *Global Initiative for Boys and Men* on state outcomes showed the need for the Commission; that an address to state representatives by Richard Reeves of the <u>*American Institute for Boys and Men*</u> galvanized the audience; and that Washington State is the headquarters of the <u>*Gurian Institute*</u>, which has been at the forefront of this work for three decades and remains a significant asset for data collection in the state and the nation.

When our group of advocates approached the congress member blocking the bill, we were armed with our data but met avoidance and neglect as the congress member referred us to data on suicide and overdose rates of girls and women. We responded that 1) female/male is not zero-sum, and 2) commissions exist for female assistance but not for males, which is discriminatory. The staffers and legislators in charge chose to avoid the male data and yet again a government agency decided against helping males. Fortunately, the Melinda French Gates foundation, also headquartered in Washington State, has taken a different path, awarding the *American Institute for Boys and Men* <u>a $20 million dollar grant</u>. Melinda Gates was moved to act because of the data on male mental health, and we boy advocates are grateful to her.

All of us in this field hope the data you are just getting started with in this book will be used in full by you to lobby the Big Three to evolve the field of mental health.

Areas for evolution include:

- Evolve brain science forward into deeper understanding of the male brain, without excluding the female brain and brains on the gender spectrum.
- Reverse myopic focus in the Big Three on masculine norms theory and concomitantly increase focus on healthy male brain development.
- Exercise compassion beyond our present social dismissals of boys and men as either inherently defective or too masculine.

Wherever you look at data in our world—whether in medical, climate, psychological or neuro-biological science, male mental disease reflects ways in which human nature is not being served by a society. As Michael will detail in the next chapter, the etiology of *male-type depression,* a mental illness central to diseases of despair, cannot be treated fully, healed, or even substantially curtailed if we remain male-avoidant in contemporary culture. We must treat male mental disease and difficulty with as much compassion as we do female.

Chapter 3

Diagnosing and Treating Male-Type Depression

"We need be careful how we deal with those about us, when every death carries to some small circle of survivors, thoughts of so much omitted, and so little done."

–Charles Dickens

(This essay is useful for general readers and parents, and particularly to therapists, social workers, college students in various disciplines, and those involved in suicide and drug-addiction prevention.)

TRACY, **18,** CALLED HIS PARENTS to say he was not doing well in college. "I can't take it," he said, "I have to get out." After insisting he keep trying, his parents did finally relent. They sent him a ticket to come home and he did. Three days later, in his bedroom, he hung himself.

"We missed the signals," his parents told me (Michael), still grieving. "But all along, he was such a normal kid. He was beautifully sensitive, a real talker. We thought once he came home, he would be okay." This boy's parents and community–well attached to him–nonetheless missed his sex-specific, male-type depression.

Cory, 15, took his girlfriend breaking up with him very hard. His mother, as most parents would, assumed his puppy love was part of his maturation. And Cory, like Tracy, was a "good talker" (his mother's words to me at a social gathering, as she told me Cory's story). "He said he was okay and he seemed to be okay." Gradually, though, she said, he became increasingly angry. One day, after being suspended from school for fighting, he told his mother he wanted to "really f—k up Mr. Halliday" (English teacher who set his suspension in motion). A month later, Cory attacked another boy with a knife.

Approximately 1 in 5 Americans struggle with a serious mental health issue and many of those people are depressed males. As Sean has outlined, male suicides and overdose deaths have become a silent epidemic. Some depressed males are publicly violent in ways that shock our nation, including school and workplace shootings, as we noted in Chapter 1. The accused school shooter in Parkland, Florida, Nicholas Cruz, had allegedly been in and out of the mental health system, yet his real mental condition was not fully understood, and necessary intervention did not occur. With accessibility to weapons, he concocted and refined his plan and finally, carried out his slaughter of children and adults.

Boys, Girls, and Depression

Most research on depression, like "Why is Depression More Prevalent in Women?" Paul R. Albert, *The Journal of Psychiatry and Neuroscience*, points out that women and girls are nearly twice as likely as boys and men to experience depression (at approximately a 5.5 to 3.2 ratio respectively). Girls and women absolutely struggle with a great deal of depression, but data on depression is incomplete because the depression measured in studies like Albert's is "overt depression," or "reported depression." This kind of depression is seen by researchers and clinicians because women and girls (and boys and men who have overt depression) present to clinicans with its symptoms and often are able to present it verbally (they talk about it). "Covert depression," on the other hand, which is biologically favored by males, is a different thing. Once this kind of depression is factored into statistics, the statistical female/male gap diminishes or disappears. Millions of males with covert depression are suddenly seen.

Try This
Is A Child in Your Care Depressed?

To ascertain whether someone in your care is depressed, you and your clinicians will tend to look for these symptoms:

- excessive rumination (constantly thinking and talking about negative thoughts, especially about a recent occurrence or trauma)
- expressed feelings of guilt, sadness, or shame perhaps about a trauma (e.g. being bullied or hurt and expressing the hurt to others; the expression can happen in person or via social media)

- headaches or other physical pain noticed by or brought to the attention of parents or friends
- relatively constant irritability and/or overreaction to others in social interactions
- noticeable lethargy
- ennui that becomes relatively impossible for loved ones to ignore
- insomnia on the one hand or too much sleep on the other
- suicidal thoughts or attempts—the attempts will likely bring attention to the problem and generally lead to treatment.

If you or anyone you know fits these symptoms, it is essential to get help immediately.

In reading this list, you might have noticed that all or most of the symptoms emerge into a diagnostic framework because they are communicated verbally by the depressed person. They fit under the category of "overt depression" or "reported depression." It may take a while for parents, teachers, or counselors to realize this child or teen is overtly depressed, but thankfully, the realization does often occur, and help, hopefully, is forthcoming. Boys and men often do not fit the pattern of communication in the list, however. Sometimes, even when they do communicate their feelings—as did Tracy, Cory, and the Parkland shooter–parents, teachers, and mental health professionals often miss the extent of the brain distress the male is experiencing because so much of it is covert at a neural level.

If We Could Just Get Males to Talk About It....

We have, for a few decades, chosen to culturally assess natural male under-reporting of their own hurt and sadness as the negative result of what we frame as masculine social norms. We claim that males are less likely than females to talk about things because of the emotion-erasing pressures of masculinity.

A headline in *Harper's Bazarr* reflects this position: "It's Time to Let Boys Be Girly." The author says, "We've taught men to reject traits like gentleness, empathy and sensitivity. But if men don't have the means to deal with their anger and frustration in a healthy fashion, it can have deadly consequences."

On the Today Show five boys, one author, and one expert posited that males kill people because they have been indoctrinated to not cry or show feelings of kindness and friendship. The pressures of masculinity, the guests said, cause male suicide and homicide.

On an *NPR's Hidden Brain* episode, *The Lonely American Man*, "Boys get the message at a young age: don't show your feelings. Don't rely on anyone. This week, we take a close look at misguided notions of masculinity in the United States."

Promundo, an international organization focusing on gender justice, published a report with this abstract: "The research, conducted with a representative, random sample of young men aged 18 to 30 in the US, UK, and Mexico, reveals that most men still feel pushed to live in the 'Man Box' – a rigid construct of cultural ideas about male identity. This includes being self-sufficient, acting tough, looking physically attractive, sticking to rigid gender roles, being heterosexual, having sexual prowess, and using aggression to resolve conflicts."

This report is presented as a "study" but, like the pieces in *Bazarr*, on *Today*, and on *NPR*, it is an opinion piece created from anecdotal interviews with a small sample of individuals who agree with the ideological principle of masculine/male defect. Many well-meaning reports like these use soft science and culture-opinion, leaving male-type depression invisible. Perhaps all of us can understand the idea that "social constructs" force some boys into boxes, but as we noted in Chapter 1, masculine boxes do not create brain disease. Male-type depression, like male violence, is a biochemical and neural condition, a disease with etiology, and we must look empirically into the male brain to discover it, as we will do throughout this book. To do this, we will need to consciously set aside the masculine-defect conception of male depression and violence that exists in the "Dominant Gender Paradigm" (DGP). This term is my amalgam term for academic approaches to males and females that hyper-rely on the politics of masculinity, masculine social norms theory, and social constructivism (that we are who we are not by nature but almost solely because of our social constructs). When our society attaches male problems to the DGP ("males are suffering because of masculinity") we misread or don't read male signals. Meanwhile, we blame males/masculinity/boys/men for "toxic masculinity" and then in a cruel solipsism blame that professed toxicity for the existence of male depression. This circular reasoning convinces legislative leaders, like the Committee Chairs in the Washington legislature Sean discussed, not to act on behalf of boys and men who are, in the millions, covertly depressed.

Is a Boy in Your Care Depressed?

Males participating right now in the opioid epidemic have *covert depression*, what I call *male-type depression*, but we who care about them, legislate around them, or avoid them don't realize their depression because 1) parents and others have not been taught by academics how to assess male-type depression adequately, 2) the males themselves don't tell us how they feel because they don't know and don't have word-emotion access in the brain, and 3) males feel temporarily better when they self-medicate with substances, porn, other addictions, or violence.

Percent of U.S. Opioid Deaths by Sex and Year 2018-2022

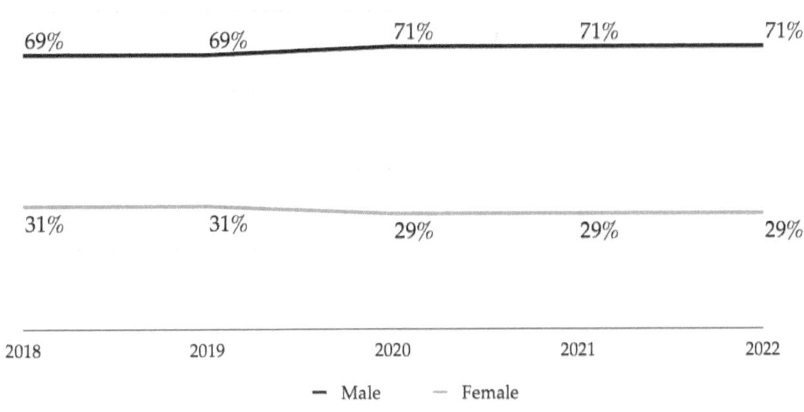

Source: Kaiser Family Foundation
https://www.kff.org/other/state-indicator/opioid-overdose-deaths-by-sex/?
dataView=1¤tTimeframe=4&sortModel=%7B%22colId%22:%22Location%22,%22sort%22:%22asc%22%7D

Brain-sex differences, pre-set in utero by gene markers on the X and Y, provide a nature-base for male/female differences in neurochemistry and blood flow in the following parts of the mid/lower-brain that involve feeling/emotion experience first, then verbal expression:

- insula
- anterior cingulate cortex
- amygdala
- hippocampus
- caudate nucleus
- nucleus accumbus
- cerebellum.

Male/female differences (sexual dimorphism) exist when we measure upward activity in the brain to executive functioning, verbal/word areas of the orbito- and prefrontal cortices, and Broca's and Wernicke's areas in the top of the brain. Two overall male/female brain differences significantly impact the way depression is experienced and expressed by males.

First, the male brain generally utilizes up to 7 times more gray matter activity for its mental processing of intelligence and emotion while the female brain utilizes up to 10 times more white matter activity. Gray matter activity concentrates in one or more "splotches" of the brain (areas of activity) while white matter spreads activity throughout the brain. The female brain generates more interconnectivity in the brain by which to study its own depression via significantly more white matter activity.

Second, the female brain generally has verbal (word) centers in both hemispheres while the male brain generally lateralizes/compartmentalizes verbal activity mainly on the left side of the brain. Heightened white matter activity and bilateral verbal centers in the female brain enhance female verbal expression of feelings/emotions, giving women a profound verbal-emotive (words-for-feelings) advantage. Researchers have found these male/female verbal-emotive differences throughout the world with a 1 in 5 to 1 in 7 exception rate. This means, as psychologist Joann Deak, author of *Girls Will Be Girls*, has put it, around 10 – 20% of males may verbalize more feelings at any given moment than females but those exceptions prove the rule, which is: in a majority of cases females will outperform males in verbal processing about what they feel.

These brain differences provide a baseline for understanding male-type depression. Recently, neuro-scientists at the National Institute of Mental Health began to look at the brain differences as they studied men returning from war with severe depression. It is now clear to the scientists that male depression does not necessarily present, express, or even terminate in the same way that female depression does. Many of the depressed veterans were not initially diagnosed as depressed because diagnosticians are trained to look for overt (more female) not covert (more male) depression and clinicians are trained to work with brains that produce words and word-for-feelings which a lot of depressed male brains do not do.

Try This
Answer These Three Questions in Clinical Teams

*Will our medical and psychiatric society admit diagnostically that there is something called "male-type depression" and that its incidence-rate is reaching crisis proportions in America?

*Will our whole culture see beyond our culture-based approach to what causes male depression, i.e. see beyond the "pressures of masculinity" and the Dominant Gender Paradigm to issues in the male brain that males by nature hide from us?

*Will our government and clinical associations invest in training parents, teachers, mental health workers and policymakers in male-specific depression assessment and treatment modalities?

A New Paradigm for Assessing Male Depression

In the late 1990s, I changed my clinical paradigm in large part because I saw that male- and female-type depression often needed sex-specific understanding in three areas:

- Presentation
- Assessment
- Treatment

If you are a clinician, *How Do I Help Him (2011)* is a clinician's guide to working with boys and men in counseling and psychotherapy, a book of strategies for working with males in distress. These strategies evolved in part from my paradigm changes regarding how I provided counseling to males in the 1990s. My first strategy-shift was to re-assess normal clinical evaluation protocols to discover general, female- and male-type depression. Here are two interconnected tools I use that come from a brain science perspective.

Try This
The Ten Questions Life-Story Assessment Tool

If a parent, teacher, or provider feels even a whiff of intuition that a silent (or talkative, but unfocused) boy may be depressed, you might change your assessment package to these questions and answers about his present and past daily living.

1. Is the boy absorbing environmental neuro-toxins that can trigger lowered testosterone/hormonal imbalance?
2. Has the boy experienced significant trauma, e.g. abuse or bullying, or divorce trauma?
3. Does the boy have a head injury? Has he suffered concussions in the past?
4. Has the boy witnessed homicide or other acts of significant violence?
5. Is the boy engaged in excessive social media use and screen time?
6. Even if he is on social media/internet (thus seeming to interact with others), is he isolating himself from family and from in person activity with close friends?
7. Is he spending too much time with substances, alcohol, video games, gambling, or pornography?
8. Does the boy perceive himself as a social, academic, financial, or physical failure?
9. Is the boy obese or significantly overweight, and/or does he suffer from insomnia?
10. Does he lack attachment to necessary caregivers and mentors—often, especially, a lack of father or father figure in his daily life?

Is he acting out or promising to act out in significant ways (making threats, very angry).

Both females and males can experience these issues but male physical, hormonal, emotional, and cognitive systems experience and, quite often, *act out* these sufferings in male-specific ways. Assessing the potential for depression by assessing the life-story of the boy can be crucial, especially with males who will simply never tell us in words what they feel when we want them to. If a "Yes" is the appropriate answer for two or more of the above list, he may be depressed even if he does not tell you he is, and some of these items, like brain injuries, can act as solo potential indicators of mental illness. By using this tool among parents, teachers, and counselors, you can collectively decide a Yes to three or four of the list apply–if so, there will likely need to be intervention on his behalf to connect and reconnect him with relationships, treatments, and activities that help ameliorate the depression.

The Reading Male-Signals Tool
(aka, Seeing Through the Masks Is Our Job As Much As His)

While using the first tool and this second one, we can certainly ask a boy what he feels. At the same time, this second tool, like the previous one, assumes:

- boys and men will not naturally, or even with pressure, talk to us about their feelings as much as females do in the aggregate, even accepting a 1 in 5 exception rate;
- they will not do so mainly for neuro-biological reasons rather than mainly from cultural constructs; and
- talking is just one way of expressing feelings of sadness and depression anyway. Boys show us their emotions, quite often, by "doing" or "not doing" (action or withdrawal).

Try This
The Male-Signals Assessment Tool

This tool studies external activities and signals.
- If the boy is angry a lot, especially more than he was previously, he may be clinically depressed.
- If he has just lost a significant peer attachment, e.g. girlfriend/partner, he may be situationally depressed.
- If he has just lost an adult attachment, e.g. contact with Dad, Mom, parent-like mentor, he is likely depressed.
- If he has been humiliated (ostracized from) his crew/best friend/peer group, he may be depressed.
- If he is of age to work but is unemployed and unable to find work, he is likely depressed.

- If he is unmotivated in school and under-performing academically without compensating mission, purpose, or focus, he is likely at least mildly depressed.
- If he has become obese and/or unable to self-motivate and perform at something useful physically, he may be depressed.
- If he is addicted to or abusing porn, substances, alcohol, video games, or involved in another addiction, he is likely depressed and self-medicating.
- If he is becoming increasingly lonely, isolated, and not relating well to primary attachment assets (e.g. parents, team members, friends) he is likely depressed.
- If he is only or primarily relating to others via online and social media rather than in person, he is likely depressed.
- If he is obsessed with weapons, revenge plots, or extreme ideologies, he is very likely depressed.
- If he is not sleeping, not exercising enough, eating poorly (eating junk food but little nutritional food), he is likely depressed.
- If he has absorbed one or more head traumas, he may be depressed.
- If he has engaged in the performance arms race in school (grades, test scores) or as an athlete and perhaps failed to get into the college of his choice or has been kicked off the team, he may be at least temporarily depressed.
- If he is living in poverty, especially an ongoing cycle of poverty, he may be depressed.
- If he has been sexually or physically abused, witnessed the murder of a parent and felt powerless to save her/him, or has been significantly bullied, he is likely depressed.
- If he has been humiliated in school via cyber-bullying or being outed or sexually compromised, he is likely depressed.

If on top of two or more of these, if he says he is doing fine, we may want to wonder if he is depressed.

This tool overlaps with the previous tool to give parents, educators, counselors, and psychiatric professionals a different angle on this work. While a boy may not be depressed even if he fits some of these categories, erring on the side of "he may be depressed" may be an important move, especially with the depression epidemic we are facing among children today. Since increased anger and/or withdrawal are generally signals of sadness, hurt, and potential depression in males, you might be able to use the tools to diagnose depression and not need the male to tell you at length that he is sad or hurt; instead, you might accept that the anger or withdrawal constitute male expressions of hurt, sadness, and potential depression, and feel empowered to help the boy right now. As you move in this direction, you may notice that the boy's/man's/male's stress hormone level may be constantly high; his serotonin may not re-up-take as it should; he may be a low methylator (impaired methylation results in decreased production of dopamine); in various parts of the brain, axons and neurons are not transmitting correctly all adding up to his being neurally and biochemically depressed behind his anger and armor.

How to Treat Male-Type Depression

As it is with so many other parts of our educational, mental health, and social systems, if we do not train professionals and parents in sex-specific developmental signals (*sex-specific evaluation and assessment*), we will tend to miss real and actual signals our males are sending. Missing those signals because of our own lack of knowledge regarding the male brain, we might distract ourselves by blaming "masculinity" or just blaming the males themselves, things we do not generally do with girls and women who are hurting. Our blame of males constitutes systemic neglect of healthy male development, yet we think we are doing the right thing for everyone by falling back into "masculine norms force him to not tell us what he feels," and similar abandonments that evolve even farther into blame of males in general. The psychology field and the general public will need to end this blame and shame practice if we are going to really get at treating male-type depression.

Try This
To Treat a Male Who is Depressed

- Make sure he is in the care of psychiatric professionals—get him any help he needs, from medication to supplements to counseling to lifestyle changes to social interaction.
- Use brain scans if affordable and possible, like those done by Amen Clinics, so that you can look at the exact parts of the brain involved in the depression.
- Use gene and blood testing to discover exactly which medications might be most useful for treating *his* depression, medications that may fit *his individualized genetic structure.*
- Try to discover whether he is allergic to a certain food, then keep that food away from him, e.g. gluten is a substance well known to trigger or amplify male depression.
- Connect this male with other males who have been depressed and come through; let them mentor him.
- Keep him away from weapons, guns, and implements that can become dangerous to an impulsive person–as a depressed male, he may have trouble controlling impulses.
- In safe and reasonable intervals, continue to confirm that he has not set up a plan for suicide or homicide.
- Remove the substances that are co-morbid with the depression (drugs, alcohol, other addictions).
- Limit screen, Smart Phone, video games, and Internet Use– excessive screen use can be comorbid with male depression.
- Increase social contact with two or more well-attached adults and two or more well-bonded peers.
- Give him purpose, mission, and meaning through service- work, e.g., visiting elders in nursing homes, caring for pets, caring for others.
- Allow no locks on bedroom doors (know where he is and what he's doing as much as possible) for at least a two- month trial period from the day of intervention.
- Increase his exercise time to at least two hours of healthy and, at times, intense exercise per day.

Cut out junk food, plastics, non-organic food (or at least some of these) to reduce environmental neurotoxins that may be negatively affecting his cells.

Brain-based research consistently shows the power of exercise to help combat depression. As neuro-scientist Daniel Amen recently put it, "Exercise appears to affect, like an antidepressant, particular neurotransmitter systems in the brain, and it helps patients with depression re-establish positive behavior. Exercise helps keep your psyche fit. It's an effective, cost-efficient treatment for depression and may help in the treatment of many other mood disorders."

Meanwhile, Getting Him to Talk to You…

Admitting that male-type depression often does not come with words-for-feelings does not mean we shouldn't keep trying to "get him to talk about it." Here are eight strategies that help get males to open up who might not otherwise talk with us. These are not a substitute for treatment for depression but practicing them can up your chances of increasing male words-to-feelings ratios on average.

Try This

- Avoid too much eye-to-eye contact when asking him about his feelings; do more shoulder to shoulder contact (e.g., talk with him while you are driving to the grocery store).
- Use parallel and/or competitive play, such as chess or poker, while talking about how he feels.
- Say "What do you think about that?" much more than "How did that make you feel?" especially in the early stages of assessment and treatment.
- Ask him to analyze what motivated him or another person to do a specific thing, e.g. "Why do you think Allan attacked you on social media?" Be concrete.
- When talking with him, remember that *fear and courage* are deep themes for males. Targeting them can help him express himself verbally, i.e. "What are you afraid will happen if

you ___________________?" "I see you as really courageous and brave, do you see yourself that way?"

- Use peripatetic interaction and counseling, i.e. begin your talk therapy with him while walking together, side by side, rather than only sitting down in a closed room.
- Do something physical together that uses game theory before getting into deep work, e.g. shoot hoops, throw a ball together, play a video game as preamble.

Ask him to draw what he is feeling, make an audiotape of himself talking and/or a video on his phone to illustrate how he is feeling. Use multimedia to get him going.

Two clinical settings that have explored sex differences in depression are Amen Clinics (www.amenclinics.com) and The Center, A Place of Hope (www.aplaceofhope.com). I have personally trained staff at The Center, A Place of Hope. I am hopeful that every clinic, school, and health-related institution will train its staff in sexual dimorphism and male-type depression. If we can all push through thin DGP paradigms about masculine norms to see the actual boys and men in our society, we can utilize new training and new approaches that are fully truthful about males. This will save male lives and it will help girls, women, and everyone else in a family and community who interacts with our hurting and depressed young males.

Chapter 4

We Can't Save Lives if We Won't Admit the Problem

(This essay is useful for general readers and parents, and college students in various disciplines, as well as educators, policymakers, therapists, social workers, data scientists, and economists.)

TO HELP OUR BOYS AND MEN in the early twentieth century, we need to become "data wonks," at least a little bit. I (Sean) have spent more than my fair share of time looking at data to create state and national reports on the state of boyhood in America. I use a fairly simple methodology to present male and female outcomes. Throughout this book, I will help you to do this, too, because data matters both on its face and in its depth of purpose. Looking at suicide and overdose data is only one way of looking at what is happening to our males.

The Data Conflation Trap

Often, the data you find in studies and news reports is not disaggregated for sex. This means that a huge data set we need, *male*, we don't get. Even more subtle, when data is not disaggregated for sex but is disaggregated for another factor, e.g., ethnicity or race, our lack of data on males actually increases as an issue we must face. For instance, recent data sets revealing American Indian /Alaska Native (AI/AN) peoples to have higher suicide rates than any other racial group, while very useful, is also misleading because race or ethnicity is used as the common denominator when, in fact, sex (male) is the greater factor of ten.

When researchers avoid the highest factor for political purposes, they are caught in the Data Conflation Trap (DCT). The data analyst decides which

35

detail is needed for the narrative, and makes sure the data fits. The analyst is helping a race or ethnic group but the highest factor in the despair, male-type depression, which took most of the lives by suicide is not focused on. Social change for males does not happen because the data does not speak for the hurt and the fallen.

As a citizen scientist, you can study local, state, or federal reports online to capture deaths of despair among males. You can do this by finding the *intersection* of race/ethnicity and sex/gender, as I did here.

U.S. Suicide Deaths from 2018-2022 by Race and Sex

Race/Ethnicity	Female		Male		Percent of Male Deaths within Race
	Deaths	Deaths / 100,000	Deaths	Deaths / 100,000	
American Indian or Alaska Native	768	12.5	2,255	37.6	75.0%
White	38,680	7.8	146,789	30.1	79.4%
Native Hawaiian or Other Pacific Islander	81	5.3	338	21.9	80.5%
Black or African American	3,339	3.1	13,604	13.7	81.5%
Hispanic /Latino Only	4,538	3.0	18,715	12	80.0%
More than one race	733	3.8	2,221	11.9	75.8%
Asian	2,027	4.0	4,771	10.3	72.0%

Source: CDC Wonder Database
Not Hispanic or Latino https://wonder.cdc.gov/controller/saved/D176/D356F737
Hispanic or Latino https://wonder.cdc.gov/controller/saved/D176/D356F738

Male suicide deaths cut across all racial lines. Suicide is a predominately male outcome. Of the 14 sex and race-based classifications, the three groups with the highest number of deaths per 100,000 are accented with heat mapping. **79% of all suicide deaths are male.**

Let's Analyze a Study Together

Let's analyze a study together to move our culture beyond the DCT. In September of 2022, the Centers for Disease Control and Prevention (CDC) published "Suicides Among American Indian or Alaska Native Persons." Demographic factors regarding suicide among AI/AN persons included age, nonmetropolitan and metropolitan geographical areas, history of mental health, substance abuse history, non-Hispanic AI/AN persons, relationship problems, and intimate partner abuse. Here is language from the Discussion section.

Analyses of characteristics of and circumstances preceding suicide among AI/AN and non-AI/AN persons in participating NVDRS jurisdictions during 2015–2020 identified many differences, including higher odds of relationship and substance use problems and lower odds of physical, job, and financial problems;

known mental health conditions; and any history of mental health or substance use treatment among AI/AN decedents compared with non-AI/AN decedents. Although direct comparison of circumstances between studies is not possible, these findings suggest a similar pattern observed in a previous analysis of suicide in 18 states among non-Hispanic AI/AN persons compared with non-Hispanic White populations, during 2003–2014 (2). Those findings also indicated higher odds of relationship and alcohol problems and reduced odds of known mental health problems, current or past mental health or substance use treatment, and physical, job, or financial problems. Toxicology results from the earlier study also followed the same pattern as those observed in the current study, including higher odds of positive alcohol, amphetamine, and marijuana toxicology results among AI/ AN decedents, and reduced odds of positive opioid and antidepressant test results, compared with non-AI/AN decedents.

You have likely noticed no mention of males, the highest factor of ten, yet.

The current study found higher odds of suicide among AI/AN persons across a range of relationship problems related to intimate partners, family, other relationships, interpersonal violence victimization and perpetration, and death of friends or family members by suicide. Similarly, more alcohol and other substance use circumstances, including those of an acute and more chronic nature, were observed in this study, as were criminal problems, although the nature of these problems was unknown. According to previous NVDRS reports, approximately one half of persons who die by suicide do not have a known mental health condition (4). This study found that only 41.5% of AI/AN suicide decedents had a known mental health condition. This might be the result of less available or accessible mental health services, especially in rural areas, and therefore fewer diagnoses. Post-hoc analyses controlling for metropolitan status did not change these results, suggesting possible contribution of other factors.

There is still no mention of "male," but males account for 78.2% of the deaths within the AI/AN population. Suicide deaths over the same time period as the study (2015-2020) at five-year age groups show more male AI/ AN suicide deaths across *all* age groupings ranging from 2.2 times (those 15-19 years-of-age) to 5.5 times (those 55-59 years-of-age). Overall, for every 1 AI/AN female who died from suicide, there were 3.4 AI/AN males, and 15-19 year-old males were significantly higher than any female groups.

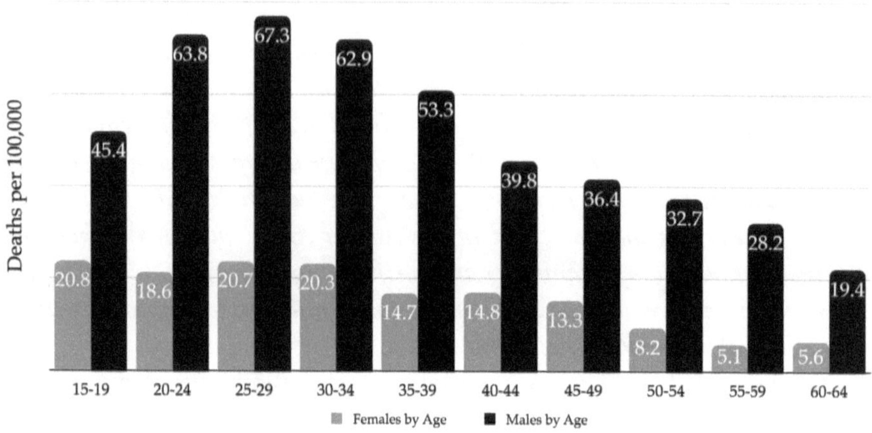

Source: Centers for Disease Control and Prevention

Neglect of males is common in the Data Conflation Trap. While focusing on AI/AN suicides higher among males across all age groups is useful and important, most of the suicides discussed in the study are male. Adding males to the study would do no harm and only help researchers, diagnosticians, and treatment specialists, but males are absent. If every study like this added "males," legislators and others in the Big Three could focus social capital on the primary factor in suicide overall—males in distress. Adding a focus on males would not require researchers to nullify any findings about race/ethnicity; rather, it would open up the possibility for others to dig more deeply into the reasons, including but not limited to male/female brain differences and male-type depression, and thus give visibility to the whole problem we face with suicide in depth rather than only looking at a part of it.

A Conversation I Had Before School One Day

When I taught high school English, I tended to arrive early to school, usually around 5:30 A.M. This helped prepare me for my day and allowed me to get a bit of work done before the students flooded the classrooms and hallways. On many occasions, at 7:00 or right after, I met students sitting in the hallway, which led to a brief exchange and, sometimes, a conversation.

One particular morning, a student of mine was sitting outside my classroom very early. The halls were empty, so we struck up a conversation sitting on the floor, facing a row of lockers across the way, talking shoulder to shoulder. I cannot remember what we were talking about until the conversation changed and Billy started talking to me about his suicide attempt two years earlier. He spoke openly as if he had known me for years. I sat quietly and listened until he hesitated, looking for a paternal affirmation. I told him what a pleasure it is to have him as a student and to know him as a fine young man.

He asked me a question about my own teen years and partying. My answer was honest, but not too openly revealing.

"I always feared I would use partying as a way to escape despair instead of facing my own challenges head-on and spending my time more fruitfully."

He sat quietly.

I continued.

"I worried that my own despair might lead me to other things, like too much partying or too much of something else."

After a moment of reflection, he nodded his head.

"I do the same thing."

I felt the mood change as if a burden lifted off him.

I stood up to get to work saying, "You're a great kid, Billy. Thanks for sharing this part of your life with me. If you ever need to chat, I'm here." That morning a male-male bond was formed with this boy, and he did later talk with me more about his life.

Despair as Cause: Suicide, Overdose, and Alcohol as Effect

When it comes to discussing diseases of despair, suicide, overdose, and alcohol use are often discussed as individual afflictions, as if suicide is its own category, and drug addiction and overdose is its own category, and alcoholism and alcohol death is its own category. Though there is value in looking at these diseases and deaths of despair independently, it is equally important to look at the three as one collective category, which is what I was tacitly doing with Billy, a boy who had questions about all these categories in one.

Despair is the disease and suicide (ideation, attempts, and deaths), overdose, drug addiction, alcoholism, and alcohol deaths are each and all potential consequences—not just of addiction genetics that a person may carry, but of the despair that may trigger those genetics to express themselves in the male. In a sense, despair is the disease and these outcomes are the effects of the disease, or at least comorbid with the disease.

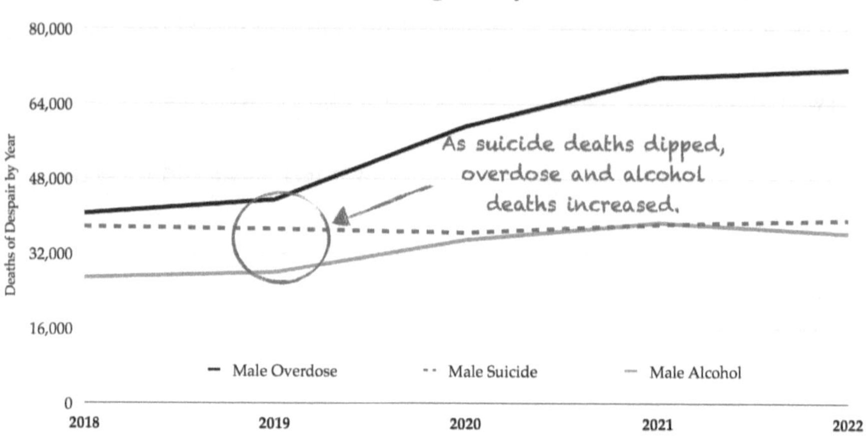

U.S. Male Deaths of Despair by Year 2018 to 2022

Even in years when one category of despair, suicide, decreases, another area of despair, overdose deaths, increases, and vice versa year after year. The despair has not gone away. From 2018 to 2020 the U.S saw a dip in the number of suicide deaths, but during that same time period, there was a dramatic increase in overdose deaths and a noticeable increase in alcohol deaths. Similarly, from 2021 to 2022, there was a slight decrease in alcohol deaths offset by a rise in suicide and overdose deaths. Even as alcohol deaths decreased from 2021-2022, they did not return to lower levels similar to those in 2018. The important point here is that, each year, male deaths of despair increase in one or more of their categories of outcome. Thus, when we look at total deaths of male despair statistics, they should give us significant pause. We are losing tens of thousands of males to depression and despair but can barely bring ourselves as a culture to notice.

The graph pointing this out avoids the DCT by showing male-specific results of male despair. (I will go more deeply into the fentanyl crisis, which adds more fuel to this fire, in a moment). Whatever the death of despair statistic we have available to us, when we disaggregate numbers with race and sex intersecting, males in all races present higher rates of deaths of despair compared to their female counterparts. All agencies and institutions involved in reports regarding the diseases of despair should start using graphs that avoid the DCT so that we can all see the collective result of despair among the highest population of deaths: males.

Recognizing other groups, such as transgender, is important, as well, yet even there, disaggregating transgender groups that recognize the sex/gender of surveyed individuals is crucial so that we avoid the DCT. In Los Angeles, there were 4,012 homeless deaths from 2020 to 2021. Eighty-two percent of those deaths were male and eighteen percent were female. When it annotated its tracking mechanisms, the Los Angeles County's Public Health Department ensured that "male includes transgender male and female includes transgender female." Actual data on males is again conflated here–biological males whose gender is female are considered biological females and biological females whose gender is male are placed in the male demographic but sex and gender are not the same thing. Transgendered people whose sex is male have a mortality rate three times higher than transgendered people whose sex is female and whose gender is male according to a recent study in the *Journal of the American Medical Association* (JAMA). This makes unfortunate sense–the brain, bloodstream, and cells are still male, so these trans women, still male, have higher suicide and death rates three times higher than the trans men who are female.

Why do transgendered females (sex-male) have a mortality rate that is three times higher than a transgendered male (sex-female)? (In a later chapter, "Does the Child Have Brain Sex Dysphoria or Gender Dysphoria?" Michael provides language and research critical to moving our understanding of sex, gender, and sexgender into the future.) If we keep moving farther away from studying and understanding our males, whether they are gender nonconforming, trans, gay, or questioning, the more we avoid targeting treatment to the source code of the issue–our males.

Tables You Can Use for Your Citizen Science

For your use and the use of any agency or institution working in the area of mental health, I am providing tables geared toward objectively presenting information regarding deaths of despair. Please feel free to make the tables age specific, e.g., grouping 15-24, 30-39, 50-64, and so on. You can also use percentages, raw data, and whole numbers transparently on these graphs so that people can see the data immediately. Here are two tables. I will provide more tables in Part IV.

Number of Deaths of Despair of by Race and Sex (Year)

	Suicide		Overdose		Alcohol	
	Male	Female	Male	Female	Male	Female
African American Female						
African American Male						
American Indian or Alaska Native Female						
American Indian or Alaska Native Male						
Asian Female						
Asian Male						
Filipino Female						
Filipino Male						
Hispanic or Latino Female						
Hispanic or Latino Male						
Pacific Islander Female						
Pacific Islander Male						
Two or More Races Female						
Two or More Races Male						
White Female						
White Male						
Not Reported Female						
Not Reported Male						
Total Females						
Total for Males						

Deaths of Despair by Sex and Gender (National or State) Year(s)

	Suicide		Overdose		Alcohol	
	Sex Male	Gender Female	Sex Male	Gender Female	Sex Male	Gender Female
Transgender						

Deaths of Despair of Transgendered People by Race, Sex, and Gender

	Suicide		Overdose		Alcohol	
	Sex Male	Gender Female	Sex Male	Gender Female	Sex Male	Gender Female
African American Female						
African American Male						
American Indian or Alaska Native Female						
American Indian or Alaska Native Male						
Asian Female						
Asian Male						
Filipino Female						
Filipino Male						
Hispanic or Latino Female						
Hispanic or Latino Male						
Pacific Islander Female						
Pacific Islander Male						
Two or More Races Female						
Two or More Races Male						
White Female						
White Male						
Not Reported Female						
Not Reported Male						

Digging Deeper into DCT and Overdose Deaths

Not only do boys and men of all races have higher rates of fentanyl and other overdose deaths than girls and women, but males across all racial groups account for 63% to 81% of fentanyl and overdose deaths within their own race. Male overdose deaths also cut across racial lines with AI/AN, black, and white males dying at higher rates than all female groups.

U.S. Drug Overdose Deaths from 2018-2022 by Race and Sex*

	Female		Male		Percent of Male Deaths within Race
Race/Ethnicity	Deaths	Deaths / 100,000	Deaths	Deaths / 100,000	
American Indian or Alaska Native	1,860	30.2	3,066	51.2	62.9%
Black or African American	18,607	17.2	50,453	50.8	74.7%
White	84,689	17.0	183,699	37.7	68.9%
Hispanic /Latino Only	9,856	6.5	38,911	25	79.4%
Native Hawaiian or Other Pacific Islander	98	6.5	336	21.8	77.0%
More than one race	1,550	8.1	3,077	16.5	67.1%
Asian	697	1.4	2,830	6.1	81.3%

Source: CDC Wonder Database
Not Hispanic or Latino https://wonder.cdc.gov/controller/saved/D176/D399F461
Hispanic or Latino https://wonder.cdc.gov/controller/saved/D176/D399F460

*Note: Overdose deaths only include unintentional overdose deaths to avoid duplicating suicide overdoses. Male overdose deaths cut across all racial lines. Overdose is a predominately male outcome. Of the 14 sex and race-based classifications, the three groups with the highest number of deaths per 100,000 are accented with heat mapping. **71% of all overdose deaths are male.**

You can be a citizen scientist regarding presentations of overdose data by providing legislators and other stakeholder in the Big Three with this data. You can dig deeper into this issue with the stakeholders by pointing out that when, in 2022, there were 46.6 overdose deaths for every 100,000 black people, leaders came together to build helpful and important new programs specifically for black women. Meanwhile, if that same data was disaggregated by sex, we would see 71.8 overdose deaths for every 100,000 black males and 23.3 overdose deaths for every 100,000 black females, more than three times as many black male deaths. Social assistance should not be a zero sum game. While the 46.6 number was an average of females and males and very helpful, the 71.8 overdose deaths per 100,000 for black males compared to 23.3 for black females should have alarmed stakeholders and funders.

Michael and I hope your combined efforts across the country and the world make sure everyone is reading data on males, too, so that it will lead to helpful programming for males and not just females or other groups. "Male" must become a significant part of our social investment if we are to treat and curtail deaths of despair. As we will explore throughout this book, there are political impediments to caring for our males, but enough is enough. At some point we must rise up together to say to the Big Three, "Look at the data," and "Let's do something now."

How to Further Pursue the Data Where You Are

To do my data work at the Global Initiative for Boys and Men, I have needed state or city level data by race and sex. And to get it, I need to request the information for sex assertively because that data is often not readily available on websites. Sometimes, I have to file Freedom of Information Act requests, which you can do from home. In many cases, data is available if you write emails and letters, make phone calls, and search through websites without needing to file a Freedom of Information Act request.

An Example of Citizen Science in Action

In April of 2023, I responded to a post by Richard Reeves, President of the American Institute for Boys and Men, on X (formerly Twitter). In his post, Reeves had provided a pie-chart showing that 2/3s of COVID deaths were male. My response to his post included a graph that showed COVID deaths by sex and age at different age groupings. In response to my post, Todd Zywicki, a law professor at George Mason University, made a comment that encouraged me to dig even more deeply into the particular area of infant respiratory deaths. I dug and the data showed that infant males (those under one-year-of-age) were considerably more likely to die of respiratory diseases than infant girls, and that it has been that way for decades.

Percent of Infant Deaths by Sex from Diseases of the Respiratory System 1968-2020

56%	58%	59%	59%	59%
				Median
44%	42%	43%	41%	41%

— Infant Boys   — Infant Girls

1968-1978	1979-1988	1989-1998	1999-2009	2010-2020

Source: Centers for Disease Control and Prevention, National Center for Health Statistics. National Vital Statistics System, Mortality
https://wonder.cdc.gov/controller/saved/D16/D339F371
https://wonder.cdc.gov/controller/saved/D76/D339F373

Because medicine has improved, the number of infant deaths of boys and girls has decreased significantly with each passing decade. In 1979, there were 1,062 infant boys and 827 infant girls who died from respiratory diseases. By 2020, that number decreased to 180 infant boys and 128 infant girls. The consistent factor, however, has been more males than females dying, as the most recent 2022 data showed. Respiratory deaths for infant boys were 215 and infant girls 150. Males are clearly more fragile than we tend to realize.

As you obtain and work with data on sex and gender, you may find what Michael and I have found: the politics of masculinity and the Dominant Gender Paradigm leave out male-type depression, the male brain, and male diseases of despair from policy-making and funding, a systemic practice that results in boys and men getting inadequate care, and thus dying all around us. And as you go forward, remember that most counselors, psychiatrists, and medical professionals do not access the data I have been looking at with you. They get the data in front of them that the Big Three provides them. We can help them by being citizen scientists who dig for this data. By showing them what is going on, we can get better treatment options for our own child who has a mental illness, and/or help build and fund programs that will rescue our boys across the board from mental illness, male-type depression, and deaths of despair.

Essential Questions

- Are studies I am reading disaggregating data for sex and at the intersection of race/ethnicity and sex/gender?
- Are the studies adding a person's developmental age to the equation, i.e., disaggregating data at the intersections of age, race, and sex when working with specific populations?
- How can I discover data myself that includes sex differences or develop that data myself by adding sex difference to data about socio-economic conditions?

Are there other "citizen scientists" I can band together with to ask on social media, in classes and seminars, at city council meetings and other forums regarding data on the male mental health crisis that will inspire leaders to discuss deaths of despair from the viewpoint of sex?

Chapter 5

What Was The American Psychological Association Thinking?

> "I believe in the difference between men and women. In fact, I embrace the difference."
>
> –Elizabeth Taylor

(This essay is useful for general readership, and may be especially useful for parents, counselors, social workers, mentors, and in high school or college courses in psychology, sociology, and gender studies.)

IN 2019, THE AMERICAN PSYCHOLOGICAL ASSOCIATION published its "Guidelines on Practice with Boys and Men." I (Michael) was one of the clinicians asked to write a response. Before sharing that content with you here, I want to feature something very relevant that Sean did a few years ago. This is an example of therapeutic gut instincts working to save a boy in a teacher's care.

> My wife and I had just returned from a wedding. I couldn't sleep, so I decided to check my school email because I had left school immediately after classes to get ready for the wedding. I don't remember the time, but it was late, sometime between 1:00 AM and 2:00 AM. A male student of mine had sent a group email to all his instructors about feeling depressed and heading home for the weekend, giving physical illness as the reason he was not in class that day. Something about the email did not sit well with me. It included no overt show of depression, but my guts tightened as I read and then reflected on it.
>
> I decided to call the school's health office where I spoke with a mental health professional. It didn't seem like that person

could do anything right away, but it was a restless night for me. I couldn't sleep, I woke up early, I decided to call the parents even though I had handed my instinct off to the school counselor. It was somewhat early to call someone on a weekend, but my guts still ached.

After we talked, the boy's parents called him and made up some reason as to why they needed him to return home with the car. When he did return home, they asked him about the email and he cried with them and shared his pain, his shame, his sadness. The student did not return that semester so that he could get care for his depression. From the parents I learned later, just before we talked, the young man had left the house on his way to take his own life.

A young man sending an email about feeling "a little bit down" to a group of instructors he has known for approximately a half-of-a-semester could have been "nothing," but it seemed like a cry for help to me, and out of the norm for this student who was, for the most part, quiet, reflective, but not uncheerful. Making the call to the parents is one of those things I will never forget in my teaching career. In writing this book, I have asked myself, "Why of all the instructors who received the email from the boy was I the only one to pass the email to school officials then call the parents?"

My answer is: my immersion in the male brain data and science we are writing about in this book. If I had not become sensitized to male-type depression, I don't think I would have reached out to school officials. If I was not looking at the boy as a *male* who 1) does not tend to tell people what he is feeling by nature, 2) might need different psychological interventions than a girl, and 3) is not suffering because he tends toward "the masculine" (which this boy did not) but might be a male in crisis, I don't think I would have intervened.

Tony was a 14-year-old boy who walked into my (Michael's) counseling office with a lot of issues. Short for his age and not yet visibly pubescent, he had been diagnosed with ADHD and his parents felt that he might be depressed. Tony was like hundreds of boys and men I've seen in my clinical practice: if a counselor shows that he or she knows how to work with a young male, Tony will work with us; if the counselor doesn't, he wouldn't. Like Sean in his school, in my counseling practice, I look at boys as males and try to understand them from that vantage point.

The first thing I did with him was to walk outside (peripatetic counseling) so that we could talk shoulder-to-shoulder. Because the male brain is more *cerebellum-dependent* than the female (it often needs physical movement to connect words to feelings and memories), we sat down to talk *after* our walk had finished. As we sat and talked, we tossed a ball back and forth like fathers often do with children in the backyard. This combination of cerebellum-activation and spatial involvement helped his male brain move neuro-transmission between the limbic system in the midbrain and frontal lobe at the top of the brain where word centers are. Over the months that we worked together, Tony and I also used visual images, including video games, to trigger emotion centers and neural pathways between emotions and words. We discussed manhood a great deal, since Tony and every boy is longing for mentoring in the human ontology of how to be a man.

I've seen hundreds of girls and women in my therapy practice. Few of them needed walking, physical movement, and visual-spatial stimulation to help access memories, emotions, and feelings because most girls are better able to access words-for-feelings than boys and men while sitting still. Girls and women naturally grow language centers on *both* sides of the brain, thus they connect both sides of their brains to memory, emotion, and sensorial centers. The male brain mainly has word centers on the left (more on this in Part III). Even more intriguing, perhaps, more of the female brain operates in the frontal lobe (where word centers are) at its baseline. If counselors want to be effective with the whole gamut of males, we need to work with, not against, the male brain, which means we can't hyper-rely on words while sitting in a chair for fifty minutes.

The Mismatch of Counseling Psychology with the Male Brain

Wherever I travel to speak, I hear, "Why don't boys and men go to therapy or stay in therapy like girls or women do?" Most literature from the Big Three argues that "masculine training keeps boys and men from opening up," but the real answer is that for fifty years we've set up counseling and psychological services for girls and women, for the female brain, more than for boys, men, and the male brain. In a sense this is ironic, since counseling and the field of psychology should be about very little else except how to treat the brain, but "Come into my office," we say kindly. "Sit down. Tell me how you feel." This modality will not work for millions of boys and men. Not only won't it work, but these boys and men will realize, quite quickly, that they are failing out of counseling and therapy in the same way many of them are falling behind or failing in education and in our schools. The counseling psychology modality is "verbal-emotive" (words for feelings) first, and does not include enough action, movement, challenge, and immediate problem-solving. After a week or a few more in this counseling, males leave the therapy office, or they withdraw from therapy even if they are still forced to sit in the chair by mom or a spouse.

Once again, our lack of focus on *male* is hurting our boys and our social systems. Perhaps you have been told that medicine, psychiatry, education, and most things in our culture are set up for males not females, but in our males' lived reality, the problem is just the opposite: we have not taught psychologists and therapists about the male brain. We have not taught them how to work with males in particular. The counseling profession skews female, with only 15% of new counselors male, 85% female, and with voluntary clients in therapy mainly female for decades.

Given this reality, it would have been most useful if the American Psychological Association provided training on males and the male brain in its Guidelines for Practice with Boys and Men (www.apa.org/about/policy/boys-men-practice-guidelines.pdf.) but it did not. The document began by pointing out the boy crisis we've explored in this book, then fell into a masculinity/ideological swamp. The document tells us that males are born with dominion created by their inherent privilege while females are victims of this male privilege. It continued to argue that masculine privilege roots all or most masculine issues (suicide, early death, depression, substance abuse, family break ups, school failure, and violence). The assumption that all systems skew in favor of males–including schools, homes, and public policy–was so deeply entrenched in our culture already, the writers of the APA Guidelines never had to prove it and so they did not. They just pushed forward with the politics of masculinity.

Perhaps most worrisome: the APA should be a science-based organization, but the APA guidelines lacked hard science. Ruben and Raquel Gur, Tracey Shors, Louanne Brizendine, Sandra Witelson, Daniel Amen, and the hundreds of scientists worldwide who use brain scan technology to understand male/female brain differences do not appear in the Guidelines. Practitioners like myself, Daniel Amen, M.D., and Leonard Sax, M.D., Ph.D., who have conducted multiple studies over three decades in practical application of neuroscience in schools, homes, and communities are not included. The brain differences I introduced in my discussion of male depression were not discussed, e.g., that the male brain is more cerebellum dependent, utilizes more gray matter activity than the female, and has a lower baseline word-to-feeling ratio. Nor were the male brain characteristics discussed that I will detail much more deeply in Part II. The American Psychological Association charged with treating and fixing our brains did not adequately delve into the human brain in general nor discuss the male brain in particular.

Instead, the Guidelines authors pushed the Dominant Gender Paradigm (social constructivist) idea that maleness is socialized and that it is badly socialized via masculinity. Stephanie Pappas on the APA website summed up the APA definition of masculinity as "marked by stoicism, competitiveness, dominance, and aggression, and, on the whole, harmful." Our job as therapists, she and the other authors admonished, was to remove the harmful masculinities while preserving in boys and men the ideologically approved masculinities. Specifically, the goal of the counseling psychology profession should be to remove competition, aggression, male ways of doing emotions, and social power from male development.

I can think of very few documents that are better examples of the Big Three's use of the Dominant Gender Paradigm than this one. The Guidelines condemn the very parts of males that can help boys, men, and everyone around them succeed, heal, and grow–the motivation that comes with competition, the assertiveness that comes with healthy aggression, the male way of doing emotions and feelings, and the male drive to advance and succeed. Had I as an adolescent boy been a client of an APA directed counselor, I would have been let down by my therapist. Like Tony, and like the boy Sean helped, I experienced significant child abuse and sexual abuse as a young boy. I was also a sensitive boy then teenager who needed therapy to help me tap into male strength and the arc of manhood. While he helped me "develop my feminine side" in the 70s and 80s (which I am certainly glad of), I could not have healed from significant childhood trauma nor become a resilient man without therapy regarding maleness, manhood, strength, aggression, power, and compartmentalization of trauma. Focus on manhood by one therapist helped me as a male to be both expressive and stoic when each was needed, competitive enough to survive and thrive in a complex world, and resilient in a way that might look, at times, like dominance, but in the end was my way of serving others, and aggressive enough to be assertive when my family, my community, and I myself, needed help.

I write gratefully about this manhood-focused therapist, Mr. Ramirez, in my 2024 memoir, *The Storm in My Mother's Eyes* (michaelgurian.substack. com/). A strong and sensitive man, a Vietnam veteran, he knew that I was on a journey of manhood and that maleness and manhood were healthy. He did not limit masculinity or manhood to what the APA limits it to, and he used intuitive best practices with me *as a boy* to help me free my soul. Now a counselor myself, I can see what he was doing: my maleness and his manhood were ontologies he was helping me to learn; they were not socially limiting "masculinities." As *ways of being,* manhood and maleness transcended race, creed, ethnicity, or sexual orientation by committing a boy to a quest for resilience, trauma-response, perseverance, a work ethic, the ability to love in an adult way, service to the disadvantaged, and the self-sacrifice incumbent upon men throughout the lifespan.

As I read the APA Guidelines with sadness, I thought of Mr. Ramirez. Were he still alive, he would find them anathema to working with boys and men. He would say, "What is the APA thinking? Shouldn't every professional in the psychology field, and parent, mentor, or friend want to embolden confidence, assertiveness, competitiveness, protectiveness, and success in our males?" To him, as to me, not the erasure of maleness, but the development of maleness–of manhood–is required of boys and men in a society, including inside the counseling office, if we are to rescue our sons from suicide, school failure, addiction, deaths of despair, depression, anxiety, and the male loneliness each APA guideline purports to address.

While the male journey is not perfect, and while expanding what "masculine" and "man" mean to a given family and person is a point well made by the APA authors, hooking male mental health and our system of mental health professionals into an ideological trinity of DGP ideas

- masculinity is the problem.
- males do not need nurturing in male-specific ways because men have it all in our society anyway
- manhood is not a way of healthy being but a form of oppression

ignores one of the primary reasons for the existence of our psychology profession: to help boys and men find strength, purpose, and personal confidence during what is, for them, a complex *male* journey through their difficult lifespan.

Essential Questions
If you know a boy or man who has been to a counselor, ask them these questions:

- Did the counselor understand you as a male–a boy or man? If so, were you inclined to stay in counseling longer? Did you look forward to counseling with this mentor?
- What made this counselor "boy- or man-friendly"? Can you describe the techniques s/he used or uses to bring the best out of you?
- Or did the counselor not understand how to work with you as a boy or man? How can you tell s/he did not understand you?
- What was it in the counseling that made you want to quit?

About the counselors you know, and about their training for counseling, you can ask the same questions, though tactfully, and perhaps silently.

- Did the counselor get training in the male brain?
- Does this counselor lose boys and men who quit earlier than they should because they do not feel understood by this counselor?

Do boys and men seeing this counselor say, "This is a waste of time," and quit when they really mean: I am not safe in this office because I, including my maleness and what it means to be a man, are not understood by this person?

Chapter 6

False Allegations, Suicide, Opioid Deaths, and the Self-Medication of Boys

"I am not interested to know whether vengefulness is in my heart or not. I am going to act rightly regardless of whether I like it or not."

–Mahatma Gandi

(This essay is useful for general readership, and may be especially useful for parents, high school and college students, media and communications classes, law-enforcement, social workers, and policymakers.)

IN 2002, BRIAN BANKS, a rising football star at Long Beach Polytechnic High School in California was falsely accused of rape by Wanetta Gibson. Brian Banks spent nearly six years in prison and another five years on probation. The false allegation derailed his academic and athletic aspirations at the University of Southern California, where he made a verbal commitment and was offered a full scholarship. Banks was a 16-year-old when he was falsely accused.

Banks' story played out like many that begin with poor due-process procedures, young men ill-equipped and ill-funded to navigate the judicial system, prosecutors and defense attorneys ready to move a case along, and false victims who make allegations for a variety of reasons—some for financial gain, others for spite, and some from their own mental illness. While every true allegation reveals a hurt victim who needs our help, every false allegation hurts not just the falsely accused person but other actual victims, male and female, of rape and assault by creating a lack of trust in victims down the line. Every false allegation, too, can result in addictive behavior, self-medication, and suicide among the males who are falsely accused, unfairly attacked and shamed, and significantly depressed. For Banks, tragedy continued as Wanetta Gibson and her mother Wanda Rhodes sued the school district and won a $1.5 million settlement upon Banks' criminal sentence. Fortunately, later, the Long Beach

Unified School District then filed suit against Gibson and "won a $2.6 million default judgment against [Gibson] whose false rape allegation in 2002 cost the school district money and landed a fellow student in jail," according to Greg Mellen of the Press-Telegram in Long Beach, CA. Neither Gibson nor her mother received jail time for the allegations that derailed the life of a 16-year-old boy and drove him toward despair. You can read Brian Banks' story of his ten year battle for exoneration in his memoir, *What Set Me Free: A True Story of Wrongful Conviction, a Dream Deferred, and a Man Redeemed.*

An Easy Target, the Privileged, Defective, Unworthy Male

In November of 2022, Bafana Sithole (a 17-year-old pupil from Hoërskool Kriel High School in Mpumalanga, South Africa) took his own life after false allegations by a girl left him in such despair and shame that he felt he had no other option. Even despite Sithole's suicide, there were no charges filed against the school girl who said her accusation against him was just a joke about being raped by him. With high school and college aged boys accounting already for the overwhelming majority of suicides in their age groups, it seems most productive for media, communities, schools and mental health professionals to address all of what is happening in these boys, but our system is not prepared to address the different crises that make boys and men so vulnerable to shame then suicide. Behind the false allegations leveled against young men like Banks and Sithole is the power of rumors that swirl on campus and in social media, power that comes from assumptions in the system that males are destructive anyway, masculinity is predatory, and boys are inherently dangerous.

We must protect girls and women from bad men, but when false allegations and dangerous anti-male spin comes at the expense of boys and men, we need to look closely as a civilization at what we are doing to our males. Are we helping males feel worthy or trying to prove the case in the Big Three that they are unworthy? Has our social consciousness become so jaded as to argue, simultaneously, that "males have it all," while also arguing that they have no real worth? In England recently, three Asian men tried to end their own lives after Eleanor Williams, 22, falsely accused them of rape. According to Helen Pidd of *The Guardian*, Williams made claims on Facebook "of being raped and trafficked by an Asian grooming gang [that] sparked a worldwide solidarity movement with its own line of merchandise, 'Justice for Ellie', and ignited community tensions in her Cumbrian town...." It turned out that Williams had become a serial accuser of rape over a number of years; she was ultimately sentenced to eight-and-a-half years in prison. The accused men have not fully recovered from the incident and are struggling to regain normal lives in a community that now sees them as defective, dangerous, and unworthy.

Most boys and men will never commit a crime. We all know that. But the Dominant Gender Paradigm regarding males and masculinity is so embedded in public consciousness, young males are easy targets. College campuses and Title IX policies have lately joined in the DGP to move schools away from due-process for accused males by expanding staff positions empowered to expel males without civil liberty protections. Leaving males this vulnerable happens from tacit social pressure we must grapple with.

Underneath individual false allegations is the lack of trust in the public consciousness for all males. Mechanisms from within laws like Title IX that make discrimination by sex illegal will need to be put in place to protect our boys and men equal to girls and women, even if we instinctively see women as victims. If these mechanisms do not exist–if we do not protect the worthiness not just of each woman but also of each man–we risk individual catastrophe for increasing numbers of males.

Is There a Rape Culture on Our Campuses?

Heather MacDonald is a social scientist tracking those catastrophes. In the *Diversity Delusion*, she discusses what she calls "the Campus Rape Myth Culture" revealing how agencies manipulate data to promote a false and hyperbolic narrative of male unworthiness and violence; how policymakers, media, and academia have bought into the unworthy male; how allegations are left in the hands of university administrators who are ill-equipped to handle such allegations, and forced to rely on "believe the victim" when the accused is an unworthy male even when the allegations against that male are false. MacDonald writes, "The federal Clery Act requires colleges to report the number of crimes affecting their students. From 2005 to 2016, campuses got safer. Total crimes, including burglary and crimes of violence, dropped 43.5 percent from 2005 to 2016. Such increased safety contradicts the dominant narrative and is therefore ignored. When it comes to sex crimes, both the federal government and local campuses regularly fiddle with the categorization of campus sex crimes to get the numbers up. In 2014, federal authorities changed the reporting category of "Sex offenses—Non-forcible" to the inherently vague "Fondling." The reports increased 6,000 percent, from 59 non-forcible sex offenses in 2013 to 3,614 fondling incidents in 2016. Even with this more expansive classification, and the efforts of campus authorities to come up with even more categories of sex offenses, the total number of Clery sex offense reports in 2016 was 10,297.

"Corroboration is not required. A defendant can be cleared and the accusation against him will still be entered into the Clery tally. Those 10,297 reports include all alleged improprieties against males, females, graduates, and undergraduates at 6,500 institutions. By comparison, if the one-in-five figure of campus assaults were correct, there would be between 300,000 and 400,000 sexual assaults on female undergraduates alone each year. In 2017, the American Association of University Women complained that rape numbers were still too low. Among college campuses (including branch campuses of a central institution) with enrollments of 250 students or more, 73 percent reported 0 rapes in 2015—a wholly unacceptable 'picture,' as the AAUW put it."

One of the most egregious examples of false allegations destroying male lives came through a *Rolling Stone* article about the University of Virginia where a jury ultimately awarded $3 million to Nicole Aramo, a university administrator, after "finding *Rolling Stone* and reporter Sabrina Rubin Erdely defamed Aramo." You can access this story throughout media archives and see the hyperbole used in false accusations, then the diminutive stories written once the allegations were proved false. Some "studies estimate that between 4-6% of people incarcerated in US prisons are actually innocent," according to the Georgia Innocence Project, but estimates vary widely, with reports suggesting anywhere from 2% to 10% of incarcerated males wrongly convicted. While the Georgia Innocence Project makes a point of focusing on race, and the plight of black males is very important, males (sex) is the most likely factor for false accusations, convictions, incarceration, and suicide by shame and despair.

Males and Self-Medication

In June of 2024, 18-year-old actor Tyler Sanders died from a fentanyl overdose. His parents opened up to the media about the loss of their son, hoping to inspire national discussion on depression, substance abuse, and self-medication among young people, especially young males who feel unworthy and are depressed. "Tyler was an ambitious, hard-working actor who was dealing with deep and persistent depression," his father said. "Although actively seeking treatment, Tyler struggled to find relief and chose to experiment with drugs. Tyler then fell into drug use, not as a way to have fun socially, but rather as an attempt to overcome his profound mental health struggle. Tyler's Mom said, "I want others to understand that we are a family much like all other families who never thought this could happen to us."

According to an *L.A. Times* article, "A recent report found that 13 times as many people lost their lives in L.A. County to fentanyl in 2021 as in 2016. The drug was involved in more than half of all overdose deaths, and was especially prevalent among teenagers: Among 12 to 17-year-olds who died of an overdose, the vast majority — 92% — tested positive for fentanyl." Self-medication is a primary method for males to deal with male-type depression and its attendant shame. Data on drug-overdose deaths nationwide can reveal to us, if we let it, how hard opioids have impacted boys and men. In 2009, there were approximately 23,000 male overdose deaths, 13,000 of them from opioids. By 2022, there were over 78,000 male overdose deaths, and over 58,000 of those deaths came from opioids.

While some opioid use is recreational and experimental–teen males lacking impulse control and/or seeking temporary pleasure–much of it is self-medication for anhedonia and social isolation. Approximately 1.2 million boys and men have died of overdose and suicide in the 15-year span from 2009 to 2023, even after accounting for any overlap between suicide deaths that are a result of overdose. According to the National Institute of Health, "about 5% to 7% of overdose deaths are recorded as intentional. Because it can be difficult to determine whether overdose deaths are intentional, the actual numbers are likely even higher." The graphs below focus on all types of drug overdose deaths, with opioids, natural and synthetic, accounting for the largest percent of the overdose deaths. As noted in Chapter 2, while the percentage of deaths from one year to the next may fluctuate, the number and deaths per 100,000 has increased steadily in the last decades. Drug use and self-medication of boys and men continues to increase worldwide decade to decade.

Graph Indicating the Percent Increase or Decrease in Overdose Deaths from Previous Year, Number of Deaths from One Year to the Next, and the Number of Deaths per/100,000 from Year to Year

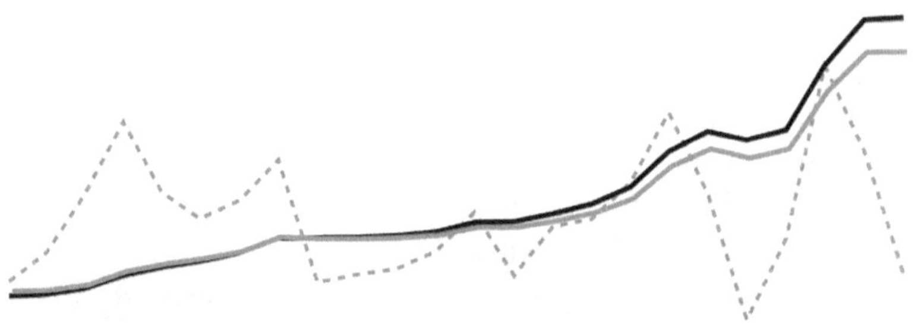

The purpose of this graph is to show the erratic nature of the political narratives that discuss the increases or decreases in overdose deaths from any one given year to the next. **In truth, overdose deaths have increased every year, accept two, in number and per 100,000 since 1999. 2018 saw a 3.8% decrease in overdose deaths, 2,483 fewer deaths.** The second, 2007, was statistically insignificant, a 0.1% decrease, 25 fewer deaths.

U.S. Overdose Deaths by Year from 1999-2022

Year	Number of Deaths	Number Increase from Previous Year	Percent Increase from Previous Year	Deaths Per 100,000
1999	19,128	N/A	N/A	6.9
2000	19,720	592	3.1%	7
2001	21,705	1,985	10.1%	7.6
2002	26,040	4,335	20.0%	9.1
2003	28,723	2,683	10.3%	9.9
2004	30,711	1,988	6.9%	10.5
2005	33,541	2,830	9.2%	11.3
2006	38,396	4,855	14.5%	12.9
2007	38,371	-25	-0.1%	12.7
2008	38,649	278	0.7%	12.7
2009	39,147	498	1.3%	12.8
2010	40,393	1,246	3.2%	13.1
2011	43,544	3,151	7.8%	14
2012	43,819	275	0.6%	14
2013	46,471	2,652	6.1%	14.7
2014	49,714	3,243	7.0%	15.6
2015	55,403	5,689	11.4%	17.2
2016	67,265	11,862	21.4%	20.8
2017	73,990	6,725	10.0%	22.7
2018	71,147	-2,843	-3.8%	21.7
2019	74,511	3,364	4.7%	22.7
2020	96,096	21,585	29.0%	29.2
2021	111,219	15,123	15.7%	33.5
2022	112,109	890	0.8%	33.6

Source: Centers for Disease Control and Prevention, https://wonder.cdc.gov/controller/saved/D77/D413F149

Percent and number increases (in the graph above) should be compelling political talking points regarding male self-medication and male crisis but they are not, unfortunately, or at least they are not compelling enough for leadership to create social change.

Black Males and Suicide

In 2023, MSNBC's Joe Scarborough interviewed actor Courtney B. Vance who lost his father and godson to suicide. Vance had released his book, *The Invisible Ache: Black Men Identifying Their Pain and Reclaiming Their Power,* written with co-author Dr. Robin L. Smith. In the interview with MSNBC, Vance focused on suicide in the black community specifically. "Don't hide your grief or your shame," he and Scarborough said. "Hiding grief and shame is something we men are particularly good at, of whatever race." Males may not express grief and shame verbally–until they write a suicide note. While alive, they may show us their depression covertly via self-medicating, which is a theme in Vance's book, and which shows up statistically in overdose deaths. Black and Native American males die from overdose at rates higher than any other demographic group, approximately 51 per 100,000 population for both groups. Black males are also susceptible to the consequences of false allegations and other male social stigmas that potentially lead to addiction and suicide.

Percent of U.S. Black Suicide Deaths 2018-2022 by Sex

80.9%	81.4%	82.3%	81.8%	81.3%

19.1%	18.6%	17.7%	18.2%	18.7%

2018	2019	2020	2021	2022

— Black Male Suicides   — Black Female Suicides

Source: Centers for Disease Control and Prevention
https://wonder.cdc.gov/controller/saved/D157/D402F740

Our culture knows something is going on with our males. In certain pockets of culture, we take a glance at the problem, as, for instance, black male overdose death increase and media report it, but we don't focus enough on male development itself as a core issue, nor on each aspect of the male's sense of unworthiness–whether from false allegations, mental illness, lack of purpose, loneliness, addictive disorder, or shame. The state of our males should get reported much better than we report it, and to that end each of us as a citizen scientist will need to lobby the Big Three via universities, governmental agencies, and the media to notice the abysses in which boys and men travel. Our male mental health crisis involving depression, suicide, overdose deaths, and shame and the profound sense of unworthiness boys and men experience today cannot be solved if we avoid focusing on our males with the same depth and inward eye we use to focus on our girls and women.

Essential Questions

In your book group, family, professional learning community, or agency meeting, I hope you will ask and answer these questions.

1. In the media I read and follow, are male issues discussed or are they avoided? If avoided, who in the media can I approach to change that avoidance? In social media, what platforms can I use to present the kind of material in this chapter for root-cause discussions regarding male life?

2. Have I seen false allegations made against males in my community? If so, how can I help the accused males at the outset, before they become significantly depressed from shame, to guide them toward resilience?

3. How can I bring women's groups into this discussion about males without allowing "masculinity is bad" or the more hidden concept of "males as unworthy" ideas to paralyze the kind of social change?

If I see any child self-medicating, who will I bring into the family to help me address the internal issues this child is facing? Who can help him or her to deal with shame, grief, anger, and sadness at the level of trauma and resilience so that the self-medication can end?

Chapter 7

Understanding and Uplifting the
Science of Male Fragility

"And if you think tough men are dangerous, wait until you see what weak men are capable of."

–Jordan Peterson

(This essay is useful for general readers and parents, and particularly useful to college students in various disciplines, medical school classrooms, educators, law-enforcement and criminal justice personnel, policymakers, and schools of psychology.)

MALES DIE FIVE OR MORE YEARS YOUNGER than females. Each time I (Michael) look at death rates, I feel my own destiny calling out to me. The chance that I will die before the women around me is obvious. Among African Americans, the death number nearly doubles to a nine year gap. In suicide, accidental death, deaths on the job, overt depression, chronic loneliness, school-life, and in general social-emotional difficulty, male biology is fragile. In some ways, it is more fragile than female biology. I think many people sense this already. You have probably noticed that females live longer, suffer less suicide, die less on the job and die less quickly from disease on average; that females mature their social-emotional development and frontal lobe connectivity more quickly than males, do better in school on average, and use words better, on average, than boys; and that males wear armor but are in many ways quite fragile. In our contemporary culture experiment, new parents report wanting girls rather than boys because they perceive girls as more useful or just for gender political reasons. Do these parents also suspect, even if subconsciously, that girls are less fragile than boys, and thus easier to mature?

A hundred years ago or in China a few decades ago, boys were favored and "boys ruled," but things have changed in the last four decades. Statistics and parent preferences are shaping a new world in which girls can be said to rule. While many females are more fragile than many males and while each person is in some way more fragile than another person, male fragility must now become a crucial human topic if we are to rescue our sons just as we made women's fragility a crucial human topic more than fifty years ago and now live in heightened sensitivity to women's needs and vulnerabilities.

Unfortunately, the Big Three's obsession with "masculinity" and "privilege" as the causes of our social problems accompanied our new sensitivity to girls and women and now continues in a way that mainly avoids the science of male fragility. As such, it disallows a human discussion about male fragility culture wide. But without this discussion, we will not develop the empathy we need to rescue our sons.

The Science of Male Fragility

In this book you've seen graphs and charts comparing males and females in various areas of life. Here are graphs that combine mortality rates. Even when we remove the three leading causes of death for males in these age groups, male mortality rates are still 2 and 2.3 times higher than female rates.

Mortality of 15-19 Year Old Males and Females per 100,000 population (Not Including Overdose, Suicide, and Homicide Deaths)

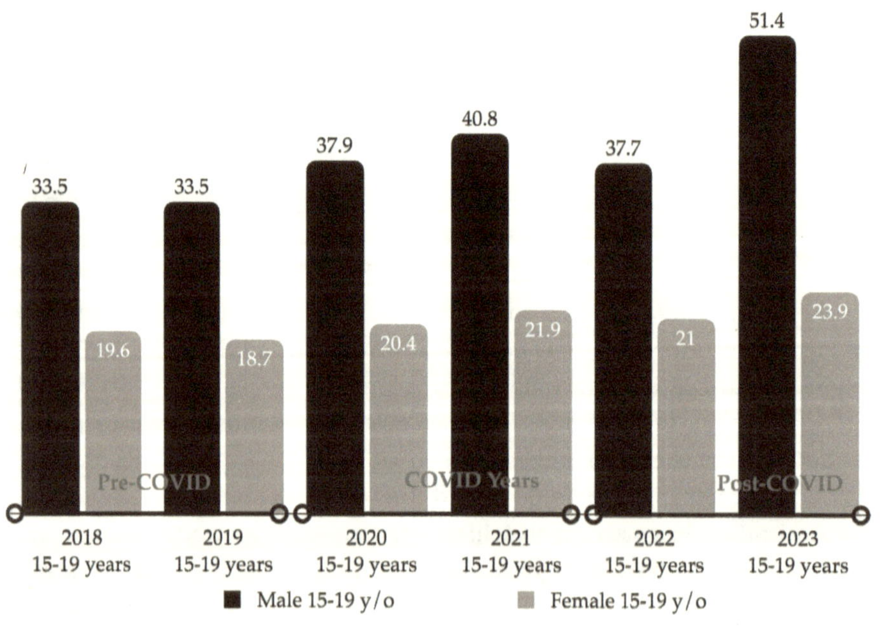

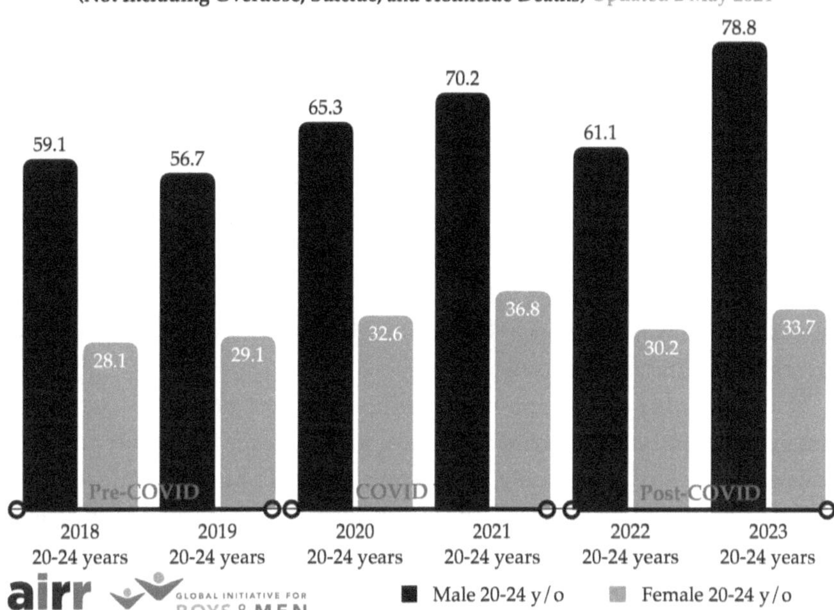

If we add back in the mortality rates that include suicide, overdose, and homicide, the mortality rates of boys and young men compared to girls and women are even higher, as you saw in previous chapters. While there are many ways to look at the fragility of a sex, death rates are one of the most dramatic. Since 2003, because of genome mapping, we also now have available to us another way of using the science of male fragility to help define and map that fragility. We can look at chromosomes (females are XX, males are XY) and notice that people with a Y (males) have a 25% higher infant mortality rate than people with an X (female) because of the smaller and more fragile Y chromosome. This chromosomal fragility follows each male throughout his life, reflected most dramatically in his higher death rates that include suicide, overdose, homicide, and death by natural causes, but also in the covert depression, school failure, and many other markers we are exploring with you throughout this book.

But males don't look as fragile as females might look physically. Males are bigger, females are smaller (on average). Males have more muscle mass (on average), more fast twitch muscles (on average), larger bodies and brains with more mass than females on average. Our fragile males appear bigger and stronger. These males have ten to twenty times the amount of testosterone in their bodies and brains than females, and testosterone is a root biochemical cause of male armoring, height, weight, and the "strong" appearance of the male in comparison to the physical female, so the male look of armoring and strength will probably never go away.

But *why* did nature set males and females up in this different way in the first place? What is the root cause of these sex differences? The primary evolutionary reasons for male armoring ("toughness") are for sexual attractiveness to females and more subtle: nature has compensated for the fragile Y. Our boys and men are wired to bulk up and/or work to be "strong" so that the male body, male "self" (their psychological structure), and the Y chromosome can survive and thrive. Testosterone wires the male body and brain *in utero* toward this end. Throughout life, testosterone compensates for the fragility of the male chromosome.

Scientific study of inherent male fragility, like the analysis we are providing throughout this book, is critical, Sean and I believe, to rescuing our sons because so much of human life hinges on the fragile male chromosome even when we don't realize it. School shootings, war, violence, high risk behavior, financial and business sectors, education and parenting, marriage and work... there is no part of human life that does not intersect with the fragile Y and the stronger X.

But Wait, Isn't All Science About Males Already?

To admit that the Y chromosome is more fragile than the X is a crucial step in understanding our boys and men scientifically and in sympathizing with them individually. Utilizing sciences that intersect with the male brain, sexual dimorphism, male mental health, and male genetics is necessary in our very scientifically inclined new century to rescue our sons, but our cultural obsession with masculine social norms gets in the way. We avoid male fragility by focusing on social constructs that exaggerate male strength and power.

To take into our minds and heart that suicides, overdose deaths, school failures, and even male violence and rage might connect with Y fragility, we need to remove a smokescreen the Big Three uses—the false assertions of male hegemony in life and in science. "Why study males when the world is set up for them anyway?" "Let's study girls and women, not boys or men." "Science is all about males already." "Males dominate health care research." While research in the medical sciences in the past focused on males for reasons of administrative ease, protectiveness of women, and gender bias, things have changed. Progress in health care today increasingly involves females more than or rather than males. Our governments and communities have formed and funded thousands of federal, state, and local agencies to help girls and women. Hundreds of hospitals and clinics specialize in women's medicine and women's services. Executives at managed care companies know that it would constitute political disaster to put "Men and Boys Clinic" on the side of a building. In health care, "the future is female" is a growing reality.

Our national attention to the medical and psychiatric science of female development is welcome and will not abate, but we should be honest about our lack of sympathy for male fragility. "Men have it all" and "everything serves men anyway" made sense fifty years ago as a slogan. But unfortunately, for the Big Three, it is still the norm mainly because our cultural attention goes to powerful men leading businesses and government. These visible men do not appear fragile and in many ways that they are not, but the visibility of these men adds to the smokescreens not just about "masculinity" and "patriarchy" but in the cultural trend toward seeing powerful males as dominant enemies of the rest of us. By their visibility, we become distracted from the millions of males who are fragile and unsuccessful—unemployed, underemployed, listless, purposeless, addicted, suicidal, under-educated, mentally ill, lost, broken, and unable to get help in systems ostensibly set up for them as males.

Our "Enemy" Is More Fragile Than We Think

Our males became the enemy in the Big Three around five decades ago, but fragile male biology, untempered unless we temper it, and dangerously lonely unless we give it purpose, will burn down our houses with its hot anger and paralyze our social functioning with its cold pursuit of isolation and withdrawal. Making males and masculinity the enemy via gender politics can work for a graduate thesis, but it cannot work for a society built to help everyone in need. Shootings and gang activity, crime and punishment, male failure in schools and preschool-to-prison-pipelines, racial and gender inequities, bullying, homophobia, and transphobia will all continue, not abate, until we make male neurobiological development one of the most important scientific discussions of our age. To do this, we will have to look at hard science more than soft constructivist sociology. In hard science, we will find our boys and men open and vulnerable.

Did You Know?
Studying Male Fragility

Studying the science of male fragility means studying these things.

- Fragility effects of biological neurotoxins on male testosterone levels and the male brain (average male testosterone levels are presently 30% lower than thirty years ago), effects that are dangerous not just because of low sperm motility but because of the cellular link between low testosterone and depression/violence.
- The fragile mismatch of educational and social services institutions, e.g. counseling systems and schools, with the male brain; systems are set up much more for strong girls and women than for fragile boys and men.
- Fragility effects of individual male trauma and traumatic poverty on the male brain and male mental health–including the alignment of low testosterone with trauma-response and then depressive disorders among males.
- Fragility effects of under-attachment to mothers in some cases and effects of more general father-loss in approximately ⅓ of our males, including lack of father figures and lack of shared parenting/shared custody to compensate for fragile male neurobiological development after divorce.
- Fragile co-morbidity in etiologies of male mental illness, the male depression spectrum, covert male depression, and brain disorders predominating in severity in males such as ASD (autism spectrum disorder) and ADD/ADHD.

The fragility effect of generalized lack of resilience development in children today, including lack of male purpose and identity development; this is resilience-deprivation that leads to male anhedonia.

A powerful exercise for ongoing discussion in your community is to change the sex in the above list to "female." Once you do that, you will likely see no cultural objection to saying, "Our culture needs to address female depression, mother loss, women's trauma, and girls' issues in schools." Women and fathers of daughters like myself have joined together to advance female empowerment and will continue to do so. My books on girls and women (*The Wonder of Girls* (2002), *Leadership and the Sexes* (2009), *The Minds of Girls* (2018) have focused on women's empowerment through the lens of the very powerful female brain. Other authors have focused on female empowerment with sociological framing. But we are all united in helping girls and women to survive and thrive by expanding definitions of "girl" and "woman" to include holistic models of what is female. None of us treat "femaleness" or "women" as the enemy, no matter the science we use to help. When we see female fragility, we move to protect and assist it to thrive and be resilient.

We have seen female fragility as a culture and now must also see male fragility. Women were never our enemy, nor are men. Our males are our lovers, parents, children, friends, coworkers, students, teachers, soulmates, and leaders who can be quite fragile, and because they are fragile—both inside and out—they need us. These males are more physically aggressive than females on average; they use fewer emotion-subtle words than females do on average; they have different resilience needs and experience male-specific empathic responses. All these differences that might empower an individual male are also part of the male fragility spectrum. We must see it better than we do.

The Testosterone Test

When I speak in communities, I challenge audiences to look at the science of male fragility by taking a "testosterone" test with me. Specifically, I ask the group if testosterone causes violence. Nearly everyone who answers the question says, "Yes, the higher the testosterone, the more violent the boy or man." I then ask if the group would say that testosterone levels are too high in our males today. Most people who respond say "Yes" because they see so much male violence (which they associate with high testosterone) in the news, in video games, in movies, and because they see bigger and more armored football and basketball players today than they remember from their childhoods. Surprise comes when I note the things I noted with you earlier.

> **Did You Know?**
>
> 1. Rather than being "up," male testosterone levels are 1/3 lower than they were in the 1980s.
> 2. Low testosterone is often more dangerous than high testosterone because it is co-morbid with under-motivation, anxiety, irritability, rage, and many other psychological and physiologic etiologies.
>
> In terms of violence, low testosterone often leads to more violence than high testosterone because the lowered brain chemistry and compromised cellular function contributes to male depression, which is comorbid with male violence.

Some people in the audience, most of whom are women, may have heard me speak on this topic before but this time, they say, "I got it." The science runs counter to what they are seeing in social media and culture and bears repeating so that it sinks in. As we explore these points together in that room, most people who speak up end up saying something like, "Oh, okay, I see now, that does make sense." This is true especially for those people who know an underperforming, depressed, fragile male.

Together in these rooms we are doing citizen science. The audience sees: male mental health issues in general are potentially connected to low and fragile testosterone levels and have ramifications for every aspect of life—loving, parenting, mentoring, working, physical health, interest and talent, schooling, opportunity, relationships, resilience, and empathy. In a couple hours, a few hundred of us take a foray (the first for some people) into the science of male fragility. "That makes sense" about testosterone becomes "that makes sense" about the fragility in males.

Because many of my speaking and training engagements are in schools, I have seen the education sector absorbing the science of male fragility better than other sectors. Some schools and districts are investing in science-based teacher and counselor training on male/female brain. (To get to know some of them, check out Part IV of this book, my previous books such as *Boys and Girls Learn Differently*, and www.gurianinstitute.com/success). From Head Start through high school, these schools have enacted equity, gender, achievement, and behavioral initiatives to include male fragility training. When these systems, administrators, faculty, parents, and community members are trained in brain science and practical strategies, they see the power of citizen science at work.

These people are no longer paralyzed. Just the opposite. They see test scores and grades improve for *both boys and girls.* Discipline referrals go down by half or more for all children as the system now utilizes the science of male fragility. Bullying rates go down and student behavior improves across the curriculum. This happens because most of the issues that modern schools face, both anecdotally and at a data level, surround boys' performance and behavior. The staff discovers that altering the system to include the male brain and the science of male fragility alters the system positively for everyone else, too.

President Donald Trump announced in 2024 that he would like to see some sweeping changes in the way America educates our children. Sean and I hope the new Trump administration will be bold in recognizing sex-difference in our schools. We hope, too, that Congress will join the President in helping to fund programs that use a boys and girls learn differently approach that works best for educating boys, girls, and everyone on the spectrum. We hope, too, that from now on all future administrations and Congresses will do the same.

Uplifting the Science of Male Fragility

More than a century ago the philosopher Hannah Arendt took on the ideological frameworks of her time by saying, "Modern ideology has become the knowledgeable dismissal of the visible." When we get too ideological, we dismiss what is right in front of us. The fragility of males is right in front of us, but we neglect and avoid it. The dominant themes of 'toxic masculinity' and 'masculine privilege' have a bit of worth, but they do not solve our social problems because they dismiss the fragile male, the boy who is suffering, and the man who is adrift. Whether you are pro or con about patriarchy or pro or con about masculinity and masculine roles, Arendt cautioned us all to look beyond ideological frameworks toward actual human nature.

Once we accept that males are fragile people just like women and that, just like women and girls (and just like everyone on the gender spectrum), they need specific things from our society, we can use citizen science to compel structures into the society that solve the deep issues we face, many of them around boys in our homes, schools, and neighborhoods. Decades ago, in Arendt's time, we wondered if we had the courage to focus on our girls and women as females with distinct and sometimes fragile *female* assets that are essential to a good society. We did, and we still do. Now the question is, "Will we have the courage to focus on our boys and men as males with distinct assets, fragile needs and profound vulnerability?"

Part II: Boys, Sexual Dimorphism, and the Culture of the Exception

"More than 99% of male and female genetic coding is exactly the same, but that 1% percentage difference influences every single cell in our bodies—from the nerves that register pleasure and pain to the neurons that transmit perception, thoughts, feelings, and emotions."
    –Louann Brizendine, M.D., Professor of Neuropsychiatry at University of California – San Francisco, Founder of the Women's Mood and Hormone Clinic, and author of *The Female Brain* and *The Male Brain*

Introduction

The life of the adult male begins at the moment of conception, when the sperm that fertilizes the egg provides its X or Y chromosome. The fetus is flooded with hormones that develop the physiologic and brain-sex of the child. Even XXY and XYY (intersex) children are flooded with one of the two sex's hormones more than the other. These sex-based genes and hormones don't determine the full person the child will become, but they format the particular sex through which the child will react to stimuli in life, experience excitement, feel depressed and challenged, encounter health and illness, and absorb emotional moments.

In the case of boys (including intersex and the gender spectrum), the Y chromosome causes the testicles to drop at between 4-8 weeks in utero. It is from there that the 10 to 20 times more testosterone in his male body and brain moves and flows. As he experiences good education or bad, new things or old things, success and failure in the various stages of his lifetime, he is doing so from the inside out, as a *male brain* with *male hormonology*. This is the "nature" of the boy that will be nurtured in family systems and then discover the culture's wealth of stimulants and frameworks from which he will resiliently, we hope, take what he needs and to which he will give what he can.

Nurture and culture will matter greatly to him. No biological organism exists outside of its environment. Nurture and culture help shape the clay of the boy into the form and face he will use to meet the world, but his brain construction based on his fragile Y chromosome is the original driver of his emotional, physical, relational, and social life. Human sex is one of the three original elements of human development (the other two are personality genes and physiologic genetics), thus we can't serve boys and men unless we understand his brain from the inside out, which means understanding *sex differences*. Just as girls need certain things in their developmental arc from nurture and culture to thrive as women, boys need nurture and culture to help shape body, personality, and sex which is male. Just as girls need us to nurture their nature, so do boys.

The Power of Sexual Dimorphism

To rescue our sons, let's now focus on sexual dimorphism in Part II of this book. If you have heard on social media or elsewhere that sexual dimorphism and sex differences are a myth or are dangerous, you have heard or read ideological fervor used to negate sex in favor of the DGP, social role elevation, the politics of masculinity, and weak constructivism rather than good science. While our males today are capable of and indeed often thrive in post-feminist social roles, social roles are only a part of a boy's internal life. If we do not understand boys as *males with male brains,* we will continue to create more male mental illness, violence, struggle, and malaise.

Feminist sociology, from which the dislike of sexual dimorphism comes, has strong control over the Big Three and specifically dislikes the concept of sexual dimorphism. Feminist sociology posits that there can be no equality without sameness and further posits that hard-wiring is a myth, only soft wiring via masculinity is character forming. This has led to an accepted vision of the male as a home for defect. But sexual dimorphism is a very real thing, not "done" or "old" or unneeded; the male brain is quite real (so is the female brain), as we will explore in depth in Part II. The brain is a tool of scientific strength and usefulness, and a tool of boy-rescue. Whether you are a parent, teacher, coach, community leader, extended family member, journalist, podcaster, business owner, mentor, or friend, you are in some way trying to mature the boys around you into men. You have made a primal commitment, not just to your son, but on your family's behalf, to everyone in the society.

In The Essays That Follow, Michael and Sean Will Explore:

- The human brain, sex on the brain, and gender nonconforming brains.
- The use of the term "cisgender" and pronouns.
- How our society uses sociological reasoning to create a culture of the exception.
- What happens to our sons when words are equated with violence.
- How school culture often treats male brains.

The abandonment of males and females that occurs when we ignore or socially negate sex differences.

Chapter 8

Why I Do Not Generally Use "Cisgender"

(This essay is useful for all general readers and parents, and particularly to leaders in The Big Three (academia, government, and media), including policy makers and college classes in medicine, psychology, therapy, social work, and gender studies.)

I (MICHAEL) WAS IN A DISCUSSION with a colleague recently who used "cisgender" to identify me, herself, and nearly everyone. When she asked me why I winced at the term, I said, "While I respect your use of it, for me 'cisgender' is inaccurate because it assumes that everyone is defined by *gender* when, in fact, everyone participates in *sex*. Gender is an add on we've developed in post-modern culture, but sex is the human baseline."

"No, not only is that old-fashioned," this professor of sociology and women's studies said, "but..." she went on to accuse me variously of being anti-future, anti-women, anti-LGBTQIA+, anti-queer, and transphobic.

I responded when she had finished. "As a child advocate, I am an advocate for *all* children, including trans, gay, intersex, and gender nonconforming, but human sex exists in 2024 just as much as it did in the past, and as much as it will in the future. It is an immutable biological reality that predates our present experiments with gender. The term 'cisgender' is not accurate to that reality because of the assumptions about sex as a culture construct. Gender is a culture construct, not sex."

"That is a patriarchal concept and pure mansplaining," she pointed at me. "Using 'sex' implies that reproductive biology has the final say in the conversation. This is something men have done for centuries to keep women second class, but sex doesn't control us. Identity—what the mind thinks—that matters more than biology."

I countered. "So, if I think I'm perfect, I'm perfect, by your logic. If I think I'm good at something, I'm good at it. But in fact I'm not perfect and I might not be good at that thing I think I'm good at. Similarly, thoughts about gender identity can change, but your sex is your sex, even if you have gender dysphoria. Doctors need to know your *sex* to treat you for illness—gender nonconformity comes second or is not necessary for physiological treatment of disease unless you call attention to it."

"Biology no longer matters to a post-feminist conversation. In fact, what you're saying is wrong for new research, social justice, and social change. Our identity matters, how we see ourselves, and how we make the culture we want to live in—not which reproductive organs you have."

I tried a different approach. "You, me, women, men, and billions of people fight for equal rights for *girls and women*. We aren't fighting for equal rights for social constructs like 'femininity' or 'gender'—we are fighting for women and men to be social equals because women are a biological sex that was kept unequal via sex roles that disempowered them. Those sex roles had a gender element to them as we feminists started using 'gender roles' and 'gender stereotypes' in the 1970s, but women were never a gender. They were and are a sex. To reduce them now to social constructs of gender becomes reduction to a social identity defined by a few people in power and tosses out decades of feminist success for girls and women."

She had heard this point before and was ready for it. "Not if you take 'sex' out of it—just realize that we are fighting for women as a *gender,* and we will keep fighting our fight because it is definitely not over."

"We will keep fighting our fight, but issues arising from men playing women's sports show a different picture. Girls and women are being supplanted by biological males because women and men are not genders, they are sexes. While nurture and culture do matter to everything that is human, our *nature* will always be our baseline. The culture part—the social construct—comes third in what shapes us, just as it did during the patriarchy, and just as it did a million years ago. Our differences in brain biology and genetics need to come first if we are to fully gain equality for everyone."

She started to interrupt, but I asked her to let me finish.

"To say that there is no sex in the brain, only gender identity, avoids four decades of brain scan evidence showing male and female brains sex differentiated—sexual dimorphism. Scans of fetal brains show male/female brain-differentiation *already obvious in the eighth month of a pregnancy, before children are born.* 'Gender' exists, yes, but it comes later, just like culture comes later. First, we are male and female, and we are male and female before we come out of the womb."

"That's bogus," she said. "Our brains only differ in tiny things like brain size. What scans are you talking about?" I listed scans from dozens of research institutions like University of Cambridge, University of California-Irvine, Vanderbilt, and others in Japan, the Netherlands…dozens of countries. Then I asked her whose brain scans she had looked at, from which university, which hospital, which expert. She admitted to not studying brain scans but she said she knew they are not important because "there just aren't any differences in our brains to speak of."

Again I countered. "All the fMRI, PET, and SPECT scans of male and female brains show significant differences. The sample sizes are in the millions. These scans show differences occurring on a male and female brain spectrum, including some people in human populations who occupy a position of 'bridge brain'. Their brains are still male or female but bridge between the sexes by having more characteristics of the other sex brain. Some LGBTQIA+ people are bridge brains who nonetheless have male and female brains. And LGB people gain their sexual orientation genetically; they are not a 'gender' making a 'choice.' They have a hard-wired sexual orientation. While 'gender' might depend on what you say it is, homosexuality is hard-wired at the same time in utero that sexual dimorphism is hard-wired—in the womb. The brain, again, trumps gender."

"You are just making this stuff up," she said. "Sexual dimorphism is a myth of the patriarchy. You're pretending something is science when it's just crap. Cisgender is the right term for you and all of us who are not gender fluid."

Again, I disagreed. "Given the existence of brain scans for sex-differentiated brains, the academic term 'cisgender' implies *gynandromorphy* which happens in some species when both female and male organs are present in equal measure but does not happen in humans. In humans, even a hermaphrodite or intersex person with both sets of sex organs still leans toward one brain sex at various times of development. While 'gender' may be accurate for discussing fluid social roles, gender dysphoria, and gender exploration in some people, 'sex' applies to *all* people; thus, to me, 'cis*gender*' is not the correct universal terminology. 'Male' and 'female' with room for variety of manifestation via gender exploration seems more accurate."

An even more contentious back and forth led to no ground gained for either of us, so we walked away. But this dialogue and others like it have shown me the anti-science approach that some people are taking to sex and gender today—and some of those people are academics with powerful positions in the Big Three. Their approach began in academic sociology and has spread through advocacy channels. Soft science gets used by these people to try to erase hard science. Sexual dimorphism is considered anathema, enemy, "patriarchal," anti-trans, transphobic, etc. when, in fact, neuroscience is a healthy way of advocating for all children, including trans, gay, and gender-nonconforming.

Experts Weigh in on the Science of Sex and Gender

In few places are "boy" and "girl" (sex) more important than in schools that disaggregate their data for sex, as Sean introduced in Part I. They do this to discover where each population is having difficulty, in what classes, and in what environments. Boys generally have more trouble in nearly every area of school than girls from preschool through high school, while girls tend to have trouble in some specific areas. After looking at their own data, school districts are often very interested in how boys and girls learn differently, how the male brain and female brain (sex) need differentiated learning in some areas, especially those of acute distress.

When I speak at schools and conferences, I quote other experts in the field to help audiences see how clear sexual dimorphism is to scientists. Despite arguments in the media or in gender sociology regarding cisgender and gender, sexual dimorphism is robust.

Did You Know?
Experts on Sex and Gender

- "There are 10 trillion cells in the human body, and every one of them is sex-specific. We've had a unisex vision of the human genome, but men and women are not the same in our genome, and men and women are not the same in the face of disease. All our cells know on a molecular level whether they are XX or XY."
  –David C. Page, M.D., Professor of Biology at the Massachusetts Institute of Technology (MIT) and Director of the Whitehead Institute.

- "More than 99% of male and female genetic coding is exactly the same, but that 1% percentage difference influences every single cell in our bodies – from the nerves that register pleasure and pain to the neurons that transmit perception, thoughts, feelings, and emotions."

<blockquote>
–Louann Brizendine, M.D., Professor of Neuropsychiatry at University of California – San Francisco, Founder of the Women's Mood and Hormone Clinic, and author of The Female Brain and The Male Brain
</blockquote>

- "The X chromosome has about 1,000 genes; the Y has 70. The X is one of the biggest chromosomes; the Y is short and stubby. The X contains extremely significant genes: genes that make and maintain the brain and control immune function... All my (male) cells are using an identical X – the one I got from my mother, so, if that X has any problems – genetic mutations, spelling mistakes in the genetic code – tough luck for me. But a woman has two Xs: one from her mother, one from her father. So, if one X has a problem, the healthy X can compensate."
  <blockquote>
  –Shäron Moalem, M.D., Ph.D., author of *How Sex Works and The Better Half*
  </blockquote>

- "Sex differences in the brain are real at the molecular level, for instance they are now found in mechanisms of pain, effects of stress, how an autism-linked gene regulates neurophysiology, how an intellectual disability-linked gene affects the biochemistry of synapses...and much more."
  <blockquote>
  –Catherine Woolley, Ph.D., Professor of Neuroendocrinology, Northwestern University
  </blockquote>

- "Biological sex is either male or female...sex is defined by gametes, which are mature reproductive cells. There are only two types of gametes: small ones called sperm that are produced by males, and large ones called eggs that are produced by females. There are no intermediate types of gametes between egg and sperm cells. Sex is therefore binary."
  <blockquote>
  –Debra Soh, Ph.D., *The End of Gender*
  </blockquote>

Human beings are sexually dimorphic. Our chromosomes set us up that way *in utero*. We develop during our lifespan as male and female in body and brain, even as particular brain characteristics in a male or female lean toward spectrum extremes or middles.

Dimorphic doesn't mean stereotyping. It doesn't mean one boy-type, one girl-type, with no variety. Sexual dimorphism creates averages and means for male and female on the *brain sex spectrum.* There is no way around sexual dimorphism (except social constructivist argument), because our genes are sexually dimorphic (X and Y). Genes make our bodies and brains dimorphic (with variety). Our culture might refine us in various directions but we are not genetically wired by cultures, which is why I don't generally use the word "cisgender." Gender is a word about cultural identities that can keep us from realizing who our girls and boys and women and men are.

"It's old fashioned not to use 'gender'," my interlocutor was saying, implying that I am not including LGBTQIA+ people. Not in the least. As I argued back, homosexuality (LGB) is genetically wired into the brain at birth. Trans (T) brains, too, our newest science is showing us, are also wired before birth. Thus, it is incorrect to think that the existence of trans people means "gender" is what matters. A trans person who transitions does not transition *between genders,* but *between sexes.* Puberty blockers, hormone therapy, and surgery allow him/her to match body and brain by restructuring the body to fit the brain already housed in the skull. This is not a "gender" change; it is a change of *physical sex* to match *brain sex.* I advocate for trans rights by pointing people to brain scans that show the reality of the trans brain. Keeping trans linked to "gender" in sociological terms keeps it in the realm of "choice" like homosexuality used to be misconstrued, but showing with brain science that trans involves sex allows for clear personhood and identity.

Meanwhile, in all this, gender is not sex. Gender (gender nonconforming) is a personal and social experiment with identity construction. When children present to parents and then clinicians with gender dysphoria, responsible professionals treat it as depression, first, because dysphoria is depression; meanwhile, professionals, parents, and the child work to learn, over a healthy period of time, if this personal identity-exploration is more than an internal way of dealing with depression—for instance, whether the child is gay; whether the child, once old enough to choose, will proceed forward with transition (a trans person has brain-sex dysphoria rather than gender dysphoria, which we will explore later in this Part); whether the child will remain gender non-binary but not transition the body, thus remain their birth sex; whether the child will return to an equilibrium as male/female (sexual dimorphism) which most gender fluid children do after a period of time. It is hard-wired trans adolescents and adults who do not tend to end their depression with a return to equilibrium in their birth sex.

The population of gender fluid people is small worldwide, but provides expansive and experimental frontiers. Supporting gender exploration compassionately with the leading edge science is an important part of the human endeavor today. Gender dysphoria and gender fluidity are not going away, especially with so many people carrying negative views of previous social roles and limitations associated with "woman" and "man." At the same time, if we are going to be citizen scientists who are adept at systems analysis in families, schools, organizations, neighborhoods, and communities, we must not forget that boys and girls learn and grow differently because they are, by nature, different sexes, with all the brain differences attached to sex–white matter and gray matter activity working differently, testosterone levels differing in brain cells, verbal center and hemisphere differences, and connectivity differences.

Unfortunately, for political reasons, along the same line as the Big Three hyper-use of "cisgender," universities mainly avoid sexual dimorphism. Our academic culture has decided we should avoid dealing with the male and female brain so as not to appear anti-trans or politically incorrect. As I mentioned, though, when a school district or school provides Boys and Girls Learn Differently training/support for its staff before or during the school year, it garners positive results for all students, whether male, female, gay, trans, or gender non-conforming. In this work, "cisgender" does not need to be used—or if it is used, I express caveats alongside the word so that listeners, constituents, and people in the grass roots don't think that by covering "gender" every child is being helped. If gender is covered but sexual dimorphism is left out, only a few children will be helped because most children will remain unaccounted for.

Help Right Now If You Have an LGBTQIA+ Child

If you have a child or know a child who fits in what we now call the LGBTQIA+ universe, I want to take a moment to delve into categories and provide practical support to your child and family.

Lesbian, Gay, Bisexual. Like heterosexual, LGB is hard-wired in the *sexually dimorphic nucleus of the anterior hypothalamus* (a part of the brain toward the middle of the skull). A child may or may not know that he or she is gay until adolescence, but by adolescence or somewhere into adulthood, she/he will most likely know. What is already hard-wired genetically into the hypothalamus often gets triggered and expressed when adolescent hormones wash through. As I mentioned before, LGB (Lesbian, Gay, Bisexual) are not a "choice." They are part of who the person is, in the core of the brain, just like heterosexuality is. Approximately 5 – 10% of humans and mammals are LGB.

The Trans Brain. This brain is also not a "choice." A trans brain shows up on scans as an *extreme bridge brain* (a brain that looks like it is right in the middle of the sex-brain spectrum between male and female). While "trans" is the contemporaneous word used by children and adolescents for nearly every brain difference, only around .3% of human beings scan as trans. Most children who tell us they are trans will end up later saying they are gay not trans. This is another reason that knowing the categories is crucial: we must be careful in how we study, treat and care for our gender dysphoric children by not jumping to the conclusion that they are all trans. I will go back through all of this and add more in Part III when I go even more deeply into changes that I am asking of the medical community in the language of diagnosis. But knowing these categories at the outset helps us to avoid overreacting or under-reacting to a child who says, "I'm gender nonbinary." It helps us take time (6-18 months) to explore with the child whether he or she is gay or straight, trans, or gender nonconforming. We affirm the child's or adult's self-exploration along all the categorical lines with Time on our side for full discovery.

To provide hormone therapy and transitional surgery to a gender nonconforming or gay child who is not trans can be dangerous to that child both as an individual and within the child's nurturing system. At the same time, to withhold transitional resources from trans emerging adults can also be dangerous to them and our systems, including higher suicide rates in this population, as you've seen reported in the media. Meanwhile, in one recent study, "Individuals who underwent gender-affirming surgery had a 12.12-fold higher suicide attempt risk than those who did not," so we must be very careful with children whatever direction we take them. It is not necessarily true that providing immediate gender-affirming care to young children saves our depressed children from suicide. At the same time, to shame our children for exploring their gender can also backfire.

Gender Affirming Care and Biological Intervention

As mentioned, "trans" is being used to include lots of people who are not trans. I would estimate hundreds of thousands of bridge brains are being called trans (or calling themselves trans) when they are not trans. Because of our mushy self-reported categorizations, we must postpone, whenever possible, significant biological intervention for children and teens who present with *gender dysphoria*. The statistical likelihood is that the child telling us they are trans is gay and/or bridge brain—a young mind involved in exploring a new, adolescent identity they are calling "gender nonconforming," "gender nonbinary," or "trans." Beginning in universities and medical and mental health clinics, and spreading from there through government and media, professionals and policymakers should study both sex and gender to help children and parents distinguish *sex, sexual dimorphism, gender, trans, gender nonconforming, lesbian, gay, bisexual*—all the categories—so that adults can help children understand their internal explorations from a science-based perspective.

If we study and use all the categories of the human brain that we can, we will improve "gender affirming care" to include sex and gender, both—not just gender. Practically speaking, this would mean that for trans people we would say "sex-transition care" and for gender non-conformers, "gender exploration care." We would thus take sex denial (denying the DNA of male/female) out of social and medical policy. We would also empower medical professionals and families to work with gender exploring populations via the addition of the *bridge brain* category rather than immediately compelling these children toward hormonal intervention and transition via trans care.

The bottom line: a child telling you, a parent, or telling a doctor, or another person that he or she is trans does not mean he or she is trans. He or she might be, but statistically, it is more likely that she/he has gender dysphoria, a malaise in which she/he believes exploring gender identity will help with depression. I know that some gender affirming care advocates see sex/gender as zero sum, usually with gender being the 90% element and sex occupying a 10% category at most ("sex assigned at birth"), but both sex and gender are important elements of human development in which sex affects *all children and adults* while gender heavily affects *bridge brain exceptions.* By understanding both sex and gender, parents can remain crucial to childhood/adolescent decision-making unless the parents are abusing the children and the state must intervene.

If we don't utilize gender in our social thinking, we miss helping thousands of children, but if we don't use sex as the baseline, we not only do damage to women/girls and men/boys, but we encounter backlash against helping these children downstream. Girls' and women's rights are paralyzed in some states because "girl," "woman," and "mother" (all of which are based in sex) are encountering cultural erasure for the sake of extreme social positions on gender. Meanwhile, recent gains via school training to help boys and girls do better in schools where boys have been behind for decades are also stymied in some states by the proposed erasure of "boy" and "man" for the sake of gender affirming care.

Resolving the Pronoun Question

Once our whole society de-politicizes both sex and gender, and once we utilize science-based categories for each area of child development, we will resolve the pronoun question we are haunted by right now. "He" and "she" will go back to being used without penalty or discomfort in social discourse and legislative policy because he and she apply to sexual dimorphism (male/female) not to gender choices. Even a gender fluid person is male or female at a molecular level, so using he and she is inclusive of all, including gender nonconforming and trans children if we work sensitively with the trans population to alter speech to the other-sex pronoun after physiological transition has occurred.

Meanwhile, using he/his and she/her as our default for the sex of the person will not mean a bridge brain can't ask for "they" to be used, if possible, but "they" is awkward linguistically, so we will need to teach bridge brain children that they are resilient enough to survive if "they" is not used for and with them. They are a sex so, if they ask for "she" or "he" but neither one is used, their resilience will win the day.

Returning to the use of pronouns based on sex will allow for pulling back from political thinking that people who don't use gender-choice pronouns or "they" for male or female sex are abusive people or "transphobic." When a trans person has completed transition, he or she will likely want the other sex pronoun used (i.e., if "he" becomes "she" and vice versa). We can follow this person's wishes, and go further to learn from the trans person about brain sex via brain scans. This trans person has a lot to teach us about human variety, about the bridge brain spectrum, and about the positives and potential negatives of transition, medication, and sex/gender life-changes. The science of trans is new science—we are learning as we go. While some people are very glad they have transitioned, some people recant and are not. In this global experiment, policymakers need to collect information from the people in the trenches before quickly developing new policy around changing trends in soft-wiring regarding the use of pronouns that are not about being "cisgender" but are about sexual dimorphism.

Coed and Single Sex Schools

Coed schools absorb all sexes, bridge brains, and genders, but for a single sex school, issues about which students to recruit and include will likely be best resolved regarding sex more than the "gender identity that my child has chosen." A school's policy to not recruit a girl identifying as male into a boys' school is appropriate because the child's sex is female even though the child's social identity experimentation is presently linked to gender nonconformity. Similarly, in a girls' school, the school should not be required to take a biological male, even if that male is identifying as female or is gender nonconforming given that the child's sex is male. If a trans male during adulthood completes transition to female, she is no longer a nonconforming man, she is a woman. Because it is generally unsafe to surgically transition children, this scenario will likely be moot for most schools except, potentially, among faculty members.

Athletics and Sports

The pronoun question is a sex/gender question not just for schools but athletics. As puberty approaches, athletics and sports need to be defined by sex first, gender second, since sex is the molecular, cellular, physiologic, and neurobiological baseline of the child. A lot of informal sports and play among boys and girls is coed, of course, without negative consequence; however, by the time puberty begins, sex will need to prevail in order to be fair to biological girls and women in competitive settings. To do otherwise is to set women's rights back without good reason as girls lose in competition to boys whose advantages go beyond muscularity to comparative cardio-vascular robustness and advantages in other internal systems. For fairness to girls and women, "boy," "girl," "male," and "female" need to matter more than gender exploration and gender nonconforming identity. Sex is hard-wired, gender is explorative. Many countries and international organizations have begun to catch up to this, pulling back on insistence that a gender nonconforming boy (identifying girl) compete, in adolescence or adulthood, with females.

Maternity and Paternity

Similarly, the baseline of sex needs to prevail legislatively in matters of maternity and paternity. No language changes proposed by extreme groups in the Big Three will change that mothers are mothers and fathers are fathers as a matter of sex. In this, "gender" has little sway. While, yes, a mother can be a gender nonconforming person identifying as a man, she is still female. Equally so, a male who transitions to a female is now rebuilt to female: if this female has a child via scientific experimentation or social arrangement, she is a mother. We make mistakes that will haunt us for decades by trying to legislate "birthing person" instead of "mother" into social language. Whenever we allow culture imperatives to override nature imperatives, we create a war between nature and culture and risk significant confusion with little gain for society. To legislate that mothers are birthing persons is like legislating "they" instead of "he" or "she" with penalties for non-use of the word that just don't fit common sense and will only diminish the rights of mothers and fathers, and women and men.

If A Person Has Transitioned

If a person has transitioned, I (Michael) believe public policy must agree across the board that this person has altered reproductive organs and completed the adjustment of hormonology to become the target sex. Thus, this new man can go to a men's college; this new woman can go to a woman's college. This person will want to be called by the target pronoun, generally, "he" or "she," given the significant investment in altering epigenetics toward the brain-sex target. In other words, this person will likely not want to be "they" anymore because the sex has changed, and so has the pronoun.

We should support this woman and man by honoring their substantial personal and social investment and shifting our pronoun from he to she or she to he, even if we were adamant previously that this transition should not occur. If testosterone levels and other blood tests match baseline female levels suitable for sports competition, this woman will likely be able to compete in college and professionally with other women.

Using XX and XY to Determine Sports' Participants

I, Sean, hold a different view on sports competition. I believe males (XY) who use chemicals and surgery to take on a female identity, for a variety of reasons, even if they have fully transitioned to a female identity, should not compete with females (XX). While much of our society's debate on this has focused around testosterone levels, there are other advantages of male biology beyond testosterone levels. Attempting to create all sorts of nuances only muddy the waters and integrity of chromosomal truths. To not look at other components of male biology, such as skeletal systems and other systems complicates the matter.

The 2024 Olympic boxing controversy in which a female boxer stopped boxing after getting hit in the head by a chromosomal male, because she experienced that hit as impossible for a woman, was a recent example in a long line of examples. Over the years, we have seen women's skulls cracked, women punched with extreme force, field hockey players severely hit, female track and field competitions dominated by those with XY chromosomes, and female swimming competitions dominated by people with XY chromosomes. If a person has a Y chromosome, I do not believe he (even if now identifying as a she) should compete with biological women (XX).

Teach Sex and Gender in Sex Education Classes

Parents often ask me (Michael) when to teach kids about sex and gender. As you have likely seen, various state legislatures are taking extreme positions on this question so let me provide a science-based approach.

Your child's school already teaches sex ed in fourth or fifth grade. It is developmentally appropriate for all the categories of sex and gender to be taught by schools at that time (parents can teach it earlier if they wish). Meanwhile, if schools and districts are going to teach this material responsibly, their teachers must be provided with science-based (non-political, non-ideological) curricula and training that allows them to use hard science, i.e. to teach sexual dimorphism first, then gender development second. Teachers can be trained to teach these subjects in their science, biology, gym, and other relevant classes.

With science in tow, these teachers can explain to children on the cusp of puberty that:

- Male and female brains are set up differently with overlap
- 1 in 5 people are bridge brains–they bridge the sexes via brain biology
- 99% of people or more are not in conflict regarding their sex but around 1% of bridge brains are in conflict around their gender
- 90 – 95% of all mammals are heterosexual but 5 – 10% of mammals are gay (LGB)
- Gender is a social construct based in sexual dimorphism that also seeks to branch beyond binary social roles.

By teaching good science, teachers and parents can support everyone on the sex and gender spectrum via training and education in the same way teachers, parents, and children are trained to teach not only "the birds and the bees" but also to work with autism spectrum kids, and indeed every child, via evidence-based scientific information.

Hard-Wiring, Soft-Wiring, and The Culture of the Exception

When our Big Three bases our social and legal policy on what is hard-wired (sex) in our laws we include protections for all exceptions. Our goal is to protect everyone's civil rights in a fully democratic school and society. Laws like Title IX, as originally written, have done a good job of protecting everyone. But when the Big Three focuses only or mainly on what is soft-wired, including focusing on gender not sex, we create a society in confusion. I have named this approach "The Culture of the Exception." Confusion occurs because the Big Three are trying to alter the bulk of society to reflect a small part of that society rather than including the smaller part into the existing whole. Intuitive evidence of this Big Three overreach occurs when we look at extremes and see social policy, whether from the far Right or the far Left, that are 1) wrenched away from common sense, and 2) pressured toward what certain people want to have soft-wired into us for political or ideological reasons. What we are teaching children we need to teach ourselves as adults in the Big Three, too.

- Bridge brains constitute the lion's share of LGBTQIA+ individuals, thus, we can pull back at a macro level from political attacks and backlash against them; but meanwhile, we must not legislate or socially pressure the culture of the exception to leave the whole out (sex) to accommodate dominance of the part.
- There are exceptions to every rule in science, exceptions we can learn from and absorb into the mosaic of society and policy, but these exceptions always prove the existence of the rule, so we can assert minority interest and bring social empathy to the minority's exceptional needs without trying to erase the rule.
- Given that most trans and gender-nonconforming children present to health professionals with gender dysphoria (depression), we should treat the dysphoria first and foremost, before doing anything else. To treat depression, we must use everything in our arsenal from all our mental health assets, not just a particular approach we now call gender-affirming care.

Some people will be angry at my positions (and Sean's). Some of you will feel that we should do whatever someone in the LGBTQIA+ community, someone trying to assert the culture of the exception, says we should do because this person or cohort says we should do it. Others will feel that we should do nothing to accommodate vulnerable LGBTQIA+ populations. Exceptional people are our brothers, sisters, colleagues, friends, and children who expand our personal and social boundaries not only on behalf of themselves and their own mental health, but also as an experiment in culture we need to respect and explore as we move forward in human evolution.

How we treat our children is always the knife-edge of a spear, even as we protect our children from every battle we can. The human mind that is safely entrenched in what has worked for a million years–*sex difference*–is also experimenting with building a larger bridge between the sexes than before as it expands human ingenuity. A double blind study is occurring right now in the sex and gender of our children and adolescents. Let's take control of the experiment by removing confused social policies that don't respect the scientific basis for sex, while also enjoying the evolving wisdom that our next generation is bringing into the expanded journey of human freedom.

Essential Questions

1. What is sexual dimorphism?
2. How is it different from gender?
3. What do we mean by the difference between hard-wiring and soft-wiring? Why is the "wiring" analogy useful in talking about sex and gender?
4. How is it good for girls to talk about sexual dimorphism when we are creating policies for sports and competition so that girls and women are not discriminated against and underserved?
5. How is it good for boys to talk about sexual dimorphism in school systems and other social institutions that are undeserving them?
6. What is the "culture of the exception?"
7. What roles do universities, government, and media often play in keeping sexual dimorphism out of policy discussions, thus neglecting what boys and girls need?

Chapter 9

When a Student Is Suspended for Using the "Wrong" Pronoun

"Free speech is the whole thing, the whole ball game. Free speech is life itself."

–Salman Rushdie

(This essay is useful for all general readers, and particularly useful to parents, child advocates, educators, students, college courses, administrators, and school board members.)

I (SEAN) LIVE IN CALIFORNIA where schools have seen an increase of the non-binary population by 1,642% from 2019 to 2023, according to data provided by the California Department of Education. In an attempt to navigate new challenges in this increase, we are seeing significant overreach among administrators, a kind of hyper-protection in the culture of the exception of people who have not been harmed by harming boys who are as confused as the adults are. The culture of the exception, and the harm, appeared in the case of John Dow, a student in Livermore, California whose words set off a series of actions that brought the culture war home to him and his family.

John's suspension from school started when he and another student were sitting together at the beginning of a class and noticed one of the students walking into the room looking different than before. "Jane" had decided to start using male pronouns and identifying as male. John's friend asked John, "Why does Jane look like that?" John responded by saying, "He used to be a girl." This factual comment was overheard by another student, who reported it to the school's Vice Principal via email. A firestorm ensued over John's common sense answer. Official school documents were generated that called John a "bully" who "created an unsafe environment that does not demonstrate... PRIDE." The school suspended John without telling John's mother why. The school just told her that her son was waiting at the school to be picked up.

When I met John, I broke the ice by asking him what he was reading in school. He said John Steinbeck's *Of Mice and Men*. When I asked him some questions about the book, he was reluctant, at first, to respond, but eventually he shared some of his thoughts as we sat across from one another tossing a tangerine back and forth. I could see that this was a boy who cared about school. I saw a 14-year-old boy at a defining moment in life–a moment when a boy can become caught between caring about his academic future and feeling betrayed by education itself. John feigned indifference about his suspension for self-protection, but he was clearly shamed by it, and I as an adult could see that he was unreasonably shamed.

As I explored this case, I saw the school's disciplinary action summary. In it, the vice principal only included the phrase "used to be a girl" to forward a narrative that aided a disciplinary action around the notion of bullying. By taking "he" out of the sentence, the vice principal could argue some animus in a 14-year-old boy she had suspended for no sin, and certainly no bullying–a boy simply trying to reconcile sex and gender without having had the kind of important school training on each part of the distinction that Michael discussed in the last chapter. John was labeled a bully and an ensuing parent-school clash occurred in which this boy's life became very difficult at school. His simple non-aggressive words made him a casualty in the culture of exception framework we are seeing around us today in which there is pressure to pit sex against gender, despite that gender is a part of sex, not the other way around.

In investigating this case, I learned that John had known Jane since early childhood. He knew Jane before she started to experiment with using he/him pronouns. The school discipline and suspension referral did not include the fact that "he used to be a girl" was a kindness in its context, something factual that made complete sense to John and would have made sense to everyone around him, both children and adults, who knew Jane previously. John even tried to understand whether "it" was the correct pronoun instead of "she" or "he" as you can see from the documentation here.

LIVERMORE VALLEY JOINT UNIFIED SCHOOL DISTRICT
OFFICIAL NOTICE OF SUSPENSION

Education Code 48900.2

☐ (Grades 4 to 12) Committed sexual harassment to another pupil or employee – verbal or physical conduct of a sexual nature; an act which creates an intimidating, hostile, or offensive environment.

Education Code 48900.3

☐ (Grades 4 to 12) Caused, attempted to cause, threatened to cause, or participated in an act of **hate violence**.

Education Code 48900.4

☑ (Grades 4 to 12) Intentionally engaged in harassments, threats, or intimidation directed against school district personnel or pupils, that is sufficiently severe or pervasive to have the actual and reasonably expected effect of materially disrupting classwork, creating substantial disorder, and invading the rights of either school personnel or pupils by creating an intimidating or hostile educational environment.

Education Code 48900.7

☐ Making terrorist threats against school officials and/or school property.

Education Code 48901.5

☐ Possession or use of any electronic signal device in violation of District Policy and Regulation 5131.2 (includes cell phones).

Factual Explanation of Incident (must include date incident occurred):

DATE: TIME:

During ▇ period on Tuesday, 11/7/23 ▇John Dow▇ told a student that another student "used to be a girl." The student ▇John Dow▇ was referring to uses he/him pronouns. The comment was overheard by other students in the classroom. ▇John Dow▇ was also overheard referring to the student as "it." ▇John Dow's▇ comments create an unsafe environment and do not demonstrate Granada PRIDE.

☑ The student's explanation of the incident was heard and considered before suspension was imposed.

TO THE PARENTS: This suspension has been issued in compliance with Education Code Sections 48900-48915 and 35291. The teacher of any class from which a student is suspended may require the suspended student to complete any assignments and tests missed during the suspension. Supervision of the student is the responsibility of the parent/guardian during the suspension.

During the suspension, your child must not be on or near any school campus and may not participate in any school-sponsored activities.

_______________________________________   11/9/23
Principal or Designee Signature   Date

Telephone contact with parent by: **Jessica Mann**   Date: **11/9/23**   Time: **1:00pm**

Denial of a Child's Right to Education

The culture of the exception is ideologically bound to narratives, hyperboles, hyper-sensitivies, and fears of cancellation. School administrators feel institutional permission, even pressure, not just to punish a boy for no solid value, but also to suggest—in the process—that not only does gender-identity trump sex on its face but that talking about biological sex is bullying. Within a few days, a boy's right to education is lost temporarily, in the matter of felt time, but for longer in felt shame.

Did You Know?
John's Suspension Timeline

1. November 7th: John uses the words "He used to be a girl."
2. Ms. Mann receives an email sometime after school hours from a third party about John's comment.
3. November 9th: John is pulled out of class at 9:50 AM.
4. John sits in the main office for approximately one-hour-twenty minutes before meeting Ms. Mann.
5. Ms. Mann meets with John for approximately 15 minutes, where the vice principal tells John he is being suspended.
6. The student is then asked to give a written statement.
7. 11:25: John's sibling receives an email from John that he is being suspended.
8. 11:30: Sibling contacts father about John's suspension.
9. 12:25: John's mother receives a voicemail from the vice principal that John was suspended and to come pick him up.
10. 1:15: John's mother picks up the message after finishing work. The father is never contacted by the vice principal or school administration.
11. 1:30: John's mother picks up her son from the office. The mother does not receive any suspension paperwork.
12. John shows up for practice and is told to go home because he is suspended. The student and parents were not informed about John's ineligibility for practice.
13. Although the suspension notice states that students "may not participate in any school-sponsored activities," the parents did not receive the suspension notice until a week after the suspension.
14. November 16th: Parents receive a copy of the suspension-notice in the mail.
15. February 2: Parents receive John's November 9 witness statement.

In a follow-up email two months after the suspension, the vice principal wrote that John "was provided an opportunity to provide his side of the story," but according to John and his family, John was only given the opportunity to give a written statement *after* the suspension had been determined. The vice principal justified the suspension via "zero tolerance" policies for "harassment." The legal definition of harassment specifically involves repeated actions that cause substantial emotional distress without any legitimate purpose. John did not harass Jane. He did not harm her repeatedly. He did not cause substantial emotional distress. The legitimate purpose of his answer to his friend was to try to figure out what was happening right in front of him.

Removal of John from class and athletics and making him sit in the administrator's office for the week are now being explored by the family as potential violations of the Equal Education Opportunity Act and FAPE (free appropriate public education). Complicating matters, John has an Individual Education Plan (IEP) that requires particular accommodations to equal classroom instruction. Those accommodations were not made for John during suspension even though that time-frame was one in which he needed to prepare for finals. Because he could not go to class, he was not able to fully prepare for finals.

John's IEP also notes that he has a degree of "impulsivity" that may lead him to "blurt out…and act before thinking." The school has the IEP but did not seem to make the connection between blurting out a common sense comment and impulsivity. John's IEP also notes difficulty for John with "fluid reasoning," the "ability to reason, make inference, and solve novel problems using unfamiliar procedures of information." Making John wait an-hour-and-twenty minutes in the main office and then asking him to proceed through unfamiliar administrative processes without a guardian present is a mismatch with the IEP. The school's decision to remove John from his English class for a week hangs on the simple words, "unsafe environment," but this catch-all, while useful when children truly are unsafe, is not useful in the ways it is used to disproportionately impact boys. If the school felt comfortable letting John wait unattended for an-hour-and-twenty minutes in an office, it must have felt that he was not a threat. Both emotional damage to John and potential academic distress in the face of the finals he could not prepare for adequately become hidden damage to this boy. The school system is now being assessed for causing damage to a boy with an IEP via an extreme institutional response, a zero-tolerance policy for free speech.

What Is "An Unsafe Environment"?

Zero-tolerance policies in general pertain to ensuring safe environments. Enlightened school districts have moved away from zero-tolerance policies, but on minute aspects of gender and sex, we are seeing zero-tolerance policies supercharged again, even though, in California, for instance, suspension rates are double for boys. This matches the national average, state by state, in overuse of suspensions among boys. The California Department of Education warned schools about disciplinary practices among those "overrepresented in suspension statistics" in August of 2019 when the Department enacted its "State Guidance for New Laws on Discipline," "We are writing to you today regarding the implementation of new laws regarding disciplinary practices consistent with our shared view that all students—particularly African American students and others overrepresented in suspension statistics— deserve a school environment that fosters their social-emotional well-being and academic success."

Some suspensions are needed, of course, so what is "unsafe?" What is "safe"? How do we apply common sense and science to "unsafe" and "safe" so that our national suspension rates for boys and boys of color do not continue to escalate?

The first thing we have to do is acknowledge this as an issue facing *males*. As the California Department of Education data showed, many suspensions of boys are hyper-punishment and hyper-discipline of males because they are male. School administrators are not trained in male brain development, do not understand boys' actions, approaches, words, and these administrators overreact not just to the boys but to the administrator's own lack of understanding, with punitive rather than restorative measures.

In John's suspension notice, the vice principal at the California school blamed John for "comments that create an unsafe environment." The dictionary definition of "safe" is "protected from or not exposed to danger or risk, not likely to be harmed or lost." For Jane, the school would have been a safe environment without the suspension of John. Jane was not exposed to danger or risk by John and was not likely to be harmed or lost because of John's comment. There was no harassment here, no bullying, and no unsafe environment, but John was nonetheless suspended.

Because John's words were not verbal threats and since John had not been involved in any physical forms of violence, his parents and John were right to push back on "unsafe" and they were also right to push back on the administrator's response to their pushback, "But words are violence, and

John's words were violent." John's words were not directed at Jane nor did they violently condemn Jane–they were an attempt to reconcile the girl that John grew up with and the person now using male pronouns. When social systems coach administrators and everyone, for that matter, to believe that words are violence, boys are the main kids suspended.

Boys by nature tend to speak more impulsively than girls, especially an IEP boy like John. Schools are chartered with serving all children but do not understand, or administrators avoid understanding, the consequences of pushing boys toward unhealthy behaviors via suspension and expulsion, especially boys with already negative personal experiences in the educational system, as IEP children can often have. Adding insult to injury throughout John's process, the school continued to justify the suspension with "bullying" as justification. Onward it went, from harassment to unsafe-environment and from bullying to violence. A boy who did no harm was not just considered "insensitive"; he was labeled a bully.

My Citizen Science with the Vice Principal

In an email to the vice principal, I played the role of citizen scientist by first asking respectful questions specific to this case. I then looked for a broader understanding of the suspension process by asking:

- Are students asked if they want to have a parent or guardian present before or while they provide a written statement to administrators investigating the occurrence?
- Are parents informed about administrative investigations into their children before, during, or after an occurrence?
- Is the district responsible for providing comparable classroom instruction to a student with an IEP who is removed from class?
- I low does the school district define "unsafe environment?"
- What district mandate allows for non-threatening words to be deemed violence?

If you have a son like John who has been accused, suspended, expelled, or otherwise punished in the school system, you can modify my questions and add your own. If your son did something clearly wrong, he needs to be accountable, and suspension, expulsion, or other discipline may well be warranted. Parents can often be of the most help to the school and the child by supporting the authority of teachers and administrators who are doing a good job for our children.

At the same time, if you have a son who is treated like John was, you and your child might be part of a trend that harms our young males especially. You may need to lobby the school district to come to terms with its subjective, highly unscientific approach to suspension policy. You might need to hold the district accountable to define its terms and conduct its own internal study of "bullying" and "unsafe environment." You have the right to call the district out if the males in your life are being unfairly treated, especially when they are punished for just trying to understand what sex and gender are.

When Schools Look More Deeply at Sex Differences

Let's switch gears now to schools that do not overreact–schools that inculcate male/female brain difference (sexual dimorphism) into their discipline systems. Often their motivation to do so has come from looking at suspension/expulsion data in house, or via their district (as the State of California did) requesting that schools disaggregate discipline referrals by sex and race both. As these schools do internal research they discover that their boys are behind their girls academically (as boys are nationwide) and they discover that schools with stronger academic outcomes across the student body also tend to have fewer discipline referrals and suspensions. One primary reason: good teacher quality and strong teacher engagement lead to students engaged in learning. The high quality and engaged teachers are often the teachers who use boy-friendly strategies for dealing with academics and behavior.

Sex Difference Data Via School Districts

Via my position at the American Institute for Responsible Research (AIRR), I took a deep dive into the outcomes of boys and girls in Livermore Valley Joint Unified School District (LVJUSD), John's school. Then I took the same dive throughout California. This meant looking at results of over 22.5 million test scores from 2014–2023. This was a lot of work but well worth it for the results I discovered.

In Livermore, I saw that boys are significantly behind girls in reading and English/Language Arts at all grade levels. Looking at just over 52,000 test scores in Livermore from 2014 to 2023, I found that for every 100 boys who are above standard in reading, there are 150 girls. The scores also show that eleventh grade girls in Livermore have maintained a fifteen to twenty percent higher average in English/Language Arts proficiency for a decade; in the last two years, they have been between eighteen and twenty percent higher. I found, too, that girls are now ahead of boys in 11th grade and 8th grade math.

In other districts across the country like the one in which your children might go to school, you will find similar gender gaps. You can see some of your districts already at https://www.gibm.us/state-reports, and later in this book I will show you how you can discover the test scores in your district if I and others have not already searched there. In your own data dive, you will likely find the boys in your district significantly behind girls at all or nearly all grade levels in English/Language Arts (ELA). If you show your school principal the data (both for academics and for discipline referrals), the principal might decide to act on the data by setting up training for faculty in how boys and girls learn differently. This is a great scenario because, as Michael pointed out earlier, within a few months after the training and support, the teachers will (hopefully) be using classroom strategies for academics and behavior not used before. Here is a list of strategies used by teachers and staff at one of the Gurian Institute's Model Schools, Cherokee Creek Boys School in Westminster, SC.

Try This
Boy Friendly Learning and Behavior Strategies

- Physical stuff before class that turns the brain on and gets the wiggles out
- Classroom modifications like yoga balls and standing desks can help any boy who feels the need to move in class or any student with ADHD
- Small classroom size
- Field trips, outdoor classrooms, experiential opportunities.
- Pets in the classroom
- Studying heroes to identify role models demonstrating strong character and emphasizing the importance of living by our values
- Character education and social skills training
- Leadership and community service opportunities
- Active and diverse sports program
- Free time for recreation and hobbies
- TREKS ... weekend wilderness adventures
- Celebrations, rituals, and rites of passage to acknowledge and honor successes and milestones.
- Male mentors who serve as role models.

Michael's book *Boys and Girls Learn Differently* has more than 100 of these strategies for schools and teachers of all age groups. We'll keep sharing more of them with you in this book. Your school and your teachers will probably not do all of the strategies Cherokee Creek does nor all of the strategies in Michael's books, but once the school becomes sensitized to the mismatch of the male brain with traditional education practices it, and they, will likely institute many new strategies, and many of them, like being physical to get the wiggles (impulses) out, and having male role models, affect student behavior so much that discipline referrals, suspensions, and expulsions decrease significantly.

A Local Teacher's Feedback

Teachers themselves, once sensitized to the male brain, often see what is happening around them and want things to change. After sharing the Livermore data with an educator, I received back observations and advice that may resonate at a gut level with some of your own experiences.

Did You Know?
Observations From an Elementary School
Reading Specialist

Our schools have been built on the premise of being able to sit and listen for extended periods of time. If you did that, you most likely succeeded. We now know this is not a conducive environment for our boys. As an educator for over 20 years, both in the classroom and as a reading specialist, I have watched boys having difficulty sitting still and focusing for extended periods of time.

Walk into any lower elementary classroom especially, and you will see the boys moving more, and getting reminded to sit "properly." At the secondary level, lecturing is a common mode of instruction, with lessons often involving reading/writing long passages within a set time frame. Reading and writing are passive. We sit for extended periods of time engaged in an activity that requires focus without physical movement. It is not surprising that our boys are performing lower than our girls in this area.

Often I find that the boys referred to me for reading intervention at the lower elementary level are boys who also exhibit boy behaviors tied to their biology. As Michael Gurian has pointed out, brain science shows that boys' brains (in the aggregate) develop at different rates than girls, especially the frontal cortex which is responsible for impulse control and that boys' brains go into full rest mode more often than girls' brains. Their cerebellum (the "doing" center of the brain) is more active and needs to be more active than girls' if they are going to learn on par with girls. Boys need to be well engaged if we do not want them to do the impulsive actions we will call "misbehaving."

For these reasons, I coach teachers to use these among other boy-friendly strategies.

- Break lessons into smaller, pithier chunks (1 minute for every year of age up to 15)
- Intentionally and strategically use movement and tactile experiences throughout the period and day
- Allow the students various options to sit or stand (flexible seating) during the lesson and/or independent work

If every educator looked at the boy/girl data through the lens of brain science and sexual dimorphism, I think they would be more intentional about implementing strategies based on the science. I've found not just academics but behavior improves because of the social and institutional change the boys and girls learn differently theory and strategies bring to the school.

Here are graphs I promised you, built for my discussions at Livermore. They include all student scores by grade from 2014-2023 and also the percent of boys and girls who have scored proficient or advanced in English Language Arts in state testing that measures reading, writing, listening, and research inquiry.

Percent of Livermore Joint Unified Students who Scores Proficient/ Advanced in English/Language Artsby Grade and Sex from 2014-2023

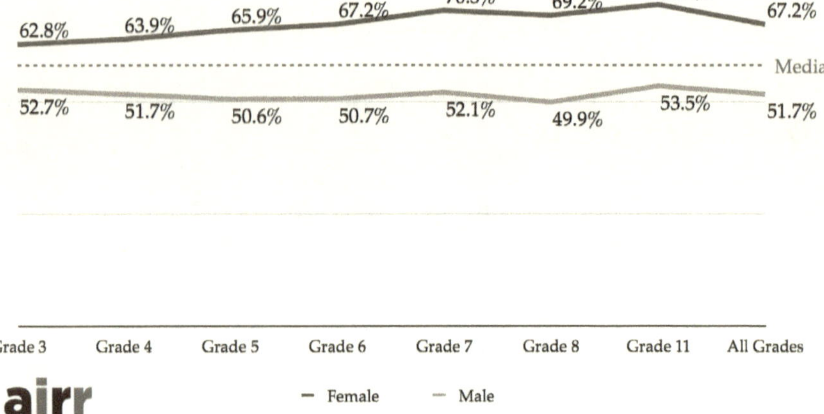

Notice the gap in ELA scores widening when boys enter middle school and as they continue into high school. Now in the table below, you can see exactly how far boys are behind girls from third to eleventh grade in reading above standard. The low reading and ELA scores are significant on their face, and they are also significant in the context of behavior. What the teacher said in the example above has been borne out by numerous studies worldwide, including the Gurian Institute's studies reported in *Boys and Girls Learn Differently*: achievement in academics and equilibrium in behavior are intrinsically linked.

Percent of Males and Females Reading Above Standard in Livermore Valley Joint Unified School District from 2014 to 2023

		Students with Scores	Above Standard	Male Deficit
3rd Grade	Female	3,654	33.5%	-9.2%
	Male	3,787	24.3%	
4th Grade	Female	3,596	33.1%	-10.4%
	Male	3,840	22.7%	
5th Grade	Female	3,631	34.9%	-13.6%
	Male	3,827	21.3%	
6th Grade	Female	3,638	29.8%	-9.9%
	Male	3,822	19.9%	
7th Grade	Female	3,676	33.7%	-10.8%
	Male	3,843	22.9%	
8th Grade	Female	3,650	36.5%	-14.1%
	Male	3,860	22.5%	
11th Gade	Female	3,641	41.2%	-13.1%
	Male	3,804	28.1%	

A review of 15.9 million student test results in California showed me that the gap between boys and girls in reading is at around double digits. Meanwhile, far too many girls, too, are faring poorly in reading.

Table 2. Percent of Males and Females Reading Above Standard in CA from 2014-2019

		Students with Scores	**Above Standard**	Male Deficit
3rd Grade	Female	1,104,140	24.8%	-9.5%
	Male	1,155,540	15.3%	
4th Grade	Female	1,115,703	24.8%	-9.2%
	Male	1,167,810	15.6%	
5th Grade	Female	1,131,385	26.1%	-10.7%
	Male	1,181,662	15.4%	
6th Grade	Female	1,129,175	21.6%	-7.8%
	Male	1,178,317	13.7%	
7th Grade	Female	1,125,567	24.7%	-9.4%
	Male	1,172,059	15.3%	
8th Grade	Female	1,115,567	27.3%	-11.0%
	Male	1,162,114	16.3%	
11th Gade	Female	1,071,101	33.7%	-10.8%
	Male	1,106,444	22.9%	

Sex Differences Matter

Every child has a right to safety in school, including Jane, but Jane was not harmed in Livermore, John was. John's school district was not well versed in boy-friendly education—the male brain was not a subject most of the teachers knew about. The teachers were sensitized well, however, to gender discussions and gender exceptions. This is one of the reasons the school overreacted to John's innocuous observations regarding sex and gender.

Livermore is just one of the districts and schools where the concept of gender, which is certainly an important one in any district, is considered much more important than the sex-differentiated learning brains of boys and girls. But when the needs of males and females at the neurobiological level are not understood, "male" is not understood. Boy is not understood and man is not understood. It becomes easier for districts to punish boys than to recognize that boys and the other students in the district need boy-friendly education, teacher training, and systems change to close learning and gender gaps, increase understanding and sensitivity, and decrease or end the boy-girl behavior gaps many districts report.

Students feel good as learners when they are learning in ways suited to them. John's school ended up feeling unsafe for John since his suspension. It is now harder for him as a boy to learn there. Improving John's and millions of other boys' downstream achievement would go a long way to change some of the problems schools are facing, but to get there, schools will have to focus on developmental tempo differences in boys and girls, sex differences in learning, and fairness and justice for all parties throughout the school's climate and culture.

Essential Questions

1. Can you identify three things that contributed to John's suspension? Could the suspension have been avoided?
2. How would you evaluate the procedures used to suspend John?
3. How do people employing the culture of exception logic disproportionately punish boys?
4. What strategies can parents and teachers all use to engage boys in learning?
5. Why is it important to distinguish ELA scores from Reading scores?
6. Have you looked at your child's school data to see the outcomes of boys and girls at all grade levels?
7. Why do you think the boy education-gap widens in middle school?

Chapter 10

Not Breast-Feeding but Chest-Feeding?
A Culture of the Exception

(This essay is useful for general readers, and particularly for high school students in science classes, college students in psychology, sociology, and biology classes, and media and policymakers)

"GURIAN, WHAT IS GOING ON?" the email began. "Have you seen this news report? Not breast-feeding but chest-feeding? What did I do with my kids all those years, 'chest-feed' them? What a sick thing to do to us moms. Why do people want to pretend there is no such thing as a mom, or dad, or girl, or boy? Frankly, I cannot believe this is happening! What universe are we living in?" A listener to our *Wonder of Parenting: A Brain Science Approach to Parenting* podcast, Latisha continued, "How did we get here? There must be some reason for these shenanigans. On your podcast, you called it 'the culture of the exception.' I can say as a mother and a woman, I find this stuff offensive. I truly think most people in the world do too, but I don't want to hurt trans people or anyone else, so I don't know how to push back on this or what to say to my kids who go to school and get in trouble for telling the truth about this stuff."

In the last five years, I (Michael) have received hundreds of emails like Latisha's. When I lecture or do media interviews, I am asked about the sex and gender confusions more than perhaps anything else. In answering questions, I often use the term "the culture of the exception" to refer to the difficulty that, for instance, J.K. Rowling (author of the *Harry Potter* books) has recently experienced. Ms. Rowling, a celebrity, told her truth—that to support trans people does not mean erasing moms and dads or boys and girls

109

because moms and dads and boys and girls are the rule, not the exception. She went through cancellation by a culture that takes exceptions to extremes.

Most people in the world are not ready to do away with mom, dad, woman, man, or boy and girl, but the "culture of the exception" pressures systems to harm boys and girls, and women and men, without scientific forethought. Latisha, Sean, I and perhaps Rowling, too, are saying: From a science-based standpoint, erasing everyone else for the sake of a minority of people just cannot work for very long. Our society is best served by bringing gender exceptions into the whole rather than trying to erase nature and the whole altogether.

The Pressure of the Exception

"Gender-neutral babies" as a trend is another example of pressure from the culture of the exception. A trend with only a small number of parents worldwide right now, it garners a lot of Big Three press and from *press* comes *pressure.* Some parents now wonder whether they are being shameful, oppressive, and abusive by loving their children as female and male. On our podcast we reassure parents that sex has not gone anywhere; in fact, there is no such thing as a gender-neutral baby except in culture conversation, because gender experimentation happens later. At birth, there is only sex. But the pressure is fierce today not just online but in our schools. Despite boys falling behind in education worldwide for decades, and even when districts disaggregate data to see the problem, they wonder, "But do 'boy' and 'girl' actually exist anymore, or are males and females 'gender stereotypes' we have to avoid in schools so that we support trans populations?" The Livermore district Sean reported on is just one of thousands grappling with the culture of the exception in the area of sexual dimorphism—the pressure to erase male/ female because that is considered the only ideologically acceptable way to help gender nonconforming and trans children.

To Latrisha I wrote back, "The science of sex and gender is one of our most empowering human pursuits—not shameful, oppressive, abusive, or stereotyping." I sent her some of the material in Chapter 8 in which I argued that neurobiological science can and should be used to protect sex/ gender diversity for *all* children and thus *all* adults. I also brought up a tool in the sciences called "prevalence inflation." It can help us understand what is happening and push back scientifically. Prevalence inflation is used in the Big Three as prevalence of cases is inflated so that exceptions-to-the-rule (the number of gender nonbinary, nonconforming, and trans) can be "shown" to have risen so high statistically that that prevalence is overtaking (or should overtake) sex and sexual dimorphism. Then prevalence is inflated further as the Big Three argues that most people in a culture, and especially most people in academics, government and media, agree with the first inflation of prevalence, even if they don't admit it.

Here's an example of the double inflation in an email I received from a school district administrator. He told me he would not disaggregate data around what was happening with the boys in his district because, "Don't you realize, Mr. Gurian, there are so many gender non-binary kids now, it makes no sense to talk about binary sex? Our admin team is in agreement on that. You are stuck in an unenlightened position." When I pressed him on how many nonbinary kids there were, he did not answer. When I asked him whether everyone on the admin team agreed that data for sex should not be disaggregated and used to bring training on boy-friendly education to the district, he said, "No, not everyone, but enough." When I asked him what science he was using to back up his prevalence inflation he said, "It's everywhere, just google it, binary male and female are dead."

He was saying that the rule, sex, should be removed from human nature, even also from "an enlightened culture" and "from science" because social pressure from prevalence inflation required this change. Once the prevalence of "there is no sexual dimorphism, there is no male/female anymore" was established, the exceptions, "we are all cisgender or gender fluid" became the new rule for him. Once the prevalence of "we are all cisgender or gender fluid" was established, "gender" became the new rule and sex was denied. This ongoing prevalence inflation allowed a reverse dominance in which the exception was seen as refined and dominant and the rule as ignorant.

Prevalence inflation and the culture of the exception led to a division of the American Medical Association, in 2020, feeling enough pressure to suggest that "mom" and "dad" should be used less or not at all and "female" and "male" should no longer appear on birth certificates. The AMA's justification was: biological terms like female and male might disturb a gender fluid person later in life when they explored their new gender identity. These AMA guidelines blasted through social media and gained enough traction that people began to wonder, "If the American Medical Association is saying it, then maybe boys and girls are not real. Maybe we shouldn't focus on them anymore." As colleges accept this prevalence inflation, so do school districts. The result: new and established teachers are not taught sex differences and the impact of sexual dimorphism, and boys just keep falling behind in grades and discipline referrals, equity and excellence directives are inadequately fulfilled, and significant issues continue to arise in boys' behavior, performance, and mental health daily.

Changing Gender Roles and The Culture of the Exception

"How did we get here?" Latisha asked. Historically, we built human cultures to advance both uniformity *and* diversity. We saw this combination as an existential element of *ontology* (the study of our way of being). Historically, not just uniformity but diversity within the uniformity mattered. Exceptions within the rule, minorities within the majority reflected and codified our core human experiences—both. States of being that were basic to us, like sex, held deep mystery, and thus rose to the forefront as we navigated them. Each person, living life within the social story, helped create each monolithic culture as each generation accepted what was useful, from their point of view, and culled what was not useful. In every generation since the beginning of time, there have been extreme ideologies that we try to pull together toward the center by building strong coalitions for social stability and, when needed, for social revolution.

Sexual dimorphism is a grounding mystery of human development that each generation has understood better than the last. Sex has always been a part of our personal and cultural pilgrimage. Previous sex roles, once useful for many people, calcified and often caused harm, especially to women and girls. The Big Three—starting in academic culture and branching out to law, government, and media—decided to change that while changing "sex roles" to "gender roles" and "sex" to "gender." The feminist revolution helped us study rules *and* exceptions, majority *and* minority, and parts *and* whole. We learned about the fragility of previous uniformities and added civil rights for minority populations and women's rights to our democratic future.

As our revolutions have proceeded forward over the last fifty years, equality for women and minorities has been occurring. Uniformity of previous female sex roles changed to diversity of gender roles and diversity of male roles followed suit. Lots of mistakes have been made in the last one hundred years, but for the most part, the culture of the exception ("women are diverse and we must support whatever a woman wants to do, no matter if it does not fit the social norm") has been a healthy pressure in both scientific inquiry and human development. Women are no longer "the weaker sex." The feminist movement that introduced the contemporary culture of the exception to social politics has by and large succeeded in using that methodology to advocate for a new and improved humanity.

The Impossible War: Sex vs. Gender

But a core mistake has been made. This feminist sociological methodology created a war between sex and gender. Whereas previous exceptions to rules were about *social roles*, the new culture of the exception is about *gender sameness.* Whereas, for much of the last one hundred years the uplift of women and girls was done to ensure equality for obvious *sex* differences between women and men, in the culture of the exception, sex has been relegated to unprovable-for-advocacy-purposes, and gender sameness has been uplifted to the only acceptable social norm.

When the AMA suggested removing male and female from birth certificates, the culture of the exception, growing directly from feminist sociology, is "how we got here." As sociologists pressured culture to change gender roles, they also pressured the "all" (sex) to be seen only through the lens of "some" (gender). "The sex of your baby" changed to "the gender of your baby." The pressure to erase "mom" and "dad" from human life, and "female and male" from science and from birth certificates, is now destructive in part because, unlike the women's equality movement, erasure of sex *cannot be anchored in the science of human nature.* When people on the political Left tell us that "breast-feeding" is anti-trans and "chest feeding" should replace it, they are calling sex dangerous or stupid, yet it is one of our three most basic human genetic components (the other two are your physiologic genetics and your personality genetics). Erasure of human nature and of common sense causes backlash culture-wide so that "anatomical sex" is held up as the *only* human element worth discussing, and "gender" is erased from discussion on the political Right.

Now we have an impossible war, unwinnable by either side. People on the political Right who argue that the minority (gender fluid, lesbian, gay, bisexual, trans, gender nonbinary) are anathema to social progress cannot win their war because these people *do* exist, do not cause harm, and have much to offer. This minority is a part of the whole so that, if we try to erase this part, we are trying to erase ourselves.

But people on the Left who argue that the minority constitutes the correct ideological whole cannot win their war because human nature and natural science prove both exceptions and rules. Unreasonable pressure of the exception and then backlash against that pressure destroy our individual and collective voice around what is true. Our children become casualties of a majority and a minority who fight this impossible war of erasure.

Social Media's Power to Negate Hard Science

Up until social media's control over social conversation, the culture of the exception regarding human nature could not prevail against nature because it could not deny *science and common sense both at once.* Now, in social media, each side of the war receives short bursts of false "facts" and impossible "ideas" blasted out as "truth" so that academics, school administrators, political leaders, and scientists fear social media's demonizing, blaming, scapegoating, and stereotyping. Social media does make it possible to deny both science and common sense.

The school superintendent did not have proof for his claims–only social media. Scientists like those at the AMA created senselessly extreme positions to build a tribe-of-the-exception on social media and got that attention. Other scientists, afraid of losing tenure, step out of the impossible war for self-protection, taking real science with them. Whether far Left or far Right, social media creates an algorithmic neural environment in which resilience often gives way to fear and self-loss. The media bombard our amygdala (a fear center in the brain), keeping it super-charged with cortisol (stress hormone). We become hypervigilant and act against the prosocial norms—the center— on which a culture's successful evolution depends.

Simultaneously, we receive dopamine rushes ("dark reward") in the brain from demonizing and hurting other people by exclusion and hate. Even if we are not violent, we become like the depressed boys in earlier chapters, hooked into the dopamine rush of social violence on social media while sapping other parts of our brains, especially the frontal lobe, of the blood flow our thinking and common sense need to thrive. If you have personally spent time with gangs and groups on social media, you have likely felt the power of expressing rage against a group that is often your rage against reality.

The Sexgender Spectrum

The social pressure to create a culture of the exception regarding sex/gender occurs concomitant with *sexodimorphobia,* the fear of sexual dimorphism. As our brains are bombarded by social media in the Big Three, our anxiety swells and not just the people pushing the culture of the exception but we ourselves become afraid of doing damage in this impossible war, whether to ourselves and our own families or to trans people. Physicians entrench themselves on one or the other side of the war out of fear and posit that "To be empathic to LGBTQIA+ people we have to no longer admit that human beings are sexually dimorphic," despite that those same physicians know that sex and gender are not the same thing.

I propose a way out of this. Let us make a language change in our culture that can start with you, Sean, and me via this book. When talking about sex, sexual dimorphism, trans, gender fluidity, or any similar topic, let's from now on use "sexgender." Despite that, these days "gender" is used for nearly everything related to sex and gender, humans possess only two sex options, male and female, pre-set with variety *in utero;* so, it is scientifically unsound to only use "gender" for sex. Meanwhile, we exist on a *male brain spectrum* and a *female brain spectrum* with four billion people on earth *on the male brain spectrum* and four billion people on earth *on the female brain spectrum* including approximately 20% *bridge brains.* Given that the word "gender" can capture some of the exceptions to the rules, especially the bridge brains, let's add sex to gender to use "sexgender" from now on where appropriate. Sexgender will encompass all human brains, whether we are talking about sex or gender in conversation, in studies and books, and on social media.

If we will use *sexgender* instead of the inaccurate "cisgender" (that denies sex), we could gain universal understanding of *both* sex and gender without the use of ideologically weighted concepts on either front. By using sexgender instead of just sex or just gender when the amalgam is what we are discussing, we will avoid leaving anyone out of the discussion. The *science of sexgender* then could place all human brains along a *sexgender spectrum* supported by hard science then augmented by soft science. Academics in Schools of Education could perhaps now find it politically correct to teach future teachers about sexual dimorphism because sexgender is inclusive of the population they are most worried about offending, gender populations. Children would not have to deal anymore with the kinds of errors that are made in schools, families, and institutions like the one involving John Dow in California, whose only "crime" was answering a logical question about sex with a 14-year-old brain's sexgender analysis.

Two Sexgender Tools

Here are two tools for you to use in your citizen science and group discussions. The first tool includes elements in the previous chapters around the four elements of sexgender. The second tool provides a snapshot of sexgender brain differences, including some I mentioned earlier, you can use here in one place to bring to your school boards and other social institutions to advocate for focus on boys' boy-specific neural and social-emotional development.

Try This
The Four Elements Sexgender Tool

In defining sexgender, we can deal with all four natural elements together, not just any single one exclusive of the others. This way we accept diversity, avoid stereotypes, and include everyone.

Physiological/Anatomical/Chromosomal Sex. X/Y chromosomes create female and male bodies, reproductive organs, muscle mass, blood content, sex-specific gametes, and sex-specific molecular structure in our cells. In *Eve's Rib: The New Science of Gender-Specific Medicine*, Marianne J. Legato, M.D., summarizes the importance of our knowing and celebrating sexual dimorphism: "Everywhere we look the two sexes are startlingly and unexpectedly different, not only in their internal function but in the ways that they experience illness. To care for them, we must see them as who they are: female and male." Notice how Dr. Legato's book title, in keeping with the politics of our times, without access to our word "sexgender," uses "gender" while in the book itself, she uses the more biologically accurate "two sexes." "Sexgender" would solve the issue.

Brain-Sex/Sex-on-the-Brain/Sexual Dimorphism. X/Y chromosomes create body and brain-sex differentiation in utero (sexual dimorphism). This brain-sex differentiation continues throughout the lifespan and includes trans and bridge brains. Louann Brizendine, M.D., has written *The Female Brain* and *The Male Brain*, two books your group can access that provide in depth analysis of brain sex in adults and children. For further reference, my *Saving Our Sons* and *The Minds of Girls*, are practical parenting resources in the sexgender area. David C. Page, M.D., professor of biology at MIT, reminds us about the source of our brain-sex dimorphism: "Our genomes are 99.9% identical from one person to the next as long as the two individuals being compared are two males or two females. But if we compare the two sexes, the genetic differences are 15 times greater than the genetic differences for two males or two females." "Sexgender" includes all of these ideas.

Evolutionary Exceptions within Sexual Dimorphism. There are and have always been exceptions in particular areas of neural and physiological dimorphism. For example, in 5–10% of us, the sexually dimorphic nucleus in the anterior hypothalamus of the brain is sized and formed for same-sex orientation (homosexuality). Heterosexuality is the rule and homosexuality is the exception, but they both exist in the brain; thus homosexuality is not mainly a "gender choice" or "culture choice." It carries a genetic component, running in families, and is hard-wired into the person's male or female brain *on the sexgender spectrum.*

Gender Fluidity and Gender. Gender is a social construct regarding roles and identity. It can be fluid as people "choose what gender to identify with," gender non-conforming, gender non-binary or "bridge brain." The child or young adult who says, "I'm gender nonconforming" may be LGBT or may be experimenting with fluidity in response to gender dysphoria, which is a form of depression, or may have experienced significant trauma, which gender nonconformity can help process and heal or may be exploring adolescent identity with *sexgender curiosity.* Gender fluid children and adults will likely scan as bridge brains on the sexgender spectrum.

Using "sexgender" includes all of these children.

The Male/Female Brain Difference Tool

Here are six male/female brain differences you can apply in your discussion groups as you learn about and help others use sexual dimorphism and sexgender for social change. I have chosen brain differences that can impact parenting, schooling, love, marriage, social progress, and social policy. You have read bits of this before in earlier chapters. I am now deepening this material for you so that you can add it to your use of "sexgender" in your meetings and advocacy work.

Gray and White Matter Activity Difference
Richard Haier, University of California-Irvine neuroscientist, has studied brain scans over the last three decades from all races and multiple continents.

He and his colleagues have discovered that girls and women utilize up to 10 times more *white matter activity* than boys and men and boys and men up to 7 times more *gray matter activity*. White matter activity moves signaling throughout the brain instantly while gray matter activity generally houses a task in a specific area of the brain. This white/gray matter activity difference is one of the reasons that traditional schooling can become a crisis point for so many boys: the school systems teach much more towards girls' white matter activity/multi-tasking brains, much less toward boys' gray matter/single-task-focused brains.

Frontal Lobe Use Difference

Richard Haier and colleagues have also discovered that 80% of female learning and intellectual activity transpire in *the frontal lobe* of the brain (where executive decision-making, impulse control, organization, and word production take place). In contrast, male learning and intellectual activity transpire only 0 – 40% in the frontal lobe. These findings have been confirmed at Cambridge University and numerous others in the brains of all races, cultures, and continents. For reasons of genetic neurobiology, males tend to emphasize learning in gray matter areas lower and further back in the brain than females do. The fact that males have more impulse, organization, and word/literacy issues than females finally made sense to interested educators when the brain scans revealed these different locations of activity in the 1990s. We came to understand that traditional schooling expectations lean toward assuming a child development baseline/tempo in the frontal lobe suitable to far more girls than boys.

Furthermore, we noticed that behavior standards and evaluations assessed boys through the lens of girls' frontal lobe activity, which led, quite often, to evaluating boys as defective in comparison to girls. "Difference," of course, is not "defect." While some male behavior must face discipline, some of the male-defect-obsessed discipline provided to boys in schools, like the story in Livermore, causes a school-to-prison pipeline. As Sean noted, when schools and teachers move toward a brain science approach to boys and girls, they diminish discipline referrals, bullying, suspensions, and expulsions, which ends up diminishing the school-to-prison pipeline.

Male Cerebellum Dependence

The cerebellum is the "doing center" at the base of the human brain. Neuroscientist Daniel Amen has conducted multiple studies including a recent 49,000 scan study of male and female brains of all races and demographics. Dr. Amen's scans show males to be *cerebellum dependent* for much of their learning and living. This means, for the male's learning brain to be activated, he often needs the movement/doing center of the brain to be activated. For equity's sake, where teaching to the girl's frontal lobe makes sense given her significant use of that cortex during the school day, teaching equally toward the boy's *cerebellum* should make sense.

One of the primary principles of a "boys and girls learn differently" approach in schools is the shared realization *a priori* among faculty that boys don't tend to sit still as well as girls for as long; when they do sit still for too long a time, boys don't learn or retain as much as girls in the aggregate. Teachers have also noticed: when boys move around the room or move near their desk, in the hallways, on playgrounds, their cerebellum is activated, and that activation sends signaling upward into the frontal lobe and other learning areas. Physical movement in boys' learning isn't just for entertainment–it is a profound learning tool.

Word Production and Word Use in the Brain

Doreen Kimura, Ph.D. and her colleagues have studied male/female brains for location of *word use and word production*. In brain scans, these researchers see language-related brain activity in girls on both sides of the brain and word activity in boys tending mainly to occur on the left side. Because girls and women do more words in more multiple areas on both sides of the brain, they often connect words to senses, feeling, and memories more than boys tend to do, with more variety, and in general, more quickly. In most schools today, "use your words" is considered the gold standard for both emotional life and cognitive education, but boys do not have as much immediate access to words as girls. They often need other strategies for accessing words-for-feelings than "use your words." When English, Social Studies, or other writing related classes require tests, homework, worksheets, papers—and lots of them–their learning is hyper-word based, and many boys will not learn as well as girls.

When, however, schools and classrooms account for male/female word use differences, they notice that the right side of the male brain (where girls are doing words) emphasizes spatial-mechanicals (objects moving in space) and visual-graphics (pictures and visuals). These teachers then allow boys to use graphic, visual, and spatial stimulants to access male right side brain function which then can stimulate male word areas on the left more frequently and fully. Especially if visual-graphic stimulation is used along with physical and kinesthetic learning, the boys end up using words commensurate with girls, thus getting better grades than before on assignments that require words and word-connection to senses and memories. Even more subtle, the more visual-spatial, kinesthetic, and physical learning used in a classroom, the more that behavior and classroom management issues dissipate or, in many cases, disappear.

The Brain Rest State

Ruben and Raquel Gur at the University of Pennsylvania were some of the first neuroscientists to study the ways that male/female brains enter *rest states*. The rest state is also known as a "zone out," "boredom," or "blank brain" state of mind. Boys' brains can enter these boredom-states numerous times in a traditional school day, especially when the work they are supposed to do is not dynamic (is "boring") and they are involved in no physical or spatial movement during the classroom hour.

While girls may feel bored in an unstimulating class, their brains do not enter the same rest/boredom state neurologically. Because of an X/Y-chromosomal/brain difference, the female brain retains information and directions the male brain loses in the rest state. The female brain continues to pursue the learning goal in front of them and can appear attentive because her frontal lobe does not become empty of blood flow when she is bored. The male frontal lobe, however, does tend to empty of blood flow ("goes blank") and thus our boys miss the lessons, directions, and learning.

When a school takes a holistic approach to boys and girls' learning it provides teacher training in many of our Gurian Institute strategies noted already in this book. The training and support work helps teachers to:

- keep boys' brains activated and out of the rest state;
- read signals in boys' eyes and demeanor that the boy is in the rest state;
- provide "brain breaks" for the students; and
- add on novel and new brain-friendly innovations to keep the male brain learning and active.

Differences in Biochemistry

Male and female molecular differences in hormonology (*brain chemistry*) have been noted by many scientists, including David Geary at the University of Missouri, and Shelley Taylor at the University of California. Over the last forty years their teams have studied the impact of evolutionary biology on sexgender. Among the brain chemistry insights they have shared is the *testosterone/oxytocin* difference. As we noted earlier, boys and men have ten to twenty times more testosterone, an aggression chemical, in their bloodstreams and brains than girls and women. Girls and women have more estrogen, progesterone, and other chemicals well known to us all, and more of a lesser-known chemical, *oxytocin,* which is a primary human bonding chemical. Dr. Taylor calls it the "tend and befriend" chemical.

Bonding and attachment are one of the most crucial human functions for life-success, but boys and girls tend to bond differently. Females tend to bond via more verbal empathy and less physical aggression. Males tend to bond less via protracted words-for-feelings and more via rough and tumble play and quick bursts of physical aggression. As Dr. Geary has noted, these sex-different bonding mechanisms fit our hormonal neurobiology. There is nothing wrong with them or their sexgender dimorphism.

I have named male bonding *aggression nurturance.* Different from the more female tend-and-befriend bonding, which tends to downplay aggression, male bonding *includes aggression* (we must remember that aggression is not violence—aggression is healthy assertiveness). The higher your oxytocin levels, the more likely you are to avoid physical aggression; the higher your testosterone levels, the more you will tend to pursue aggression nurturance. Traditional schooling punishes the aggression nurturance that boys use even though that kind of nurturance is a primary driver of resilience-building in all human beings and ought to be utilized and directed not punished.

Programs that Serve Boys and Girls
Serve Gender Nonconforming Kids Too

I hope you will use these tools and insights wherever you can. Remember what Dr. Legato said: if we forget sex, we make major mistakes in child and adult care. Similarly, if we forget sexgender, we can harm children. Since every child, even one who is gender nonconforming, is male and female, brain-based programs that serve girls will serve all girls in need, including gender nonconforming girls; similarly, programs that serve boys will serve all boys, including nonconforming boys. Our Gurian Institute field work has proven this in wisdom-of-practice research beginning with our first pilot programs at the University of Missouri-Kansas City in the 1990s. Our programs are all inclusive and help all children because they are programs involving *sexgender* thus they include male/female brain difference as the human baseline with bridge brains/LGBTQIA+ brains accounted for equitably.

Did You Know?
Training Based in Sex Differences Works to
Help Kids in These Ways

Our GI success data (see www.gurianinstitute.com) shows that use of Gurian theory and strategies by organizations, schools, and teams generate success in these categories.

- Decreasing the pre-school to prison pipeline
- Closing achievement gaps throughout the curriculum
- Turning around low performing schools
- Raising grades and test scores for all children
- Increasing teacher effectiveness and teacher quality
- Decreasing unhealthy discipline practices, especially unfairness to boys of color
- Improving girls' learning in STEM/STEAM areas
- Improving boys' literacy and social emotional learning
- Increasing parent participation in the education of children
- Preventing bullying and cyberbullying
- Using trauma-informed and poverty-informed strategies across the curriculum

Expanding diversity and inclusion for race, ethnicity, and gender

---

The gender fluid person, the exception to the rule, qualifies for voice in our culture—yet, too, especially via social media these days, social pressure to make *gender* the baseline and *sex* nonexistent makes schools, teachers, and parents afraid to help the students right in front of them–boys and girls. In their fear of getting reprimanded or canceled, they help a small group of students, not the largest group in trouble in school, boys. As fear of sexual dimorphism rules a school board or school building, gender innovations are hyperbolized and forced throughout the system. Sexodimorphobic administrators, faculty, and parents ax programs that help boys and accuse boys of crimes the boys did not commit. Sex is seen as dysfunctional and dangerous, the science of sex is decommissioned, and the school's primary issues, do not get solved.

As you help change things by encouraging institutions to look carefully at all aspects of sexgender equitably, you will be requesting that your school system pay attention to the very language it uses around sex and gender. From there, you will be asking for its structures and protocols to change toward the most holistic sexgender approach possible. Your ask is not a huge one given the proven and positive results already revealed nationwide through this sexgender approach.

Chapter 11

I Am a Boy, Hear Me Roar

"And Max, the king of all wild things, was lonely and wanted to be where someone loved him best of all."

–Maurice Sendak

(This essay is useful for general readership, and particularly for parents, teachers, students, college courses, coaches, mentors, and book discussion groups.)

A MOTHER IN A CALIFORNIA MIDDLE SCHOOL, Terrie, reached out to me (Sean) after having a conversation with a teacher that revealed what Michael calls *sexodimorphobia*. Terrie shared that she had talked to her son, Alan's, teacher to discuss Alan's reading comprehension skills. When Terrie asked the teacher about the ways boys and girls learn differently, how this might impact the boy's learning, and whether the school staff were trained in boy's learning methods, the teacher rebuked the mother. "There is no difference in the way boys and girls learn. Boys' and girls' brains are the same." Terrie learned that the teacher was repeating what she had heard in the School of Education that trained her. As Terrie pressed harder, she learned that the teacher followed people online who supported this view. But Terrie was a mom who wanted help for her son not a mom who sought to get involved in anxious or angry social politics. When she came to see me for help, she said, "Please give me a data question I can ask the teacher tomorrow, something concrete." Terrie knew: teachers and school systems need data to pressure them toward internal social change.

I suggested asking, "If there is no difference between boys and girls, why are boys behind girls in reading in our state?"

I supplied the mom with this graph from Washington State (where she lived).

Percent of 3rd to 5th Grade Students in WA State Proficient in English/Language Arts by Race and Sex from 2014 to 2022

Race	3rd Grade ELA			4th Grade			5th Grade ELA		
	Female	Male	Male (Deficit)	Female	Male	Male (Deficit)	Female	Male	Male (Deficit)
American Indian/ Alaskan Native	29.1%	21.6%	(7.5%)	30.0%	22.1%	(7.9%)	32.5%	23.5%	(9%)
Asian	75.3%	67.4%	(7.9%)	76.0%	69.6%	(6.4%)	79.3%	71.3%	(8%)
Black/ African American	41.4%	31.0%	(10.4%)	40.5%	31.5%	(9%)	43.9%	32.9%	(11%)
Hispanic/ Latino of any race(s)	37.8%	31.1%	(6.7%)	38.9%	32.3%	(6.6%)	42.7%	34.1%	(8.6%)
Native Hawaiian/ Other Pacific Islander	33.9%	26.0%	(7.9%)	34.5%	26.6%	(7.9%)	38.7%	29.8%	(8.9%)
Two or More Races	60.7%	51.7%	(9%)	60.5%	52.5%	(8%)	63.9%	54.6%	(9.3%)
White	64.7%	56.7%	(8%)	65.5%	57.6%	(7.9%)	68.7%	59.2%	(9.5%)

Percent of 6th to 8th Grade Students in WA State Proficient in English/Language Arts by Race and Sex from 2014 to 2022

Race	6th Grade ELA			7th Grade			8th Grade ELA		
	Female	Male	Male (Deficit)	Female	Male	Male (Deficit)	Female	Male	Male (Deficit)
American Indian/ Alaskan Native	29.6%	19.2%	(10.4%)	35.9%	22.1%	(13.8%)	35.6%	23.1%	(12.5%)
Asian	78.0%	69.4%	(8.6%)	80.7%	72.0%	(8.7%)	79.9%	71.6%	(8.3%)
Black/ African American	41.0%	28.3%	(12.7%)	44.4%	30.6%	(13.8%)	44.2%	29.0%	(15.2%)
Hispanic/ Latino of any race(s)	39.8%	29.8%	(10%)	43.8%	33.0%	(10.8%)	44.0%	32.4%	(11.6%)
Native Hawaiian/ Other Pacific Islander	36.2%	24.8%	(11.4%)	38.5%	27.5%	(11%)	38.8%	26.1%	(12.7%)
Two or More Races	60.5%	50.0%	(10.5%)	64.1%	52.2%	(11.9%)	63.7%	51.9%	(11.8%)
White	65.7%	54.7%	(11%)	69.0%	57.4%	(11.6%)	68.5%	56.4%	(12.1%)

Source: Office of Superintendent of Public Instruction (Washington State) **Information Request Received January 22, 2024**

You can see boys' deficits in light gray across the demographics. (I am presently working with data in all fifty states to develop similar graphs and graphics). After Terrie read the chart, she and I discussed how this tool could help parents, educators, academics, and policy makers work locally to identify the real causes of male underperformance, what Michael has called "the mismatch of the male brain and our educational system." (To keep getting more of these graphs beyond this book, please feel free to subscribe to my InHisWords.us substack).

The Academic Source of the Problem

I went through academic training to become a teacher and did not get a course in sexual dimorphism, male/female brain, sexgender, or anything similar. I only learned about gender stereotypes and changing gender roles. Like every teacher similarly trained in Schools of Education, I did not see the brain scans Michael referred to in the last chapter, nor did I hear about the huge amount of research coming from offices and labs of the scientists Michael has featured. More than 99.9% of the teachers and administrators in our schools did not get a course in the male and female brain. While young teachers are required to take courses on topics such as the "Politics of Educational Inequality" and "Education in a Global World," both worthy indeed, we are not required (nor is it available as an elective) to take a course in the one population that will give us the most confusion over our lifespan as a teacher–boys.

When I discovered the work of the Gurian Institute fifteen years ago, I felt vindicated because as a father of two sons and as a man, I had instinctively tried to teach so that boys and girls could both flourish in my classroom. When I got to know the Gurian Institute, I was surprised to see that GI has been employing their brain-differences approach for decades in coed public schools, free-and-reduced-lunch (Title I) schools, private and independent schools, religious schools, charter schools, homeschool coops, single sex schools, and universities.

I began to spread the word about this male/female brain approach, and often asked academics in Schools of Education, "Why don't you teach this?" Most of them told me what Michael has shared: sexual dimorphism, the male brain, and sexgender are too politically charged to be touched in academe. Even now, in 2025, when I discuss the mismatch of the male brain to present day educational systems, I hear, "We need to stay away from that," or "that's not proven," or "my university professors said to avoid that," or some other form of *sexodimorphobia*.

A new study out of Stanford Medical School might help reduce educators' fears. This study follows four decades of academic research from the people Michael quoted earlier (you'll find many more in the endnotes, as well) and uses fMRI, SPECT, and PET scans along with Artificial Intelligence to identify neural components that distinguish male and female brains. Cerebellum use, white/gray matter activity, frontal lobe connectivity, and the other differences Michael outlined were studied via a mechanism that disallowed either the researchers of the AI to know ahead of time if the 1,500 scanned brains in the study were male or female. Both the humans and AI were tasked with distinguishing the female and male brains solely by noticing the cerebellum and other brain differences on brain scans. Both the humans and the AI succeeded in seeing the differences and identifying each brain accurately as male or female.

The Stanford team followed up by wondering if they could create "another model that could predict how well other participants would do on certain cognitive tasks based on functional brain features that differ between women and men." They developed more sex-specific models of cognitive abilities and tested these out to see whether other human beings and AI would know the differences between the male and female brain yet again. They did. With brain sex differences further clarified by these results, the study authors were able to discuss consequences of the sexually dimorphic brains. Among those were cognitive and behavioral. About the latter, the study team wrote, "Our findings indicate that functional brain characteristics varying between sexes have significant behavioral implications."

Not just in cognition but in behavior male/female brain differences must be studied *and applied* in the Big Three—not just in schools but throughout our systems. Regarding school life, Richard Reeves, in *Of Boys and Men* (2022), suggests that brain differences in developmental tempo, especially around word production and behavior, should allow us to red-shirt (hold back) boys in kindergarten so that their brains can catch up to neural development tempo in girls' brains. This suggestion likely will not become social policy from the legislative side because it would impede human freedom overall, but some parents are already doing it with their individual sons, and getting, in some cases, good results.

The male brain is behind the female on average about 1 to ½ years in word production because gray matter areas on the right side of the male brain used for reading and writing develop later than similar frontal lobe areas in the female brain on both sides. Males are also behind females in frontal lobe connectivity development, as Michael noted in the previous chapter. If you have a late reader son who also has some behavioral disadvantages in relationships with other children, you might want to consider waiting a year to start his first-grade schooling.

When Abandonment Becomes Denigration in Colleges and Beyond

Avoiding sex differences in Schools of Education, sociology departments, universities in general, and then in our nation's schools constitutes abandonment of healthy male development. The abandonment is not malicious, but it is abandonment just the same. As boys come up through the educational system, we generally hope they will go to college but the largest gender-gap in American educational history exists right now in college access and performance. Neglect of boys, the male brain, and healthy male development ought to be addressed by academic systems before college age but it is avoided, males are neglected, and many boys grow up unready for college learning and performance.

This issue is not a small one. From 2016-2020, 2.85 million more women graduated from college than men. College graduates will make substantially more aggregate income in their lifetimes than women and men who do not graduate from college. According to the National Center for Educational Statistics (NCES), "For 25- to 34-year-olds who worked full time, year-round, those who had higher educational attainment also had higher median earnings in 2022. For example, in 2022, the median earnings of those with a master's or higher degree ($80,200) were 20 percent higher than the earnings of those with a bachelor's degree ($66,600) as their highest level of attainment. In the same year, the median earnings of those with a bachelor's degree were 59 percent higher than the earnings of those who completed high school ($41,800) as their highest level of attainment."

While not every person will go to college, still, college should be a place for males as much as it is for females. But as academics populate themes like "toxic masculinity" and push the impossible war between sex and gender, males are denigrated, unprepared, or just stay away. How should a young man in college navigate the blame and shame he hears about his father and other men? Isn't personal achievement and strong self-esteem something everyone should get behind for every young person? The Stanford study is a welcome encouragement for sexgender work from a powerful academic institution but much of what trickles through the Big Three from university campuses is male-neglecting and at times just anti-male.

The Core of Maleness

Robert Frost has a wonderful poem, "Pan With Us." It presents a world in which modernity disposes of the natural world and, in turn, destroys its connection to the human spirit– to what is unique and beautiful. I think of that poem when a boy like John is suspended for inquisitive and mental problem-solving. Some of his purpose as a young man, especially his love of learning, will be lost. He will feel himself making constant missteps in a system that is not boy-friendly, missteps that add up to cumulative shame propelled out of the Big Three that taught his teachers. As he and boys like him go through pre-K through 12 schooling then, as some of them enter college, they know something very deep is going on, something targeting the discrete and unique existence of a male.

When a boy sees the movie *Barbie*–a visual replication of a college course in radical feminist sociology–he may laugh with those around him, but when he goes home, doesn't he wonder why all the men in the movie are stupid, hyper-dominant, weak, purposeless, and exploitative? Our males do wonder why so many boys and men on TV and in social media are portrayed as specifically inferior to females. The male story coming out of academic frameworks and penetrating visual and social media is presented as academic framers want it to be presented, not with language about maleness, the boy's male soul, his life. When his parents, teachers, and college professors try to discuss "male" as an important piece of his identity, they are admonished or told to discuss "masculine stereotypes." The boy learns that "male" ought to be avoided, whether because he and maleness are too violent or not violent enough.

When people in positions of authority remove the male story, a young man recasts male purpose and a life of meaning in ways that leave a void—which is what abandonment always does. It creates a hole inside the person abandoned. Because we have millions of males with this hole, we have a hole in our culture as well.

Mark Twain has a beautiful sentence: "My mother had a great deal of trouble with me, but I think she enjoyed it." The natural and brain-based world of boy-ness is challenging but interesting. It is essential to human life and evolution. We need it for our survival and thriving. It is sex differentiated—male, equal to female–not superior or inferior but equal. A boy may not talk as much about what he feels during his lifetime as his sister or mother do; he may not sit still as well as his sister or mother; he may learn differently, think differently, feel differently because he has a male brain, but this ought not condemn him.

A Mother's Story of Her Son

I am grateful to this mother who wrote me this portrait of her son, Bradley, and her mother-son relationship.

"I have an active child and so I have learned how raising a young man takes grit, a big heart and communication. I also understand boys need hugs too. Before I understood how boys are different, I remember feeling so tired and confused as to why he wasn't satisfied with sitting still to watch a movie or staying quiet in the library or why he was so competitive. My first born is a daughter and that's all I was comparing him to. Once I realized he needed to be raised according to his male needs and desires, life started to make more sense to me as a mom. It was time to get my hands dirty!

"When he felt bored, he'd flop around on the floor screaming like he was being electrocuted. After too many days of this chaos I decided to find him a purpose every day which helped immensely with his boredom tantrum. I learned that when he is purposed he excels. What that meant for me was prepping projects and getting 'ready' for the day before he woke up (similar to a teacher's lesson plan). The moment he woke up, he hit the ground running. We went from books to art projects, to cooking, to free play, to outdoor activity, to dinner, to bath time, and he'd barely listen to a book in bed but he loved back rubs and storytelling. I had to act like a kid in order to understand him better.

"For a great portion of his young life Bradley and I spent every day digging for worms, skipping rocks at the creek, riding bikes, walking miles around the skatepark or ballparks, hiking and playing catch. He is a great cook which I attribute to the many messes he was allowed to explore in the kitchen. He's a doer so I let him 'do'! My son has always been high intensity at home, at school and in sports. He's taught me to lighten up, not take everything so seriously. Expecting him to conform to a life that doesn't scratch his brain, feels wrong. I'm exhausted as his mom in the best loving way!"

This mom understands her son! She is tracking the diverse and passionate core of maleness in him and nurturing that. While it is good for a boy to sit still sometimes, he will not sit still as much on average as his sister. As he gets to pre-puberty, he will not cry as much as his sister or mother on average. He will not have as many words-for-feelings as they have, but what a blessing he is! Kudos to his mom for, like Mark Twain's mom, enjoying hearing him roar, with a voice committed to purpose. She has done the opposite of abandonment—she has ensured the healthy development of her young male. She knows that abandonment of a boy's "boy energy," his maleness, is a bad thing not just for him, but for all of us who will one day depend on him for love, empathy, grit, and service.

Essential Questions to Try with Others

1. Twain's statement ("My mother had a great deal of trouble with me, but I think she enjoyed it") attempts to reconcile the essence and nature of the boy with the mother and society's understanding of him. Twain is not suggesting something defective in the boy but perhaps something more engaging. Can you think of

a story that shows how you learned something about yourself and your misunderstanding of a boy that in a way opened your eyes to his unique wonder?

2. How can teaching students in high school and college about the ways boys and girls learn differently build healthier relationships?

3. Pressured by our culture to neglect maleness in our boys, how do we as parents and teachers unknowingly abandon boys' needs?

4. What brain differences allow girls, in the aggregate, to better access words connected to feelings and emotions than boys?

What can you do in your home, school, or community to ensure that the male story is included and celebrated as essential to the good of the home, the good of the school, and the good of the community?

Part III: Big Three Politics That Keep Us from Helping Boys

"What we leave as a legacy is not what is etched in stone monuments, but what is woven into the lives of others."
  –Anonymous, Hanging on a Plaque in Hospice House

Introduction

WHAT WILL OUR INDIVIDUAL LEGACIES BE? How will we each weave the best of ourselves into the lives of others? What will the legacies of our social institutions be, especially those that work in the areas of sexgender?

Our contemporary social politics may claim positive gains on masculinity studies, but those same social politics ignore disturbing male outcomes; construct negative narratives of males and dismiss male struggles; underestimate male challenges and create straw man masculine constructs that deny male development its inherent needs. If we are going to rescue our sons in this era of human evolution, we must grapple with the politics of the Big Three head on so that those politics are not our main legacy. We have the right to change those politics while we are still alive.

In this Part of the book, you will read essays that help you change our national political legacy where you are. We will provide you as a citizen scientist with evidence and tools for pushing back on arguments about masculine constructs that ignore males. We will help you assist the Big Three to understand not just how but *why* academics, government, and media have placed our struggling, depressed, lonely, wavering boys into a nearly invisible demographic in political and social policy.

Michael will introduce another key term, *feminaphobia,* to help arm you for social discussions and social change. Sean will provide various ways to confront policymakers, media, and social systems that ignore hard data on male outcomes. Michael will end the section with new language and diagnostic elements that you, your educators, and your medical professionals can use to understand the males in your and their care without the weight of masculine norms theory and the dominant gender paradigm.

You don't have to be a politics-wonk to enjoy, even feel moved, by this Part of the book. You need only be open to the task of cutting through political theater that either ignores males or targets them as masculine villains. In your own family, grass roots organizations, schools, and universities, you can band together to rescue your sons where they are individually and politically. Politics matter, and we can all start taking control of anti-male politics.

Chapter 12

The Danger of Feminaphobia

> "Men have sacrificed and crippled themselves physically and emotionally to feed, house, and protect women and children. None of their pain or achievement is registered in feminist rhetoric, which portrays men as oppressive and callous exploiters."
>
> –Camille Paglia

(This essay is useful for general readers, and particularly to policymakers, media and communications organizations, school boards, college courses, group discussion, and the field of gender studies.)

THERE ARE SECRETS IN OUR NEW MILLENNIUM that the Big Three does not want shared or known. These secrets go against the headlines all around us, against the optics of visible and successful men in our companies and government, and against prevailing social theories regarding masculinity and sexgender. Sean and I (Michael) have outlined one of the secrets already: In overall physical, cognitive, educational, neurological, emotional, psychological, and health markers, boys are doing as badly as and, in far too many cases, worse than girls. Somewhat unbelievably, boys have been doing worse than girls in these ways *for more than three decades,* but our culture turns a blind eye. Male suffering has been kept a secret by the Big Three in some part to protect social assets for use by girls and women.

I have two daughters. I know they suffer as women. My late wife, Gail, suffered in her life, especially at its end, battling pancreatic cancer. Women around her, and me, and my daughters and women around you suffer. I have personally worked with schools and corporations on girls' and women's empowerment since the late 1980s. We are a hard society to live in and we have a lot of vulnerable people we must serve and assist, including girls, women, and LGBTQIA + people.

Fortunately, when our society recognizes the vulnerability of girls, LGBTQIA+ populations, women, racial and ethnic groups, indigenous peoples, and many others, our Big Three come together to help. We commit to leaving a good and strong legacy for these people in difficulty. When our culture identifies "boys," "men," or "boys and men" as an aggregate group in pain, it tends to respond by deflecting this fact with political feints such as we have mentioned already in this book: "But boys are surpassing girls, everyone knows that," "boys and men already get more of our social assets than girls," "you're wrong, boys suffer less than girls in our culture," "boys and men constitute fewer victims of violence than girls," and so on.

Our culture will not admit the depth of male suffering in part because we feel collectively (even if subconsciously) that to admit male suffering equal to female suffering would wound girls and women. This leaves the variety and depth of male suffering a continuing political secret in universities, in your kids' school, in each neighborhood, in the faith-community, in the media, and in social politics.

Recalibrating Our Dominant Gender Paradigm

Re-calibrating democracy toward truth would help us create equality for everyone, including women and girls, racial and ethnic groups, and LGBTQIA+ populations because the suffering of men, boys, and maleness intersect with every other group. Millions of suffering males create a million sufferings for others around them. One of the popular sociological models that allows political leaders to keep pursuing "masculinity" and avoiding male, is a tenet of the dominant gender paradigm (DGP) you've no doubt heard about or perhaps used yourself: *the oppressor/oppressed model.* Decades ago (and in some places around the world, still) this sociological model served second wave feminism and the civil rights movement very well, revealing the secrets of the patriarchy (oppressor) to help our civilization affect a social revolution on behalf of girls, women, and African Americans especially. Not just fifty years ago, but still today in the Big Three, it is the most popular model for discussing the intersection of sexgender, social class, and culture study.

Some girls and women are still oppressed today. Some boys and men are privileged today. At the same time, many girls are more privileged than boys, many women more privileged than men, many boys are doing worse than girls in the millions in the U.S. alone. Today, some men are against women (some men hit their wives, oppressing them, as depicted powerfully in the recent movie, *This Ends With Us, 2024*). But looking around a room, a neighborhood, a university, a government office, a family, a school, and any location where there are women and men together, we can see that most men today are not against women; very few men today, and even fewer boys, can be truthfully linked to oppressive patriarchy.

Does the prevailing theory in the Big Three still fit our human and lived experience?

If we see that it only fits certain pockets of life but not most of our lives, don't we have the right to place that theory into a box of tools useful where and when they are useful but meanwhile walk away from that box to build new tools and new theories and new legacies?

The Power of the First Secret

Sean and I, in this book, I in other books, and our colleagues in their books and articles have been detailing the first secret for three decades. Simultaneously, we've been building new tools and theories, like those you are reading here, to help you to tell the secret of male suffering in a way that inspires each person to not only give the facts to others but help others move anti-male models out of dominance in contemporary culture. Here is a quick review of what we've noted in this book already regarding the secret. I will follow each point with a challenge to the oppressor-oppressed model.

- While statistics on overt depression are dominated by girls, covert depression is dominated by boys. Covert depression is often concealed beneath anger, substance overuse, suicide, and the disease of violence. Boys and men experience suicide and substance overuse at twice to four times the rate of females, with countless males experiencing male-type depression unnamed or not diagnosed because it does not look like overt depression. Arguing that male depression comes from "masculine social norms" and "male privilege" might satisfy a university course or an APA Guideline, but does it fit real life?

- Male brains suffer mental illnesses just as the female brain can, and in some areas, males suffer more severe brain issues than females do, including behavioral, attention, substance, and autism spectrum disorders. The male mental health crisis is bleeding into nearly every aspect of human life from homelessness to family distress to violent death. Three quarters of our homeless populations are male. Is the oppressor-oppressed model the right model for our homeless, dying, ill boys and men? Are homeless males oppressors or patriarchally privileged?

- In education, girls surpass boys beginning in the toddler years and continuing through college and graduate school as boys receive approximately two-thirds of Ds and Fs in our schools and comprise approximately 85% of discipline referrals, suspensions, and expulsions. Our traditional educational system, whether in-person or online, is set up better for the female brain than the male as my colleagues and I proved in six school districts in *Boys and Girls Learn Differently* in the 1990s, and as I and many others have proven since then. Since it is mainly our boys who are failing in our schools, are those schools patriarchal institutions? Really? Are boys and men the oppressors in those schools?

- Digging deeper into state mandated testing, as Sean has done with you, boys are approximately 10 points behind girls in literacy while girls are only 0–2 points behind boys in math/science depending on the test. "Achievement gaps" in state and local standardized testing mainly mean "boy gaps," including boys-of-color gaps identifiable now in every school district that disaggregates data for sex. The Big Three likes to say our boys do badly in school because they are burdened by "masculine stereotypes," but that is not provable. What can we prove? Schooling and counseling often do not teach or counsel well to the male brain. This is not a patriarchal-oppressor problem but a professional training problem.

- In physical health outcomes, males die on average five to seven years earlier than females depending on race and ethnicity, and men dominate death rates from dangerous jobs, general injury, and violence. When I ask audiences at my lectures which sex is more likely to suffer violence in its lifetime, I mainly hear "girls and women." People are shocked to learn that boys and men on average suffer more violence than females on any given day, week, month, year, and during a lifetime. In a domestic violence situation, we may see an oppressive man with power over his wife. But in dangerous jobs, general injury, and male victimization by violence is the male who gets killed or beaten or robbed the oppressor?

Of course, we might say the victims who are suffering don't matter to the oppressor model—what matters is that most criminals are male, which proves, for some, the males-are-the-oppressor model. But since boys and young men disproportionately fill our jails and prisons, comprising 93% of the incarcerated (which translates to between 1.1 and 1.5 million males incarcerated at any given moment), do these males behind bars and impoverished males who commit crimes have privilege and patriarchal power? Or isn't the situation just the opposite: a lack of privilege, lack of power, lack of father, lack of male help and lack of hope that have created a hole inside many of our males that they fill with substances and the dopamine rush of risk-taking crimes? Devastation and desperation afflict men in this population for whom academic models of oppressor-oppressed are just more abandonment.

The Second Secret: Feminaphobia

Suffering sits, like fate and joy, at the center of our human condition, but about contemporary suffering we have made a cultural decision: because we want the privation that women experience to remain at the forefront of culture, we will keep the extent of male suffering a secret. Even more, if we do talk about male suffering, we will say it happens because men are oppressors. The data just mentioned and other data that Sean, I, and others have provided to the Big Three (for example, my colleagues and I have briefed White Houses, Congress, and the United Nations) generally does not get acted on except to hear from leaders their laments about "masculinity." Why doesn't real data sway the Big Three?

Professors, leaders, people in the media have sons and can often see male suffering around them—why do they remain intransigent about publicizing the secret and helping our hurting males?

Has the oppressor-oppressed model become so entrenched that leaders and citizens can't see what is really happening?

The answer is Yes for some, but for many, the answer needs to expand to this: even when the secret of male suffering is told and our leaders and media see what is happening, they are *afraid to act because they want to retain political and social power.* I have met leaders for three decades who struggle with fear of losing their power to complex gender issues and they suffer from what I call *feminaphobia.*

This is the anxiety that regular people in our social systems and most of our leaders feel about betraying women, mothers, girls, and the difficult-to-define "women's," or "feminist" lobby. Whereas *misogyny* is a word that defines the irrational hatred/dislike of women mostly among some men, *feminaphobia* (sometimes irrational, sometimes quite rational) makes sure our leaders construct a society that neglects, marginalizes, cancels or punishes people for:

1. Telling the secret of male suffering, privation, and abandonment in equal fullness to the sufferings of girls and women as if agreeing on male suffering equal to female will harm girls and women.
2. And constructing other paradigms for sexgender difficulty than the obviously limited, and mainly outdated male/oppressor female/oppressed model.

Because "feminophobia" and "femiphobia" connote slightly different fears, I have placed the "a" in feminaphobia so that we have a collective name for this cultural and leadership paralysis.

A Factual, Or At Least Allegorical, Meeting

A meeting in the Hillary Clinton camp during the last months of her campaign for President (2016) is illustrative. (I have been told this story from a reliable source, but given that I was not at the meeting, I will use this story as an illustration of feminaphobia rather than a personally observed fact). In the summer 2016 meeting that took place among Hillary Clinton's campaign staff, Bill Clinton asked Hillary Clinton and her staff to talk more in stump speeches about the needs of boys and men in America. Former President Clinton was saying, boys and men are struggling–if you don't at least talk about boys and men, you lose half the population. This sounds logical in hindsight and must have sounded logical to some of the people at the meeting, but after discussion, the Hillary Clinton team voted down his suggestion. Again, I was not there–this is what I've been told.

The team gave their rationale on three fronts, as I understand it: First, women as a group provided more than enough of a voting base to win the election; second, talking about boys and men would muddy the voting waters, they believed; and third, backlash from women's groups and feminists would become severe if boys and men were highlighted. History ensued as Hillary Clinton continued her almost singular focus on women's issues, and she lost the election. While Donald Trump won the election for various reasons, Trump *did* talk about male distress and, in large numbers, American men, and a plurality of women–moms, wives, partners, grandmothers of boys and men–voted for him.

Might the election have gone differently if Hillary Clinton had pushed through her campaign's feminaphobia and spoken equally to boys and men's issues? I believe so. Hillary Clinton would not have lost the female support she had anyway, and it seems logical that she would have gained both male voters and sympathetic women voters–wives, mothers, girlfriends, grandmothers, teachers and others who see boys and men suffering around them.

If this story is correct in its basic facts, the Hillary Clinton campaign struggled with feminaphobia: fear of women, the women's lobby, feminists, and a perceived stereotype of oppressed women as a voting monolith. I, a man, voted for Hillary Clinton because I felt 1) she had the resume with the most qualifications and contacts for the job, and 2) I believe our American democracy needs to join India, Israel, Turkey, England, Germany, and nearly every other democratic country in electing a female leader. To this latter point, in *Leadership and the Sexes* (2009), my corporate colleague Barbara Annis and I explored how women's leadership styles differ from men's leadership styles. Hillary Clinton would have brought her sex-specific style of leadership to our fragile republic, and I believe our culture would have gained from her acumen and intelligence.

But in voting for her, I had to sit uncomfortably with my gut sense that feminaphobia would prevail in her White House; that backlash against boys and men at the highest leadership level might increase during her four or eight years, not decrease; that the oppressor-oppressed model would rule the sexgender conversation in Hillary Clinton's years in office despite that it does not apply to most women and men in America anymore. Donald Trump won, and his administration did tell a little bit of the secret of male distress during his four years, but he and his staff, too, suffered feminaphobia–they would not take the risk of creating a White House Council on Boys and Men just as Barack Obama did not and Hillary Clinton probably would not have done. If you go to https://whitehouseboysmen.org/, you will see the most comprehensive meta-study to date on the state of boys and men in America (click "The Proposal"). Its content includes the work of 34 scholars in the field, including Dr. Warren Farrell, author of *The Boy Crisis*, myself, Sean Kullman, and many others. Warren led the effort to get this meta-study in front of Barack Obama, Donald Trump, Hillary Clinton and other presidential candidates and state legislators. None of these presidents/candidates created or promised to create a White House Council on Boys and Men.

When Joe Biden won the presidential election in 2020, Dr. Farrell sent the meta-study to the West Wing staff. Soon after, President Biden formed a White House Gender Council but without reading our meta-study, or perhaps reading it and choosing to neglect its facts. When the Biden White House was asked by a number of us to explain why the new Gender Council did not include males, two sadly inevitable answers came back:

1. women and girls are victims struggling in America, but males have privilege and/or are part of the problem (oppressor-oppressed), and
2. including issues faced by men and boys on a Gender Council would be too dangerous politically (feminaphobia).

In the 2024 election between Kamala Harris and Donald Trump, we saw these models and fears repeat along various party lines. If the new Trump administration funds a White House Council on Boys and Men alongside a White House Council on Girls and Women, we will be seeing national courage to push past the dominance of past models and political, social fears.

Sons Without a Home

Our civilization has become like a family losing its sons to disease, violence, school failure, mental illness, obesity, war or other suffering that keeps pretending our boys are doing fine. When our sons run away from home to find help or turn around to hurt us in their immaturity and purposelessness, we seem satisfied with, "Boys are privileged," "boys are masculine" "boys are less needed than girls." We focus on female victims individually and collectively and feel satisfied, missing solutions to boyhood issues as our boys keep doing bad things. When we become self-aware about both the secret of male suffering and the secret of our own feminaphobia, that awareness doesn't last. Things must be better than we think, we muse, or it's the boys' faults anyway, or we must be on the right track already because our sociological models tell us so.

While helping female victims is a sacred thing, it does not solve many of our social problems because our social problems intersect less with the oppressor/oppressed model or the DGP masculine-defect; the social problems intersect with our abandonment of healthy male development. If we will fully tell the secret of male suffering, we are more likely to study areas of concern like unemployment and corporate greed, violence against others and violence against oneself, school failure and workplace failure, under-motivation and lack of social relationships, fatherlessness and substance use diagnoses, and drug overdose deaths and homelessness, but even then, we have to push through our feminaphobia to get leadership to act. Obsessed with the oppressor-oppressed model, feminaphobic at the leadership and policy levels, we are right now basically paralyzed where boys are concerned, and the bad things just keep on happening, even after we've tossed our sons out of the house.

Freedom Feminism

To change course, you and Sean and I must tell the two secrets fearlessly in the grassroots. We must build support for social change through non-profits, school boards, neighborhood programs, and our own protest movements (In Part IV, we will share organizations already doing this with you so that you can reach out to them and model from them in your community). When you see a White House create a Gender council that doesn't include men, call them on it, as Sean, Warren, I, and others have done. When you see state legislatures avoid male issues, confront your legislators and, if needed, vote differently. In media and social media, one post at a time, push back on the overuse of oppressor/oppressed and masculine-defect models. One email at a time, confront local, state, and federal feminaphobia.

Millions of people will be with you. Most women know that men and boys are suffering. These women want to help sons, brothers, husbands, and fathers. Women and men can force school districts to push beyond feminaphobia and ask for a focus on boy's mental health and increased school success for boys. At your local college, you can ask for new paradigms including resources of boy rescue you find in this book. *Freedom feminists* like Christina Hoff Sommers, Danielle Crittenden, Naomi Wolf, Warren Farrell, myself, Sean, and others are allies with you in this effort. We try to help map the course of boys' rescue unencumbered by the oppressor/oppressed, feminaphobic, culture/gender war.

Freedom Feminism by Dr. Sommers is a powerful read along these lines. Sommers distinguishes a "freedom feminist" as someone who believes in "Moral, social, and legal equality of the sexes—and the freedom of women to employ their equal status to pursue happiness in their own distinctive ways." Unlike the academic feminist or women's lobby that politicians are afraid of, "Freedom feminism is not at war with femininity or masculinity, it does not seek to bring down capitalism, and it does not view men and women as warring tribes. Conspiracy theories about universal patriarchal oppression are nowhere in its founding documents. Put simply, freedom feminism affirms for women what it affirms for everyone: dignity, fairness, and liberty." Susan B. Anthony, Betty Friedan, and most of the other early feminists were not scary feminists–they were freedom feminists.

They would cringe at the overuse of oppressor/oppressed models in the radical feminism that has control of the Big Three today. They would dispute that males are either inherently defective or inherently our social enemy. To them, academic feminism and feminist sociology would seem like "the closed system" Sommers, as a freedom feminist, calls to the carpet, "that chews up and digests all counter-evidence, transmuting it into confirming evidence." Academic feminism, especially as it is dominated by the oppressor-oppressed model, tends to work in half-truths that act as lies many people believe because the sociological frames established decades ago require frightened belief. But in the grass roots, most of us are freedom feminists like Susan B. Anthony and Christina Sommers. Let's allow the rest of the world to know that we are here fighting hard for non-discriminatory social justice for all people on the sexgender spectrum.

Collecting Your Own Data for Your Community

As this chapter ends, I hope you'll take a moment to use the essential questions tool to collect citizen science for your community and school. If you haven't already, perhaps you could start a journal on a yellow pad dedicated to "Boys Rescue Citizen Science," or perhaps write notes or dictate into your phone. Whatever way you choose to journal, gather evidence and documentation for yourself, ask others to do it as well, then come together in living rooms, in faith community social halls, in PTA meetings, and elsewhere to share the data you have gathered. As data gets shared you might form a parent-led team to log into your school district's website to discover data in your schools (Sean will teach us all how to do this much more in Part IV).

As you sift through data, you will probably notice more male failure on school district websites than female. With that data and your own neighborhood and community data, you can talk to administrators and leaders. You can, together, show superintendents, schools board, teachers, counselors, legislators, and policy-makers that they do not need to be feminaphobic because you are not. You are their voters, employers, colleagues and community members. You are citizen scientists in a fragile democracy. You will not vote these people out of office for helping boys, too. You are here to support leaders in setting aside old sociological models, and you want the secret of male suffering to get told and acted on with as much rigor as study and actions on behalf of other suffering populations.

Essential Questions

1. Overall, what is happening where I am—in my schools, my communities? Who is getting in the most trouble? Who is doing the most damage?
2. Overall, in what ways do I see boys and healthy male development abandoned in my neighborhood? Which boys don't have dads or positive role models? Which boys are in prison?
3. At my school's awards and graduation programs, do I notice more girls than boys succeeding? Do I see young women going to college and less young men doing the same?
4. Do I know a boy in my own family or in a friend's family who is getting Cs, Ds, and Fs and could be doing better if teachers were trained in how boys and girls learn differently?
5. Which children around me are the most hooked on binge drinking, marijuana, vaping, harder drugs, and pornography? Which kids are most listless, even purposeless, in their teens? Which kids are unmotivated to do much else besides gaming?
6. When I look at the suicides in my town, which sex is ending its life more frequently? Which sex is the victim of homicide and violent crime most often in my city and near me?
7. In my own home, if I have multiple children, have I found myself saying to a friend, "My girls are taking over the world, but about my son…I'm worried."
8. What statements are boys and girls around me making about their friends and classmates? What are they posting online?
9. What websites are my males going to get inspiration for survival—and are those websites healthy for them as young men?
10. Who can I form a parent-led team with to lobby my son's school, district, and even legislature to take better care of our males?

Chapter 13

The Silent Killer, Males Left Out of National, State, or Local Budgets

(This essay is good for all general readers, and particularly useful to voters, parents, media and communications, people in the social sciences, policymakers, college courses in economics and political science, and book group discussions.)

THE BIDEN ADMINISTRATION released its proposed Budget of the U.S. Government for fiscal year 2025 in March of 2024. The recognition of women in the budget was impressive, with numerous budget lines for programs meant to improve the lives of women and girls via education, business, health, counseling and training resources, girls in STEM, work and apprenticeship training programs, the *Department of Labor Women's Bureau*, women's gender-specific care, Pell Grants, maternal care, women veterans' healthcare, social services, opioid response for women, women's housing, global women's health, and more. The first lady, Dr. Jill Biden, was also budgeted to head up a $12 billion initiative to "transform women's health research and benefit millions of lives across America," something highlighted in the President's State of the Union address in 2024.

There is no question that a nation should spend budgets on improving and assisting the lives of girls and women. We have enough resources to do so. Missing, however, were budget items to help males. The Biden administration said it was concerned that "despite making up more than half the population, women have historically been understudied and underrepresented in health research" (2025 Budget) which was factually correct fifty years ago when the oppressor-oppressed model ascended in academe, but it has been incorrect for the last three decades. The CDC, a federal agency, concluded in 2018, "There is no evidence of systematic under-representation of women in clinical trials." A false claim was not needed to spend money on women and girls because our culture is already purposed to do so.

Unfortunately, we are not politically purposed to do the same for males. Masculine social norms, male privilege, and oppressor/oppressed models work with feminaphobia to keep boys, men, and males out of health and wellbeing budgets. Presidential administrations and state legislators fall into "men have it all anyway" traps, and really mean, "we'll get too much flack if we spend money on male development and health, so let's not include males." This is what we see in not only the 2025 budget as a whole, but especially in the mental health and substance abuse items in the budget. That budget area orders the Department of Health and Human Services to use its money to "Expand Access to Treatment for Substance Use Disorder" (81) by "investing in a new technical assistance center to strengthen health providers' understanding and treatment of women's mental health and substance use."

Let's pull this out for a moment and study it. While the desire to help women struggling with substance abuse and mental health is worthy, male disparities in mental health and substance abuse are far greater than females nationwide—and worldwide—as per the federal government's own data at the Centers for Disease Control. In this CDC data, males account for 73% of overdose deaths (not suicide related) and 79% to 80% of suicide deaths each year from 2018-2023. The CDC reports **570,000** male overdose and suicide deaths over that time, a number that is much larger than the combined female and male populations of 300 American cities. The recognition of unique female challenges in mental health and substance use—but not male—reveals the power of feminaphobia and old sociological modeling. Policymakers must know the data since it is offered by their own agencies, but they are compelled to recognize sex-based differences in areas of mental health for women and neglect sex-based differences when males are at stake.

Percent of Unintentional Overdose Deaths by Sex and Year 2018-2023

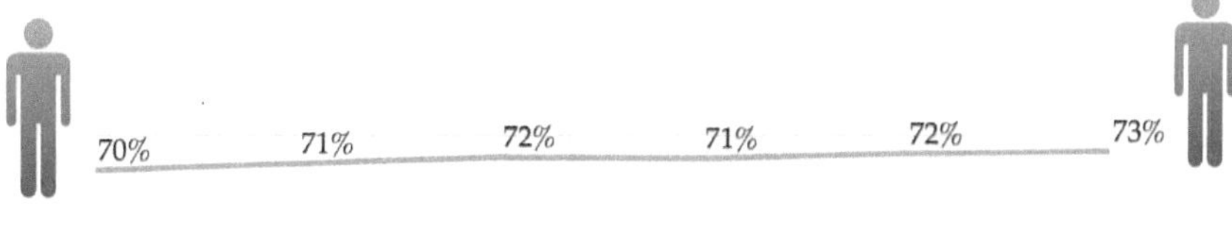

Note: *indicates provisional data.
Source: Centers for Disease Control and Prevention (Downloaded May 16, 2024)
https://wonder.cdc.gov/controller/saved/D176/D392F257

Male Drug Overdose Deaths Cut Across All Racial Groups (2018-2022)

Race/Ethnicity	Female		Male		Percent of Male Deaths within Race
	Deaths	Deaths / 100,000	Deaths	Deaths / 100,000	
American Indian or Alaska Native	1,860	30.2	3,066	51.2	62.9%
Black or African American	18,607	17.2	50,453	50.8	74.7%
White	84,689	17.0	183,699	37.7	68.9%
Hispanic /Latino Only	9,856	6.5	38,911	25	79.4%
Native Hawaiian or Other Pacific Islander	98	6.5	336	21.8	77.0%
More than one race	1,550	8.1	3,077	16.5	67.1%
Asian	697	1.4	2,830	6.1	81.3%

Source: CDC Wonder Database
Not Hispanic or Latino https://wonder.cdc.gov/controller/saved/D176/D399F461
Hispanic or Latino https://wonder.cdc.gov/controller/saved/D176/D399F460

*Note: Overdose deaths only include unintentional overdose deaths to avoid duplicating suicide overdoses. Male overdose deaths cut across all racial lines. Overdose is a predominately male outcome. Of the 14 sex and race-based classifications, the three groups with the highest number of deaths per 100,000 are accented with heat mapping. **71% of all overdose deaths are male. (Updated Nov. 30).**

Percent of Suicide Deaths by Sex and Year 2018-2023

Note: *indicates provisional data.
Source: Centers for Disease Control and Prevention (Downloaded May 16, 2024)
https://wonder.cdc.gov/controller/saved/D176/D392F257

Male Suicide Deaths Cut Across All Racial Groups (2018-2022)

Race/Ethnicity	Female		Male		Percent of Male Deaths within Race
	Deaths	Deaths / 100,000	Deaths	Deaths / 100,000	
American Indian or Alaska Native	768	12.5	2,255	37.6	75.0%
White	38,680	7.8	146,789	30.1	79.4%
Native Hawaiian or Other Pacific Islander	81	5.3	338	21.9	80.5%
Black or African American	3,339	3.1	13,604	13.7	81.5%
Hispanic /Latino Only	4,538	3.0	18,715	12	80.0%
More than one race	733	3.8	2,221	11.9	75.8%
Asian	2,027	4.0	4,771	10.3	72.0%

Source: CDC Wonder Database
Not Hispanic or Latino https://wonder.cdc.gov/controller/saved/D176/D356F737
Hispanic or Latino https://wonder.cdc.gov/controller/saved/D176/D356F738

Male suicide deaths cut across all racial lines. Suicide is a predominately male outcome. Of the 14 sex and race-based classifications, the three groups with the highest number of deaths per 100,000 are accented with heat mapping. **79% of all suicide deaths are male. (Updated Nov. 30 2024).**

The Silent Killer

You can access the budget online yourself as a citizen. Our feminaphobic political landscape created a 2025 $7.2 trillion budget with no programs funded specifically to address the disparities of boys and men in the United States. Despite our male (and female) mental health crisis in America, we funded work for girls and women but no budgeted training for male mental-health and social service providers to specifically work with males.

Hopefully, the new Republican administration and Congress (2025) will push beyond feminaphobia to understand sex-based differences in male and female mental health; from there, to propose and implement a new budget that fits the needs of both sexes. Hopefully, too, all future presidents and congresses will focus on boys and men at risk with equal ferocity to our national focus on girls and women.

In Washington State, we saw an example of the same feminaphobia and the influence of the old male-oppressor/oppressed-female paradigm when Representative Bill Ramos and Senator Sam Hunt (two committee chairs) suppressed the hearing of a bi-partisan bill in both houses to create a Washington State Commission on Boys and Men. It would have been the first State Commission on Boys and Men's Health in the nation and had a noninvasive mission: to gather data, study the data, and assist existing agencies in boy's and men's wellbeing. Washington, like most states, already has commissions to help girls and women.

The decision by Ramos and Hunt to avoid bringing the bill to committee mystified many Democrats and Republicans who saw the commission as equality under the law and a moral and ethical responsibility in a state in which boys and men are facing significant issues. You can see extensive coverage of this effort in our Global Initiative for Boys and Men state report on the Status of Boys and Men in Washington State (www.gibm.us/state-reports). I and others contacted Ramos and Hunt multiple times to beg them to reconsider, given that the bill itself *had bi-partisan support.* Neither of the policymakers responded to questions, either avoiding the issue or afraid to deal with it. In so doing, they joined a long line of leaders who practice a politics of abandonment toward males. Our GIBM and other data sources on male distress disaggregated not just for sexgender but also for race and ethnicity keeps piling up on the desks of these leaders. But fearful of perceived voting blocs and locked into outdated sexgender models, they deny the data in their policy making.

Helping Boys of Color Without Federal Budgets

Fortunately, an exception to male abandonment in budgets occurs regarding black and brown boys. President Obama's My Brother's Keeper program is the best example: using corporate donors, President Obama founded the program to send money into non-profits and communities around the country. My Brother's Keeper has been a boon for work with boys of color. Meanwhile, because President Obama could not risk a significant federal budgetary item focused on male development (it would be, his staffers must have thought, political suicide to do so), corporate donors were required to provide the money for My Brothers Keeper. Taxpayer dollars could not be risked or approved to help boys and men, even boys of color.

Michael told me about a conversation he had with a Department of Justice director a few years ago. Michael asked him why federal budgets did not fund assistance for boys and men like they did for girls and women. The official responded, "We do budget for males–in the Department of Corrections budgets." The official was not being flippant or disrespectful, just realistic of the present political climate: money on males can be spent if it is spent on housing males when they commit crimes. One could argue that our military budgets comprise "money spent to help males," and that money does help males, but it is money spent not on males specifically, but on helping women and men in the military. It is not comparable to federal or state money spent specifically on girls and women to help them with STEM, education, mental and physical health, and family development.

Returning to President Biden's proposed 2025 budget, women and girls were mentioned eighty-one times, gender was mentioned twenty-two times regarding trans/LGBTQIA+, underrepresented groups like black and brown children were mentioned sixteen times collectively, but males were not mentioned–they were abandoned. For decades, presidents on both sides of the aisle have rejected boys and men in their budgets. When males are mentioned, it is in the context of men and women collectively, as in men and women in the military or working men and women. Boys and men as individuals with specific needs in areas such as education, physical and mental health, and job training are ignored. Is there any way around realizing what is happening politically? Just as racism can be systemic, the neglect of males is systemic. Calculations for federal and state budgets begin among academics who focus on female deprivation connected to previous oppression and are themselves feminaphobic. Their information, data, and suggestions go to politicians and governments and those reports and their outdated, fearful messaging is reinforced by media coverage.

We in the grass roots will need to write an onslaught of emails, letters, and texts to presidential and governmental offices to point out how unfairly males are absent from Big Three equations. At some point, politicians will take notice of our voting bloc. We are probably the largest voting bloc out there, people who care about both women and men.

Essential Questions

1. Why is it important to include more content on the outcomes and needs of boys and men in presidential speeches and in policy conversations? How can you make this happen?
2. How has ideological capture and feminaphobia paralyzed the Big Three nationally and also right near you?
3. How can you have a conversation about feminaphobia and federal and state budgets without harming girls and women's issues and needs?
4. How do the suicide and overdose data listed above reveal a systemic problem when it comes to boys and men's mental health? Why do we ignore it? What are your solutions?
5. Why is it important to discuss the outcomes of boys and men in ways that do not look toward distracting masculine norms theory for solutions but instead focus on sex-based differences and needs?
6. The United Nations Office on Drug and Crime states that "men are 5 times more likely than women to inject drugs." Why are males worldwide more likely to inject drugs and why is the U.S. largely ignoring this problem with its own boys and men?

Chapter 14

**When America Embraced Wonder Woman
and Forgot G.I. Joe**

> "SEC. 3. (a)(1) Except as otherwise provided in this title, every male citizen of the United States, and every other male person residing in the United States, between the ages of eighteen and twenty-six, shall be automatically registered under this Act by the Director of the Selective Service System."
>
> —From the 118th Congress 2D Session H. R. 8070

(This essay is useful for general readers, and particularly useful to students in high school and college classes on media and communications and gender studies and the social sciences, as well as policymakers.)

As a child, I (Sean) grew up playing with G.I. Joe and Action Jackson figures. For hours I created military missions that placed my action figures (and, thus, myself) in challenges against dark forces. When I started to grow out of the action figure phase of life, a new superhero emerged on television, Wonder Woman, played by Lynda Carter. I remember her golden lasso, her bracelets to block the bullets of menacing antagonists, her American flag outfit, and the music and theme song. Right there in my lifetime, action figures, like all of life around us, evolved from an old world of men only in the military and certain workplaces to women and men together in work, heroic quests, and real life.

When I work with boys and men today I often feel human evolution in the work. Some of our gender politics are locked back in the Action Jackson days when there was no Wonder Woman, but much of our DGP, our masculine norms theory, and our feminaphobia around boys and men's needs comprise a phenomenon that we can understand historically but must alter to fit *our present reality.*

In the 2020s, we are facing what evolutionary biologists call "evolutionary drag." When something that was important to evolution in the past is still considered important in the present (even though it has mainly subsided as an environmental phenomenon), it drags down its present society. In this drag on a social environment, upward, progressive functions are paralyzed and the culture dragged backward and downward by thinking that disallows assistance to huge swaths of humanity. Because the old oppressor-oppressed model–in part, developed to convince people to no longer attach their admiration to GI Joe, the military, the establishment, John Wayne, the patriarchy, and our violent past–was in some ways useful in the recent past, but because it still dominates the Big Three models and policymaking, it is mainly dragging the West down in our new century.

Our parents know now: GI Joe action figures are not dangerous, and Wonder Woman is a welcome figure for both boys and girls. Parents also know: boys tend to turn every stick they touch into a sword or gun and girls less so. This is not a masculinity problem, since it is rooted in a sex difference in the right side of the male brain where spatial-mechanical areas of the brain trigger the male cerebellum to move objects in space. Our schools are not failing at fairness by leaving girls behind, as they did a hundred years ago–now, they are failing at fairness by leaving boys behind. Most of our leaders at the very top are still men, but women now account for the majority of medical students, law students, biology graduate students, college students, and graduate students. In some pockets of culture, like football and the military, more men ascend to higher positions, but women join and enjoy those opportunities. In some pockets of culture, like teaching and medicine, less men and more women populate employment and service. The Western world has changed. In America the patriarchy may exist in some pockets, and certainly exists in a movie like Barbie, but in real life, throughout the country, patriarchy is not dominant. Yet feminaphobia and oppressor/oppressed models tenaciously place evolutionary drag on the Big Three.

A Human Story

I want to briefly add my insights to Michael's on this historical drag because my brief look backward can help you as a citizen scientist to lobby leaders with your own grass roots human stories that will help wrestle leadership free of paralysis.

Hoping to evolve our educational responsibilities toward fairness in the 1970s, our culture reacted correctly to the fact that men outnumbered women in college by a margin of nearly sixty-percent to forty-percent.

The oppressor/oppressed, male privilege, and patriarchy model worked to mobilize an increase of K-12, college, and professional opportunities for girls and women. Less than six percent of Americans (25-29 years of age) held a bachelor's degree or higher in 1940, and the percentage was even lower in 1920. By 2013, thirty-four percent (34%) of Americans had a bachelor's degree or higher, and women held more of those degrees (57%) than men (43%).

Our movements in these positive directions actually began in the '40s. Modern technological advances, a booming post WWII economy, the contributions women made to the war effort, and the advent of birth control were huge pieces of our evolving (since the industrial revolution fifty years before) departure from a formerly agrarian society that relied on large extended families in which each member, filling specific roles, contributed to family survival. Going away to college was not the journey of most Americans in the agrarian and early industrial economy. Sex and gender roles were survival mechanisms for our families and groups. In 1920, the life expectancy for males was 53.6 years and 54.6 years for females. Death rates of males and females were similar because many women died in childbirth. As medical science removed that crisis from female development, life expectancies related to sexgender shifted. Now the life-course of women changed dramatically, with women living nearly six-years longer than the average male.

This and other big shifts began after WWII but exploded in the 1960s and 70s. Tribal and extended family emphasis continued, but they were mitigated by the industrial economy that broke families into different groups based on the city or region of work. Given the classroom and school structures of that time, and given girls access to them, it is unsurprising that by the late 70s and early 80s, girls began to outpace boys in K-12 education. Title IX in the mid 70s had a profound effect on equality for girls and women in education, sports, and culture, as well. *Ms. Magazine* debuted in 1972 with Wonder Woman on the front cover–near her photo the slogan, "Wonder Woman for President." The magazine published Gloria Steinem's articles, "On How Women Vote" and "Money for Housework." Second wave feminist ideas took hold not only of culture but in laws and politics, starting in academe which provided useful theory for inspiration. It became a nearly universal academic, thus socially dominant theory, that males oppressed women. Women were assisted now in society as victims so that they could advance into "a male dominated world" and reshape it away from patrix to something more egalitarian and, in some quarters, more matriarchal.

On the policy front, federal programs such as the *Women, Infants, and Children Nutrition Program (WIC)* were funded and implemented as women and the women's lobby continued to mobilize. *The Women's Bureau* that had been established but underfunded by the *U.S. Department of Labor* in 1920 advanced hundreds of women's programs and initiatives throughout the 1980s for *"promoting employer-sponsored child care, introducing child care at occupational training center sites, working more closely with women serving on corporate boards and in high-level management positions to help others move up in the management structure, and launching studies on the employment-related needs of women veterans, immigrant women, dislocated women workers, displaced homemakers and older women, and the career transition problems of women."*

We can look back and see 1980 as a pivotal year, especially on the education front–the first year women outnumbered men in undergraduate fall enrollment. Just under 500,000 more women, who were first graders in 1968, went to college than men that year. By 1990, a decade later, 1.2 million more women than men went to college. The Western world was well headed in a new direction that built policies to move even more women through successful education and into the workforce. In just a few decades, Western cultures had adopted a newly empowering national attitude toward the education of women and girls, which helped females immensely, and which continues to this day. Meanwhile, males were already disappearing, and doing so unnoticed. In 2019, men accounted for only 41% of all college degrees. From 2016-2020, women earned 2.8 million more associate, bachelor, master, and doctoral degrees than men (*National Center for Educational Statistics*). This is good for women, we can say, but not good for men since, as we've noted, a college degree means more income over the lifespan—money the man will most likely spend not on himself alone but on feeding, clothing, and advancing his wife, children, partner, and other loved ones.

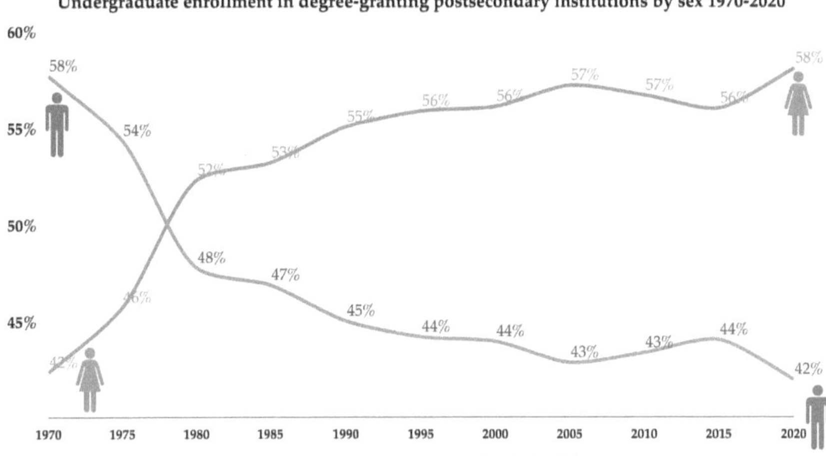

Prepared by Sean Kullman (Source: National Center for Educational Statistics)
https://nces.ed.gov/programs/digest/d21/tables/dt21_303.70.asp

The Changing GI Bill

America saw educating women as a civic responsibility after World War II and it saw educating men from World Wars, the Korean War, and the Vietnam War as a helpful recompense for serving in the military. For college, "2.2 million [WWII] veterans utilized their G.I. Bill, with over 1 million veterans crowding on American campuses during 1947-48." These veterans accounted for "49%" of college admissions. Some of them were women, but the overwhelming majority of GI Bill veterans were men whom our government helped to get college degrees so that they could support their families as the country moved into a more industrialized economy throughout the mid century.

In the last fifty years, this war/veteran/college link has diminished for males and not been replaced as we've noticed by watching male college enrollment keep diminishing despite the Iraq and Afghanistan wars. Social changes brought positives to many girls and women (and some boys and men), but a nurturing attitude toward males, like the GI Bill, has mainly disappeared from national politics. The sociological models in second wave feminism provided early thinking on how to empower females but the academics, government, and media pretty much stopped thinking about what would happen to males–or who our males really are–beyond inherently limited arguments over masculinity. While first wave feminism asked for equality (respect for both women and men), second wave feminism, unfortunately, evolved to empower females by disempowering males. This central point of our present evolutionary drag locks in feminaphobia, the DGP, systemic oppressor/oppressed models, and abandonment of males.

"Male" Expanded into Race and "Masculinity"

As the patriarchy and male privilege and dominance dissipated and women and girls ascended toward parity, academic theory splintered into theory around the destructiveness of traditional and masculine social norms and the intersection of destructive masculinity with the effects of slavery, racism, and colonization. Protection for women and minorities became protection from "white male privilege" then, it became, "not just the patriarchy and white men but the core of maleness itself, which is, from a social constructivist standpoint, "masculinity' is inherently destructive and must be removed." Each social thinker in this sociology defined masculinity negatively and their self-defined "masculine social norms" were pilloried as socialized norms used by males to be dominant over others and oppress women and minorities.

Because the job of second wave feminism was not perceived by sociologists to include scientific study of males themselves but, rather, to cast males as sexist, dominant, and systemically racist villains, the tacit decision had already been made from a theoretical standpoint to present males as oppressors and females as oppressed. From there, "Marriage is rape" could coexist with feminist reality and masculinity became universally dangerous in the Big Three, and the study of masculinity became "enough study of males" toward the goal of removing it from human social development.

Though "gender stereotypes" are ostensibly anathema to the social revolutions of the last fifty years, "masculinity" became culture stereotyping of males, as male development was neglected in our society, and our sexgender social capital regarding males was spent arguing over stereotypes of males. Meanwhile tens of millions of males are trying to grow up well, get into trades, go to college, raise children, and live with purpose and service. What started out as protection and assistance for girls and women and led to programs implemented to support and uplift them unfortunately evolved into accusing boys and men of ongoing, negative masculine stereotypes. This turned to arguing over those stereotypes, not paying attention to males themselves–we are now at a zenith in this evolutionary drag and political paralysis.

Conferred Associate, Bachelor, Master and Doctoral Degrees in U.S. by Sex in 50 Year Increments

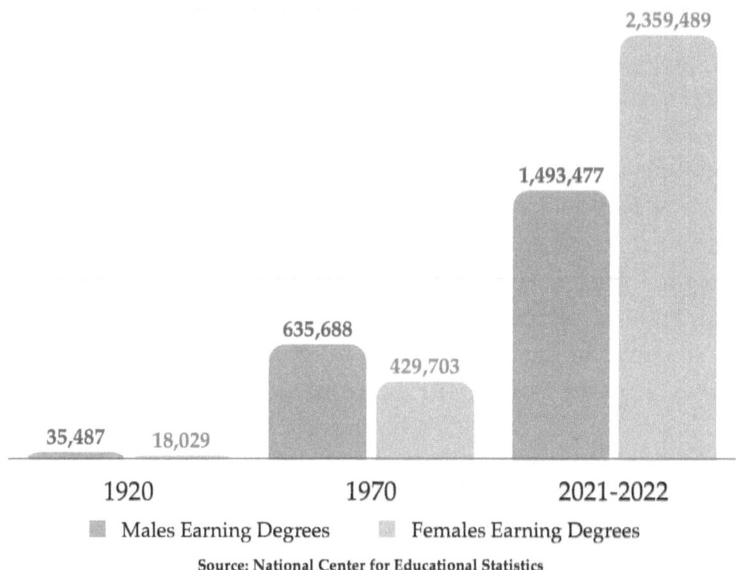

Some barriers still exist for women, but the world is not now what it was in the 1920s, 40s, 70s, or 90s. Women advance careers, wait later to have children, make their own roles in all aspects of culture, run their own businesses, lead companies, and embrace opportunities. Girls are not ignored today–they are ubiquitous in voice and passion, especially in media and social media. Women's needs are also well represented in budgets, jobs, stories, and iconography throughout the Big Three. Second wave feminism created and continues to encourage a women-friendly culture of which we can all be very proud. When our individual girls and women suffer–and they do–we marshal social resources to help them.

The Simultaneous Evolution of Male Outcomes by Race

Our embrace of Wonder Woman was and still is a needed and wonderful thing, but was it morally sound to embrace her diverse talents and iconography while developing only one angry culture theory to fit boys and men? Or, put another way, if we think that we did need to advance Wonder Woman by attacking and abandoning GI Joe fifty years ago, should we continue that practice now? I can help us answer both questions with "No" by looking, among other things, at data at the intersection of sex and race issues.

Simultaneous to the oppressor/oppressed paradigm's use in empowering women, it was used for racial justice where it continues to be used as the West works on our systemic inequities by race. Meanwhile, when we look at sex and race data in the same frame, data on racial suffering shows significant male suffering. In other words, problems facing boys and men are universal to their sex even when proportionally different in race. Black males, for instance, die at higher rates from overdose deaths than white males, but black and white males die at higher rates than all female groups disaggregated by every measure of race/ethnicity and sex. LGBTQIA+ suicide data is also clear—a higher proportion of children and adults with gender dysphoria end their own lives than non-trans children. At the same time, when these rates are compared to all males, males again dominate suicide statistics. "Male" is the common denominator in whatever our angle on these statistics.

While it is appropriate for our local, state, and federal politicians to support members of the LGBTQIA+ community, women, and all racial groups, avoidance of "male" is a heavy weight on evolutionary drag. Our fifty years of moving from "empower women now"—to "empower women and minorities by fighting against men and males" to "empower women and minorities by making males and masculinity defective, dangerous, and unneeded in society"—has led to ignoring the well-being of an entire group (males) in the Big Three because of "masculinity" or "patriarchy" stereotypes of those males. When we embraced Wonder Woman but tossed out G.I. Joe, we evolved to leave male issues unhealed for the sake of social categories more popular or more politically correct than male—but it is our males who are in trouble and causing trouble, not their "masculine stereotypes." Male issues don't get corrected because the social root cause of male issues lies not in masculinity nor even race but in social abandonment of the developing male himself.

Three Root Causes and Three Solutions

Profound examples of our cultural abandonment of males appear in three areas especially clearly: school discipline practices, father deprivation, and police reform. Let me explore them more deeply with you here as each of them have mainly evolved over the last fifty years to avoid "male," but once male is added into them, boy rescue occurs.

The Proven Disciplinary Practices Solution

We looked briefly together at disciplinary practices a few moments ago. I mentioned that the California Department of Education, like many around the country, informed their schools the State was "implementing new laws regarding disciplinary practices, consistent with our shared view that all students—particularly African American students and others overrepresented in suspension statistics—deserve a school environment that fosters their social-emotional well-being and academic success." Throughout the country, it has been important to look at how many boys of color are being disciplined because it is a useful data point in changing social systems away from potential racial oppression. Good strides are being made in various states and districts to address discipline disparities as part of the pre-school-to-prison pipeline.

Meanwhile, the widest gap in discipline referrals and systems is not race but sex. Males comprise between 70-75% of suspensions and expulsions nationwide. This gap starts very early, with three males suspended or expelled from pre-schools for every one female. As mentioned earlier, fearing accusations of discrimination by women's groups, afraid that Title IX applications might accuse schools of gender stereotyping if they concentrated on male/female gaps, and noting significant cadres of boys of color being suspended and expelled, legislators passed laws and policies that singled out boys of color. These policies do some good but leave out the cadre that is most affected by discipline practices–males.

What policy might address ALL "boys"?

The Gurian Institute (GI) has shown: the mismatch of the male brain with the traditional schooling system is the cause-and-effect solution-variable that *all* school districts can control for, a variable not locked into race but inclusive of race. You can access some schools' success data on www.gurianinstitute. com/success/ and in Michael's books such as *Boys and Girls Learn Differently* (2011). This book reported results from six school districts that the GI pilot conducted through colleagues Patricia Henley and others at the University of Missouri-Kansas City. When schools are trained in how boys and girls learn differently, this data shows, and when they are supported in making school-wide systemic change via understanding of the male and female brain, discipline referrals go down exponentially *for children of all races and ethnicities.* Newly trained educators, who get training they were not allowed in most graduate schools, teach better to both boys and girls, see playground, hallway, and classroom behavior management expectations change, and student discipline improves. Because the systems now include the male brain as comprehensively as they already, inherently, include the female brain, the systems see cognitive, social-emotional, and behavioral gains.

These gains start all the way back in preschool as the GI has discovered while working with the Greater Phoenix Urban League, City of Phoenix – Head Start, and Booker T. Washington Schools to roll out GI Pilots at Phoenix's preschools. Marion Hill, Head Start Program Coordinator in

Phoenix, captured the data this way to Michael, "We called GI in to help us address the preschool-to-prison pipeline and racial equity issues. As soon as we trained our staff in the Gurian Boys and Girls Learn Differently® theory and strategies, we noticed positive changes for not just children of color but for all children. We had far fewer discipline and behavioral referrals when the GI team was providing us with their model and support."

Father Loss (Dad Deprivation)

Father loss and dad deprivation is another sex-based issue in social statistics that gets missed when we avoid dealing with sex, male, as a major factor in systemic suffering. The male brain, like the female, needs male influence to help it naturally mature. Males especially, given their high testosterone and other neural factors outlined in Part II, are more likely to act against systems and rules when paternal nurturance is not forthcoming. This awareness is true of all peoples whatever their race or ethnicity. It is true for females, as well, but the destruction females commit when raised in dad deprivation is not as noticeable as the destruction males often commit.

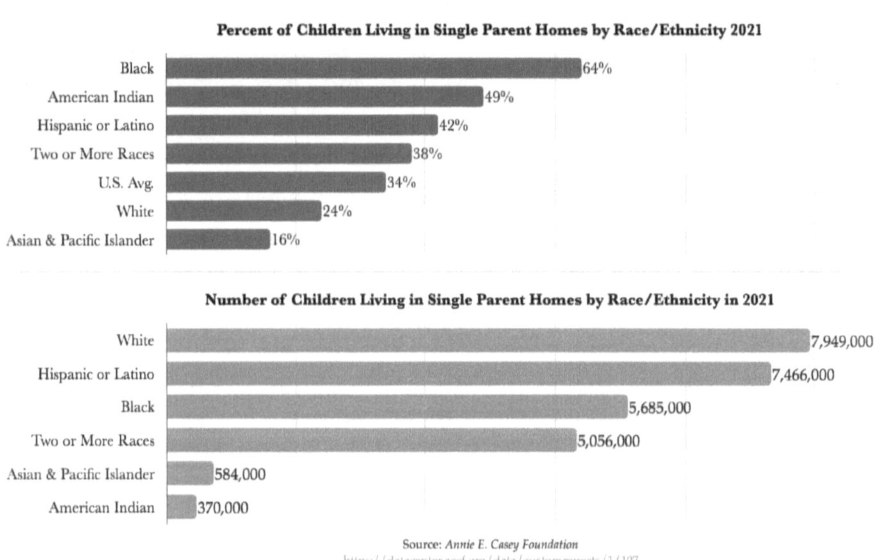

Source: *Annie E. Casey Foundation*
https://datacenter.aecf.org/data/customreports/1/107

Dad deprivation can be measured statistically via race and ethnicity but, as the graphs show, the issue crosses races and ethnicities–it is a *male* deprivation issue in homes and communities.

Marion Hill talked with Michael recently about why his fathering program, M.A.N.C.A.V.E. (which has now joined with the organization,

Dad Together), is having so much success in helping boys become better disciplined at school, confirming the point about sex difference as the common denominator. "We bring together issues of race, ethnicity, and brain science with an emphasis on the male brain. Using the GI resources and our own, we train parents in nature, nurture, and culture because we know the data on fatherless homes. These homes affect boys significantly regarding impulse control and self-regulation, and we know the data on differences between ongoing trauma markers for boys and girls from fatherlessness. To us, the challenges we're addressing with men and fathers today are more than about just one factor like race–they are *male* challenges."

Data on Police Shootings and Race

Like our school systems, our judicial system is trying to figure out ways to serve the populations that most need serving, and just as the education and non-profit sector can be hampered in dealing with male issues, the judicial Big Three is also politically suspicious of dealing with sex as the causal factor.

The George Floyd murder compelled our culture to look much more closely than it had on the plight of black males on our streets, in our police cars, in our jails and prisons, and in the criminal justice system as a whole. Boys of color and black men, we have learned, are more likely to be profiled, stereotyped, and scapegoated by some police than whites, and violence like what George Floyd experienced has occurred with other black boys and men. Because of our national reckoning, these harmed black boys and men are no longer invisible, and police reform is a national requirement.

Meanwhile, for decades, males of all races have been both victims and perpetrators in police actions. Even before George Floyd, the *Washington Post* Fatal Force Database and Dr. Roland Fryer, an economist at Harvard, studied police data for racial differences in assault and violence. According to Fryer, "On the most extreme use of force – officer-involved shootings – we are unable to detect any racial differences in either the raw data or when accounting for controls." Fryer showed that black males were treated differently when it came to lower forms of force like frisking, which black males experience more than white males; meanwhile, he found that it is actually *males* who are involved in officer shootings, not just black males or males of color. I have gone through the *Washington Post* Fatal Force Database as well and my research, below, shows that the underlying cause of fatal police shooting is a violent (usually male) perpetrator who is armed and/or attacking an officer.

Police Shooting Deaths as a Percentage of Violent Crime Arrests 2015 to 2019

Race and Gender	Deaths as a Result of Police Shooting	Violent Crime Arrests by Race	Police Shooting Deaths as a % of Violent Crime Arrests
Asians	80	29,361	0.27%
Blacks	1,087	721,708	0.15%
Hispanics	784	398,650	0.20%
Native American	72	38,804	0.19%
White	2,176	1,149,980	0.19%

Source: https://www.gibm.us/news/police-shootings-and-violent-crime

Number and Percent of Police-Shooting-Deaths by Race and Sex from 2015 through April 2021

Race and Sex	Total Shot & Killed	Killed While Armed and/or Attacking Officer	Killed Unarmed/Other/ Undetermined	% Killed while Armed and/or Attacking Officer	% Killed Unarmed/ Other/Undetermined
Asians Males	100	90	10	90.00%	10.00%
Asian Females	4	4	0	100.00%	0.00%
Black Males	1,454	1,428	26	98.21%	1.79%
Black Females	51	44	7	86.27%	13.73%
Hispanice Males	1,024	973	51	95.02%	4.98%
Hispanic Females	31	28	3	90.32%	9.68%
Native American Males	83	71	12	85.54%	14.46%
Native American Females	5	5	0	100.00%	0.00%
Other Males	44	37	7	84.09%	15.91%
Other Females	3	3	0	100.00%	0.00%
White Males	2,716	2,532	184	93.23%	6.77%
White Females	170	154	16	90.59%	9.41%
Unknown Race Males	547	513	34	93.78%	6.22%
Unknown Race Females	13	13	0	100.00%	0.00%
Total of All Males	5,968	5,644	324	94.57%	5.43%
Total of All Females	277	251	26	90.61%	9.39%

Sources: Washington Post
https://www.washingtonpost.com/graphics/investigations/police-shootings-database/

Police reform and support of police is needed in many cities. White males do not experience as much harsh police intervention as black males. A black mother or father may have a talk with their son about how to act around police that is perhaps different from the talk a white parent has with their white son.

Meanwhile, data shows that the primary issue on our city streets and in our courts and prisons is the issue of *male* development. Were police and judiciaries to study the population they deal with most–males–they would be motivated to obtain training that helps them de-escalate situations involving *males,* including how boys and young men react differently to stress than females, experience trauma differently, and act out differently than females no matter their race.

Did You Know?
Interactions with Law-Enforcement that Lead to
Fatal Shooting as a Function of the Threat Level

Many of the conversations regarding police shootings fail to address the threat level to police officers and civilians. The *Washington Post* (WAPO) database only lists an assailant as attacking an officer at the moment an officer discharges a firearm; it does not take into account the actions prior to the shooting, the history of the person, nor the threat that person brings to an interaction with an officer or civilian.

The shooting of Phillip Rhoades in West Virginia in 2017 happened after an initial attempt to serve multiple warrants on Rhoades, who faced 22 charges, and was living at "a home without the owner's permission." He used at least four stolen vehicles on July 25, 2017 to escape officers and attempted to attack an officer with a stolen truck. In a later and similar pursuit on August 2, 2017, Rhoades used a stolen vehicle to evade police before a foot chase that led to the shooting death of Rhoades. His threat level in the WAPO database is listed as "other," and his "armed" status is blank.

My analysis and WAPO database numbers indicate that police-shooting-deaths occurred in situations where the person killed possessed a weapon, was attacking an officer, or posed a consequential threat to a civilian *at least* 94% of the time. Police-shooting-deaths are directly related to high level threats to police officers and civilians. In June of 2023, I downloaded the newest WAPO data to look at fatal police shootings by race and sex since May of 2021. "Threat level" was no longer a qualifier in the database. I reached out to the *Washington Post* and asked about the removal of this qualifier, but I have not received a reply.

Boys of All Races

Boys of all races are behind their female counterparts in reading, high school graduation rates, college enrollment, college graduation rates, graduate school graduation, law school and medical school graduation, yet also overrepresented in homicide, overdose, suicide, and dozens of other health outcomes. When disaggregating data by race and sex both, boys and men are behind girls and women throughout majority and minority demographics. Boys need our attention and love within racial groups and also from a universal standpoint. When our culture invests in mobilizing male-friendly school training, male-friendly work with father enhancement, and male-focused training for police in male mental health cues, we assist in making the whole social system safer and more equitable.

As the Big Three uses narratives that merely or mainly promote socially constructed concepts of oppressor/oppressed, privilege, and gender toxicity, social concern for males devolves into one Scarlet M: Masculinity. Males are limited to

1. the oppressor role if we talk about boys and men as males, and/or
2. a racial group of males but not males as a whole, and/or
3. emotionally repressed masculinity (he doesn't talk about his feelings or cry) as the cause of his problems.

Males in the narratives are, thus, limited to oppressors, repressed, or suppressed along masculine lines. This leaves the Big Three in evolutionary drag regarding males, despite the millions of males around us all who are not doing well. When America embraced Wonder Woman in 1972, it did some righteous things for women. But the movement negated G.I. Joe and his brothers, fathers, and friends–it abandoned his sons, and thus has brought with it a spiritual sickness.

Here are some questions you can ask in your families, book groups, and organizations to gather more data for citizen science.

Essential Questions

1. Do I believe boys and girls handle challenges differently? If so, how and why?
2. Do I believe men and women handle circumstances differently? If so, how and why?
3. How do I explain to others that male suffering is real and needs our help?
4. How is male suffering different from female suffering?
5. Can I have a conversation with others about suffering that stays focused on male suffering without males being verbally attacked or abandoned?
6. How do race and sex interact in each area of focus? Will answering questions of sex also help with the notion of systemic racism?
7. How does a boy's suffering align with and also differ from a man's suffering?
8. Where does the oppressor/oppressed model work and apply around me? Where does it not apply?
9. What new models, like the GI work and M.A.N.C.A.V.E., can we use to help both our women and men and girls and our boys?
10. Should schools teach students how to interact with law-enforcement with the help of law-enforcement?

Chapter 15

Digging Deeper into Our Spiritual Sickness Regarding Males

"A joyful heart is good medicine, but a crushed spirit dries up the bones."

—Book of Proverbs

(This essay is useful for general readers, and particularly for students in high school and college, media and communications, the social sciences, parent groups, faith-based communities, schools of divinity, and classes in media literacy.)

SOMETIMES I (SEAN) BROOD OVER IMAGERY in William Blake's poem "The Poison Tree."

The Poison Tree

I was angry with my friend;
I told my wrath, my wrath did end.
I was angry with my foe:
I told it not, my wrath did grow.

And I watered it in fears,
Night and morning with my tears:
And I sunned it with smiles,
And with soft deceitful wiles.

And it grew both day and night.
Till it bore an apple bright.
And my foe beheld it shine,
And he knew that it was mine.

And into my garden stole,
When the night had veiled the pole;
In the morning glad I see;
My foe outstretched beneath the tree.

Throughout his poems, William Blake wrote about spiritual sickness. In this poem, the poison tree is a symbol of moral failure and its consequences. Reading it this way, I find relevance to the Big Three's lack of humanity and ethical failure to support males. Attitudes planted deep in our cultural psyche allow anger at patriarchal archetypes of past centuries to grow into indifference toward male suffering now. This present-day moral failure brings us a dismissive posture to real human suffering.

Acknowledging Cultural Misandry (Prejudice Against Males)

Throughout human history, targeted anger at a social group has occurred so that our moral efforts of compassion would help ease a different target group's pain. Rebellion against oppression has been a spiritual quest. As the targeted pain and suffering eased, and the cause of the rebellion was fulfilled, the anger should have subsided, and it has for many people. Anger has been used for millennia in this way following a pattern of collective spiritual passion for confrontation and social justice, then, when we saw our foe outstretched, dead, at the foot of the tree, we celebrated the empowerment that made this victory possible.

In the case of male-female relationships, however, targeted anger at the patriarchy led to significant social change but also expanded to anger at all males pretty much all the time. *Misandry* is the definition's term for anger and hatred of males. Males individually and collectively have become the poison society is enraged about even after social change occurs. New visions of social issues and new moral efforts to help males get lost in our constant social re-immersion in the dominant and seething anger at males—what is now a culture-wide misandry.

Domestic Violence and Identity Politics

Philip W. Cook's book, *Abused Men: The Hidden Side of Domestic Violence,* is a powerful read. The book does not downplay that women are victims of domestic violence, nor that it is our sacred duty as a society to protect women. Rather, the book helps us understand misandry as, early in the book, Cook discusses how female perpetrators of domestic violence were recognized by Erin Pizzey in the 1970s, but Pizzey was ostracized for this recognition. Recognizing that domestic violence hurts both women and men did not align with the rage at males that early domestic violence thinkers utilized for persuasion of others. Pizzey's idea that male and female domestic abuse was a mutually combative environment, in many cases, did not fit with the oppressor/oppressed model, the DGP, or the politics of masculinity.

Yet Pizzey was a woman and very well qualified to understand domestic violence–she opened the first women's refuge in the United Kingdom in the 1970s. She reported, "Of the first 100 women that came into the refuge, 62 were as violent or more violent than the men they left…. As soon as I got the big house…I said I need a house for the abused men…" (See her interview at the ONRECORD podcast with Erin Pizzey beginning at 21:30).

Domestic abuse and violence programs to protect women are well funded and need to be. Too many women are hurt by abusive men. Our discussion here is not zero sum: we must help women. But we must also understand how anger and rage at males overlooks suffering in all forms, and thus keeps us from helping all people who need help. Prejudice against men via misandry allows for males to be cast into a singular identity–masculine villain, poisonous, toxic–and females into the single identity of "victim of toxic masculinity." Misandry makes masculine, men, and males bad or wrong, thus in need of change, and feminine, women, and females fine as they are, in need of voice and the joy of expression.

Did You Know?
Miriam Webster Online Dictionary Sample Sentences

Subtle differences exist in dictionary examples given for "masculinity" and "femininity." In Miriam Webster's online dictionary, masculinity, inherently faulty, needs to change while femininity is not and does not–except to express itself with more empowerment

Masculinity
1. "Other successful films this year showcased a less angry, more accommodative masculinity, said Taneja (Vineeta Deepak, Fortune, 2 Jan. 2024)."
2. "The filmmaker narrows his focus to Fritz and Kevin, whose relationship is poisoned by toxic masculinity and irrational resentments (Thomas Floyd, Washington Post, 19 Dec. 2023.)"

Femininity
1. "Representing these women through my lens is to breathe life into a powerful form of femininity (Caterina De Biasio, Vogue, 27 Dec. 2023)."
2. "There's a performative femininity about Gracie, right? (Hedy Phillips, Peoplemag, 1 Jan. 2024)."

Adverse Childhood Experiences and Boys

John Dow (who chose to use a pseudonym) regularly witnessed his mother physically and emotionally abusing his father. "My mother physically abused my father several times a week," he told me, "and that doesn't include emotional abuse. After watching it for years, I developed a tendency to instinctively resign emotionally as an adult and in my marriage. My father always told me to keep a low profile in my marriage. I think it's been unhealthy and the reason I crave intimacy with my children and wife. I'm worried it's seen as controlling on my part but it's not my intention. I just want a more intimate relationship with my family."

John is luckier than most and credits finding a wife with empathy, which continued even after she personally witnessed the harmful environment John grew up in on her first visit to his parents' home. "After witnessing my family's dysfunction, she nearly broke up with me. I guess I was able to charm her," he said, knowing that her staying with him had much to do with her empathy and his ability to introspect and break the cycle.

John's fear and emotional resignation speaks to both a hesitance of men to come forward and the failings of the institutions around men to openly address male suffering. Given our misandry and evolutionary anger at men, a general reluctance prevails on the part of government, academia, and media to pursue inquiries into male victimization by women, even though research has shown that mothers are nearly twice as likely (39.4%) as fathers (21.5%) to perpetrate violence against children, according to the 2018 Child Maltreatment report by the U.S. Department of Health and Human Services.

U.S. Percentage of Child Victims Maltreated by Mother, Father, and Other Categories

Category	Percentage
Mother alone	39.4%
Father alone	21.5%
Both Parents	21.3%
Mother and Nonparent	7.1%
Father and Nonparent	1.3%
Mother, Father, and Non Parent	1.1%
Other	8.3%

Source: U.S. Department of Health & Human Services, Administration for Children and Families, Administration on Children, Youth and Families, Children's Bureau. (2020). *Child Maltreatment 2018.*

John, who witnessed the abuse of his father by his mom, suffered trauma during her abusive episodes. "We never knew when the switch would turn, and she'd beat me and my brother." This kind of trauma (like the trauma experienced by girls in similar situations) is one of the reasons for the development of the Adverse Childhood Experience Survey. The Centers for Disease Control (CDC) and other researchers developed the ACE survey and ACE training for mental health professionals. The agency certainly knew that suffering is not zero sum. Yet while the survey includes an important question about witnessing a mother, stepmother, or girlfriend being abused by a man, there is no similar question that asks about witnessing a father, stepfather, or boyfriend being abused by a woman. Thus, interviewers in the survey are provided a survey item "mother treated violently" but not "father treated violently."

Suffering is not zero sum in real life but in materials created first in academe then spreading throughout government and media we see reminders of codified practices that ignore or dismiss male suffering for the sake of ballasting male-oppressor/female-oppressed paradigms. How much anger (misandry) and fear (feminaphobia) must there be in people and their systems to neglect millions of male victims? By failing to ask children about witnessing the abuse of fathers/stepfathers/boyfriends at the hands of mothers/stepmothers/girlfriends, the CDC contradicts its own reason for existence by missing adverse childhood experiences that shape children's lives and impact health risks into adulthood. This national zeitgeist leaves boys, like John, whose later lives are impacted and often ruined, largely in the shadows.

These male victims are not going away. Academics need to study all of them from all sides so that social policy can be equal and complete. Many academics are trying to do that on a daily basis but are hindered by the codified tools. In 2018, Michael Windle, et. al. completed a study of "2,969 college students from seven universities in the state of Georgia.... Data collection began in Fall 2014 and consisted of individual assessments every four months for two years," to provide "a multivariate analysis of adverse childhood experiences and health behaviors and outcomes among college students." He and colleagues relied on the ACE Survey that quantified "mother treated violently" but not father treated violently. This meant that the study lacked a huge data set.

When I saw that this study relied on the incomplete ACE surveys, I dug deeper. I learned that the CDC wants the ACE survey to be used widely and thus, "ACE questionnaires are not copyrighted, and there are no fees for their use." That is an important service to all of us, but the outcome is that the CDC encourages the use of an incomplete questionnaire even knowing, as they must, that fathers and males are impacted by intimate partner violence. They provide a tool to researchers that ensures male suffering will not be included in studies involving ACE well into the future.

When I pointed this out to the CDC, I heard back, "the study is referenced on the CDC's website because of its historical significance to the field." There was no answer to my question about why the CDC continues to allow researchers to ignore intimate partner violence against males that impact children who witness it. I can only assume that encouraging the use of the incomplete survey places ideological and political benefits to an institution, despite that every person's, including males', adverse childhood experiences are not treated equally.

The ACE survey is valuable, no doubt, but why not change it to include males as specifically as females? The Global Initiative for Boys and Men pressed at the CDC to do just that. We asked the organization to either remove the original questionnaire from its website or include this as a visible infographic on its website:

"The original ACE Survey did not address the abuse of fathers, stepfathers, and mother's boyfriends at the hands of mothers. Therefore, intimate partner violence information against males was not collected, which is the reason the CDC has added a more inclusive and gender-neutral question in an updated survey."

The CDC "shared our notes with researchers" and eventually removed the flawed survey, but the replacement survey does not provide focus on male victims.

Villains, Victims, and the Poison Tree

The male/oppressor and female/oppressed paradigm is so accepted as dominant social theory, and so well ballasted by feminaphobic anger at males, and so utterly connected to obsessions with "flawed masculinity" that misandry appears both overtly and hidden throughout the Big Three. When reporter Maggie Angst of the *San Francisco Chronicle* wrote about the sharp increase in overdose deaths in 2023 in San Francisco, she focused on an increase in black deaths and in women's deaths. Meanwhile, she did not report that males died of overdose more than any other group: 83% of the deaths in San Francisco were male! In terms of race the most overdose deaths were among white males. Ironically, the title of the article was, "New data shows grim tally for S.F.'s worst year for overdose deaths. These groups were hit hardest."

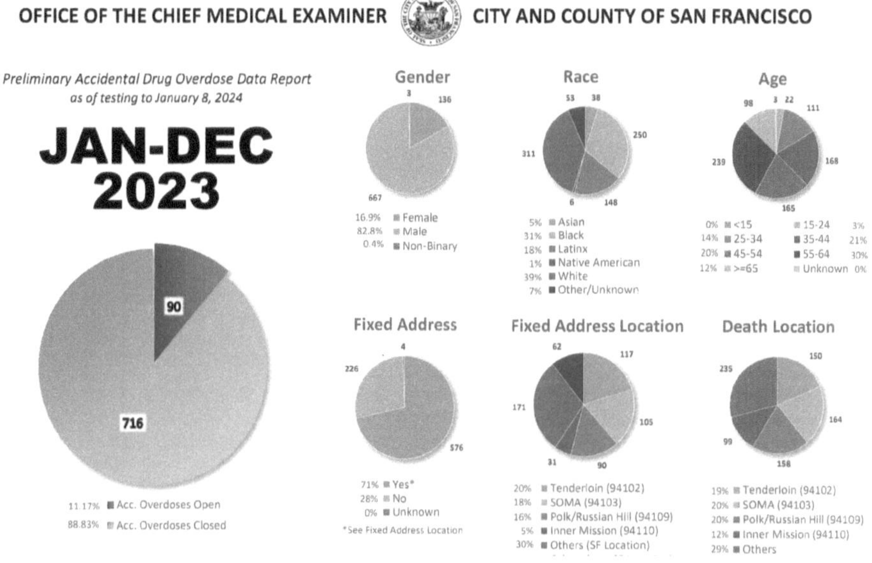

Every race and every woman's suffering should get our attention in a democracy, but to abandon males so completely, and to add abandonment of a race (white) to that first abandonment, is not democratic. "Male" and "white" should have been what the article was mainly about, but the newspaper operates with just enough misandry and abandonment of males to deny the larger statistical truths—both the first and second secrets Michael discussed. As in Blake's poem, and as we are seeing throughout our culture as males take out their self-professed, redemptive anger on the rest of us, the initial anger behind the hyper-use of zero-sum villain/victim (masculine bad, women good) narratives cannot help but create more poison, more rage, and more victimization among all groups.

Overdose Deaths as Another Case Study in Avoidance

Many people will look at graphs and see the real data but still say, "But isn't the anger and misandry justified?" Going further, "Isn't it good politics to twist data and narratives against males and white males? Males and masculinity deserve our anger anyway because of the patriarchy." Our answers to these questions should be No. In 2025, the facts don't justify calcified rage. Our culture does not have a single stereotyped culprit to hold up as the villain anymore. Believing that we do, and acting or avoiding from that misandry, is Blake's poison now.

Our boys and their parents are gradually seeing it everywhere. Returning to San Francisco for a moment, look at male overdose deaths. They increased 30% from 2022 to 2023 (from 514 deaths to 667 deaths) compared to female overdose deaths that increased 3% from 132 to 136 deaths.

Table 1. CA Suicide Deaths from 2018-2022 by Race and Sex

Race/Ethnicity	Male		Female		Percent of Male Deaths within Race
	Deaths	Deaths / 100,000	Deaths	Deaths / 100,000	
White	10,104	28.5	2,802	7.9	78.3%
American Indian or Alaska Native	76	19	30	7.3	72.2%
Native Hawaiian/Other Pacific Islander*	63	17.3	14	Unreliable	81.8%
Black or African American	774	14	234	4.2	76.9%
More than one race	353	12.4	120	4.2	74.7%
Hipanic	4,001	10.2	911	2.3	81.6%
Asian	1,414	10	579	3.7	73.0%
All Deaths (Percent Male)	**16,785**		**4,690**		**78.2%**

Source: Centers for Disease Control and Prevention Wonder Database

*Note: Indicates percent determined by number instead of cohort/100,000

Table 2. CA Overdose Deaths from 2018-2022 by Race and Sex

Race/Ethnicity	Male		Female		Percent of Male Deaths within Race
	Deaths	Deaths / 100,000	Deaths	Deaths / 100,000	
American Indian or Alaska Native	287	71.8	122	29.9	70.6%
Black or African American	3,409	61.7	1,253	22.6	73.2%
White	14,451	40.7	5,463	15.5	72.4%
Native Hawaiian or Other Pacific Islander	114	31.3	31	8.4	78.8%
Hipanic	9,493	24.1	2,103	5.4	81.7%
More than one race	661	23.3	305	10.6	68.7%
Asian	954	6.8	221	1.4	82.9%
Total Deaths (Percent Male)	**29,369**		**9,498**		**75.6%**

Source: Center for Disease Control and Prevention Wonder Database
*Note: Indicates percent determined by deaths/100,000

This California data is replicated in the national data I presented earlier, data constantly updated on the CDC website for each state (https://wonder.cdc.gov/). When males read news reports about this kind of male suffering, reports that do not mention "male," they (and women who love them) feel betrayed. And they are being betrayed. The lack of fairness in much of the media around social empathy for males ought to be visibly mourned by men and the women who care for our sons. Not just in California but throughout the nation, misandry is a subtle way that boys are abandoned.

To assert true democracy, each person, group, school, agency, conference, and neighborhood must now confront its own ideological anger at ancient males; its rage about the patriarchy; its dislike of masculinity; and its simplistic emphasis on males as oppressor-sociological-villains. Anger at males that may once have seemed righteous has become an illness we carry in our soul now. Michael is right: We in the grass roots need to convince leaders to look carefully at our invisible males; to see what is happening more clearly; to deal with facts and their own fears, phobias, and ill-willed outrage.

Ultimately, in a deeply spiritual sense, we and our leaders must rethink the ancient foe who is now dying at the foot of the tree and on our streets every day.

Essential Questions

Each one of us, including Michael and myself, can gain from holding up a mirror to our own potential complicity in neglecting males.

Here are some questions Michael and I grapple with as part of our own spiritual growth.

- Which men am I angry at from the past or the present?
- Which women am I angry at from the past or the present?
- In what ways does my anger at a particular man cloud my judgment about the needs of men and boys?
- In what ways does my anger at a particular woman cloud my judgment about the needs of women and girls?
- What man do I need to forgive so that I can move forward with more clarity about male suffering?
- What woman do I need to forgive so that I can move forward with more clarity about female suffering?

Chapter 16

The Death of 17-Year-Old Jack and the Story that Followed

> "Then she went off and sat down about a bowshot away, for she thought, "I cannot watch the boy die." And as she sat there, she began to sob."
>
> –Book of Genesis (21:16)

(This short essay is useful for general readership, and particularly useful to media and social media influencers, as well as college and high school courses that involve media literacy.)

LAWRENCEVILLE SCHOOL IS A CO-ED SCHOOL located on a sprawling 700-acre campus near Princeton, New Jersey. It is one of the nation's top private boarding schools. In April of 2022, Jack Reid, a 17-year-old student, took his own life after false, rape allegations led to incessant bullying and despair. I (Sean) mentioned him in Chapter 6. As part of its settlement with his family, the school acknowledged institutional failures that led to Jack's decision to take his own life. The school has committed to preventing these types of outcomes in the future, including the endowment of a new Dean of Campus Well-Being who will focus on mental health as part of a long-term solution.

Despite the tragic event at Lawrenceville, much of the media coverage did not address the disparities that exist when it comes to teen suicide, something that mainly kills boys. In Jack's case, a terrible, perfect storm occurred: his male-type depression wasn't understood, false allegations were made against him because he is male, and his mental health went further unchecked unto death. Meanwhile, all around him, the apparati that should have helped him instead assumed his male/masculine guilt. Out of habit, the DGP (dominant gender paradigm) around him, obsessed with masculine defect, ignored Jack's vulnerability. The school and community ran with the false allegations unable to notice that Jack, a young male, was victim not oppressor.

Percent of Suicide Deaths of 15-19 and 20-24 Year-Olds by Sex in U.S. 2018-2022.

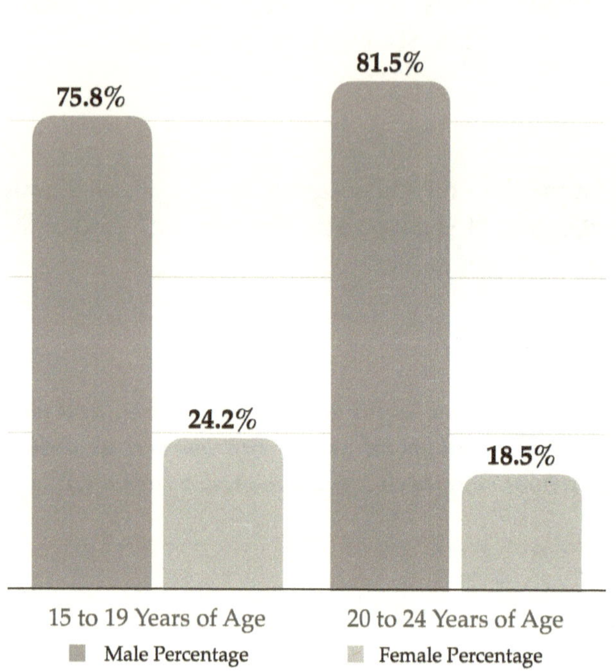

Media Politics Around Males

Throughout this book, Michael and I (Sean) have been developing the idea that people who advocate for boys face a relatively monolithic "Big Three" (academics, government, and media) that avoids male suffering, villainizes male development, and abandons our boys. The situation at Lawrenceville, and the reporting around it, seem to me a profound example of the politics of masculinity clouding judgment in the Big Three–not just in a school, in this case, but in national media. While sex is the single most important core element of suicide, media reports on Jack's story avoided it: The *New York Times*, *New York Post*, and the *Daily Mail* acknowledged the bullying that Jack experienced after the false allegations, and the *Daily Mail* focused on the false rape allegations that triggered the bullying campaign, but only the *Daily Mail* mentioned Jack's sex, despite the predominance of male suicide in local and national statistics.

The *New York Times* article mentioned the loss by suicide of this 17-year-old teen, but did not present data on male suicide deaths. Rather, the article left the impression that females are more vulnerable to suicide this way. "The coronavirus pandemic exacerbated an already worrying mental health emergency among teenagers, made worse by a severe shortage of therapists and treatment options and insufficient research to explain the trend. *Nearly three in five girls reported feeling persistent sadness* in 2021" (*my emphasis*).

The Times is right that we have a therapist shortage and that girls report feeling persistent sadness, but the article was ostensibly about a boy who took his own life after false allegations, so using data regarding male outcomes while also recognizing female outcomes would have made the most sense. A 15-19 year-old boy, in an age bracket Jack fell into, is more likely to take his own life than a female *across any five-year age grouping*. Avoiding male and avoiding disparities in suicide deaths speaks to the larger social motivation to avoid reporting disparities that show profound male suffering.

Others in our field are seeing this same issue with the media that Michael and I have seen. Richard Reeves of the *American Institute for Boys and Men* took notice of the article I wrote in May of 2023 about Jack ("How false allegations led to the deaths of 17-year-old-boys from different continents"). The two of us spoke a day or two after it was published and the tendency of the media to engage in a type of selective and deceptive reporting when it comes to male and female suicide data. Reeves complimented the piece because–although it acknowledged the greater male disparities– it did not discount female mental health as an important issue.

Suicide Deaths per 100,000 Males 15-19 & 20-24 Compared to Female Age Groups

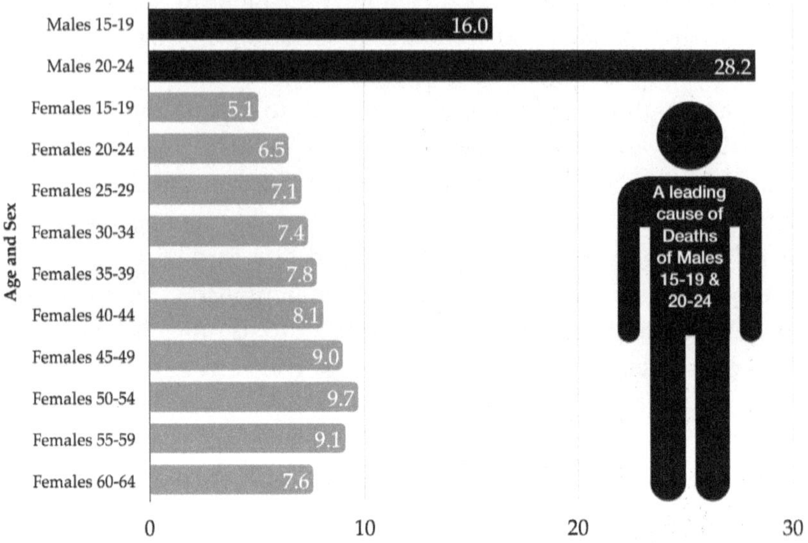

Source: Centers for Disease Control and Prevention Wonder Database
Note: Female groups over age 60-64 continue to trend downward.

Nearly a year-and-a-half after our conversation and my article, Reeves noticed a similar and fallacious approach in the *New Yorker Magazine* in an article by Andrew Solomon, "Has Social Media Fueled a Teen-Suicide Crisis?" Like the *New York Times* article about Jack mentioned above, Solomon's article leaves the same impression—that the teen suicide crisis is a predominately girl problem. Reeves notices this and responds to it in his *Of Boys and Men* substack, October, 2024. "It is essentially impossible to come away from this essay without a strong sense that the teen suicide crisis is, in fact, a teen girl suicide crisis. That is absolutely false. In fact, for every five teenagers dying from suicide, four are likely to be boys."

The media leans heavily on abandoning boys and men via a particular narrative that is at best misleading and at least irresponsible, given that suicide data and despair in general shows how desperate many boys and men are. As so many people in the media suppress male suffering, I hope the frustrating presentation of teen suicide in two major publications, the *New York Times* and *New Yorker Magazine*, will inspire all of us to see why citizen science is so important. It is critical to expose this type of misleading storytelling in our major publications to the public, in our classrooms, to our policymakers, and to the newspapers and magazines we subscribe and do not subscribe to. We can call them to the carpet for this kind of "reporting."

#BringBackOurGirls, but Forget about Our Boys?

In 2014, the *#BringBackOurGirls* campaign captured the world's attention by doing the same thing we've just looked at regarding teen suicide. When 276 schoolgirls were abducted by Boko Haram (a terrorist organization) in Nigeria, Michelle Obama, the First Lady, and the United States government joined with celebrities and world organizations to get financial and organizational support to bring attention to the plight of girls in war-torn Nigeria and to help and free them. This action was a profoundly important endeavor but unmentioned was the fact that more boys and men were kidnapped, beheaded, forced to become soldiers, and experienced other human atrocities, including sexual assault, than the girls. For every one of the 276 girls mentioned in the #BringBackOurGirls governmental campaigns and media, there were 36 kidnapped boys (a 10,000 to 276 ratio).

Two years later, in 2016, a report in the *Wall Street Journal* addressed these 10,000 kidnapped boys of Boko Haram, but the reaction to this male suffering was mostly tepid, and died out quickly in the Big Three. There was no campaign to *#BringBackOurBoys*. The campaign on behalf of the girls was very much needed, but shouldn't the media and our governments have acknowledged and helped the boys, too?

Similarly, in stories regarding human trafficking worldwide, the media, government organizations, non-government organizations (NGO), and academic institutions do not provide as much (or, at times, any) financial support to recognize boys and men in war-torn countries who face terrible atrocities. The power of oppressor (male)/oppressed (female) and villain (masculine)/victim (girls and women) paradigms and models are vast in social consciousness, paralyzing not just local organizations or governments from helping males but also the media apparatus from fully reporting male suffering.

Are Males Disposable?

Beneath our lack of sympathy there might also be something else, something Dr. Warren Farrell calls "the disposable male." Boys and men are disposable in our consciousness, Farrell argues, because they sacrifice themselves physically in war and fatally at work for their societies and to feed their families. They have done so from the very beginning of human civilization.

When boys today die from suicide, overdoses, mental illness, and other multiple causes at alarming rates but those deaths (and other suffering) do not register with the media as *male* issues or *male* suffering, Farrell's assertion that we think of males as disposable in comparison to females rings true. Perhaps the conviction that "males have it all" and "males are bad" have joined with the practice of male disposability to create a consciousness in which "males either have it all or are bad—or if not those two things—they are disposable anyway."

Jack at Lawrenceville was a male betrayed by the system that was supposed to be safe for him, his community, and his school. As he was falsely accused and each new injustice kept compounding on his innocence, he was seen as inherently bad by some people who are misandrist to males, not seen as a victim by people who see female suffering but avoid male suffering, and perhaps seen as disposable by others.

Our hatred, dislike, avoidance, and neglect of males does not feel like sickness to us because the politics of oppression, masculinity, and even of disposability, make it seem like it is necessary that our culture neglect male wellness. Pursuing the idea that our neglect of males might heal culture of past detriments, we allow boys' suffering to go unnoticed in systems that do not understand males, sometimes falsely accuse them, exploit and kill them, and feed further into their disposability. Yet as our world becomes increasingly chaotic every day, don't we need successful, loved, and helpful males more than ever before?

Essential Questions

Here are questions you can ask when reading, watching, listening, or engaging with news, podcasts, lectures, policy actions, and debates to pay close attention to the number of times male and female are mentioned and the way male and female outcomes are presented.

1. Does the media you are watching, reading, listening to, or participating in fail to mention the word male, boy, or man, or fail to address quantifiable outcomes when it is apparent males and females are impacted? (Think of the *New York Times* article about Jack's suicide that mentions female depression during Covid but does not mention male suicide deaths nor that males comprise 2/3s of Covid deaths).

2. Does the article only look at race/ethnicity without adding sex to the analysis when sex is the statistically most important factor? (Think of the *San Francisco Chronicle* article failing to mention that 83% of the city's overdose deaths were male.)

3. Does the media use a title that attempts to change a predominately male problem into a female problem? (Think of the *PBS Frontline* article "Why Afghanistan's Children Are Used as Spies and Suicide Bombers" when 99% of the victims were boys and the article's title should have been, "Why Afghanistan Boys Are Used as Spies and Suicide Bombers."

4. Does the media focus on social constructs of the masculine (toxic, patriarchal, and historically privileged) as its primary way to avoid talking about sex-based differences and sex-based root causes?

5. Are ideological points of view presented that dismiss males? (My essay above, "The Silent Killer, Males Not Written into National, State, or Local Budgets," provided evidence of this practice at the government level.)

6. Does the media discuss "women" or "women and children" but not discuss men or boys? (Mentioning boys and men equal to girls and women does not diminish the suffering of girls and women.)

Chapter 17

Does the Child Have Brain Sex Dysphoria or Gender Dysphoria?

(This essay is useful for general readers and particularly for counselors, therapists, doctors, psychiatrists, college courses in nearly all fields, educators, the media, and parents.)

TRAVELING RECENTLY, I (MICHAEL) happened to sit on the airplane next to a sociology professor at a well-known university. Like the professor I reported about in "Why I Generally Don't Use 'Cisgender'," this professor was what I call a "sexender," but I didn't know that until she heard what I do for a living and said, "Oh," not happily. Her point of view in our ensuing argument was not just "academic" for her: she told me that her daughter had gender dysphoria. In the dialogue captured here, I will use **M** for Michael and **S** for the sociologist.

First, though, what is a "sexender?" Sexenders tend to be *sexodimorphobic*: they fear sexual dimorphism, which is, as we've explored earlier, the concept that humans have only two choices for sex, male and female, despite that our brains, just like our bodies, exist on a spectrum of variety and diversity for both male and female.

In their fear of sexual dimorphism, sexenders argue for delegitimizing the word "sex" (except to denote romance or the sex act) in social and political conversation. They often believe, as this professor did, that those of us who use "boy," "girl," or "sexual dimorphism," are transphobic, inherently anti-feminist, anti-LGBTQIA+, neurobiologically, medically, physiologically, psychologically, and educationally just wrong.

As our argument began, this sociologist noted how useful social media is in confirming the veracity of her opinions. She suggested that social media ("the new social construction device") proved that getting rid of "falsely binary male and female from parenting" would become our human future. "Social media is good for spreading the word," she said. "We will end the use of 'mom' and 'dad' soon, or at least we should do that if we are going to say we are an empathic society."

Here is more of our dialogue:

M: "Empathic for whom?"

S: "For everyone. The truth is, we are all gender non-binary, gender fluid, and even bisexual. The science on this is clear."

M: "So, we should say a person is feeding a child from 'their' breast and the activity is 'chest-feeding'?"

S: She nodded in agreement. "Getting rid of 'mom' and 'dad' will protect everyone from feeling pressured to be binary, male or female, in life. Getting rid of 'breast-feeding' will finally create a healthy, fully diverse society."

M: "But you're saying that not including males and females is healthy diversity even though deleting male and female will then exclude most people in the world? So, in your mind, excluding males and females is healthy *inclusion*?"

S: "To have a diverse society, we have to stop focusing on male and female. This is what the *AMA* is trying for when they say we shouldn't put 'male' or 'female' on birth certificates anymore."

M: "But only a small group within the AMA suggested it. It is a relatively far-out option that does not fit common sense. The brains and bodies of our children are male and female at conception–how can getting rid of male and female be real *diversity*?"

S: "Sexual dimorphism is a myth. Anyway, even if it did exist it can potentially shame gender fluid children and adults. Whether a baby has a penis or vagina does not matter–that child might end up gender nonbinary later in life so we should stop imposing male and female on that child from the beginning. And male and female are just stereotypes, anyway—getting rid of male and female will free everyone up."

M: "But your own child—you said she has gender dysphoria. Doesn't that mean she is a female facing depression that includes dysphoria about feeling somewhat male? And if she is trans, wouldn't she have brain sex dysphoria, not gender dysphoria?"

S: She had not heard the term "brain sex dysphoria" before, but "No," she insisted, "the problem is that my daughter was misnamed 'she' at birth by us parents because of binary societal pressure. I'm ashamed that I gave her a girl's name and raised her a girl. If they had been born into a society without male and female, they would never have suffered the depression and discomfort of gender dysphoria."

"That statement is not true because its causation is not supportable," I wanted to say, but this was not the moment.

Gender Dysphoria or Brain Sex Dysphoria?

The term I used in that conversation, "Brain Sex Dysphoria," is not in the Diagnostic and Statistical Manual for Mental Disorders (DSM), the manual we in the psychology field use to understand, diagnose, and propose treatment for mental health issues. Right now, when doctors, therapists, or others diagnose a disease, disorder, or mood issue related to sex and gender, the DSM provides "gender dysphoria" as the catch-all.

I am uncomfortable with the hyper-use of "gender dysphoria" because it is not inclusive enough, from a hard science perspective, of all children and adults. As I noted earlier, sex comes first, gender comes later. Sex is both the house and it is a lot of what fills the rooms of the house genetically via cells, muscles, skeleton, brain centers, emotions, perceptions, interactions, relationships, and so on; gender can help fill some of the rooms with furniture and art, with its perceptions and interactions, but it is not the house itself. So, to group everything with "gender," even including a person's whole identity, means significant social confusion in families, schools, medical clinics, and therapy offices about what we are dealing with when a child presents to us with gender dysphoria.

To help create more clarity, I have developed the term *brain sex dysphoria*. I place it next to "gender dysphoria" in my clinical practice and social conversations because I believe "brain sex dysphoria" helps the medical and psychiatric professions, as well as parents and children, to distinguish who is trans and who is exploring, for a time, a gender nonbinary identity. While some children and adults who present with gender dysphoria have brain sex dysphoria, most do not. In someone with brain sex dysphoria, depression and confusion include having a brain that is more female in its structure and function than the present male body (or vice versa, more male in its structure and function than the female body); some, if not all, of these brain-sex dysphoric children will present as gender nonconforming to parents and professionals but are actually *trans*—they have brain sex dysphoria.

If this child has brain sex dysphoria and is trans, certain medications (and, later, perhaps surgery) will likely become necessary. If a child is not trans, however, those same medications and procedures may do the child harm. A child with gender dysphoria can be treated for depression in multiple ways without invasive surgery.

Ending Sex-Ending

To distinguish brain sex dysphoria from gender dysphoria, our profession must agree that sex and gender are not the same thing. The sociologist on the airplane did not agree with that. She belonged to a political force, increasingly powerful in the Big Three as we've noted, that is attempting to erase "male" from conversation and, to some lesser extent, "female" too. As a sexender, she wants to make "gender" the catchall for both sex and gender; clinically speaking, she wants to call everything gender and gender dysphoria. She is not alone in confusing sex and gender as we see in studies like this one in which the authors mean *sex* (as the first word in the title implies) but also use *gender*: "Psycho*sexual* Aspects, Effects of Prenatal Androgen Exposure, and *Gender* Change in 46 XY Disorders of *Sex* Development" (italics mine).

This is a very useful study, but it adds to our social confusion about what is sex and what is gender. I hope we will end the confusion by sticking with good science. Sex is pre-set in utero in *all* of us, even children who will later present as trans, lesbian/gay/bisexual, and gender fluid. Most of these exceptional children are their own sex but they have *bridge brains* (brains that bridge between the sexes on brain scans). Scans of fetal brains show male/female differences (sexual dimorphism) in neural function before children are born (M.D. Wheelock, J.L. Hect, E. Hernandez-Andrade, and colleagues, April 2019, Sex differences in functional connectivity during fetal brain development. *Developmental Cognitive Neuroscience)*. Sex is binary, gender can be fluid.

The sociologist did not believe me on fetal sexual dimorphism, even when I showed her the fetal brain scan results in the PowerPoint on my laptop.

"Those are fake," she said accusingly.

I challenged her to get online and look up the study, which she refused to do. Instead, she pressed forward with sexending by noting that "gender differences" is now used more than "sex differences" in studies and literature because "gender" is the word that should be used everywhere because sex is "over and done." I agreed with her about the use of "gender" instead of "sex" over the last two decades. My Gurian Institute team and I use "gender" quite a bit as in "gender differences" or in "learning through a gender lens." We use gender because "learning through a sex lens" implies a sex act, which we do not mean to imply, and because "gender differences" is indeed the popular term for differences between women and men, and boys and girls.

But still, I tried to point out, it is crucial we all know what we mean by sex and gender, and it is crucial we expand word use and definitions by using "sex" as in "brain sex" more not less. If we can agree that gender is useful but also that sexual dimorphism is useful, we will better serve all people, including LGBTQIA+ people.

Defining Brain Sex Dysphoria

The sociologist insisted that her daughter had *gender* dysphoria, nothing else. Yet her daughter was already engaged in hormonal and surgical transition into male. When I asked more questions about the daughter, I felt sure the daughter had *brain sex dysphoria* and, thus, was definitely *trans* rather than mainly *gender nonconforming*. I tried to say this diplomatically by suggesting that the daughter might have something even more intransigent than gender dysphoria, but our discussion ended. As I reflected over the conversation, I hoped her daughter did have brain sex dysphoria. If not, gender assumptions might be doing this young woman harm by confusing gender with trans—by attaching her to surgery that could have negative side effects.

To make sure we don't confuse trans and gender nonconforming from now on, we need to add brain sex dysphoria to the medical and psychiatric science of sexgender by adapting other definitions. Let's first look at a definition of "gender dysphoria" that I've combined from Wikipedia and the DSM (*Diagnostical and Statistical Manual for Mental Disorders*).

"'Gender dysphoria (GD) is a facet of modern human biology which is believed to be derived from the sexual differentiation of the brain. DSM 5 states, 'GD involves a conflict between a person's physical or assigned gender and the gender with which he/she/they identify.'"

Now let's alter this to include sexual dimorphism and brain sex dysphoria.

"Brain Sex Dysphoria (BSD) is a facet of modern human biology derived from sexual differentiation in the brain that occurs when the brain of the individual acts significantly more like the brain of the other sex than average or typical for their own sex. Further, while *DSM* 5 uses 'Gender Dysphoria' (GD) as the common term used for all BSD and GD, GD does not account for brain sex dysphoria. GD should be used to measure a conflict between a person's sex-derived sense of gender and the gender or genders with which he/she/they may later identify. BSD should be used for individuals who are trans."

To be accurate to existing science, and to help protect our males and females, I hope we will no longer group all sexgender dysphoric children under "gender" categories. By expanding our diagnostics to help us understand who is trans, LGB, bridge brain, and/or gender nonconforming, we would do better for *all* LGBTQIA+ children, and every other child by accurately diagnosing each element of the brain. We would understand, too, that "boy" and "male sex" and "boy energy" and all these terms regarding *sex differentiation* are important to schools and institutions that serve our children.

Ultimately, using "brain sex dysphoria" in our diagnosis and our literature will translate to children knowing who they are when they feel that their brains run counter to their bodies. If the child has BSD, a diagnosis of gender dysphoria will be replaced or adapted toward BSD. For Bruce Jenner becoming Caitlyn Jenner, it appears to me–admittedly, from afar–that BSD was the issue. If a child has gender dysphoria not brain sex dysphoria, though, personal identity experimentation has likely come from internal pressure around sexgender's identity speculation, and/or from others via social contagion, and this is normally coupled with depression. This gender experimenting child, who likely does not need trans protocols, would likely need treatment for the dysphoria.

Progressing Our Language and Diagnosis Beyond Gender

Language can become politics and politics become language. In this article from the *National Institute of Mental Health,* notice the political tension between sex and gender that ends up being resolved inaccurately toward gender and away from male or female–away from sex. These paragraphs border on dense semiotics, but please wade through them with me.

"The process of sexual differentiation refers to the development of differences between males and females, which are widely observed in nature and also concern humans. One of the most sexually dimorphic human traits is gender identity, defined as the inner sense of self as a female, a male, or as an alternative gender different from the male and female ones."

In this paragraph, the researchers accurately define what is going on internally but feel pressure to place 'gender identity' as an inborn trait when they say, "self as a female, a male or as an alternative gender." This is inaccurate: female and male are elements of sex and thus they are not parallel to "alternative gender."

The paragraph continues: *"In cisgender individuals, gender identity develops in line with the assigned gender at birth and is stable throughout life."* In this language, sex has become gender in two ways, first, via the increasingly used "cisgender" to include all male and female individuals despite that "cis-sex" would be more accurate or no "cis" at all—just "male" and "female." The second way appears in "assigned gender at birth." **Sex** is assigned at birth, not gender; for accuracy, the language should read "assigned sex at birth."

The paragraph continues: *"On the other hand, transgender individuals may persistently or transiently identify with a gender that is different from the one assigned at birth."* For accuracy, this ought to read: *"On the other hand, trans individuals may persistently identify with a brain-sex that is different from the one seemingly attached to their genital sex."*

Overall, too, our present use of "transgender" in the Big Three is incorrect: the trans person is experiencing trans*sexuality* in the brain, but the word "transsexual" has a recent negative history. To avoid inaccuracy and the negative history, I use *trans* for a person who presents with brain sex dysphoria.

The study continues: *"According to the Diagnostic and Statistical Manual of Mental Disorders 5th version (DSM 5), we refer to Gender Dysphoria when the incongruence between the experienced/expressed gender and the assigned one leads to clinically significant psychological distress and impairment in the main areas of functioning. In some cases, this distress may lead to the desire for a social and/or somatic transition through a gender affirming hormonal treatment and surgery."*

In this language, we come to the crux of what can bring harm to both children and adults. Inaccurate groupings in "gender affirming" and "gender affirming care" are so thin, so amorphous, they lead to use of interventions for gender dysphoric children that may be dangerous to them but may be necessary for trans children, i.e., hormone therapy and surgery.

It is crucial to remember that hormonal treatment, matched with surgery, works to alter *physical sex.* When researchers and physicians talk about "gender affirming surgery" they are hopefully talking about brain-*sex* dysphoria and *sex* reassignment, not "gender," because surgery to affirm "gender" is not needed by the depressed child's brain that is not trans. Unfortunately, because the Diagnostic Manual only includes "gender dysphoria" as a diagnosable condition, all presenting LGBTQIA+ children and adults are required to fit under gender dysphoria, a category that erases sex from the conversation and moves a child, family, hospital, physician, therapist, and governmental agency toward a category for depression so broad as to invite significant diagnostic mistakes.

Our general lack of diagnostic accuracy has been forced into medicine and child development via various pressures in the Big Three, all of which connect with the sexodimorphobia we've discussed already, the fear of sexual dimorphism. As this fear pressures everything toward "gender," boys and girls, males and females, enter murky territory.

What, Then, Is Gender Identity?

"Identity" is one of the most popular words in social discourse today. We want to know who we are because knowing who we are can help us assert ourselves frankly and successfully in the world. Germane to every stage of human life is "identity development," and perhaps in no stage more than in our long human adolescence (between ages 12–22 or so). "Gender identity" has become a popular word in this context. Adolescents and others want to know who they are from the sexgender standpoint given that sex and gender roles have been shifting so much over the past few decades.

Meanwhile, human beings do not have one identity. We are each what the philosopher Jean Paul Sartre called "a bundle of selves." So are our children who will have many identities that evolve and shift over time, identities they experiment with, identities like gender that are soft- not hard-wired. One way we know the difference between hard and soft wiring is that most adolescents diagnosed with gender dysphoria and/or who say they believe they are trans end up reporting to clinicians, parents, and friends within a year that they are not trans, they are gay. For a time, they experimented with a gender identity of "trans" or "gender nonbinary," but as identities shifted, they realized the power of their own hard wiring, the identity that is built in, their sex (male or female) and also, now, the hard-wiring of same-sex romantic orientations (gay/lesbian/bisexual). Their "gender identity" evolves or changes during adolescence from "I'm definitely trans" or "I'm definitely gender nonbinary" to "I'm gay" and "I'm a bridge brain male," or "I'm lesbian" and "I'm a bridge brain female."

As I've already noted (perhaps too repetitively but because I am very concerned about this), if we use invasive therapy on someone who is LGB or Q+ but not T, we may permanently alter that child's brain and physiological development, and often with permanent damage. As our society has done with Ritalin (misdiagnosing many children, especially boys, with ADD or ADHD and drugging them when many of them did not have the brain disorder), and as we have done with anti-depression medications recently, giving children as young as 5 or 6 these medications before a safe diagnosis for depressive disorder justifies the use of hormonally invasive anti-depression medications, so we are now doing with gender dysphoria–trying to alter children biochemically without accurately diagnosing their hard-wiring, and thus, what each of them need from us. For children with gender dysphoria, it is often best to treat the depression and other concurrent presentations (ASD, ADHD, anorexia, bulimia) rather than to try to alter their hard-wiring for sex so quickly.

Further Thoughts from Sean on Bridge Brains and a Brain-Sensitive Tact for Our Children

I join Michael in his concern about our children.

The "Cass review" is an independent review of gender identity services for children and young people published in 2023 which you can find online. It is perhaps the most comprehensive review of the use of puberty blockers and surgeries for children to date. After the researchers conducted extensive research, they proposed the same cautious approach to treating those who believe their sex does not match their new gender identity as Michael has proposed. The number of children turning to puberty blockers and surgeries in the U.S. is alarming to me, given that most of these children are going through depression and/or a normal process of self-understanding regarding sex. The Cass review and Michael's research are helpful in proposing that the more we help each child understand his/her brain-sex to include bridge brains, the more he and she can reconcile identity questions and quiet gender influenced depression.

Most males on the more extreme end of the male brain spectrum and most females on the more extreme end of the female brain spectrum do not require transition away from their functional brain/body's sex (XX or XY). They may well not need puberty blockers, hormone therapy, or surgery. A boy who is highly sensitive and reports "feeling more like a girl" need not become a girl or be encouraged to do so when another option exists: adults helping him understand that his *male brain* functions in a way that allows him to explore and express feelings more like a female brain than other boys might. Helping him understand that his brain functions *on the male brain spectrum* helps him reconcile feelings and interests. He understands that even if he doesn't always feel what he thinks other boys are feeling, he is still a boy. Years later, he may look back on his explorations from the position of a sensitive man who became a musician or teacher and father. He may remember an adolescent time when he had more female friends than male (he will likely have had lower testosterone than other males). He may have realized during that time that he was and is gay. Feelings of "being more like a girl" are well within the range of the male brain spectrum. We most effectively help him by helping him see what is hard-wired and what is soft-wired.

The same holds true for a girl who likes rough-and-tumble play more than some boys, who may like "boyish" toys, who may like to wear clothes worn by the boys she hangs out with, who sometimes feels like her brain is more a boy's brain than a girl's as she seeks her identity. She is most likely a bridge brain girl. She might grow up to become an athlete who craves physically competitive environments, and/or a mom, a corporate leader, a teacher or anyone else who, upon looking back at her interest in boyish things, can now see it as well within the range of the female brain spectrum. We best help her as an adolescent girl to see all that she can during her adolescent explorations. Just as we help quiet the boy's anxiety at "feeling like I have to become a girl," we can give the girl tools to quiet her anxiety at feeling that she must become a boy to not feel sad or anxious anymore.

Michael's "bridge brain" term ought to be used in all households and throughout The Big Three, I believe. As an educator for decades, I have worked with children whose brains operate at the middle of the sexgender brain spectrum—I have met many bridge brains and so have you. Michael's term allows our communities to help children find peace within themselves as they understand the brain-reasons for their predilections, interests, attractions, and thoughts. "Bridge brain" allows their exploration to be normal on a brain sex spectrum that matches chromosomal sex so that the young person does not have to feel at odds with themselves. "Bridge brain" is highly inclusive and excludes no one. Helping children reconcile their anatomical, brain, and physical sex allows us as caring adults to be a part of their identity development. A trans person may well seek transition later in life, but for most gender questioning children, teaching them how the human brain works, inclusive of bridge brains, helps them move beyond the notion of a wrong assignment, which is gut-wrenching for them, and toward the practice of healthy living in the brain and body that has been theirs from birth.

Revising the *DSM* Will Revise Cultural Politics

To come to grips with the extent of our misdiagnoses, we will have to transcend the sociologist's concept–popular in social media–that "You are transphobic, patriarchal, sexist or anti-LGBTQIA+ if you argue the importance of sex." We can do this by going all-in on real science, which means adding things like brain sex dysphoria to our linguistic and diagnostic protocols and bridge brain to our common parlance. On the medical side, if we change the *DSM* to include brain sex dysphoria, the study we analyzed above might read this way.

"According to the *Diagnostic and Statistical Manual of Mental Disorders 5th version* (*DSM 5*), we refer to Brain Sex Dysphoria (BSD) when the incongruence between the anatomical and brain sex experienced by the child or adult leads to clinically significant psychological distress and impairment in the main areas of functioning; and we refer to Gender Dysphoria (GD) when child or adult's gender constructions reveal clinically significant psychological distress and impairment in the main areas of functioning. In many cases, brain sex dysphoria may require hormonal treatment and surgery; gender dysphoria, however, will likely not be treated with these practices."

Once brain sex dysphoria is available to clinicians, parents, and children, all the tools available to us as clinicians, parents, and children will be seen through four brain-based categories, including bridge brain, rather than just the softer category, gender dysphoria.

Try This
The Four Categories Tool

As it is useful to you, try to ascertain what is happening in your child or a child you are serving by dividing the child's presentation of "gender dysphoria" into its four elemental sub-categories.

Gay, Lesbian, Bisexual. If the child is in pre-puberty or adolescence (around 9 or older), clinicians and parents can work to discover if the presenting dysphoria links mainly to the disconnect of the LGB attraction with the more typical heterosexual attraction among peers. If so, self-affirming counseling will likely be needed including family education about homosexuality and hard-wiring in the brain, but medications such as hormone blockers and pre-surgical practices will likely not be needed.

Brain Sex Dysphoria. As the child presents with gender dysphoria, parents and clinicians can work to discover if the child is trans by using neuropsychological batteries and, if available, brain scans. If the child is trans, hormone therapy in mid or late adolescence might begin, then surgery during adulthood might occur. Because the child is presenting with depression (dysphoria), traditional treatments for depression can also occur simultaneously or before invasive treatments.

Gender Dysphoria. This diagnosis would put the child in a category of sex- and gender-confusion that is concomitant with depression but not indicative of trans. Because gender dysphoria is linked to identity questions that blend sexes and genders, some of the treatment may include self-affirmation as gender fluid, some may connect with LGB education, and some may include traditional treatment for depression and other co-occurring issues, but invasive hormonal therapies and pre-surgery practices will likely not be needed or advisable.

Bridge Brain. Most children presenting as gender dysphoric are depressed but not trans, LGB, or gender fluid, and nearly all have bridge brains (they exist close to the middle of the male/female brain spectrum). Treatment for these children includes treatment for the depression as needed, and counseling and mentoring that helps empower these children as bridge brains that lean toward the other brain-sex but are not trans (including counseling around internal assets), so that the child does not feel so anomalous in the human condition as to need invasive intervention.

In all cases with all children and adults, suggestions in this book should not be construed as a substitute for diagnosis and care by your own or the child's medical and psychiatric team.

Political Assets and Liabilities in Working with Gender Fluidity

Some political advocacy agencies have argued that the number of gender fluid people in the U.S. (and the world) is 20% (see, for instance, "The CEO Who Transitioned," *WSJ*, Vanessa Fuhrmans, September 14, 2020). Common sense, personal experience, and citizen science reveal this number to be inflated because if it were real, 1 in 5 of us would be gender fluid, and we are not seeing that around us. In statistical terms, 1.4 million people may be trans in the U.S., according to University of California data, but many of this number are gender nonconforming not trans, thus, most of this 1.4 million will likely fit in the gender fluid or bridge brain category. In other words, we just don't know how many gender fluid people there are worldwide.

But one thing is certain: gender-fluid, gender nonconforming, gender ambiguous, gender dysphoric, queer, questioning people are a minority with a lot to offer the majority. Like LGBT and bridge brain people, gender fluid and nonconforming people have existed throughout history. They dress like people of the other sex in public sometimes (actors, artists, for instance) and/or in private. They build our roads, fight our wars, raise our children, and suffer pain from people who do not understand their identities or their alteration of sex-specific social costuming. While gender fluidity is not a new phenomenon, it is less hidden than it was 100 or even 20 years ago. People experimenting with gender identity are important people, and with existing suicide and depression rates for trans, LGB, and Q+ children clear to us, we need to give these children our support and protection.

To do this, I hope we will come together to agree on expanded rather than restrictive politics of LGBTQIA+ that involves *both* sex and gender not just the too-broad "gender identity." I hope the Big Three will start training parents, clinicians, teachers, children and citizens in all the categories–brain sex dysphoria, gender dysphoria, bridge brains, LGB, trans, male and female– because every one of these categories are parts of human identity and thus are important.

Of course, the way the training is done matters.

A Teen Case Study

A 13-year-old girl recently came home from Biology class to report to her parents that her teacher taught a lesson on gender fluidity in class. The teacher told the class that pronouns like "he" and "she" are "outdated." "You need to pick your pronouns," the teacher said. "'He' and 'she' may not work for most of you anymore." Later it was learned that the teacher's comments were gleaned from a workshop the teacher found on social media in which the trainees were instructed that there is no sex, just gender. Many of the students looked at the teacher blankly, some agreed, and some went home to complain to their parents.

This teacher was well-meaning but untrained in the complexity of what he was discussing in class. When the teacher experienced significant backlash, the school system could have realized: Parents will support gender fluid children if there is a "both sex and gender" approach, but the school did not use that approach and so the parents tore apart the "it's only about gender" approach. Parents are smart. They can see when people in authority are trying to force a culture of the exception into society (pretending that the exception, gender fluidity, is the rule). Parents are also suspicious when people in authority use social media or other resources that lack in-depth scientific backing to exert the pressure of the exception, and they will backlash. Many parents hearing about this girl's Biology class sensed a layered irony: a biology class and biology teacher avoided using actual biology in favor of using social media sociology and political pressure.

Using Science Rather Than Social Contagion to Help with Identity

For thirty years, I've presented scans of male and female brains to teachers, parents, and students in K–12 schools. Both the adults and the students are intrigued as they recognize themselves in the male/female brain scans. By late elementary school, too, adults and kids recognize gender nonconforming students; they recognize variety on the brain spectrum from scans that include themselves.

Brain science like this can be used to help communities deal with the social contagion that Brown University public health professor Lisa Littman noticed in schools ten years ago. She saw a child tell others that he or she is trans, then this self-diagnosis was accepted as the young person's identity. Littman developed the term "rapid onset gender dysphoria" (ROGD) for this phenomenon, which involved girls especially. Abigail Shrier has written powerful articles on this, including, "When Your Daughter Defies Biology" in the *Wall Street Journal* on January 7, 2019, and "Top Trans Doctors Blow the Whistle on 'Sloppy' Care" in *The Free Press* in 2021.

The sex spectrum of male and female is one of the core elements of pre-teen and teen identity, especially because of the wash of male and female hormones (sex-based biochemistry) in each blood and brain system. It is no wonder, then, that ROGD activates in the pre-teen and teen years. As adolescents develop their identities, you can be empowered to help them with the science in this book, science that is brain scan based, to avoid their locking into one identity just because others are doing it. While you may not have brain scans in your home, you can work with many pieces of the puzzle at once, teaching kids that:

- Most of the newly gender nonconforming children are not trans, even if they request affirmation as trans, thus, most are not brain sex dysphoric but are gender dysphoric and/or questioning;
- All children need help that can include affirmation of who they now say they are but also might include challenge and direction

to be sure of who they are ("Are you LGB?" "Are you trans?" "Are you a Bridge Brain?" "Are you gender fluid?") during their time of treatment for their depression, anxiety, or other issue;

- Everyone needs help understanding, from a brain science point-of-view, how children might fit into a new trend in the school which means discussion of the science, the trend and the social contagion can occur at once without shaming or belittling.

An example of empowered parents came to me from the parents of a 14-year-old girl who was set to go to a dance with a group of friends who had all announced that they were gender questioning (social contagion). The parents did not have an objection to this dance until they learned that another girl who is gay requested that their daughter go to the dance with her and go separate from the group.

"This feels like a date," the daughter said, "and it makes me nervous."

Though the daughter saw herself as gender questioning, she knew she was not lesbian, so the family joined together to tell the other girl that dating is not allowed in the family until 16, which was true. This strategy allowed the parents to take the fall on no-dating. In the end, all the girls went together as a group. Knowing about ROGD and knowing that the other girl was gay helped this family without attacking anyone in the social group. Knowing about ROGD also kept the parents and their daughter from investing too far into the politics around gender dysphoria that they had seen on social media.

Wisdom From Teachers Themselves

A retired middle school teacher and counselor, former Gurian Institute Program Director, and Positive Discipline Board Member, Eva Dwight spoke with me recently about her experience with ROGD. "In my last few years in the school systems, gender fluid expressions had already begun in earnest. We had 7th and 8th graders sorting through atypical identities, embracing the differences themselves but also reflecting peer pressure. Many of them were sorting through things like, 'I'm friends with kids who might be atypical, so I will be atypical myself, or at least experiment with being atypical, but I really don't know what I am, but I have to sound like I do, and this is a way to do that.' These kids did not need a well-meaning adult to say to them, 'Let's try hormone medication on you,' at least, not yet. Their struggle was with adolescent identity experimentation, normal for any teen, and they were choosing sex and gender as part of that.

"I think, to some extent, many people don't realize the normalcy of all sorts of exploration in any child at any time. When I work with kids and parents around this, I see significant confusion and anguish for kids and parents because they are not taught what you are explaining in your work. The parents, and the kids in the cases I'm talking about, thought 'LGBTQIA+' is all one category–they didn't realize there are brain differences between gay, bisexual, trans, gender fluid, etc. This is why I think it is best for adults to find a professional who can help the presenting teens to understand and define themselves *using real brain science*. This process will take time and patience. These growing and developing children are changing rapidly. We do them a disservice by going along with whatever they say as children."

Eva's wisdom is shared by many people. Everyone I speak with in the educational sphere has begun to wonder about social contagion, and everyone wants to do best for *all* kids. As the adults in the room, or in the house, the school, and the community, we have a lot of wisdom to bring to bear on children who are searching through identities.

But Is It Even Fair for Adults to Play a Guiding Role When a Child Says, "I'm ___________"?

In no previous era would this question arise, but Eva is hinting at it, and you've probably heard it asked. The very parents, teachers, and mentors who have always been responsible for guiding children through their childhood journey in the past, now feel politically (and medically and governmentally) pressured to believe they are abusive of children if they think like Eva thinks.

Here's an example.

I went to a school district to consult on gender issues just before Covid struck. Part of why I was called in was that the community saw ROGD especially among girls. The superintendent told me, "If a seven-year-old says they are transgender, we should just say okay, and that is that. I'd be worried about too much political outrage from some parents if we did anything else." This school leader felt that the school had a legal obligation not only to stay out of medical questions but also stay out of any questions that connect with a child's identity development. I understood his position, but in my consulting, I argued against it, especially as regards the care of younger children. "A five, seven, ten-year-old most likely cannot know if he or she is trans yet," I pointed out. "Parents and adults are morally and psychologically obligated to study and help this child over time."

Part of my consulting during my district visit involved helping the professionals to modify the tools in their own existing district toolbox. I suggested an updated checklist of protocols for professionals and parents of children who present with gender dysphoria and/or gender fluidity.

Try This
Discuss All Brain Options

- Talk with the child and parents about *all* the options including gay, trans, bridge, nonconforming, and fluid in each specific category before going any further.
- Utilize biochemical analysis, including blood tests of testosterone and other hormone levels that 1) indicate range of male brain and female brain in the child, and 2) provide insight into whether unbalanced hormone levels are partially causing gender dysphoria.
- Utilize personal statements, including patient journals over a multi-year period before confirming trans while affirming the child as depressed, dysphoric, (thus receiving treatment) and gender fluid if necessary.
- Utilize parental and community member observations of the child from various sources at home, in school, among the child's friends, and among extended family to help create a treatment and affirmation plan so this child is not alone in exploration and treatment.
- Minimize invasive biological intervention until mid- or late-adolescence unless it is very clear that the child is trans and/or it is clear that hormone treatment is necessary to treat hormonal imbalances and/or depression.

The superintendent's less nuanced protocol, e.g., "affirm the child no matter how young as trans and begin hormone therapy," may be politically correct and socially pressure-filled, but does not distinguish well enough between children in need. The one size fits all, "everyone is gender fluid" or "everyone gender fluid is trans if they say they are," leaves too many children and families in distress. It also impedes political help for boys who are *sex* not a "gender identity," boys we are already abandoning in our national politics.

A Treatment Timeline

In calling for changes in both our cultural politics around LGBTQIA + and changes to the *DSM*, I am asking professionals to utilize a timeline for treatment that will affirm a child's search for identities in stages.

First Stage: Pursue Psychological and Medical Evaluation for Six Months or More with Simultaneous Treatment for Depression as Warranted. Psychological assessments of the child take time and involve interviews, conversations, journaling, and analysis of genetics, hormonal, and neuro-physiological components like those in the box above.

The Cleveland Clinic (https://health.clevelandclinic.org/research-on-the-transgender-brain-what-you-should-know/) looks at the usefulness of brain scans and might be usable in this stage. "When we look at the transgender brain, we see that the brain resembles the gender that the person identifies as," Dr. Murat Altinay says. "For example, a person who is born with a penis but ends up identifying as a female often actually has some of the structural characteristics of a 'female' brain. And the brain similarities aren't only structural. We're also finding functional similarities between the transgender brain and its identified gender," Dr. Altinay says. "In studies that use MRIs to take images of the brain as people perform tasks, the brain activity of transgender people tends to look like that of the gender they identify with."

For accuracy (and if "brain sex dysphoria" existed in *DSM*), this second paragraph would likely read: "We're also finding functional similarities between the trans brain and its identified *sex,*' Dr. Altinay says. "In studies that use MRIs to take images of the brain as people perform tasks, the brain activity of trans people tends to look like that of the *brain sex* they identify with" (additions and italics are mine).

Of all existing treatment tools, I think brain scans might end up being the most helpful for determining a trans adolescent or adult, but many cities don't have them available. Thus, six months or more of assessment and "watching" time, with simultaneous treatment for depression or anxiety seems crucial to me. During this time, clinicians can work with children and families with help like, "You could indeed be a gender nonconforming child, but your brain may not be trans, and here's why. Let's look together at this material." If helpful, the family and child can read this chapter and/or https://gurianinstitute.com/at-what-age-should-a-child-be-confirmed-as-transgender/. Adolescents can understand everything written in this chapter or that blog post.

Moving, anecdotal support for taking time to assess and treat the child appears in a letter to the editor in the *Wall Street Journal* (January 19, 2021) submitted by a Nurse Practitioner Bob Beerman (who uses the popular "gender" but means, in my language, "sex").

"In my 37 years of practicing medicine, I have had approximately 25 patients who were unhappy with their birth gender."

Some of them, he notes, moved toward surgery.

He describes two who "spent north of $500,000 of insurance money for urogenital surgery, plastic surgery, and hormonal treatment. Both later asked how to change back to their original, biological gender."

Brain sex dysphoria, which may end up needing surgery to align with the body, and gender dysphoria are still anomalous in human evolution. When something is anomalous, we should assess, affirm, decide if treatment is needed, and practice a deep patience that protects the child.

Second, Utilize Puberty Blockers and/or Hormone Therapy After Wait-and-See. Over six months to a year or more, you have perhaps affirmed the child's gender exploration, set a treatment plan for the depression and other issues, and you are assessing what comes next. If significant use of puberty blockers can be postponed until the child is old enough to have gone through some puberty, that would be ideal for the child's skeletons, tendons, hormonology, brain chemistry, and brain, in most cases. Meanwhile, it is not uncommon for puberty blockers to be used for trans teens, and for other teens whose depression and/or gender dysphoria are so acute that the puberty blockers (hormone therapy) assist in treating the neurochemistry of the depression.

Puberty blockers and hormone therapy are juggling acts and every ball in the air carries risks. Sometimes we might have saved a suicidal child from suicidal depression with use of puberty blockers (to get more on this viewpoint, you might go online to read, "Rain Before Rainbows: The Science of Transgender Flourishing"). Other times, the hormone therapy leads to what Dr. Beerman described—a child's sex is assaulted by the therapy, and the child, once an adult, regrets it. If the child is not suicidal but is trans, starting puberty blockers early in the treatment process might be important to consider, but if the child is gender dysphoric and not trans, puberty blockers may give some help regarding the depression, but that same help might be achieved via other kinds of hormone balancing depression medications that are not as physiologically invasive.

Did You Know?
Some Possible Long-Term Effects of Puberty Blockers

- Delayed growth plate closure
- Lower bone density
- Less development of genital tissue.

Some Possible Short-Term Effects
- Headache, fatigue, insomnia, muscle aches.
- Changes in weight, mood, breast tissue.
- Spotting or irregular periods if puberty blockers don't suppress periods.

Other potential effects from long term use, especially if coupled with surgery, can include infertility, sexual dysfunction, inability to orgasm, and reproductive health issues.

Sometimes I read or hear on social media that "taking time to see if a child needs puberty blockers is analogous to saying that since a gay person is choosing to be gay, he or she should be converted out of that choice." Obviously, this is a false claim, since being gay does not require medication, and puberty blockers are medications. If, without study and time, we target a five or eight or ten-year-old with invasive medication, we might be doing the very thing we have finally stopped doing with gay people: invading the child's natural development with potentially excruciating consequences to that child.

That said, if hormone therapies are used carefully in the care of your child, you may not need to fear their effects, at least in short term use. Dr. Deborah Gore founded and led a trans and gender nonconforming clinic. She told me, "If the child does need puberty blocking hormones, those medications can be like taking meds for depression or like taking puberty blockers given now for young patients who are starting puberty very early. Their use can be reassessed by the child, family, and physician after six months, but if used like many kids are already being prescribed the blockers for these other health reasons, they are probably fine."

Third, After Six Months to a Year of Puberty Blockers or Other Treatment, Reassess. Dr. Gore's point about reassessment cannot be overstated. It is crucial in treating early puberty, male-type depression, female-type depression, brain-sex dysphoria, and gender dysphoria that we constantly reassess. Also important: early puberty itself, as well as other hormone flow and balance issues, can affect teens in ways that look like and likely are dysphoria or depression. I cannot say enough: mood and self-development issues caused by hormonal activity in adolescence may be a piece of the puzzle—we need to look at them before, during and after the use of puberty blockers because of the co-morbidity of gender dysphoria and depression.

Overall, both Time and Team are crucial: a whole *team*, including parents, children, and clinicians that takes the *time* to assess, treat, and affirm the child's evolving identity and personal development. Because there are so many possibilities when dealing with children questioning their sexgender, parents and caregivers need to be both careful and resilient against social pressures that immediately try to take the child in one direction or the other.

Protecting All Our Children

Our culture is generally a supportive one, and our science is meant to be supportive. Like our laws, science should support both majorities and minorities. It should provide pathways to protect everyone in need.

If we try to erase sex, ostensibly to uplift gender, we set women's rights back, and we lose millions of our boys whose sex is at the crux of their issues in their school and other systems. Girls and boys need and want to become women and men with all gender exceptions noted. The majority needs to continue developing toward adult purpose and adult goals of sex because societies flourish when sex, man and women, male and female, are part of adulthood.

Meanwhile, if we try to negate gender exploration–the minority–as inherently harmful, we create divisiveness in our culture that is unnecessary and dangerous to numerous children. As this divisiveness pushes extreme politics, we enter dangers like pushing some LGBTQIA+ activists and some physicians to consider many children as candidates for potentially life-altering treatments when they are not or pushing active opponents of gender fluidity conversations to limit the rights of the gender fluid. Best would be to understand what both sex and gender are, how sexgender works, and how important each part of the puzzle is to empathy and care of our full diversity of children.

Essential Questions

1. Do I know a child who has been diagnosed with gender dysphoria but likely has brain sex dysphoria or is gay?
2. In what ways have sex and gender become so politicized that we lose sight of the human beings we are trying to help?

3. What modifications to "gender affirming care" would I like to see practiced by medical and psychiatric professionals?
4. How can I help all children by bringing "male" and "female" back into the political conversation?
5. Do I see social contagion in my school or community around trans or gender fluidity?
6. How will I help my child to understand both sex and gender?
7. Can I tell my own story of identity development in adolescence to children so that they understand the many stages of identity experimentation they will go through?

Part IV: The Seven Point Plan to Rescue Our Boys

"The world is upheld by the veracity of good men: they make the earth wholesome…the search after a great man is the most serious occupation of manhood."

–Ralph Waldo Emerson,
"It Is Natural to Believe in Great Men."

Introduction

You may have noticed media, social media, and even some books on boys saying, "Well, we don't really know what works to help boys." This sometimes reads, "Nothing is proven yet to help boys except to remove masculine social norms," or "We really need more study on what works before we can say for sure."

With sixty years in the field between us, Sean and I (Michael) no longer agree with these statements. I have been involved in multiple programs nationally and worldwide already proven to help boys, their families, their schools, to gain positive human outcomes. The straw man argument in the Big Three that we don't know what works is, to me, a part of the politics of masculinity that this book has been confronting with you. The straw man argument against proven solutions allows for the writer or social thinker to conclude that the vague "confronting masculinity" is the only thing that works; yet, as we've shown, those politics mainly paralyze male development, even if useful in microsystems. Straw men politics are not enough to rescue our sons, not enough to build family, school, neighborhood, and social life that helps boys to be "great men."

This final part of the book shows that we *do* know a lot about what works to help boys and that a lot has been proven to help boys already. While it is always good to further study boyhood, let's support existing and nascent programs that take on male mental health and sexual dimorphism together. The programs, insights, and frameworks we will feature in Part IV *embrace nature, nurture, and culture*—not just culture and masculinity study. As Sean and I explore dozens of these boy-friendly programs and frameworks with you, we hope you will not just join with them in your community if they exist there, but also form your own versions of them in your world so that you can bring the best of what they stand for into the individual lives of boys in your care.

Part IV lays out a seven plank practical plan for rescuing, nurturing, raising, educating, and supporting our boys.

1. *Raise Boys in a Three Family System* that keeps male nature in mind–this can mean increasing boys' human contact by adjusting their device use and providing *male* motivation and reward in family life.

2. *Care For and Mentor Our Difficult and Hurt Sons* via seven elements of help and healing without succumbing to the paralyzing dominance of ideological politics in social program development.

3. *Train All Educators in How Boys and Girls Learn Differently,* boy friendly education, and proven practical strategies for better cognitive and social-emotional learning across the curriculum.

4. *Help Teachers and School Staff to See the Boy Crisis* in their schools and communities via new tools for teacher and school-wide evaluation based on sex. This will help communities with girls' and trans issues as well.

5. *Disaggregate Education and Other Social Data for Sexgender First,* and then combine this data with race, ethnicity, and other important elements of being–Sean will show you how to do this in your world.

6. *Change College Environments to Be Both Female and Male Friendly,* including changing academic politics to better connect academe to the trades and to workplaces, including apprenticehip programs.

7. *Build New Boy-Friendly Programs and Support Existing Boy-Friendly Programs,* including rites of passage programs and programs that build spiritual development into the maturation of boys.

If we do these things in our society, we will not only raise fine young men at our own micro level but also rescue our modern sons *en masse* from the abandonment and rejection they may feel as social members now. In their own way, each of these boys will then have the chance to become a great man.

Chapter 18

Raise Our Boys to Thrive in a Three Family System

> "There comes a time in every rightly-constructed boy's life when he has a raging desire to go somewhere and dig for hidden treasure."
>
> –Mark Twain

(This chapter is useful for all readers that cross domains of family, extended family, and community.)

HOLDING YOUR OWN CHILD in your arms is a miracle. Holding your grandchild is, too, as I've (Michael) recently learned. In June of 2024 I arrived in Seattle where my daughter, Gabrielle, gave birth to Lev Micah Quen-Murray. The hospital, the C section, the smells and sounds, the anticipation and nervousness, the yearning to protect and support, the deep call from the soul to be a part of the miracle of birth flowed through me as they all had back when Gabrielle, my first child, was born 34 years before and then Davita three years later–another C section, another birth, another miracle–then again in August of 2024 when Davita gave birth to her daughter, Effy Gail Herrington.

The miracles of my grandchildren's births were amplified, I think, because just before my daughters became parents and I became a grandfather a deep loss attached itself to our family. My children and I lost my wife, their mother, Gail, in the summer of 2023. Gail and I had been together 39 years and married 37. Pancreatic cancer took her swiftly and painfully. Just a few weeks after Gail died, Gabrielle got pregnant and then, two months later, Davita followed. Our family believes (without scientific proof but with spiritual happiness) that Gail watched over our daughters and their husbands from her mysterious perch; gave to them the lives that she, ready to retire from her counseling practice to take care of grandchildren, wanted most in her elder years: the miracle of grandchildren.

217

As I get older (66 now) and look back on a lifetime of service in the field of child development, I am even more inclined to see the life of each beautiful, fragile child as miraculous. We will all make mistakes raising our children so why not start out with a sense of the great and the grand, a belief in the miracle? Why not keep trying to feel the joy of life accompany us through a tough journey of parenting, life, love, and, inevitably, too, loss? Perhaps the best parent I have ever met was my wife, Gail, and even she made mistakes as a parent, but she never lost sight of the joy she wanted children to experience. Human beings think about what we're doing as parents more than our animal siblings do in the natural world. This chapter will add to those thoughts. I hope you will never let all your thinking erase the sense of the miracle you held in your small and trembling hands as you began the journey of parenting your children.

Rescuing Our Boys in a Three Family System

In *The Wonder of Boys* (1996) I introduced the concept of *The Three Family System* as the strongest system available to us for raising healthy children. I gave proof of concept from our human past via the field of anthropology: when all of our ancestors and relatives raised healthy children, whatever their race, culture, or continent of origin, they did so in *three families: a nuclear unit, extended families,* and *tribes.* In the last thirty years, proof of the three-family-system concept has continued via others in the fields of anthropology, psychology, and medicine. Children raised in three families have the best outcomes in adulthood because they mature their boys not in isolation but with male fragility constantly mentored and directed toward the common good of becoming a man.

What is a man?

A man is a *loving, wise, and successful male adult.*

Every boy will become a male adult because biology will propel him through puberty (even a trans boy will become a biological adult). Does every boy become a *man?* He does if the three families work in tandem to raise him through challenges, education, moral development, and the passions of love. Three families together make him into a man. "It takes a village," translates in my model to, "It takes a healthy three family system."

The Three Families

Mothers and fathers are the child's first and most significant caregivers. On them he will place his greatest trust, as will the siblings he is raised with.

Single parents and gay/lesbian couples also form a *first family* (nuclear) family. They know the importance of two-sex (sexually dimorphic) influences as they ask their male friends and other male mentors to help them nurture this boy through adolescence. Among the hundreds of single mothers and lesbian couples I have interviewed in my career, only one, politically motivated, disagreed with, "When my son started moving through puberty, I knew that I (we) needed to make sure he had good men in his life." Boys need healthy moms and dads wherever they find them.

The good men who join the nuclear unit become *second family members*. These are caregivers and relationship builders, grandmothers and grandfathers, aunts and uncles, best friends, parents of best friends, coaches, favorite teachers, other mentors. Like the limbic system of the brain wraps around the brain stem, the second family wraps around the first family to protect, provide for, nurture, challenge, and grow the boy into a healthy man. Sometimes, a boy who lacks a healthy second family will find an unhealthy second family in a gang.

Faith-communities, schools, media, culture, academe, government institutions, neighborhoods and communities form a *third family*. This communal family gives a boy his tribe, his rites of passage, the boy-into-man journey of sports, his skill building, games, spiritual process, and other supportive practice focused both on persons and also on the raising of *males* into adulthood. While parents give the most intimate care to the boy, extended family give care and skill-building as well as moral development, the tribe gives the boy a sense of purpose and belonging and mission that become an integral part of male motivation and focus.

This third family wraps around the second and first families in the same way the top of the brain wraps around the limbic system that wraps around the brain stem. A family's and culture's sacred job includes shaping maleness into what is useful to compassionate service of family and world. As social media and media take up more and more of our children's time digitally today, some healthier third family elements have decreased in influence. This is a trend we all must continue to be vigilant against. We want a boy's third family to like him, to think he is worthy. If the third family is denouncing him for being male, we must try to keep him safe from those attacks, too, or at least train him about how to respond.

Bi-Strategic and Multi-Strategic Families

In all our families, we need to make sure our sons have *bi-strategic parenting*. The lesbian parents who sought male help for their son sensed what most parents sense, that moms and dads parent differently. Mom and other women tend to provide *maternal nurturance.* Dad and other men tend to provide *paternal nurturance.* Of course, because each nurturer is a unique person, together we all provide *multi-strategic* parenting, but meanwhile, parents, grandparents, other family members, coaches, and other close mentors employing their myriad strategies for resilience-building will often lean toward maternal or paternal nurturance.

Did You Know?
Maternal and Paternal Nurturance Are Different

For reasons primarily of brain biology, but also of nurture and culture, these patterns exist worldwide. In Part II, I provided many of the sexually dimorphic reasons for this via X and Y chromosomes. For instance, girls and women do words on both sides of the brain with connectivity to emotions on both sides, but males tend to do words/connectivity on the left not on the right; females develop frontal lobe connectivity earlier than males; moms and women utilize 10 times more white matter activity (spreading data throughout the brain instantaneously) whereas the male brain utilizes up to 7 times more gray matter activity (focuses and lateralizes brain activity, with less internal variety of input); and males have 10 to 20 times more testosterone in their blood and brain than girls and women, which channels their lives more through rough and tumble aggression whereas females utilize more oxytocin in their bloodstream and brain, a bonding chemical that tends to elongate intimately sensorial bonding experiences. All these differences add up to maternal and paternal patterns.

Maternal Nurturers/Mothers Tend to:

1. Bond with kids in a *greater variety* of ways than dads
2. Provide more constant *hands-on* and *needs-based* attachment
3. Emphasize *multi-tasking* development
4. Help children and others express emotions in *words*
5. Search for methods of *direct empathy*
6. *Relinquish personal/daily independence* to meet others' needs

7. Treat others as *public allies* even if privately they dislike the other person
8. Promote development through *verbal encouragement/ praise*
9. Help kids feel *better and feel more.*

Paternal Nurturers/Fathers Tend to:

1. Bond with kids in *shorter bursts*
2. Teach more order and *pattern thinking* via ritualized action
3. Downplay *emotion,* up-play *performance*
4. Promote *risk-taking and independence*
5. Expect/enforce discipline – *provide contests/tests of skill*
6. Fight against *personal/group vulnerability*
7. Guide kids toward *authority-thinking*
8. Encourage *immediate action* as path to self-worth
9. Help kids feel *stronger via a smaller feeling/emotion array than women tend to use.*

Children develop best when they get all 18 of these elements from parents via *bi-strategic parenting*–two parents. If the mom is more paternal and the dad more maternal, there is nothing wrong with that. What is important is that kids are getting different parenting tendencies both as bi-strategic fundamental practices and as 18 micro-practices.

It is one of the social myths of our time that moms and dads (or two moms/two dads) must parent the same way, and if they don't, they should be accused of being "inconsistent." While children need parents to share values consistently, children do NOT need parents to parent in the same way. Just the opposite: as the fatherhood and dad-deprivation research has shown for fifty years, children need different parents to *parent differently* so that the child's development (specifically, his/her connectivity between the midbrain and frontal lobe) happens sooner rather than later. In other words, if everyone parented the same way, children would not mature well.

If one parent coddles the child, we hope the other parent does not (as much).

If one parent uses more empathy nurturance, we hope the other parent uses more aggression nurturance (remember, aggression nurturance is not violence).

If one parent defines protection of the psyche of the child as letting the child do whatever he wants, we hope the other parent defines resilience as challenging the child to grow up via work ethic.

Whatever the differences in parenting, as long as neither parent is abusing the child, parental difference is generally useful to the maturation of your child, and bi-strategic/multi-strategic parenting has proven useful since the beginning of time.

Solution-Oriented Parenting Resources to Help the Three Families

Over the last three decades, I have researched and written a book (or more) from every angle of child development to assist the three families in raising, educating, and counseling their sons to thrive. Each of these books is solution-oriented and they are all still in print, if you would like to delve deeply into each topic. The list of topics include what I have been asked about in my clinical practice, in my travels to hundreds of communities, and via our podcast, *The Wonder of Parenting Podcast: A Brain Science Approach to Parenting*. These latter questions have mainly come from moms about raising boys, but fathers, extended family members, educators, counselors, and policy-makers have also inspired me to fulfill these topics and resources.

Try This
Use Gurian Resources on Helping Boys Thrive

- *The Wonder of Boys* covers core topics on raising boys in one book with help targeted more toward raising younger boys.
- *A Fine Young Man* focuses on helping boys in the stages of male development from pre-puberty through adolescence and into young adulthood.
- *The Good Son* focuses on moral development, emphasizing social-emotional development as part of character development, not a replacement for it.
- *Saving Our Sons* focuses on new research in male development with chapters on motivating boys via stages of healthy digital use in two year increments.

- *Boys and Girls Learn Differently, The Minds of Boys,* and sequels in this group of books, written with my colleagues in the education field, cover each part of the school-home connection, from Pre-K through college.
- *The Purpose of Boys* focuses on how to help boys find meaning, mission, and a sense of purpose.
- *The Prince and the King* focuses on the stages of the father-son relationship, and on father-loss and the father-wound.
- *The Invisible Presence* focuses on the stages of mother-son relationship, including mothers' relationships with young adult sons.
- *Raising Boys by Design* is for Christian readers, co-authored with Christian Psychologist Dr. Gregory Jantz. You'll find core themes of boyhood in this book from both the scientific and religious perspective.
- *How Do I Help Him?* is for counselors, psychiatrists, medical professionals, and anyone working with boys in clinical practice. Parents often read it, too, as they select a counselor for their son to determine if the counselor might work well with boys.

As you may have seen in the list of titles at the beginning of this book, I have also written books on raising girls, on marriage and relationships, and on empowering women in the workplace. Most of those are still in print, should you want to access them.

Because my books are strategies–and solutions–oriented, if you decide to delve into them whether as a parent, spouse, extended family member, or professional, you will take away dozens of tools and resources to use right away in your three family system.

Imprinting Social Theory on Three Families

A pregnant mother with a boy growing inside her knows him intimately before he enters the world. Then his 4-D ultrasounds show her and the boy's father various facial expressions responding to the foods that mom eats and the smells that make their way to him through her amniotic fluid. Mom feels him kick and move. The boy will remember Mom's heart beat after he leaves the womb.

The baby will also come to know the father's voice, and differentiate touch and smells associated with him. Fathers who talk and read to the fetus are already communicating, letting the boy hear the male voice connected to life, essence, and soul. The father will become, most likely, the primary model of maleness the boy will wonder over, disagree with, agree with as this man does his part to help sculpt the boy's brain and body into manhood.

These parents generally know, at a gut level, that "my son is different from my daughter," or "this is a boy," or "he's all boy some of the time but other times not…" or "he is male." Parents are generally un-political realists: they live the life of the child, whoever the child is, whatever his or her sex, accommodating and shaping that child's approach to the future world. Second family members, too, generally follow this model as well–grandparents play a caregiving role in the life of the boy, establishing a rich legacy of truth, love, and compassion that accepts the boy for who he is while also mentoring, teaching skills and hobbies, listening and talking. Today, some grandparents are first family, if parents are unavailable; or they are hands-on childcare providers for busy, two-parent working families, single parent homes, or adopted children, and foster children. These second family members generally know that this boy is a boy and want to help him become a man–a loving, wise, and successful male adult.

In the first or second family, external ideas can sometimes enter the child-raising, ideas like, "a boy is not a boy, not a he," or "males are inherently defective so we need to re-engineer them," or "males are bad guys, stupid, worthless," or "he's too masculine," or "he's not masculine enough," but these ideas from the outside are generally sorted through and tossed out, at least for a while, because the intimacy and love the caregivers have for the boy is love of the son as a *boy*. Even when the first and second family experiment with input from some people in the third family, e.g., "We don't want him to be masculine," or "I think he's too male," still, most first and second family members try to protect the boy from this confusion by focusing their child on boyhood rather than on cultures of the exception or other culture-constructs. All this because there is significant DNA inheritance behind the male focus that generally encourages the first and second family's approach to their young males.

In the past, not just the first or second but all three families focused on "boy" somewhat relentlessly because by the time the male reached what we call adolescence, the family and community already needed him to protect them, provide for them, and soon, sire children that the parents, grandparents, and uncles and aunts would care for while the boy finished growing up. There was less culture influence in our human past, very few books and little media, no social media, internet, journalism, and little external social construction and deconstruction of family or boy. For most of our human past, while some males did bad things, maleness itself was an asset supported, challenged, and mentored by all three families.

In our human past, too, cultures and third family communities understood that males did bad things because they were not matured well; they were not taught values of manhood well enough, values of strength, security, confidence, empathy, care, service, protection, resilience, and love. Our ancestors knew, as the African proverb says, "If we don't take good care of our males, they will burn down the village." Three families united in growing males into good men because they had to do this to survive and thrive. The three families used various touchstones for healthy male development that I have updated here.

Try This
Teach Ten Touchstones of Healthy Male Development

In all three families, these ten primary principles of healthy male development are ones families have taught boys to be and do throughout human history and still want to teach. I initially provided these to readers in *The Wonder of Boys* thirty years ago and have updated them to fit our post-modern era.

These are the ten root principles of a sacred male role I ask us to name Husbandry (so that we can see past "masculine role" politics). By focusing on husbandry as the target of manhood, we can gather families together to teach healthy touchstones. If you and the three families around you teach boys these touchstones, I believe your boys will have the most success in life—and through them, your family and community will thrive as well. These touchstones fill in after "Become a man who…"

1. Seeks balance of family devotion, life-sustaining work, and personal spiritual development.
2. Provides for, protects, and nurtures those he is called to love.
3. Actively participates in not just one but three families.
4. Lives in concert with the natural world, including discovering solitude in nature with which to both recharge his soul and internally solve issues in his life.

5. Seeks equal partnerships with women, girls, females, and sexgender exceptions.
6. Seeks and finds male kinship systems–other men to share life with, support, and be supported by at the primal level of maleness.
7. Lives as an agent of service, social dialogue, and social change–always with the purpose of serving.
8. Knows the epic and healthy story he is living, including his own evolving identities.
9. Takes the time with family and community to enjoy the fruits of his labor.
10. Is open to change and when necessary is open to letting go.

Third family influence on raising boys into men changed quite a bit starting around a hundred and fifty years ago, in some ways for the better in children's lives, and in some ways for the worse. As the third family became a monolithic industrial then post-industrial culture it found a vehicle and a voice for constant streams of new social ideations such that family wisdom often got (and gets) denigrated or replaced by the excitement of ideologies in the Big Three. Starting around sixty years ago, these ideas were generated first at universities, then moved into government and media, then started to influence family and social systems away from healthy male development. Feminist shifts were and are generally good for humanity as a whole because they are generally good for girls and women and somewhat good for boys and men, but they also created harm for males in the three family system, as we've analyzed in this book.

When Gloria Steinem famously said, "A woman needs a man like a fish needs a bicycle," some feminists applied this toward the degradation of males and even the erasure of *male* in the third, then second, then first family. But until the last twenty years or so, this third family degradation of males was not a denial of *sex* because female was still sacrosanct as sex. Quickly, though, and couched in "masculinity" discussions and the culture of the exception, degradation of *male* has evolved and continues in the third family–even moving into second and first–with a vengeance.

The DGP, Especially Media, as Third Family

If you are raising children, you may not have the time or energy to fully feel the influence of culture on your daily family tasks, but they are there. You might seek out faith communities that help you enjoy good values or help you fend off some of the values you and your children are getting through the media. You might align yourselves with certain tribes in social media that fit your family values. Especially via TV, Google, YouTube, Facebook, Instagram, journalism, Tik Tok, and social media, you might ask questions and get culture-answers from people you don't know, academics and psychologists with websites and programs, government agencies that exist to help you, and other organizations with resources. Parents today are intimate with the third family through devices–and so are our kids and grandkids.

If your son has early access to devices for information, communication, and entertainment, the third family culture-influence can significantly denigrate his journey of self-respect and his respect for others. From media and culture, he can learn about his excessive privilege as a male or about his abject worthlessness as a male and, often, both at once. He may also learn to treat women badly, to be selfish rather than of service, to destroy nature rather than protect its solitudes. Each boy today tries to figure out where he stands in all frays, and many boys sit on their couches somewhat defeated because they cannot win as males either or whichever way. Boys often read third family influence as saying, "You should exist in limbo, and your manhood may not be needed anyway."

This is especially true if the boy does not have healthy and intimate female and male influence in the first and second families. While in the past males and fathers have often been away from families for work or war, and while fathers often died in these environments leaving their children with moms and extended family members (fathers being gone and away from children is not new), what is new now is the third family denigration of males, men, fathers, and male fraternity to such an extent that males exist degraded. Yes, it is true that some males "have it all," but they are not necessarily the young men in your care. Actions crucial in our human past such as the mentoring of maleness into the ten touchstones of healthy manhood have become, in some DGP controlled landscapes, the rotten fish the bicycle does not need. How does a family navigate this?

By *choosing* the third family influences that are most healthy for your son as a young male. This may mean raising your children with constant dinner table discussions about "male," "female," "gender" and "what messages are males getting that are unhealthy in our culture?" "What is a man?" "When do you become a man?" "Who are the men you admire?" "What influences exist around you that are derailing you from healthy maleness and manhood?" Discussions on questions like these *in all three families* might become a discussion of healthy masculine training in certain communities or of unhealthy denial and degradation of males via masculinity politics throughout the culture.

Raising your son in the healthy and safe three-family system you have chosen in which the ten elements of healthy male development are touchstones *and repeated discussion points* will help your son build resilience even through life-derailing traumas, including the trauma of being confused about what a healthy male is. And when trauma does occur in a boy's life, you will have a healthy three family system around you to provide the seven elements needed to heal the male heart and soul that Sean will explore in the next chapter.

Essential Questions and Try This
Seven Best Practices in the Three Families

Given where we are now in relation to boys and men as a society and given the proven viability of a three-family-system for raising boys into good men, here are seven best practices you can put into place right away that I am wrapping around questions.

1. *Have you ensured that your child has a strong and healthy nuclear family, however it is formed, that includes both maternal and paternal nurturance?* It is useful to focus on keeping both the mother and father intimately attached with your son. Exceptions to this, of course, would be significantly unhealthy, mentally ill, or violent parents who will likely need to be removed from care of the child, but we must remember: a mom-deprived or dad-deprived son is at more risk for many possible difficulties later in life.

2. *Have you planned your boy's development with your own sense of the stages of male development in mind?* For instance, if you are a mom, you can plan on how to remain close with your son throughout your life but also, how you will let your son go into the arms of healthy men (fathers, male role models) as the boy becomes a tween and then a teen. Mom is not devalued or disengaged in male adolescence, but Mom's

relationship with her sons involves her own emotional journey of separation from the boy so that males can join her in training him to become a good man. For Mom to let him go, though, she needs to make sure there are healthy men around him. I hope you will plan that out from very young in the boy's life.

3. *Are you controlling your son's screen and device use?* It will be best not to give your child significant use of devices, screens, gaming, internet, YouTube, Tik Tok, etc. until he is well into puberty and adolescence. Excessive device-use in toddler and early years (parents giving their children their phones to play with in restaurants) becomes gaming at 5 or 6 and then screen time in excess of 2 hours a day (not including at school) by 7 or 8, then social media overuse at 9 or 10, and so on. We must remember that healthy cognitive, social emotional, and physical development of boys–healthy maturation into adulthood–is affected to the danger point by excessive device and screen use. In *Saving Our Sons,* I provide a staged model for device use in two-year increments from birth to adulthood.

4. *Have you provided your sons with healthy second family influence and healthy activities to fill in the time he would be on devices and screens?* For the three hours per day that boys are on screens right now, you might substitute three hours of activities with peers, skill building with grandparents, time with family members, church and youth groups, martial arts, sports and athletics, music and dance–activities that have built into them second family mentors and coaches from whom the boy can learn healthy manhood.

5. *In what ways can you substitute healthy third family systems and institutions for screentime?* You can advocate in your schools for healthy and boy-friendly classrooms (we will provide even more practical strategies for this in the next chapters). You can provide large group activities for boys through athletics, orchestra, band, other clubs, Big Brothers Big Sisters, Boy Scouts,

and other similar male mentoring for all boys and especially for fatherless sons. You can join your sons to government and non-profit programs in underserved communities that help you raise your boys. You can enter faith communities to help your boys gain moral, spiritual, and social development.

6. *Are you being wary enough of the danger of environmental neurotoxins on male brain development?* Because the gut microbiome is a second brain, you can protect your sons from junk food, high fructose corn syrup, soda and pop, too much sugar, picky eating (boys need all the food groups as much as possible even if they have a brain disorder like autism that may be comorbid with picky eating). As a family, you can eat healthy meals with your children during the week and do so without any devices at the table–just talking together, socializing, resolving conflicts, listening, being together in the journey of male development.

7. *Can you do all these things for your daughters and other children, as well?* Healthy practices and systems for male development will also help girls and young women, and boys and girls with gender or brain-sex dysphoria. "Male development," "female development," and "gender development" are all interconnected because every child is humanly interconnected. Differentiated development by sex does not negate humanity–it increases human safety and human development across the board.

Chapter 19

Provide Seven Nurturing Elements to Boys Who Are in Trouble

"In ordinary life, a mentor can guide a young man through various disciplines, helping to bring him out of boyhood into manhood; and that in turn is associated…with building an emotional body capable of containing more than one sort of ecstasy."

–Robert Bly

(This chapter is useful for general readership, parents, and professionals involved in education, social work, and the court system.)

IN SPRING 2024, I (Sean) held a roundtable conversation with parents and members of the community in Livermore, California. Supported by The Global Initiative for Boys and Men, National Coalition for Men, and the American Institute for Responsible Research, the roundtable provided parents, grandparents, teachers and others a sense of the educational landscape for boys in K-12, in the trades, and in postsecondary education. I wanted those in attendance to interact, ask questions, and provide insights themselves, as citizen scientists. In the Livermore roundtable, as in others around the world, it was palpably clear that people in the grassroots care a lot about children, are very smart, and are frustrated with what is happening around them to our boys.

A woman named Christine stood up to speak and she made people cry, laugh, and open their hearts to the struggles of boys. She reminded me of the mothers I grew up with in Northeast Philadelphia who could put a boy in his place in the blink of an eye without making him feel angry or ashamed of being a boy. He knew her caring was genuine, especially when he was in the wrong or simply uncertain. Christine told us that she worked with child welfare students and had done so for 17 years. "I hang out with the ones who are undesirable, the ones that get into trouble, that don't have fathers in the home." She smiled, "one of these 'bonus sons' I snatched up–he is like my own son now." This boy was not an adoptive or fostered son; he was a mentored son, a second family boy who became almost a first-family boy for Christine. He became a boy given possibility and hope at a time when he was headed in the wrong direction.

Christine works with girls, too, professionally, but made a point at the event to say that "most of these lost kids I work with are boys, and they have been for many years. I try to help them get a high school diploma, and many of them do, but I got a couple of my boys sitting in Santa Rita Jail, Pelican Bay, San Quentin, Folsom—for murder." Her tone said, "I can't save everyone." Then Christine returned to talking about her bonus son who grew up like many of his peers, "with a single mom, living in a car for three years while in elementary school. People didn't know he was homeless. It was hard because I watched adults in our school go after him because they didn't like him. He was Hispanic, he hung around gangs, and they all thought he was a piece of crap. I pushed him to get grades. I pushed him to go to class. I pulled his grades weekly. I pushed him to do sports. But people make it hard for these guys to do it…. Most of my kids will not go to college but maybe I can get them to go to a trade school."

Christine and her daughter joining her spoke truth about the educational and life outcomes of boys growing up in fatherless homes whose educational experience is disrupted by poverty, homelessness, abuse, gang life, and a lack of direction. While these circumstances can impact all children, boys are more likely than girls to be suspended, land in juvenile detention, and land in prison as adults. As we've noted, the school-to-prison pipeline is an overwhelmingly male problem.

Percent of Suspensions, Juvenile Detentions, and Prison Population in Select States that are Male

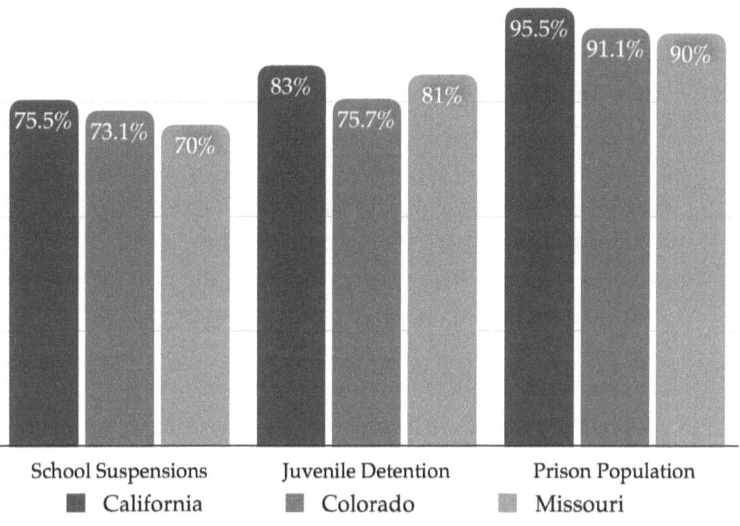

Source: Global Initiative for Boys and Men State Reports
https://www.gibm.us/state-reports

What worked for Christine to help this "bonus son"? What works to help these millions of boys on our streets? Christine and many others are essential to the three family structure that Michael discussed in the previous chapter and they have shown us what works.

Try This
What Works for Our Traumatized Sons

- Provide homes for these boys with their relatives even if in another state or with other families (e.g. families of their peers) or foster and adoptive families or with "bonus" families to get them off the streets and into *healthy male developmental frameworks.*
- Adjust police, criminal justice, and court systems to understand *male nature, nurture, and culture—all three.* This training encourages police to handle boys differently and family court judges to order shared custody when

appropriate, including more time with the father or grandfathers, uncles, and other surrogate fathers, especially once boys reach pre-puberty and puberty years.

- Focus the boy on education as *a place of belonging*—that means building schools and apprenticeship programs that understand boys, including training for teachers on boy-friendly education and encouraging the development of male teachers and male teachers of color in school systems.

- *Provide safety nets for these traumatized boys* via boy-friendly social programs, mentoring agencies, and psychiatric and counseling systems while coaching the boys toward resilience and independence so that they can grow beyond their safety net in full adulthood.

- Counter gang affiliation with *healthy adult male group affiliations* via faith communities, secular men's groups in government and non-profit agencies that are devoted to the healthy development of boys, male-friendly options in prison systems, and male-friendly treatment facilities.

- *Provide one healthy father or male role model for every boy in our culture.* This means supporting programs like Big Brothers and Big Sisters by becoming a Big Brother or volunteering in church so that every boy without a father or estranged from his father has a second father to become a primary second family support to him. This also means that all fathers and male role models will provide rites of passage programs with middle school then high school age boys. We provide the names of some of these already successful rites-of-passage programs in our last chapter.

- *Provide alternatives to unhealthy masculine norms where we see them*, including where we see boys embracing male bravado as the only framework for their being. Programs like M.A.N.C.A.V.E. featured earlier in this book, which has just merged with Dad Together, take on issues of boys and the male brain while also confronting unhealthy masculine norms.

In reference to one of the points in the box: the inclusion of more male teachers in school systems is part of an expanded effort to offer new career paths for men and a way to help our boys learn with diversity that teaching is a career choice they, too, can make. I am all for these efforts. At the same time, let's be careful not to say that women can't be good teachers and counselors of males.

An elementary school teacher, a friend, has four sons. She told me that she was not as good a teacher as she is now until she had boys and, thus, had to learn how the male brain works. She told me she wished she learned about brain-sex differences during her teacher training in college, but it was a topic openly ignored. Decades later, she is now well versed in the boys-and-girls-learn-differently brain-based perspective and shares her knowledge with younger teachers in her school. In trying to get more male teachers, we mustn't forget that most teachers are and will likely be female. Let' not ignore or neglect teaching the teachers we have—many of whom are moms like this woman—brain-friendly best practices to use at home and at work with boys and young men.

Similarly, in the counseling, social work, and psychology fields—more males will be helpful, but most practitioners will continue to be female. As we work to get more men and men of color in education and counseling, we must simultaneously encourage all colleges and training programs to provide counselors and educators with the training they need to work effectively with boys and men at a baseline—and then with boys and men who have been traumatized. Women will always be on these front lines.

On the seventh point in the box, about masculine norms, Michael has shared with me that we must understand where the "hypermasculine" boys and men are coming from when they take on unhealthy masculine norms after or during trauma. Clinically, he has found, as have many other clinicians in this field, that these young males go into survival mode, like Christine's bonus son. These boys in survival mode need identities of male empowerment just like every boy does, but they need them quicker than other boys might because of poverty, abuse, dad deprivation, homelessness, violence, or other trauma. These traumatized boys do not have the luxury of a long adolescence in which to become a loving, wise, and successful male adult. By the time they become tweens, many of them have already taken on survival-identity elements that will, at first, save them; including one of the most dangerous, a gang affiliation. From the outside we may condemn them for "becoming too masculine" and for joining gangs, but from where they live, that kind of life feels like the best way to survive, even thrive.

Gangs use similar patterns as human traffickers to hook, victimize, and burden society. They take young people away from healthy society and prepare them for lives of crime and exploitation.

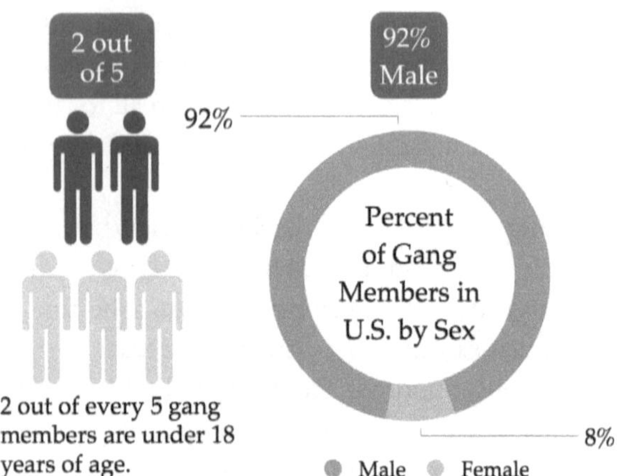

2 out of every 5 gang members are under 18 years of age.

Source: National Gang Center
https://nationalgangcenter.ojp.gov/survey-analysis/demographics#anchoragebyareatype

Healthy maleness is a part of every boy's survival, and unhealthy maleness gets added on by traumatized boys and by non-traumatized but immature boys who try to speed up their survival maturation via unhealthy "masculine" development. Christine, smartly, saw her bonus son as a *male* who needed the seven elements we just listed. As she gave him the first six, she could work with him to deconstruct some of the male stereotypes (the seventh) that he had to gravitate toward for survival up till then. She worked on getting him a home, social services, good education, male role models, and over time, a new and better life. By taking this "bonus son" on as a beautiful project of personalized male development and growth, and by bringing healthy male mentors into his life, she bought him the time to thrive in a society that had rejected and abandoned him.

Essential Questions

- Does your community or school have third-family support systems in place that can directly target traumatized boys for survival and thriving?
- Is your community and school system successfully hiring teachers who understand the intersection of 1) brain-sex difference training and 2) how trauma affects boys' learning and male brain development?
- Does your church or faith community have a male mentoring program that helps guide boys and young men, especially those without fathers/male figures in their lives, toward healthy male development and purpose?
- Do you know if boys in your school and community are affiliated with gangs and what alternatives does your school/community offer for healthy male mentoring and peer bonding than the gangs?
- Does your school system identify boys (and girls) who come from fatherless homes as "higher risk" for poor school and behavior performance, and is that school system providing mentoring and services to these children?
- Does your school have an active relationship with the Police Athletic League (PAL)? Does your community have a PAL program? These programs can help bond citizens with police in ways that further community safety.

Chapter 20

Train All Schools in Boy-Friendly Practices

"Tell me and I forget. Teach me and I remember. Involve me and I learn."

–Benjamin Franklin

(This essay is useful for general readers and particularly useful for PTAs, educators, school administrators, and school boards.)

BY THE TIME I (Sean) met Michael Gurian in person, I had heard about his work and the Gurian Institute's professional development already. I knew that, for three decades, Michael and the GI (Gurian Institute) team had codified best practices for educators, parents, and mental health counselors–best practices now being taught in some university courses (though for reasons of gender politics we discussed in Part III, still too few). Gurian-training and interventions work to help *all* children because they target sexgender to include racial and ethnic diversity. GI training covers nature, nurture, and culture, which is inclusive of both majority and minority populations.

GI's most used programs are:

> Boys and Girls Learn Differently®
> The Minds of Boys and Girls®
> Helping Boys Thrive®

I learned about Michael and GI when I was at a school that required students to give up their elective course senior year and take a remedial course in Math or ELA (English Language Arts. These students were not scoring proficient or advanced on the Pennsylvania System of School Assessment (PSSA), Pennsylvania's state testing in K-12 education. At the beginning of the year, just before I taught one of the two sections in ELA, I looked at each student's previous performance. This pre-assessment gave me a chance to identify specific skill deficits in boys and girls and to offer up a curriculum that worked best to prepare them to retake the test at the end of the year.

I was blessed with an administration that allowed me to develop my course to include *attention to learning differences between the sexes.* From reading specialists and special education teachers who often use Gurian programs and training (in part because 75% of special education students are boys), I learned about the book *Boys and Girls Learn Differently.* From there, I learned about the Gurian Institute's best practices trainings. Because my reading class was populated mainly by boys, I wanted to make sure I was teaching them well. I integrated Gurian's best practices with my own strong intuitions as a teacher to build my own boy-friendly classroom.

Try This
What Works for Challenging Boys

- I allowed the students to focus on short stories, articles, poems, and informational texts that boys and girls *wanted* to read. Books about "doing stuff" help engage boys (science fiction, fantasy battles, How To books on building and exploring). Girls might like these, but girls also tend to gravitate toward books that are more relational and verbal and are longer with more words.
- I let my students (and encouraged them) to move around in class as much as they wanted to. My room, fortunately, had access to classroom arrangements that did not force sitting down in rows for long periods of time. As you learned in Part 2, without moving around, many boys will at some point in an hour go to a "rest state," the boredom state wherein they learn little or nothing. The female brain does not generally go to this kind of rest state even while sitting for long periods of time, but girls can get bored, and can enjoy moving around, too, so the strategy assisted them, as well.
- Graphic organizers, drawing, and reading graphic novels were all allowed and encouraged. Because so much more of the right side of the male brain is devoted to graphics and pictures (the right side of the female brain uses some of this right hemisphere space for word centers), GI strategies

> focus on use of graphics, pictures, videos, visuals, and kinesthetic and graphic art to stimulate the male brain as holistically as the female brain is, generally, already stimulated with purer verbal (written, spoken, and read) input. Using a lot of graphics in my class led to much better final papers.

- I utilized competition among individuals and groups of students somewhat like the Houses in *Harry Potter* novels to motivate my learners. While competition is useful for girls and everyone, males often need competition urgently–for self-motivation, reward-seeking, to get better grades, and to do the work. When Michael has been asked if more competition in schools and classrooms will go against the concept of cooperative learning, he says, "No, because competition done right is the epitome of cooperative learning." Individual students and their teams must cooperate to compete.

Boys and Girls Learn Differently by Gurian and his GI colleagues (Jossey-Bass/John Wiley, 2001, 2011), and the series of workbooks and further books emerging from that original work, include more than a hundred strategies like these for pre-K through college classrooms. You can also look at one school that employs them in all classrooms by visiting the Crespi Carmelite High School website (www.crespi.org). There you will find the White Paper that Michael and his colleagues wrote about Crespi classrooms and culture after studying Crespi comprehensively. There are many good strategies reflected in that Paper.

In my classes, I made sure to include digital flexibility, too–allowing students to download articles for further reading. I used boy-friendly strategies to help students develop topic sentences, understand the definition of a word they did not know by using context clues, research the author of the article, and discuss his/her point of view. To avoid my students misconstruing this remedial class as time off, I read every article they read and I read their responses then interacted with the students about them. This helped me to form relationships with each student, which is another teacher effectiveness strategy our boys especially need: they need teacher rapport and respect.

Overall, a teacher who uses boy-friendly strategies tends to get more respect from students than one who does not because the teacher is showing the learners: "I understand and respect you by letting you learn the way you learn best."

By the end of that ELA course, 97% of students passed the state test, with a few of the students scoring advanced. These students told me they remember this class as one of their best that year. Throughout the process of teaching these difficult students, I was thrilled to observe a room in my school transform from an initial place of "failing students" into a home for healthy learners.

Try This
More Strategies from a Gurian Certified Trainer

Jessica Biel is an Educational Specialist in Adolescent Male Development and a Gurian Certified Trainer in North Carolina. She has provided us with these strategies for boy-friendly curriculum, classroom management, and counsel.

1. *Word of the Month.* This has been one of my most successful tactics in changing focus and behavior. I sit with the student until we decide the word of the month. Sometimes he tells me what the word is, and sometimes, in observing his behavior, I make the suggestion for the word, and we go from there. Then I draw something that would be a good visual and have him explain it to me. I draw the diagram to build a higher register of understanding. We are purposeful in using a word that is current to what he is experiencing in life at that moment.

For example, *ownership*: We chose this word as this student was constantly shifting blame and not taking responsibility for himself. The visual was the word OWNER next to a picture of a ship. It was understood that once you take "ownership" of you, the issue, the responsibility, the avoidance, your "ship" begins to navigate correctly. My student added things to the picture about navigation, water, and rough seas. Since we live near the water, boats are common in our community's life. This added relational value: the word had the potential to come back around in school and real-life application.

2. *Brotherhood.* Public school settings can be unfriendly for boys, but I have seen many behavioral issues reduce dramatically when there is a safe space for the fellows to come to do schoolwork, let off steam, and eat lunch together. Oftentimes, in afterschool activities, a brotherhood is built. For boys who need extra help, I use a place within the school and school day. I allow the boys to be boys, but the boys may not say anything to disrespect any female or bad-mouth any administrator. They can vent and joke with each other, though, and have honest conversations about their intimate relationships, talk about "adult" issues, and cry if they need to.

Over the years, I have discovered that, while many brotherhood alliances are led by men, a strong woman who allows the teen age group to build brotherhood within her presence is also a good thing. Women have a lot to teach boys about boundaries, chivalry, respect, what a healthy supportive female looks like, the art of husbandry that Michael Gurian talks about in *The Wonder of Boys*, and how to experience positive rejection/realignment by an older female (who is not their mom!)

3. *Philosophical Wisdom.* I provide the boys with true quotes from identified philosophers, the Bible, Buddha, and others in all cultures. Any teacher or mentor can do this. You can also develop your own "line," insight, or piece of wisdom. For example, I gave a student who was going through a difficult time this line that I came up with one morning: "At the heart of any wound is the answer." I asked for his response. He came back with, "In the middle of difficulty lies opportunity." I responded with "After opportunity comes vision." He replied, "I'm going to think about this today."

At the root of this strategy is not just the sharing (and creating) of human wisdom with boys and not just passing this wisdom into them but also compelling them to create some wisdom out of their own minds, their own brains. While all young men have access to knowledge, very few have wisdom yet, but they want wisdom because wisdom feeds their desire to mature and respect their world. As they interact and meditate on applications of wisdom, on values and weight, they take baby steps to mature beyond their behavioral issues.

4. *Stand Up Desks and Swivel Rockers.* Boys often need movement to be integrated with male-brain learning, so we use stand-up desks with wheels, and as stupid as it sounds, beside my desk are 2 swivel rockers that have solved MANY of my problems with boys. The boys sit and rock and soothe themselves, and then they talk. This is truly a beautiful thing to watch happening–and once they are self-soothed, they behave better and learn better.

5. *Curricula on Financial Management.* Money management is essential for young men not just for their maturation but also as an interest area. Often, parents do not teach their children money management or financial planning or how money operates, but the young men I work with are generally more concerned about making money than anything else. They need to know how finances function. We focus on this topic that is already of automatic interest to them–and so important for their futures.

6. *CTE Courses.* CTE stands for Career and Technical Education. In the state of North Carolina where I live, certain courses can be utilized in exchange for CORE classes. In my school district, Math 3 is a nightmare, so for students who show hindrance in Math 1 and 2, we use Carpentry 1 Math instead of Math 3. For most of my male students, I take this option for both Math 3 and Math 4, which improves their GPA, allows for more movement (carpentry cannot fully happen while sitting still at a desk) and improves attendance. For male students who are disengaged in general math or similar classes, CTE classes are a fantastic way of helping them enjoy school and acquire a diploma. The students also get certifications that can aid them in acquiring a job after they graduate. https://center.ncsu.edu/nccte-cms/ shows what the state of North Carolina has. Your state may have similar options within graduation requirements.

The Boy-Friendly Strategies Help Girls, Too

I remember encouraging one of my female students, Samantha (Sam) to consider moving from one English course up to my Honor's English course. She was reluctant to do so, not confident enough yet, so we worked together over the course of a year on skills that I thought helped her by using some boy-friendly strategies like those I noted above. Several years after graduating from high school and a few years after my family and I moved from Pennsylvania to California, Sam found me on social media to let me know that she had been elected to her borough's city council. She was now the youngest elected official in Delaware County and one of the youngest elected officials in the Commonwealth of Pennsylvania—at the age of twenty-two! After completing her degree in Education, she said she was going to go to law school.

I reached out to her with congratulations, and we reconnected. Then time passed and then time became a few years and then one day she reached out again. We ended up talking on the phone and she said she remembered my class. She said my teaching methods made a huge difference in her life. Now launched in her career as a lawyer in the field of educational law, she still remembered the innovations in that mainstream classroom, and how useful they were to her as a learner. I told her I was writing this book, and we talked about why the strategies work so well not just for boys but with her, too.

While I could not have predicted Sam's life course nor the positive outcomes that many of the students in that mainstream class have gone on to discover in their lives, I did have a teacher's control back then over how to help children learn essential skills to fit their learning brains. Because the GI strategies combine so well with our ultimate goal as teachers, to increase student engagement and improve student outcomes, using them was not only the right thing to do pedagogically, but also a personal joy for me. I had the opportunity to transform my classrooms into brain-friendly *homes* for my learners. Few things feel better than that for an educator committed to bringing the joy of belonging to a room full of learners.

Essential Questions
For Teachers

- Have I been trained in boy- and girl-friendly teaching strategies?
- Am I employing these strategies in my classroom? If so, how many and how often?
- As testing-time comes around, am I targeting specific strategies that help my students score proficient/advanced?
- After using boy-friendly learning and behavioral strategies, do I notice fewer discipline referrals from my classroom to the principal?

For Parents
- Are my son and his friends fulfilling their potential in school or getting into trouble and underperforming?
- If underperforming, have my son's teachers and administration been trained in boy-friendly education?
- Does my son report strategies for physical movement during learning, allowance of healthy aggression-nurturance (rough and tumble play during recess), visual-spatial tools, competition, brain breaks, and other strategies in the school?

If you as parents see few or no male-brain-friendly strategies being used at the school or in a classroom, this may constitute unfairness or bias against boys (usually inadvertent and not malicious by teachers or the system). You can form what Michael calls "a parent-led team," a group of parents of boys who give this book or Michael's *Boys and Girls Learn Differently* or *The Minds of Boys* (education-oriented books with loads of strategies in them) to the school principal.

This parent-led-team approach has been effective already in other schools and counties as principals and powers-that-be look for Title funding to bring the GI training to the school or, if funding is not available, ask you as parents if you would donate the funding. Your parent-led team can inspire the school to see the needs of boys without attacking the principal or teachers.

If you get no interest or help at all from the school administration, you can go farther up the chain in the district office. The graphics and data tools in the next two chapters might become even more useful to you as you move up the school hierarchy to get help for the boys in your school.

Chapter 21

Complete Your Own Classroom Citizen Science

> "It is not always the same thing to be a good person and a good citizen."
>
> –Aristotle

(This essay is useful for all general readers, and especially for parents, educators, school administrators, school boards, mentors, and those involved in afterschool programs.)

ONE OF THE ADVANTAGES of being both a teacher and parent is learning from daily classroom practices and bringing those practices into the home. A strategy I often used with my boy learners who read slowly or otherwise needed some assistance was to introduce them to audio books. I didn't just have them listen to the book–rather, we would listen to the audio book while following along with a physical copy of the book in hand. This is a process known as *immersion reading*. It allowed my students to see and hear the text and–with modern technology–control the speed at which an audio book (and, thus, the physical book) was read.

While using immersion learning in my classroom, I also used it with one of my sons. He had to finish a very long summer reading book during family vacation time. Seeing the dilemma, I encouraged him to use the audio version and physical copy simultaneously. Somewhat a reluctant reader anyway, he would often read less than half of a book over a long stretch of time, which created gaps in recall for him, and affected his grades. Once he decided to try immersion reading, he found himself slowly increasing the speed of the audio as he acclimated to the audiobook narrator. When I spoke with him about the book, I found that his ability to recall details and discuss them more analytically had also improved. When a very difficult second book was introduced early in the school year and the school work was seriously increasing, he opted to use the immersion reading approach.

Measuring Your Own Teacher Effectiveness

Immersion reading is just one of the leading-edge learning strategies we can all use to help boys learn better, these boys constitute most of the bad grades and lowest test scores in our schools. As we help our boys, we see changes occur in school districts and schools in these areas:

- Decreased gender achievement gaps
- Decreased bullying in the school culture
- Lowered discipline referrals to administration
- Reduced suspensions, expulsions, and fewer dropouts
- Increased student and teacher engagement across the curriculum.

If you are an educator, you can test out the strategies and measure outcomes yourself by studying each category of improvement as a citizen scientist. This helps you see which strategies are needed and helpful in your educational sphere.

You can chart, as I did in my classrooms:

1. where each student started and ended;
2. your own relationship and rapport with the students; and
3. how each student used which strategies to help them learn better.

Some students may not need any strategies–they are sponges and get great grades no matter what–but most students in my classrooms did improve in one of the five areas above by both my use of boy-friendly strategies, and by the school's systemic interest in making its educational pedagogy equally a female-brain focused/girl-friendly and a male-brain focused/boy-friendly culture.

To start out your own citizen science, pick five Gurian strategies from previous chapters, or others you know about, and use them over a month-long period. Try using some of the strategies daily (Brain Breaks only involve movement for thirty seconds every 20 minutes of classroom time, so they are an easy daily choice). Keep a chart to look at what is working (see the chart I provide below). When possible, get GI training and support in your school, even if starting just with yourself via online courses (www.gurianinstitute. com).

Classroom Management Improvement

One thing to chart is "time spent with classroom management." After using the strategies, you should find what I and others have found: classroom management becomes easier rather than harder even with students moving around the room more. Because your students are learning better, those who previously caused the most difficulty with classroom management cause less trouble with each success they have in your room. The ten to fifteen minutes you spent per hour in exasperation or anger before decreases over time and becomes a few minutes of management and direction necessary for each class transition.

Summer can provide teachers with an opportunity to learn new strategies and also to collect data regarding how you did during the past year. It may take you a few years to get a fair enough sample size for measurement, but I can say from experience, male and female differences emerge in every measurement table that disaggregates for sex in:

1. reading and math outcomes on state tests;
2. outcomes in classroom assessments;
3. outcomes on behavioral referrals;
4. athletics and sports performance (coaching and mentoring); and
5. even on the playground, at recess, in the lunchroom, in counseling, and in studying how students congregate and relate with one another near you.

Wherever you notice the need for boy-friendly strategies, you can learn, use, and measure them to help you boost student and school-culture improvement. On www.gurianinstitute.com/success/ you will find examples of the kind of success data you can collect from your school. The schools represented on that GI page have used the *Boys and Girls Learn Differently, Minds of Boys and Girls,* and for boys' schools, the *Helping Boys Thrive* models over the last thirty years.

Here is one way to do your data–an example from Gurian data for one school showing increases in reading for boys and girls. This graph is followed by another showing a marked increase in boys' scores in reading and math at a different school.

Roosevelt Middle School Reading Scores before and after Gurian Success Model on Criterion-Referenced Test (2005)

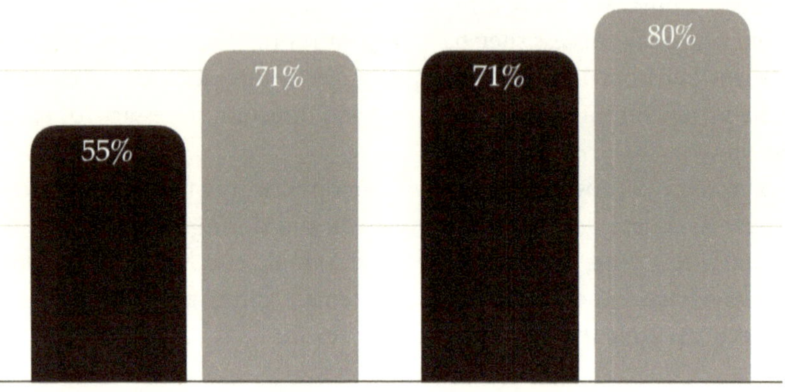

Note: Total fights on campus declined 76% from 125 to 30. The demographics of the school are 65% Hispanic, 25% White, 8% Black, and 2% Other.

Percent Increase in Reading and Math at Chattanooga Preparatory School using Gurian Success Model 2018

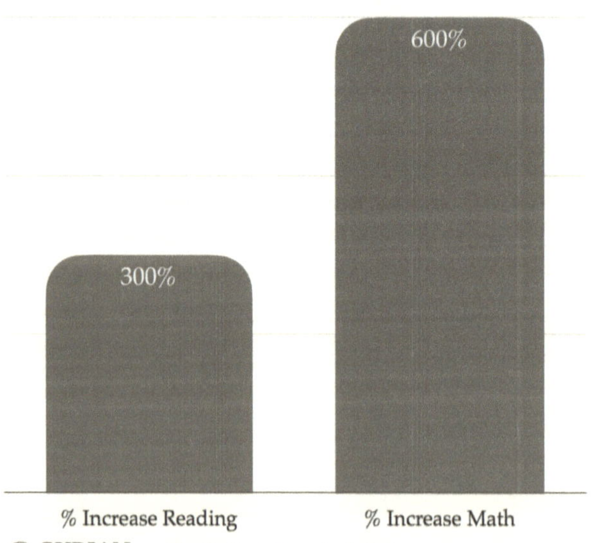

Before Any Teaching Begins…

Here is the table you can use as a teacher or teacher-in-training. Feel free to modify this table to collect data for your classrooms and school culture starting before class begins then filling in throughout the year.

Overall Assessment for 9th Grade English, Mr. Ellington, 2023-2024

Student Name	Sex / Gen	Race	Birth Month	Birth Year	Age	Family Dynamic	ELA/Math score prior	ELA/Math score with me	Reading Score on State Test Previous Year	Reading Score on State Test This Year	Grade Prior Year	Grade Current Year	My Discipline Referrals
John Dow	M	White	Jan.	2009	15	Mom	Proficient	Proficient	Basic	Basic	C+	C	3
Sarah Smith	F/NB	Asian	Sept.	2008	15	2 prnt	Proficient	Proficient	Proficient	Proficient	B	B	0
EXPAND LIST						Dad							
EXPAND LIST						Shared							

This table sets up the 300-foot view of each student's outcome in class before the year begins. By the time the year ends, it is filled in with state testing data, pre and post grades, and discipline referrals.

If you go through boy-friendly education training and support in your school training during the year, you can create a pre/post table that shows changes in grades, test scores, and discipline referrals from the year before then evolving during your classroom year (the before and after like you saw above from the GI website).

As an example, John's 9th grade English grade slightly dropped from one year to the next and he did not show an improvement in reading from the previous year. John also had more discipline referrals which might suggest he is not engaged in class. So, looking at the table, Mr. Ellington asked himself:

- Is this pattern consistent with other students in my class over the last several years?
- Do boys receive more discipline referrals in my class than in other classes?
- What percentage of my boys and girls are reading at proficient or advanced levels?

After receiving training in boy-friendly strategies and as he employed those strategies, Mr. Ellington kept answering his questions by filling in more data. One year of data told him a lot about the effectiveness of lessons on learning and behavior.

For new teachers, the table is a good way to begin a career: you start out looking for patterns in teacher effectiveness and student outcomes after each assessment. The table also encourages teachers, even math teachers included, to look at a student's reading scores.

For instance, a math teacher who assigns word problems may find that some students whose reading skills lag may be discriminated against in math class by getting the answer quickly and writing it down but getting a C because they didn't write down the whole process well. The math teacher can use the table to review his/her grading schema and perhaps to help the boy find a reading specialist.

The table can also show the math teacher that she/he needs to use boy-friendly strategies during class that will improve a student's ability to comprehend word problems—more movement and visual-graphic stimulants, for instance. These improvements generally won't happen in a classroom if a teacher is not looking for patterns. Once the patterns are seen and the strategies used, the teacher fills in more of the table with more data.

Here is a table you can use with the 10-foot view. It is designed to only measure student outcomes for in-class assessments and assignments that teachers administer throughout the year.

In Class Assessment for 3rd Grade, Mrs. Thomas, 2023-2024

Student Name	Sex/ Gen	Race	Birth Month	Birth Year	Age	Family Dynamic	Reading for Context Clues	Reading Fluency	Name of Assignment	Name of Assignment	Name of Assignment
Malcolm Jones*	M	Black	Oct.	2015	8	Mom	70%	65%	Score	Score	Score
Susan Powell	F	White	Sept.	2015	8	2 prnt	85%	90%	Score	Score	Score
EXPAND LIST						Mom					
EXPAND LIST						Shared					

Notice additional demographic features in this table. The special education student's individual education plan (IEP) is noted via the asterisk. I also include family dynamics such as single parent home with a mom, two parent home, and shared parenting where students are living with dad part of the week and mom part of the week. Every potential trauma or disruption in a child's life can affect his schooling, so I note each one. Students who have fewer resources at home generally struggle more, which makes using classroom strategies that target sex differences even more critical. When boys are dad deprived, and in arrangements where children are moving from one house to the next on a regular basis, disorganized boys become even more disorganized with homework and assignments. The more boy-friendly our teaching can be, particularly in today's different family structures, the better the struggling boy will learn.

As teachers use boy-friendly strategies, parents can be brought into connection with the school, including parents who previously thought their son was not getting a good education. The family-school connection is generally critical for helping boys and girls learn well. It can go on your chart if you wish with a column for "reached out to parents" or "heard back from parents." The more boy-friendly your pedagogy, the more it is possible the boy will go home telling parents he is enjoying your class, and the more likely it is from there that you can engage his parents in helping him to learn via boy-friendly strategies for homework time.

Comparing Outcomes Between Districts

Here is a graph comparing data from Livermore Valley Joint Unified School District (LVJUSD), Oakland Unified School District (OAKUSD), and California math proficiencies for the class of 2024 over time.

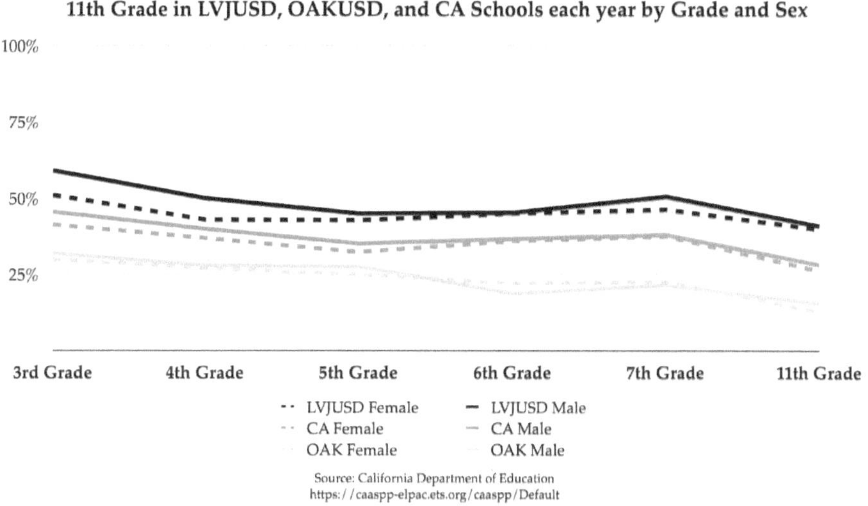

Although LVJUSD had a higher percentage of students reaching proficient/advanced in math than both the state and OAKUSD averages, the class of 2024 at LVJUSD had math scores trending downward prior to COVID and continuing to trend downward after COVID. Using this graph for our citizen science (or other comparative graphs like this) we can ask good questions as teachers and parents that might lead to the district requesting help in the area of boy-friendly strategies training.

- Why did this downward trend happen?
- What pedagogical approaches were teachers using?
- Were some teachers having more success than other teachers? Why?

- Were some teachers having more success with boys or girls? Why?
- Are the schools working on improving teacher training that result in improved outcomes?
- What new pedagogical approaches are teachers implementing?
- Are there boys and girls learn differently models in our classrooms and/or the school district?
- Do students come from a two parent, single parent, or divorced home? Does the student live with a grandparent(s), other relative, or legal guardian? How does this situation affect their learning?

As teachers, staff, administration and parents in the district answer these questions, motivation to train teachers in bias against boys, how boys and girls learn differently, healthy male development, and other similar themes and strategies will more likely occur. Then measured over the next year, data on decreased achievement, behavioral, and discipline gaps may be forthcoming. To bring parity to boys, we teachers have to generate good data, data that cries out to our districts, "We need to help these boys," "Here's how we do it," and "By helping the boys in our classrooms and culture, we bring up test scores for all students, including girls."

Generating this new data will not create any loss for girls and gender nonconforming students because helping boys is not zero sum whether in a classroom or in the data–all our students are interconnected. When we help the lowest performing group we help everyone.

Essential Questions

- What data are you generating right now?
- How can you use or modify the graphs and tables in this chapter to fit your classrooms?
- Once you generate data, what person in your system can you go to with the data?
- How can teachers and parents work together to present the data to the people who control teacher programming and training?
- How does my data and my district's data compare to other schools and districts? If the other district is doing better, what measurables can I determine regarding how they are helping boys and girls to learn better?

Chapter 22

Compel School Boards to Include Sex Differences in Annual Reports

> "The current plight of boys and young men is, in fact, a women's issue. Those boys are our sons; they are the people with whom our daughters will build a future. If our boys are in trouble, so are we all. In the war against boys, as in all wars, the first casualty is truth."
>
> –Christina Hoff Sommers

(This essay is useful for general readers and particularly for parents, members of the community, educators, school administrators, school boards, church leaders, and students in college courses.)

IN JUNE OF **2016,** I (Sean) attended my sons' Moving Up Ceremony at their K-8 Catholic school. Hundreds of children sat in assigned church pews by grade level ready to move to the next grade. In a beautifully symbolic (and physical) ritual, each grade level was called and that level stood up *en masse* then moved to the newly assigned seats. They received applause from the entire student body, faculty, staff, parents, grandparents, and others each time the move was made.

Some students received academic awards during Moving Up. Science or language arts academic awards were given to students in grades 6-8 for having the highest marks in a subject and a Love of Learning Award was given based on a child's enthusiasm to learn. One by one, a child from each grade was called up to the altar of the church to receive this Love of Learning award. By the time the last recipient was called, there was an altar of girls not boys. It looked to the audience, and the students and faculty themselves, like the girls loved to learn and boys did not.

When I brought this to the principal's attention, she saw the significance of the scene. She understood there is easily a boy and a girl in each grade who loves to learn, but they may show their love differently. She saw immediately how messaging and symbolism are powerful tools. She promised to look into the situation.

But the ceremony was what it was—boys felt abandoned.

My friend, Eric, another father in our school, said to me after the ceremony, "This is what you've been talking about around boys in school for years, right? This is what it looks like."

I could only nod silently. The problem was a glaring one at that ceremony to all of us, but it had been for years and nothing had yet happened to solve the hidden crisis in boys falling so far behind—not just in learning but in community symbolism.

What Data Can Show Us About Our Abandoned Sons

In March of 2021, Pleasanton Unified School District in Pleasanton, California held a school board meeting regarding equity and discussed the disproportionate outcomes of students based on race and ethnicity. The district presented information related to suspensions, students with disabilities, graduation rates, and those meeting college readiness standards (UC A-G Requirements Met). While many on the PUSD school board seemed eager to acknowledge the disparities, too few challenged the glaring problem with the presentation. The chart did not display information disaggregated by race *and sex* and, thus, missed the larger equity gap we all see at award ceremonies and in data, *boys*.

I requested information from the district and looked at data reported to the California Department of Education so that I could present the findings in a virtual town hall in June of 2021 (Watch it here, https://www.youtube.com/watch?v=-ppC3s7eCTM&t=2s). As the two tables below indicate, the 2021 PUSD school board report and the one compiled by the Global Initiative for Boys and Men (GIBM) differed greatly. GIBM's more detailed data showed the glaring disparities when it came to understanding suspension data as a predominately male challenge, disparities that also showed up in academic data.

PUSD Equity Gaps

2019-2020 Data						
Ethnicity	Overall District Composition	Students with Disabilities	Suspension Incidences by Ethnicity	Suspension Incidences for Students with Disabilities	Graduation Rate	UC A-G Requirements Met
Hispanic	9.9%	16.29%	3.09%	5.46%	93.4%	50.4%
African American	1.38%	16.50%	10.17%	27.27%	93.3%	42.9%
Asian	45.58%	4.25%	.95%	3.42%	99.2%	83.4%
White	35.38%	11.11%	2.7%	6.45%	96.4%	69.6%

3/25/2021
Page 5 of 13

Analysis of Pleasanton Unified School District Suspension Data from 2016-2020

Ethnicity/Sex	Student Population		1X Suspensions		Multiple Suspensions	
	Total # of Students	% of Student Population	# of 1x Incidences	% of 1x Incidences	# of Multiple by student	% of Multiple by same student
African American Male	427	0.74%	56	13.11%	23	5.4%
Hispanic Male	2,918	5.03%	155	5.31%	51	1.7%
White Male	12,182	21.00%	571	4.69%	214	1.8%
Biracial Male	1,496	2.58%	65	4.34%	30	2.0%
African American Female	404	0.70%	13	3.22%	1	0.2%
Asian Male	13,028	22.46%	235	1.80%	69	0.5%
Hispanic Female	2,908	5.01%	50	1.72%	18	0.6%
Biracial Female	1,517	2.62%	19	1.25%	6	0.4%
White Female	11,021	19.00%	114	1.03%	35	0.3%
Asian Female	12,098	20.86%	47	0.39%	14	0.1%
Total Population	**57,999**	**100%**	**1,325**	**2.28%**	**461**	**0.8%**
Females Total	**27,948**	**48.2%**	**243**	**0.87%**	**74**	**0.3%**
Males Total	**30,051**	**51.8%**	**1,082**	**3.60%**	**387**	**1.3%**
Male to Female Ratio	1.1:1	1.1:1	4.5:1	4.1:1	5.2:1	4.3:1

Data Source: Pleasanton Unified School District Data Request, May of 2021 (Pleasanton, California)

The data from GIBM showed that black, white, Hispanic, and biracial boys were suspended at higher rates than any other female groups. The data also showed that black males were suspended at significantly higher percentages than other groups and that black female students were suspended more than other female groups, but the number of black female students (13 total suspensions over four years) was too small to suggest statistical reliability.

The 4.5:1 male to female suspension ratio of nearly 58,000 students, however, suggests a systemic boy problem. But none of this information was acknowledged at PUSD's March 25 school board meeting for a number of reasons:

(1) School boards are not looking at sex differences, somewhat for feminaphobic reasons,

(2) A focus on race and gender trump differences related to sex for reasons we have analyzed earlier.

The Big Three's influence extends to the largest and smallest institutions of education, and it is the reason citizen scientists are so important. As pointed out above, one of the challenges when looking at the PUSD data is the size of the cohorts, particularly when racial groups are too small. So, at GIBM, we decided to expand data inquiry statewide. As we studied statewide data, we saw that boys of all races were suspended at significantly higher rates than their female counterparts in all districts—much like the PUSD data. Black Male and American Indian/Alaska Native male cohorts were suspended at considerably higher rates than other groups.

Compiled California Suspension Data by Race and Sex from 2016-2020

Ethnicity	Cumulative Enrollment	Total Suspensions	Unduplicated Count of Students Suspended	Unduplicated Suspension Rate	Percent of Total Suspensions w/in Race
African American Female	686,790	65,879	40,288	5.9%	28.6%
African American Male	733,414	164,736	84,432	11.5%	71.4%
American Indian or Alaska Native Female	64,221	4,458	2,806	4.4%	28.2%
American Indian or Alaska Native Male	67,188	11,337	6,260	9.3%	71.8%
Asian Female	1,128,632	5,370	4,301	0.4%	18.1%
Asian Male	1,204,017	24,303	17,876	1.5%	81.9%
Filipino Female	292,820	2,400	1,986	0.7%	24.0%
Filipino Male	318,363	7,620	5,660	1.8%	76.0%
Hispanic or Latino Female	6,741,297	183,946	132,624	2.0%	25.5%
Hispanic or Latino Male	7,093,148	536,736	330,583	4.7%	74.5%
Not Reported Female	106,525	2,338	1,614	1.5%	23.0%
Not Reported Male	112,804	7,827	4,650	4.1%	77.0%
Pacific Islander Female	57,440	2,114	1,594	2.8%	27.2%
Pacific Islander Male	60,336	5,663	3,603	6.0%	72.8%
Two or More Races Female	455,795	12,424	8,168	1.8%	24.4%
Two or More Races Male	474,150	38,474	22,029	4.6%	75.6%
White Female	2,807,009	52,789	37,350	1.3%	20.5%
White Male	3,022,509	205,062	125,656	4.2%	79.5%
Total	25,426,458	1,333,476	831,480	3.3%	
Total Male	13,085,929	1,001,758	600,749	4.6%	
Total Female	12,340,529	331,718	230,731	1.9%	
Male to Female Ratio	1:1	3:1	2.6:1	2.4:1	

Source: California Department of Education Data Quest, https://dq.cde.ca.gov/dataquest/

While PUSD was focusing on DEI, which can be well intended, it largely missed the equity gap in *boys'* outcomes. Boy suspensions are higher across all cohorts and the problem relates to poorer academic performance in K-12 education that lead to more discipline referrals: boys who are not learning become boys who are failing and problematic in a vicious circle. We are sharing this data and these graphs with you from this one district to encourage you to work with your school districts to disaggregate for sex across the board and thus become citizen scientists of your community. You can begin discovering data close to home by asking:

- Do teachers make more discipline referrals for boys or girls in our school or district?
- Do some teachers have more discipline referrals than others toward boys or toward girls?
- Does my school or district actually measure these questions?

Then go onto your school district's website and spend some time searching around there to see if there is data. You should see some data disaggregation by sex but generally you won't see enough. It is your right to ask for more of this disaggregation. You can use or modify the three questions I just asked in emails that you write to the district. You can also refer the district to this book and some of the language in this chapter.

We in the grass roots need to compel our governmental and educational agencies to disaggregate by sex for all relevant questions, whether regarding academics or behavior or discipline referrals. If we don't force the issue, the districts will often not do the disaggregation necessary to bring help to our classrooms for our boys. The district won't see the problem (or they know the problem with boys intuitively but won't act on it), and your sons will fall behind or go to a school that does not respect them as male learners–and they will fall further behind from there.

College Data

The poorer academic outcomes of boys in K-12 education in California was clearly seen in college-going rates, where boys of all races are behind their female counterparts from 8% to 13% depending on the race/ethnicity. Overall, California's female college-going rates, of those who complete high school, are 10.4% higher than male college-going rates of those who complete high school. The table below helps illustrate this point. While the table focuses on high school completers in California and their college-going rates, it could be expanded (as happens in the blank second table) to include those who did not graduate from high school so that we can get a better sense of all outcomes–this comprehensiveness would show an even larger gap as fewer males graduate from high school than females.

California College Going Rates of High School Grads by Race and Sex from 2016-2020

Race / Ethnicity	High School Completers	High School Completers Enrolled In College	College-Going Rate	Enrolled In College (In-State)	Enrolled In College (Out-of-State)	No Record of College Enrollment
African American Female	50,012	32,815	65.60%	55.90%	9.80%	34.40%
African American Male	48,301	26,206	54.30%	47.60%	6.60%	45.70%
American Indian or Alaska Native Female	4,788	2770	57.90%	50.20%	7.70%	42.10%
American Indian or Alaska Native Male	4,706	2115	44.90%	40.20%	4.70%	55.10%
Asian Female	84,548	74,146	87.70%	77.80%	9.90%	12.30%
Asian Male	88,050	74,123	84.20%	75.20%	9.00%	15.80%
Filipino Female	26,616	20,663	77.60%	73.60%	4.00%	22.40%
Filipino Male	28,337	19,173	67.70%	65.00%	2.70%	32.30%
Hispanic or Latino Female	461,073	298,143	64.70%	61.70%	2.90%	35.30%
Hispanic or Latino Male	446,662	233,407	52.30%	49.80%	2.50%	47.70%
Not Reported Female	5,656	3645	64.40%	56.20%	8.30%	35.60%
Not Reported Male	5294	2984	56.40%	49.60%	6.80%	43.60%
Pacific Islander Female	4,470	2833	63.40%	56.40%	7.00%	36.60%
Pacific Islander Male	4,356	2235	51.30%	47.10%	4.20%	48.70%
Two or More Races Female	26,179	19,461	74.30%	62.00%	12.30%	25.70%
Two or More Races Male	25,125	16,410	65.30%	56.10%	9.20%	34.70%
White Female	215,038	163,387	76.00%	60.30%	15.70%	24.00%
White Male	220,656	144,983	65.70%	54.20%	11.50%	34.30%
Total for Males	**871,487**	**521,636**	**59.9%**	**54.0%**	**5.9%**	**40.1%**
Total Females	**878,380**	**617,863**	**70.3%**	**62.8%**	**7.5%**	**29.7%**

College Going Rates of High School Grads by Race and Sex from (Name of School District or State and Years)

Race / Ethnicity	Did not Graduate	High School Completers	High School Completers Enrolled In College	College-Going Rate	Enrolled In College (In-State)	Enrolled In College (Out-of-State)	No Record of College Enrollment
African American Female							
African American Male							
American Indian or Alaska Native Female							
American Indian or Alaska Native Male							
Asian Female							
Asian Male							
Filipino Female							
Filipino Male							
Hispanic or Latino Female							
Hispanic or Latino Male							
Not Reported Female							
Not Reported Male							
Pacific Islander Female							
Pacific Islander Male							
Two or More Races Female							
Two or More Races Male							
White Female							
White Male							
Total for Males							
Total Females							

Tables like this provide more immediate feedback than the reports in various districts that may include sex and certainly include race but are unlikely to include the data at the *intersection* of race and sex. If you are part of an organization (school board, PTA, community group, or research group) that needs help completing these sorts of tables in your area, district, or state, reach out to me at seank@airr.pro (American Institute for Responsible Research) to collect the data, complete the analysis, and offer solutions.

Why Is There Such a Gap in California School Districts?

What explains the poorer academic outcomes for males in California? Three things specifically.

1. Data collected in districts does not put sex first, or at least have sex at the intersection with race/ethnicity at the top of data collection and measurement analysis. Thus we cannot see what is happening in our districts to *boys* well enough to create social justice for them.
2. When existing data, either statistical or anecdotal, is analyzed by districts or others in the Big Three, and when data around males is noticed, discussion generally moves to thin masculinity arguments or other gender politics quite quickly–the situation males face remains undiscussed and thus unresolved.
3. Pedagogical and developmental approaches taught to educators in K-12 schools, in colleges, and in society avoid sex difference-training, thus the less developed academic and behavioral skill sets in males are not understood, and males become less educated, and from there, fewer college and trade school opportunities are provided to males and utilized by males.

Using tables like the ones above will help teachers, principals, administrators, school board members, and policymakers anchor themselves in *actual data* and, thus, better understand *sex-based* outcomes from district to district and state to state.

Try This
What Schools and School Boards Could Be Doing to Look at Sex Differences

The minimum that each state, locality, and district should do is here.

1. Disaggregate educational data yearly by race if applicable *and sex* always in a way that creates intersectional cohorts. Make the reports publicly available and share the information with teachers at the end of the school year and review again the week prior to students returning to school.
2. Complete yearly reports on student growth percentiles that measure teacher performance in *working with boys and girls,* and include how a teacher works with gender nonconforming students if there are enough in a classroom to measure.

3. *Recognize sex differences in outcomes* and bring training programs to schools that increase student outcomes in reading, math, and writing both in class and on standardized tests.

4. Introduce programs that measure *objective outcomes in student performance* linked to teacher self-assessments for effectiveness with each cohort–by ethnicity, race, sex, gender, and so on.

As you share the tables above and below with parents, community members, and school boards you may be able to inspire a deeper look at the core of the educational issue every district faces: the loss of boys to K-12 education and then to college. You can work with an expert to analyze the data in your school district and share those findings with teachers, administrators, and the public before implementing policies that will address challenges.

Here are two tables you can share to begin data collection and problem solving.

Math Scores (Name of District and Year)

Reporting Categories	3rd Grade		4th Grade		5th Grade		6th Grade		7th Grade		8th Grade		11th Grade	
	Males	Females	Males	Females	Males	Females	Males	Females	Males	Females	Males	Females	Males	Females
Students Enrolled														
Students Tested														
Students with Scores														
# Math Level 4 (Exceeded)														
# Math Level 3 (Met)														
# Math Level 2 (Nearly Met)														
# Math Level 1 (Not Met)														
# Proficient + Advanced														
% Advanced														
% Proficient														
% Nearly Met														
% Not Met														

To determine the percentage for each level, divide the number of students at a level by the total number of students with scores. For example, to determine the number of students who exceeded standard (Level 4): Total Students who scored at Level 4 / Students with Scores. Do the same of each level to complete the rest. Excel and Numbers allows you to simply copy the formula to the right.

English Language Arts Scores (Name of District and Year)

Reporting Categories	3rd Grade		4th Grade		5th Grade		6th Grade		7th Grade		8th Grade		11th Grade	
	Males	Females	Males	Females	Males	Females	Males	Females	Males	Females	Males	Females	Males	Females
Students Enrolled														
Students Tested														
Students with Scores														
# Reading Above Standard														
# ELA Level 4 (Exceeded)														
# ELA Level 3 (Met)														
# ELA Level 2 (Nearly Met)														
# ELA Level 1 (Not Met)														
# Proficient + Advanced														
% Reading Above Standard														
% Advanced														
% Proficient														
% Nearly Met														
% Not Met														

To determine the percentage for each level, divide the number of students at a level by the total number of students with scores. For example, to determine the number of students who exceeded standard (Level 4): Total Students who scored at Level 4 / Students with Scores. Do the same of each level to complete the rest. Excel and Numbers allows you to simply copy the formula to the right.

Most teachers and school administrators have not seen these types of tables filled in and presented during mandated teacher development and training at the beginning of the school year. Many teachers may intuitively know that boys are behind girls in reading, but they may not know that males are behind at all grade levels. They may also not know that math scores are now relatively similar between the sexes, with girls surpassing boys in some districts.

Without having data, a school district can more easily surrender to feminaphobia or the politics of masculinity or just to a generalized lack of empathy for boys. Without the sex-based data, a district will likely not mandate training in how boys and girls learn, grow, and nurture differently, which will mean not enough boy-friendly practices used in classrooms, the very practices that can help all students learn better and all teachers be more effective as educators.

At a recent educator conference, Michael noted something about this that is very important: "A school or district spends 1 or 2 million dollars on a new math curriculum, including high priced training for teachers in how to use the curriculum. Two years later, a new superintendent comes in with a different curriculum for another million dollars. Yet over these same years, data shows little if any improvement for the district in math scores. The money was spent, and the district's teachers are still, quite often, not supported in how to best teach *all* curricula, *including math,* to the most difficult population—boys. All this while training and support in the brain-friendly best teaching practices costs only a few thousand dollars, not millions. Just at the dollars and cents level, isn't there something wrong with our priorities in training teachers?"

Essential Questions

The answers to these questions will give you, and your teams, action items for meetings with your school district personnel.

- Do you know if school or school district uses tables and graphs (like the ones above) to better understand its student outcomes? Does it share those tables and graphs with the public? If not, can you go online and access them?
- Are the schools in your community/district including student growth percentiles and sharing that information with teachers specifically to help improve teacher training, teacher performance, and student outcomes?
- Are you or members of your school community unwilling or fearful of discussing sex differences when it comes to student outcomes because of potential backlash? Are you rebuffed by teachers and administrators for even broaching the subject? If the answer is yes, forming a parent-led team might be essential.
- How can you ease the fears of those who are apprehensive to look at data broken down by sex and sex/race? Can you help them see that the intersection is not an either/or but is a both/and that is useful in solving interwoven social problems?
- What contact people exist in your team and community with whom to share outcomes and findings—not just among principals, school boards, and superintendents, but also in your local papers, social media, and public meetings? Can your PTA be beneficial in this sharing and these actions?

Chapter 23

Decrease the Male-Gender Gap in College Education

> "Boys today bear the burden of several powerful cultural trends: a therapeutic approach to education that valorizes feelings and denigrates competition and risk, zero-tolerance policies that punish normal antics of young males, and a gender equity movement that views masculinity as predatory. Natural male exuberance is no longer tolerated."
>
> —Christina Hoff Sommers

(This essay is useful for general readers, and particularly for policymakers, educators at all levels, college and high school students, parents, media, and government agencies responsible for measuring outcomes.)

WE MENTIONED THAT MALES are less likely to participate in college than females and have been for the last four decades. What must happen if we hope to close that Male-Gender-Gap in college education? How do we close the gap without harming females? Why is it important to close the gap? Let's look at the data by starting with what we noted earlier: in 2022, people 25 and over with a bachelor's degree earned 67% more in weekly wages ($1,432) than a person with a high school diploma ($853). The same was true from 2019-2021. With each higher degree, average weekly earnings were more sizable if a person graduated from college. In addition, with each successive degree level (from no high school degree to doctorate) there are commensurately lower levels of unemployment. While not every child will go to college, a male gap in college is not good for millions of families because that family is robbed of resources.

Tom Mortenson (Senior Fellow of the Pell Institute and Data Analyst), Nicole Brunt (Research Associate with the Pell Institute), and Kurt Bauman (Chief, Education and Social Stratification Branch, Census Bureau) have helped me (Sean) to assess college participation rates of over 161 million 18-24-year-old dependent family members from 2012 to 2020. Using their data, I disaggregated the intersections of three things: income quartiles, race, and sex. As the tables below show, those from lower income quartiles participated in college at lesser rates than those from higher income quartiles. Black, Hispanic, and white males were always on the lower end of college participation rates across all income quartiles. Asian females also participated in college more than Asian males, but the percentage rates were around 2 to 4.5% depending on the income quartile, closer than every other group, but still, more females than males were going to college.

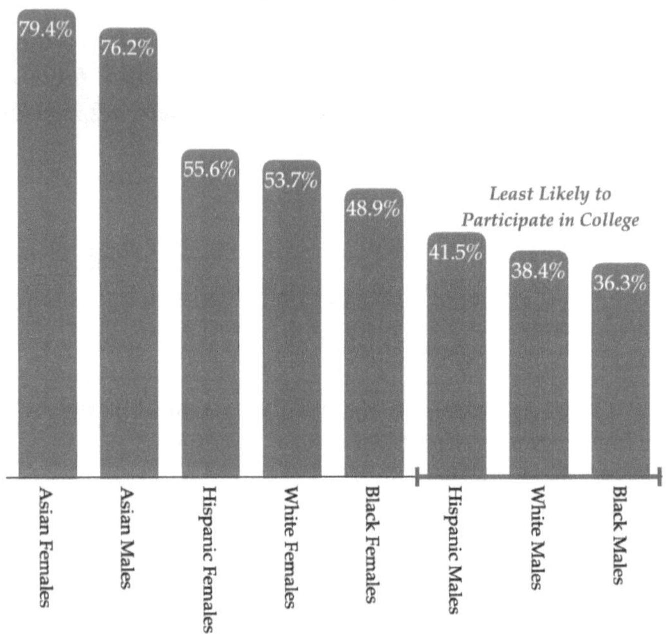

College Participation Rates by Race, Sex, and Quartile 1 (lowest) Income of 18 to 24 year-old Dependent Family Members from 2012 to 2020

College Participation Rates by Race, Sex, and Quartile 2 Income of 18 to 24 year-old Dependent Family Members from 2012 to 2020

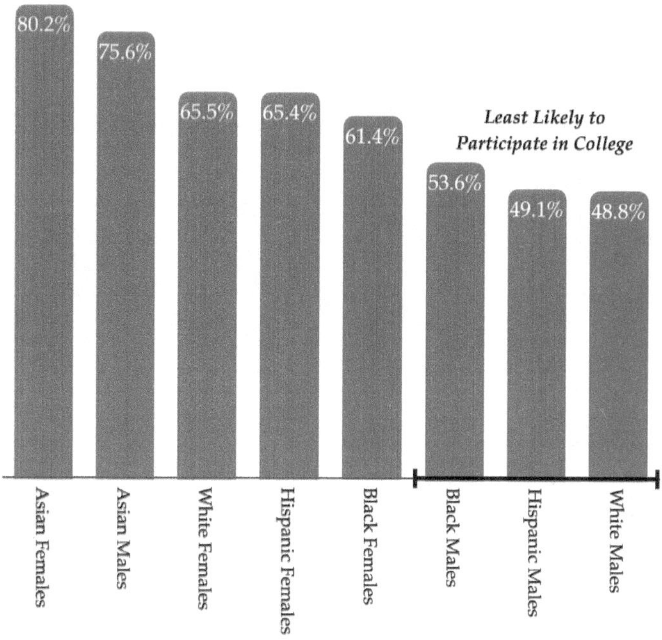

College Participation Rates by Race, Sex, and Quartile 3 Income of 18 to 24 year-old Dependent Family Members from 2012 to 2020

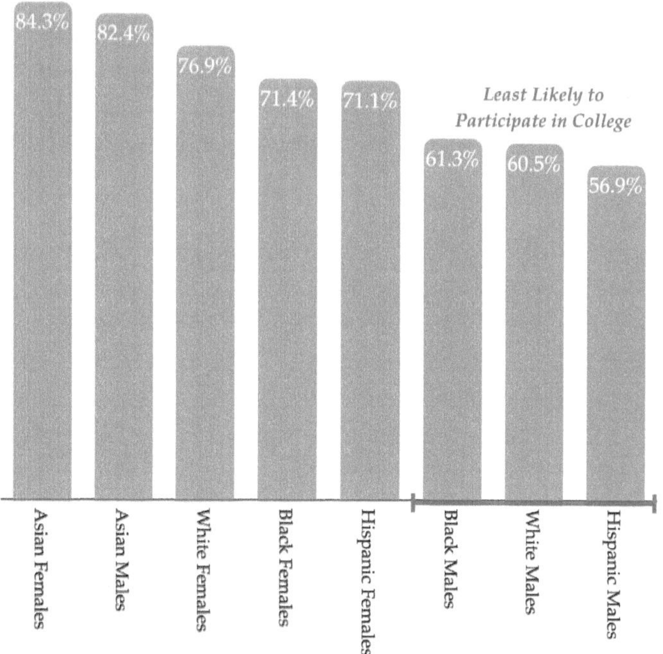

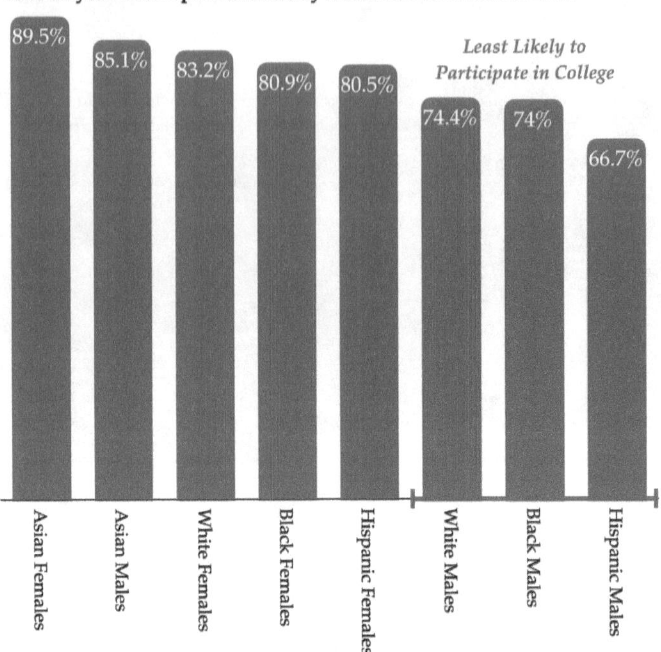

The participation rates in these graphs list the outcomes, not the reasons males are behind their female counterparts across racial groups. There are numerous contributing factors to the sex differences in college participation. To learn these factors is to begin to solve them. I'll show you what I mean as we look at them together.

We Push Trades While Overlooking the Male-Gap in Educational Skills

The lower college participation rates have in part compelled a greater social conversation around trades for young men who are not interested in or unprepared for college. This conversation is a worthy one that will no doubt continue. However, the helpful push toward trades does not deal with the underlying fact that males *as a cohort* are less prepared for college than females in K – 12 schooling. Perhaps all of us know a young male who himself knows, whether consciously or unconsciously, that he is not prepared for college. He knows he did not get as good an education as some of the people around him, especially the girls, and he avoids failing in college by not going. He likely played a part in his own lack of college preparation but so did the school system he was in, a system that did not teach as well to his brain as his sister's.

He chooses against college and goes into a trade, grateful for the availability of the trade. At the same time, he would do better financially if he went to college.

It is our job as a society to help him at least be better enough prepared for college that he can risk going. To fulfill this job we will need to make sure that encouraging trades does not displace math, reading, and writing skills in our schools, even while supporting strong education in trades by the Pell Grant Systems directing educational resources to programs that teach career-making trade skills in the technology sector. We need to do both things at once—help the teachers teach better to young males while also supporting the trades.

Increase Pell Grant Funding (Free Money) for College Males and Support Low Income Males in College

It can be difficult for our social systems to fully fathom what is happening to our young males because we lack agencies directed toward these males. The U.S. Department of Labor, for instance, has a Women's Bureau. Within it is a program called WANTO (The Women in Apprenticeship and Nontraditional Occupations). There is no MANTO program at the U.S. Department of Labor. Obviously, a government program for females is important and should be celebrated but to have no similar agency for boys is discrimination against males. Taxpayer dollars need to be used to support our sons, too. We need a MANTO program. We need to focus on apprenticeship programs too.

We can also use Pell grants to target males. Especially at the lower income levels, Pell Grants (free money) programs awarded to college students can change to focus efforts on getting more low-income black, Hispanic, and white males into and through college. Far more females than males across the demographics receive Pell Grants. In 2015-16, for instance, women received $6.4 billion more annually in Pell Grant funding than males according to data from the U.S. Department of Education.

Table 1. Pell Grant Funding by Amount and Percentage 2011-12

Academic Year 2011-12	% of undergrads with Pell Grant by sex	Undergrad enrollment by Sex	Amount awarded by sex
Females	44.8%	10,254,311	$16,538,152,781
Males	36.5%	7,822,992	$10,279,411,488
Male Gender Gap	8.3%	2,431,319	$6,258,741,293

Table 2. Pell Grant Funding by Amount and Percentage 2015-16

Academic Year 2015-2016	% of undergrads with Pell Grant by sex	Total Undergrad Enrollment by sex	Amount awarded by sex
Females	43.1%	9,962,000	$15,886,401,400
Males	34.0%	7,528,000	$9,470,224,000
Male Gender Gap	9.1%	2,434,000	$6,416,177,400

Source: U.S. Department of Education: Trends in Pell Grant Receipts Table 1.1
https://nces.ed.gov/pubs2019/2019487.pdf

This funding disparity speaks to a sex gap and a form of sex discrimination, despite that the Pell Grant program is not specifically setting out to discriminate. But our nation thinks, supports, and promotes college participation much more through a female lens than a male lens. While in 1970, males outnumbered females when it came to college participation and funding (requiring a women's rights movement to rectify disparities), within 15 years (1985), there was no college gender-gap uplifting males and since then the pendulum has swung heavily the other way as shown in the graphs in Chapter 14. Forty years into the swing, we have too little effort in our governmental systems, including in funding, to help our males, who only constitute 41% of college graduates. This sex-based discrimination can be at least partially addressed via Pell grants distributed to both sexes equally.

For this solution to gain traction, we will need to not only utilize more boy-friendly practices in pre-K to grade 12 but also increase the percentage of lower-income males graduating from college by introducing campus programs that identify at-risk male students and provide them with the skills to succeed. Every college, university, community college, or trade school needs to train its faculty and personnel to notice and help struggling and unprepared male students. Personnel should also be trained in what male-friendly strategies work to reach these struggling males. What works for young women may not work for young men.

Place an Emphasis on Increasing Male Enrollment

When a friend of mine told me about his son's nearly 1500 SAT score and 4.3 GPA at a very competitive high school, I imagined he would be accepted at California's most prestigious colleges, but he was only accepted to the least desirable school in California's system. The family had lived in California all their lives paying taxes in the state. They rightfully looked forward to the financial benefit of in-state tuition. Frustrated, the family decided to enroll their son out-of-state and made the decision to move out-of-state as well, a choice some frustrated parents are having to make when it comes to their sons' college education. In California, the numbers illustrate that male California residents are not enrolled fairly and equitably even though many certainly qualify.

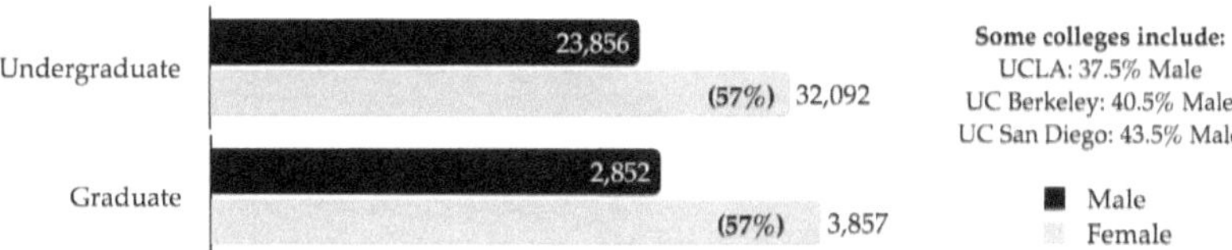

In 2022 male California residents were less likely to be enrolled at the undergraduate and graduate level than female CA residents, and while the University of California system has made efforts to expand enrollment for first generation American students and to celebrate female gains, they generally ignore the lack of male, as "nearly three-fifths (59 percent) of first-generation students are female vs. 40 percent male." Much of this data remains hard to find as reports, like the one above, because governmental agencies often avoid actively addressing male disparities. To find the data you will need to look at the smaller print and go through layers of data searches or in many cases you will need to request the data directly from educational entities via Freedom of Information Act filings.

In the spring of 2024, I contacted Ivy League colleges to ask them for demographic information to be filled into the tables below, data that looked at college demographics via the intersections of race, sex, and income.

Table 1. Percent of Freshman Class Applied, Accepted, and Enrolled by Race and Sex (Year)

Race / Ethnicity	Income Quartile 1				Income Quartile 2				Income Quartile 3				Income Quartile 4			
	Applied	Accepted	Enrolled	Avg. Tuition After Aid	Applied	Accepted	Enrolled	Avg. Tuition After Aid	Applied	Accepted	Enrolled	Avg. Tuition After Aid	Applied	Accepted	Enrolled	Avg. Tuition After Aid
African American Female																
African American Male																
American Indian or Alaska Native Female																
American Indian or Alaska Native Male																
Asian Female																
Asian Male																
Filipino Female																
Filipino Male																
Hispanic or Latino Female																
Hispanic or Latino Male																
Pacific Islander Female																
Pacific Islander Male																
Two or More Races Female																
Two or More Races Male																
White Female																
White Male																
Total for Females																
Total Males																

Table 2. Number of Freshman Class Applied, Accepted, and Enrolled by Race and Sex (Year)

Race / Ethnicity	Income Quartile 1				Income Quartile 2				Income Quartile 3				Income Quartile 4			
	Applied	Accepted	Enrolled	Avg. Tuition After Aid	Applied	Accepted	Enrolled	Avg. Tuition After Aid	Applied	Accepted	Enrolled	Avg. Tuition After Aid	Applied	Accepted	Enrolled	Avg. Tuition After Aid
African American Female																
African American Male																
American Indian or Alaska Native Female																
American Indian or Alaska Native Male																
Asian Female																
Asian Male																
Filipino Female																
Filipino Male																
Hispanic or Latino Female																
Hispanic or Latino Male																
Pacific Islander Female																
Pacific Islander Male																
Two or More Races Female																
Two or More Races Male																
White Female																
White Male																
Total for Females																
Total Males																

I requested this data from Brown, Columbia, Cornell, Dartmouth, Harvard, Stanford, University of Pennsylvania, and Yale. Only three responded, despite multiple requests for information broken down in a way that would show, very clearly, data points most colleges should be willing to explore and share with the public; and even those that responded have stalled out, withholding data on males. As I write this, the Global Initiative for Boys and Men is reaching out to a variety of congressional and senate leaders and filing a request to the U.S. Department of Education's Office of Civil Rights for this data. One university's response captured the general tenor of the problem. "Thank you for reaching out. This information is not publicly available." Here are the other two responses I received.

University 1: "The Institutional Data section of the website for [the school's] Office of Institutional Research offers a wealth of data, and you're welcome to make use of that as it's helpful in your work."

My response: "The data source did not include the requested information."

University 2: "You can find information about [the school's] program of meeting 100% of demonstrated financial need for its undergraduate students here. Race/ethnicity and sex are not considered when determining the amount of aid."

My response: The university may not use race/ethnicity and sex when determining the amount of aid, but it may accept students from lower-income quartiles in particular groups more so than other groups. In doing so, financial awards could still discriminate against groups underrepresented, like males, from the lowest income quartiles."

I spoke with a representative from one of the Ivy League colleges who noted that this type of demographic information—to his knowledge—has never been requested. While I appreciated his honesty, still, no data on male distress was forthcoming. There are walls we keep walking into as we try to address the college gender gap that mirror walls we hit with other gender gaps involving males—a combination of feminaphobia when looking into "male" data; males themselves less educationally prepared for college than females; and misandry that sees males as less worthy than females because of past wrongs. Together all this adds up to diversity becoming so selective that "diversity" does not end up including the group most disenfranchised at college and in our public schools—males.

Essential Questions

In your book group, classroom, or around the family dinner table, we hope you'll ask and answer, together, these questions, then use your answers as action items as you approach colleges to redress the gender gap and flagrant sex discrimination against males.

1. Should schools and school districts provide the Boys and Girls Learn Differently approach all the way through college?
2. Why don't universities disaggregate data on males at the intersections of income, race, and sex?

3. Who do we know in our local university that we can approach to do that and generate the data?
4. How can I help the boys around me to both go into trades and also be better prepared to go to college, even when the school system might not be doing enough for boys?
5. Who in my three family system can become my son's tutor or mentor through schooling issues not just pre-college issues but even during his college years, until he is fully prepared for a college education?

Chapter 24

Build and Support Community Programs
That Help Boys Thrive

(This essay is useful for general readers, and particularly those looking to learn more about volunteering, starting similar programs in their communities, and advocating for programs through the public or private sector, policymakers, and social workers.)

IN MY TRAVELS THROUGHOUT THE WORLD to speak and consult, I (Michael) have found the grass roots to be way ahead of a lot of people in leadership positions. The Big Three controls funding and resources and sometimes spearheads worthy projects and programs to help males, but most often the money in the Big Three does not go to helping boys. The Big Three insists, as we noted earlier, that boys don't need us as much as girls, "that we don't know yet what works for boys," that "boys already have everything, why give them special programs," or that "we just need to get rid of masculine stereotypes to solve boys' issues." Cultural paralysis leaves boys out of many layers of government. But not all. Programs do exist, and very much so in the grass roots.

We want to end this book's call to action by featuring some of these programs. To find other programs in your area, try searching things like "boys programs in _______ (type in your region)" "programs for boys near me," "boys' rites of passage programs," "boys schools near me," "boy supportive organizations near me," or use other similar search parameters on your browser. In providing you with some programs here, we hope that you will be inspired to not only utilize these healthy models of male development in your own life and community, but also to support programs like these and perhaps build your own versions or models in your community.

One example of a family building their own model occurred in Spokane, Washington. A young man, Kellen, took his own life at 19-years-of-age. His parents and extended family created the non-profit Kellen Cares Foundation to help the local community create and utilize resources applicable to the mental health of boys and families. Kellen Cares partnered with Suicide Prevention programs and speakers, the Gurian Institute's Helping Boys Thrive® program, fatherhood programs, sororities and fraternities at Washington State University, and many others to spread the word about male mental health.

Another program that started local is M.A.N.C.A.V.E. (www.azmancave. org), which we featured earlier. M.A.N.C.A.V.E. is now M.A.N.C.A.V.E. & Dad Together. The Gurian Institute has been working with this program since its inception. Marion Hill, the organization's founder, can be reached at marion.hill@phoenix.gov. He is presently expanding the program beyond Phoenix.

Other programs with which GI has partnered over the years may be known to you already. Some are:

My Brothers Keeper (https://www.obama.org/programs/my-brothers-keeper-alliance/).
Scouting USA (formerly Boy Scouts of America). (www.scouting.org)
Big Brothers and Big Sisters (https://www.bbbs.org/)
The Boys Initiative (www.boysinitiative.org)
The Ever Forward Club (www.everforwardclub.org)
The Building Boys Network (www.buildingboys.net)
The Greater Phoenix Urban League (www.gphxul.org)
Booker T. Washington Schools (www.btwchild.org)
Santa Fe Boys Educational Foundation (https://santafeboys.org/)
The Center, A Place of Hope (www.aplaceofhope.com)
ManWave in Calgary, Alberta (https://manwavemovement.com/)
Maggie Dent's work in Australia (www.maggiedent.com)
The Spokane Fatherhood Initiative (www.spofi.org).
Partnership for Male Youth (www.partnershipformaleyouth.org)
The Camino Institute (www.caminoinstitute.com)
Tim Wright Ministries (www.timwrightministries.org)

Pastor Tim Wright and I created secular and Christian Rites-of-Passage programs which you can download from Tim's website. The *Heroic Quest for Boys* and the *Wisdom Journey for Girls* programs have been used successfully in secular and church communities to lead children through rites of passage into healthy male and female adulthood.

Here are more programs that have performed well in rescuing our sons.

Mentoring and Fatherhood Initiatives

This is not an exhaustive list but represents some of the programs that the Global Initiative for Boys and Men support. Most of these programs are presented in their own words.

Boys to Men Mentoring

Location: California

Website: boystomen.org

Boys to Men Mentoring is a 501(c)(3) under the U.S. tax code that has been empowering teenage boys since 1996. The organization believes that integrity is the foundation of the Boys to Men program. A team of researchers affiliated with the Counseling Program Department of School, Family, and Mental Health Professions School of Leadership and Education Sciences (SOLES) University of San Diego completed a case study of the program and its findings were impressive.

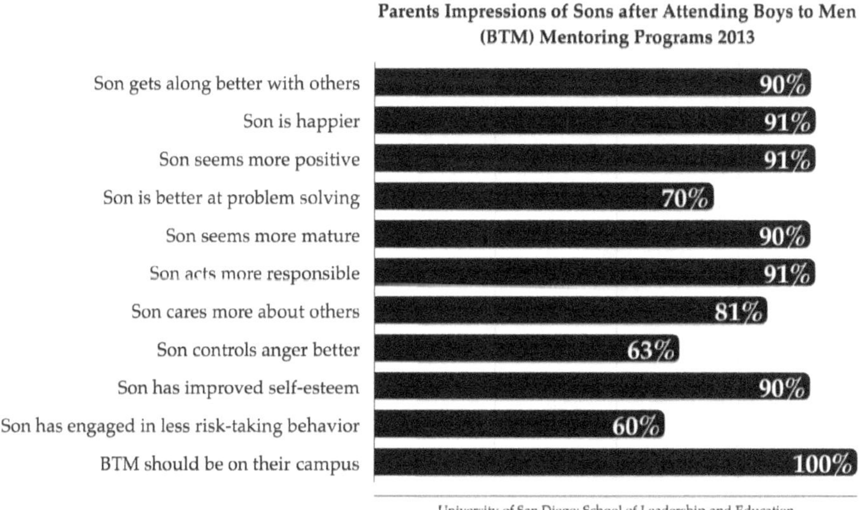

University of San Diego: School of Leadership and Education
https://boystomen.org/wp-content/uploads/2019/12/CaseStudy1.pdf

The Six Core Values of the Boys to Men Program are:
- RESPONSIBILITY – Mentees are taught that they are responsible for their own actions and choices, right or wrong. The responsibility for who they are and the man they will become falls on their shoulders. Each mentee learns they choose how they are viewed in today's world.
- ACCOUNTABILITY– Mentees learn that they have self-accountability and must take ownership over how they think, do, and feel. A man can feel anger or joy, fear or confidence; how he acts in each situation is his own self-accountability. Each mentee learns he is responsible for controlling his own emotions.
- SELF- AWARENESS – Mentees learn the importance of being self aware. They may not always succeed in controlling how they act in a situation but self-awareness helps them accept the consequences of their actions.
- EMOTIONAL EXPRESSION – This is one of the most important concepts of the program. Mentees learn about coping skills and what signs to look for that trigger their emotional responses. Techniques are taught to help control their anger in hopes of diminishing the negative consequences they are used to experiencing. These consequences include trouble with parents, teachers and school suspensions.
- THE MAN THEY WANT TO BE – Mentees learn to think about their futures and how to get there. Once a young man knows who he wants to be, Boys to Men can then look at where he is today and help the mentee build a map to travel from point A to point B. Boys to Men can then help him complete his journey.

Boys on the Right Track
Location: New York
Website: https://boysontherighttrack.org/
Boys on the Right Track is a fun, non-competitive running wellness program for young men ages 8-13. Through providing an environment that nurtures growth, fosters open communication, promotes inclusivity, and prioritizes both mental and physical health, we are empowering our boys to navigate the challenges they face with resilience so that they may thrive in our rapidly evolving world.

The program was designed to help prevent violence as well as promote healthy choices in the young men who participate. Through small groups led by trained coaches, boys learn collaboration, healthy choices, and goal setting.

They practice communication and healthy self expression while building their confidence and developing leadership skills along with fostering relationships that can last a lifetime. BOTRT has been proudly serving the Western New York community since 2013, and we are rapidly expanding our programs to other areas of the country.

Watch D.O.G.S. (Dads of Great Students)

Location: United States

Website: https://dadsofgreatstudents.com/

The Dads of Great Students WATCH D.O.G.S.® provides training content, support materials, uniform apparel and other promotional items for a campus community. Its mission is to support principals and teachers by providing willing volunteers while contributing to improved outcomes for students. Fathers, grandfathers, step-fathers, uncles, and other father figures serve on campus for one day or many each year under the leadership of a program coordinator and the guidance of a school principal or designated administrator. The program speaks directly to those caregivers and guardians who are statistically less likely to come onto campus to volunteer. D.O.G.S. has brought millions of volunteers onto campuses who use its model, tools, and support. Many of its campus programs also invite M.O.M.S. and all Heroes of the Hallway to serve under the WATCH D.O.G.S.® Program.

Key Ministry

Location: United States

Website: https://www.keyministry.org/

Key Ministry was founded to help churches welcome families of children with hidden disabilities. Since 2002, Key Ministry has provided knowledge, innovation, and experience to the worldwide church as it ministers to and with individuals and families of kids with developmental and physical disabilities. In addition to being a disability inclusion ministry resource, we find ourselves uniquely called and positioned to serve churches seeking to become more intentional and effective in ministry with children, teens, and adults impacted by mental illness and trauma. Our mission, vision, and values shape the *guiding principles* for the day-to-day operation of the ministry.

- We provide as many products and services as possible free of charge.
- Ministry is done best by a team. No person or organization gets all the gifts!
- We expand the circle of the disability ministry movement by including people inside and outside the church.

- We seek opportunities to collaborate with like-minded ministries.
- We create platforms to advance the cause of disability ministry and share them with other leaders.
- We actively seek to maximize the impact of our ministry through application of technology.

Good Plus Foundation

Website: https://goodplusfoundation.org/home

In 2010, Good+Foundation expanded programming to intentionally include fathers. Stronger fathers build stronger, more resilient families, which are the backbone of thriving communities. The more we invest in fathers and in their capacity to be engaged co-parents, the greater positive impact we see on children and families. An external evaluation of Good+Foundation's work found that 93 percent of fathers receiving donations had their relationship with their children improve while 82 percent of fathers reported improved relationships with their children's mother and/or other relatives. Additionally, 97 percent of fathers said that donations made them want to continue the life-changing programs provided by Good+ partners. Good+ continues to provide partners with workshops aimed at building capacity in areas such as father engagement and trauma-informed care. We have now provided more than 10.5 million hours of training to 25,817 social workers and other client service professionals. These sessions have also provided insights into working with diverse populations, implicit and explicit biases, and microaggressions that fathers experience.

Real Dads Network

Location: New York

Website: https://www.realdadsnetwork.org/about-us

Real Dads™ Network is a non-profit organization established in 2004 by Derek Phillips, following the success of the award-winning documentary "Real Dads-Black Men on Fatherhood" (2000) directed by Derek Phillips and Nikki Dees. The organization was founded in response to a strong need identified from the documentary feedback for a platform where fathers could share their stories, access resources, engage in meaningful conversations about manhood, fatherhood, and family, and feel connected to a positive and empowering community.

The mission at Real Dads Network is to provide support and resources for fathers and families, advocating for father involvement as essential for the development of healthy children. We believe that children thrive when both parents are actively engaged in the parenting process, regardless of their marital or living circumstances. Our vision is to foster a culture where all fathers are actively involved in parenting and are recognized as exemplary role models by society. We aim to strengthen the institution of the family by empowering fathers with support, information, resources, and opportunities to be the best for their families and communities.

- **Empower** fathers by providing them with the support, resources, and opportunities they need to excel in their roles as parents and community leaders.
- **Foster** a sense of belonging and connection among fathers, providing a platform for them to share their experiences, learn from one another, and support each other in their journey of fatherhood.
- **Advocate** for shared parenting as the standard for public policy decisions, recognizing the positive impact of involved fathers on children's well-being and development.

National Responsible Fatherhood Clearinghouse

Location: Dunwoody, GA

Website: https://www.fatherhood.gov/about-us

The National Responsible Fatherhood Clearinghouse is an Office of Family Assistance (OFA) funded national resource for fathers, practitioners, programs/Federal grantees, states, and the public at-large who are serving or interested in supporting strong fathers and families.

Fatherhood.gov is a site for:

Dads looking for tips, hints and even deals for dads and kids – find them on the *DadTalk Blog* (https://www.fatherhood.gov/dadtalk-blog) and in the *For Dads* section (https://www.fatherhood.gov/for-dads).

Fatherhood programs looking to get started or expand – check out the *For Programs* section (https://www.fatherhood.gov/for-programs).

Researchers and policymakers looking for the latest on responsible fatherhood – check out our Library (https://www.fatherhood.gov/research-and-resources/library-search).

The goals of the National Responsible Fatherhood Clearinghouse (NRFC) are to provide, facilitate, and disseminate current research and proven and innovative strategies that will encourage and strengthen fathers and families and providers of services via the following activities:

- Robust NRFC website – www.Fatherhood.gov
- Media Campaign (https://www.fatherhood.gov/for-programs/fatherhood-media-campaign) that promotes the Responsible Fatherhood field and efforts of local programs.

Social media engagement via Twitter, Facebook, Instagram, YouTube, and LinkedIn.

Development and dissemination of written products that advance responsible fatherhood research and practice.

Outreach and presentations at conferences and events.

National Call Center for dads and practitioners (1-877-4DAD411). Virtual trainings (https://www.fatherhood.gov/research-and-resources/library-search?f%5B0%5D=resource_type%3A61).

A Virtual Collaborative Community (VCC) for Fatherhood Stakeholders (https://learningcommunity.fatherhood.gov/?login=true),

Groups that Focus on Policy, Journalism, and Educating the Public

These resource organizations are involved in the political and journalistic world on behalf of boys and men. You might reach out to them for help with your own advocacy work in your community.

Global Initiative for Boys and Men

Location: United States

Website: gibm.us

The Global Initiative for Boys and Men (GIBM) supports boys, men, and families through research and advocacy. Established in 2019, GIBM is a 501(c)(3) under the U.S. Tax Code and is incorporated in Friday Harbor, Washington and Pleasanton, California. GIBM educates and collaborates with parents, teachers, educators, researchers, nonprofit and for-profit institutions, and policymakers across the country to present the most important data on the status of boys and men in schools and other areas of well-being. GIBM works closely with leading researchers, community groups, public and private institutions, and policymakers to support boys and men and the women who love them.

Relationship-building with nonprofits and for-profits allows GIBM to ensure that resources are directed toward advocacy, research, and actions that create change. GIBM's areas of research and support include:

- Education: Boys have fallen behind in K-12 education at all grade levels, and they are much less likely to enroll, participate, and graduate from college. GIBM studies and creates reports that parents, school board, teachers, and policymakers can use to better understand factors that affect boys' educational progress and outcomes. GIBM understands that boys of all races are behind their female counterparts in education.
- Mental Health: Boys and men are at higher risk for suicide, overdose, and alcohol related addictions and deaths. GIBM understands that sex-differences contribute to these risks and outcomes and many of our solutions must include that perspective along with understanding some of the social contagions.
- Financial Health and Employment: The financial health of men is ever changing in a global economy. Working class men are being hit especially hard, as are younger men who are finding it harder to gain entry to college and attain careers in trades that provide financial security. Many of these problems are structural in nature and greatly influenced by policy actions that overlook male outcomes. GIBM reveals the statistical realities about male financial health, employment, risk, and solutions.
- Fatherhood, Family, & Relationship: Father absent homes lead to social breakdowns. Boys and girls from *dad-deprived homes* (a phrase used by Warren Farrell in the *Boy Crisis*) has led to challenges in education, physical & mental health, addiction, crime, and teen pregnancy to name a few things. Family life tells us a lot about the well-being of boys and men and their socio-economic futures and needs. Relationship issues, including sexual and domestic abuse, are areas GIBM pays attention to as primary forces that impact boys, girls, men, and women.
- Criminal Justice & Court Systems: The court systems are heavily laden with boys and men who are part of a proverbial school to prison pipeline. We look at this data closely to help inform policymakers about the systemic challenges males face in education and family that lead to courts, detention systems, and prison. The court systems have historically created greater challenges for boys and men.
- Male Narrative in the Public Discourse: GIBM provides important information and solutions to those in education, media, and government to address risk, outcomes, and solutions for boys and men. Academia, media, and government tend to overlook outcomes

of boys and men or tend to under-represent their challenges. GIBM also helps educate parents and others on how to address academia, media, and government by being armed with data and solutions.

The GIBM State Reports on the Status of Boys and Men (https://www.gibm.us/state-reports) have influenced policymakers at the local, state, and federal levels. GIBM has encouraged others to imitate GIBM's model in their own community, state, and nationally. GIBM is often sought after for research and advice.

Washington Initiative for Boys and Men

Location: Washington State

Website: wibm.us

Washington Initiative for Boys and Men (WIBM) focuses on issues that impact boys, male youth, and men in Seattle, Tacoma, Spokane, and throughout Washington state. The leader of the organization, Blair Daly, says his work is a "combination of grassroots political advocacy and advocacy journalism." WIBM brings to light areas where males are struggling and monitors the successes and failures of efforts to bring about positive change. WIBM knows that equity and equality must include everyone, and it is necessary to look comprehensively at what constitutes equality of the sexes/genders. Blair Daly wrote, "All of our content fits into one or more of three categories:

- Empathy for Boys and Men — affirming the goodness of males and/or offering them empathy.
- Discrimination and Prejudice — spotlighting discrimination or misandry boys and men face.
- Gender Disparities — highlighting sex-based disparities in which males are experiencing worse outcomes."

Blair is a resident of Redmond, Washington and facilitates advice and support from local and national leaders who care deeply about the well-being of our boys, men, families, and communities. WIBM is the sponsor of a grassroots lobbying campaign to get the state legislature to pass a bill creating a Washington State Commission on Boys and Men. This would be the nation's first state commission on boys and men. Potentially, this kind of commission could exist in all fifty states and in provinces of other countries.

You can reach Blair at blair@wibm.us.

American Institute for Boys and Men

Location: United States

Website: aibm.org

Too many boys and men are struggling – at school, at work, and in their families and communities. The American Institute for Boys & Men believes many of these challenges are structural and demand evidence-based policy solutions. The AIBM aim is to inform policy and public dialogue with non-partisan research so that boys and men from all backgrounds can lead healthy, happy, and meaningful lives. Its research focuses on five key areas.

- Mental Health: Boys and men are increasingly lonely, and at higher risk of suicide and "deaths of despair." We shed light on the male mental health crisis and look for urgent solutions.
- Education & Skills: By multiple measures, boys have fallen far behind in school. We study the many factors that affect boys' educational progress and outcomes.
- Employment: Men–especially working-class men –are struggling in our changing global economy. We study structural forces–including globalization but also education and skills training–that affect men in the labor market.
- Black Boys & Men: In a time where all boys and men confront new challenges in school, work, and family life, black boys and men face certain systemic disadvantages. We pay special attention to their needs and hardships.
- Fatherhood & Family: Family life is changing, but dads matter as much as ever. We study the economic and cultural changes that are affecting boys and men at home and with their families.

Shared Parenting

Location: United States

Website: https://www.sharedparenting.org/mission

The mission of Shared Parenting is to improve the lives of children and strengthen society by protecting every child's right to the love and care of both parents when divorced or separated. The overarching goal of National Parents Organization (NPO) is to promote shared parenting by educating parents, divorce professionals, and legislators and by reforming family courts and laws in every state. We envision a society in which:

- Shared parenting when parents are separated or divorced is the norm.

- Children's natural right to be nurtured and guided by both parents is fully honored.
- Society treats fathers and mothers as equally important to the well-being of their children.
- Children are happier and more successful because their loving bonds to their parents and extended family are protected after parental separation or divorce.
- The courts arrange finances after separation or divorce so that both mothers and fathers can afford to house and care for their children and themselves.

Health and Human Services Entities

These entities often provide direct service to boys and men in need.

Philly House
Location: Philadelphia
Website: https://www.phillyhouse.org/
With 145+ years of experience, Philly House is the second oldest homeless mission in the country and the oldest in Pennsylvania, housing some 220 men each night. More than just a meal and a bed, we build relationships with our guests to give them hope and reorient their lives. Their Christian faith is the foundation of everything they do and compels them to treat everyone—their guests, volunteers and donors—with dignity, respect, and compassion.

- **What We Do:** Philly House opens its doors every day to walk alongside the homeless, hungry and hurting of Philadelphia so that they may experience the love of God through acts of mercy, dignity and respect. Our guests come for shelter and food, and also find a holistic, empowering refuge from the streets through deep, intentional care.
- **Meals:** Philadelphia's only provider of indoor meals EVERY day—365 days a year, we serve up to 10,000 meals each month to anyone who walks through our doors.
- **Shelter and Housing:** As the city's largest and longest-running shelter, Philly House provides a safe, clean refuge off the streets along with deep, intentional engagement to see a long-term impact. 1/3 of all homeless men in Philadelphia are sheltered at Philly House each year.

- **Programs and Services:** We join with our community partners to serve the homeless, hungry and hurting through a wide range of living, compassion-based programs, and services.

Philly House believes that everyone has God-given potential and the opportunity for transformation. Quick-fix charity is never the ultimate solution. We activate healing, not handouts, through deep intentional engagement so that the homeless, hungry and hurting can achieve stability and self-sufficiency.

Missouri Department of Health: Suicide Prevention for Men

Location: Missouri

Website: https://dmh.mo.gov/suicide-prevention-men

I (Sean) looked at recent suicide deaths across all ages and data, discovering that, on average, 953 boys and men die by suicide each year is Missouri. This represents a real loss for Missouri families and communities. Suicide can be prevented. This agency is answering this call. From the website: "If you or someone you know is in a mental health, suicide, or substance use crisis, reach out to the 988 Suicide & Crisis Lifeline by calling or texting 988, or chatting at https://988lifeline.org/. The Lifeline can help you get through an immediate crisis and put you in touch with resources in your community." The decision by Missouri's Department of Health to recognize male mental health is one that other states should embrace.

The Mankind Project

Location: Philadelphia and Other Places in the U.S.

Website: https://philly.mkpusa.org/new-warrior-training-adventure/

National: https://mankindproject.org/

What Is It? NWTA (New Warrior Training Adventure) is a modern male initiation and self-examination process. It is a real-time hero's journey—the challenge of a lifetime for many men. Safe, supportive, and cutting edge, it is not a retreat, a conference or workshop. It is not like anything you've done before. Many men rank this among the most powerful experiences of their lives.

What You Will Get. You'll get more than you're willing to hope for: purpose, passion, vibrancy, joy, healing, connection to self, new energy, clarity, power, freedom, understanding, brotherhood, trust. Over 60,000 men have now taken this journey, and every man's experience has been unique.

About the NWTA. This is a life affirming event that honors the best in what men have to offer the planet. We are only able to recognize the powerful brilliance of men because we are willing to look at, and take full responsibility for the pain we are also capable of creating…and suffering. This is the paradox of modern masculinity, and it is a lesson we are dedicated to learning and teaching.

At the NWTA. You'll experience a level of energy, a quality of masculinity, a deep sense of safety, joy and laughter, anger and fear, physical challenge, and a connection to life's mystery that we can't explain to you, no matter how hard we try. You'll have the opportunity to look with fearless honesty at the life you've created, and make profound choices about what you want to keep, what you want to expand, and what you want to let go of. You'll discover your unique connection to manhood, explore a new way of understanding masculinity, and step fully into the man you envision yourself to be.

Other Programs and Causes

Some programs are religion-based, like Philly House and like these, presented in their own words via emails from stakeholders.

"Christian Service Brigade is a nation-wide program in hundreds of local churches. Brigade began in 1937 and continues to be a gender-specific, intergenerational ministry building godly men of today and tomorrow. Its main office is in Hamburg, NY with an active website (CSBMinistries.org) and programs for dads and sons, men and junior age boys, and men and teen young men. My involvement in CSB for over 70 years has been as a boy, a teen, an assistant leader, a dad, a leader, and on the full-time staff. The program and leaders have made a huge impact on my life and still do!"

"Trail Life USA. We have nearly 60,000 members in 1,200 Troops in all 50 states and have an unapologetic stance on the wonder and uniqueness of boys."

"House of Timothy (www.houseoftimothy.org) is a Christ-centered residential program dedicated to helping young men heal from trauma, addiction, and other challenges. Our mission is to provide a safe, nurturing environment where these teens can grow, learn, and thrive."

Helping Boys of Color
A potential way to get funding for your boys' organization is to focus on specific populations that have been underserved. Here are some organizations that do just that.

Sims-Fayola Foundation (www.sffoundation.org) provides K-12 After School, Community Based Mental Health, and other boy-friendly programs.

Black Men Building Community (https://bmenfoundation.org/) brings together black men to build community and resources.

BMAN Advocacy (Boys Mentoring Advocacy Network, www.bmanadvocacy.org) is an international Non-Governmental Organization incorporated in the USA and Nigeria.

BOND (bondeducators.org) works toward more male teachers of color in our schools.

An example of a program in this vein that is highly local is **Saving Our Sons Now**, founded by Latronia Green, a concerned mother of sons, as a mentoring program based in New Jersey for boys ages 8-21. Ms. Green wrote, "Our mission is to help boys and young men build self-awareness, self-esteem, and self-discipline for themselves. Our vision is to see boys discover who they really are in this world, and to grow into men with purpose for their families, society, and the world. The Saving Our Sons Now program came out of a painful situation that occurred with one of my four sons. Shortly after, I realized there are so many mothers and grandmothers that faced some of the same challenges I experienced raising young men. I knew that there was something that needed to be done about these situations. So, on June 30th, 2012 we had our first meeting for the boys and we continued once a month after that. We also collaborated with similar boys' programs and community events.

"This program is designed to support and help males learn ways to turn complex issues into simple life strategies. Over the past 12 years, we have supported our boys in finding jobs, preparation training, and community service projects. We have guided them with advice from male role models, helped build confidence, and helped them find new hobbies and many other resources. Overall, we have found creative and successful ways to navigate boys on a path to becoming purpose-driven men."

Gurian Model Schools

Another place we find boy-friendly programming is in boys' schools, therapeutic boarding schools, and Gurian Model Schools. Not all boys schools and therapeutic boarding schools work from a male-brain approach, but some do. One of those, a Gurian Model School, is Cherokee Creek Boys School in the wilderness outside of Westminster, SC. GI has been collaborating with this leading-edge school for fifteen years, providing consulting and training. Check out the school at https://cherokeecreek.net/.

Here is a testimonial from parents of a boy who went to the school that illustrates how well a male-focused and male-friendly program can work to help solve the male mental health crisis.

"We are so incredibly grateful that we found Cherokee Creek Boys School. Our son was in a world of really bad hurt in so many ways when we arrived at Cherokee Creek—and the same for us, perhaps on an exponentially greater scale. We had no idea what to expect, and left the campus and our son on Day 1 with massive guilt and fear of the unknown. It became clear very early on that this wasn't CCBS' first, or even their second rodeo. The staff and faculty quickly and deftly embraced our son. They were seasoned experts in managing, working with, and helping boys in an environment that let the boys put it all on the table, testing their behavioral limits in ways that simply would not happen or have been allowed in a co-ed environment. The counseling was beyond what we expected, as was the universal dedication and support of the entire administrative, educational and support staff.

"The boys are allowed to be boys at CCBS, without the distractions of girls, and of course they push those limits, and are allowed to do so within reason. Along the way, they are counseled and redirected and learn how to comply appropriately with boundaries and limits, and how to interact with and respect male peers and co-ed adult staff. If girls were in the program, I believe it would necessitate an approach that would seriously dilute and fail to fully address the root causes of the problems and challenges the boys are suffering at this developmental stage in life.

"Boys are held accountable, and learn to accept consequences, and they are given counseling and support focused on how to redirect male-specific impulses and anger, and how to focus on finding their true potential. The boys interact closely 24/7, go on trips and outings together, and learn how to be good, dependable and supportive friends—and how to make friends without the struggles that they faced when they arrived. So many of the bonds our son has formed with his closest peers will be ones that I'm sure will last a lifetime.

"A week from now, our son will graduate, and we are very optimistic looking ahead. Sure, there are still bumps in the road, but one of the things that stands out for us is how far happier, more mature, more respectful he is—to put it mildly. And he's determined to be a better son, grandson, cousin, friend and citizen of the neighborhood and the world. He's evolved from an out-of-control boy with no foreseeable future in his mind to a confident and respectful young man, and we could not be happier with our decision to have given him the CCBS opportunity to overcome his obstacles, and to prosper now and into the future."

You can see more about Cherokee Creek and other Gurian Institute Model Schools here: https://gurianinstitute.com/gi-model-schools/. San Antonio Academy, a boys' school in San Antonio, Texas, has just recertified as a Model School. Crespi Carmelite High School in Encino, California, mentioned above (www.crespi.org) has become a Gurian Center for Educational Excellence, which includes the Model School designation. These schools and others like them have committed to brain-based approaches to male development. This means they are committed to matching the male brain with good schooling, with strong emotional development frameworks, and with physical and mental health goals for young males.

Moving Forward to Boys Health

If you are reading this book, it is likely that you live in a democracy or democratic leaning culture. For those of us in these cultures, non-discrimination is a core value. We are cultures with boys and girls and males and females in them any of whom may need our help. Equality for women should be equality for everyone, we were told decades ago, and we created organizations within and without our governments to make sure we got equality for girls and women. We are glad these existing organizations flourish and that new female-focused organizations start up almost daily around the world.

Boy-focused organizations like those mentioned in this chapter should now join girl-focused organizations in search of equality for all people. The culture imperative under which our sociological thinking labors, teaching us that everything good or bad in a child's life exists in "culture" without much input from "nature," is ultimately inadequate. Our children need help in "child" development, yes, but also in "male and female" development, which includes the sexgender spectrum. Women faced significant discrimination fifty and a hundred years ago not because they were a cultural stereotype of "woman," but because the social system was set up to hinder their female brains and bodies from excelling with the opportunities and support they deserved.

Similarly, now, while boys and men may face discrimination because of their skin color or cultural region, their discrimination also happens because social systems are not set up for them as *males*. Indeed, many existing social systems dislike, fear, reject, or abandon them as males. While culture matters for some things, it is not the foundation of everything going on with our children. To deny that "male" matters is to dangerously disavow a core answer to "Who am I?" Boys hurt themselves and others in large part because of what is in their brains–the "who." We are tasked as a civilization with unlocking Who, Am, and I, their minds, hearts, and souls for the common good.

Each organization that helps boys and men will likely be an organization battling against discrimination in some way because sexgender discrimination does inspire (or should inspire) our social will to solve problems. As secular and faith-based organizations work together (like the Spokane Fatherhood Initiative, a Christian-based organization commissioned by the state to run post-prison programs for *all* males), we should keep church and state separate in some ways, certainly, but also bring them together in other ways. We need *all* our assets to create a social revolution on behalf of males especially in a culture that thinks they need no help. In the State of Arizona's government, a division is dedicated to supporting faith-based alliances. Arizona provides a model for how to make state and church work in unison.

If new or existing organizations and programs try to rob females of girl-friendly resources or if they pretend that girls and women are not discriminated against in various human areas, these boy-friendly organizations should gain little traction. One group's suffering does not negate another group's suffering; help for one group should not negate help for another group. Equity is the art and science of helping everyone *according to their need.* Our democracies possess the social and financial capital to build equity for *everyone.* Where our females need us, we must show up whole-heartedly to help them. Similarly, where males need us, we must discover with them a new world in which resources, assets, ideas, theories, governments, universities, media, and the whole multi-family system bring equity to the boys and men on which our human future depends.

Thank you for reading this book and utilizing its tools and resources.

Please reach out to us at seank@gibm.us or michaelgurian@comcast.net.

We are your allies in fulfilling your own rescue plan for boys.

Notes and Resources

Introduction

New York University. "Why Do Some Teen Boys Turn Aggressive? The Surprising Role of Masculinity." *SciTechDaily*. July 15, 2024, https://scitechdaily.com/why-do-some-teen-boys-turn-aggressive-the-surprising-role-of-masculinity/

Perry, Mark. Phd and Mortenson, Thomas. 2021 Update: "For Every 100 Girls." *American Enterprise Institute*. November 1, 2021, https://www.aei.org/carpe-diem/2021-update-for-every-100-girls-part-i/. "In 2011, Thomas G. Mortenson, senior scholar at the Pell Institute for the Study of Opportunity in Higher Education in Washington, D.C. and independent higher education policy analyst, put together and published the 100+ item list "For Every 100 Girls…." on Education Week. In an email, Tom explained to [Perry] that "At the time I initially wrote it I was hearing and reading that boys were no different than girls, and the data I was looking at said something very different. Our differences are important, to both genders, and should be respected. Education has a long way to go to recognize, appreciate, and address these differences through educational opportunities tailored to these differences."

Hill, Marion. M.A.N.C.A.V.E. (Men All Need to Be Caring, Actively Engaged, Vested, and Encouraged) was founded by City of Phoenix Head Start Program Coordinator Marion Hill. This program helps dads, parents, grandparents, and male role models enhance their child-raising in their families and communities. Here is more from Marion: "M.A.N. C.A.V.E. & Dad Together have joined together with one vision in mind, to reach fathers and male role models. This program is designed to help fathers and male role models strengthen their relationships with their children, improve communication and parenting skills, and build a support network of other dads and men who are going through similar experiences.

"M.A.N.C.A.V.E. and Dad Together improve the well-being of children by increasing the number of children growing up with engaged, committed, and responsible fathers or male role models. We promote the importance of nurturing fathers and mothers, parenting, and healthy marriages, and in doing so, improve the lives of children and families.

"M.A.N.C.A.V.E & Dad Together provide nurturing programming, one-on-one or group mentoring for fathers, and male role models to help them navigate the challenges of healthy masculinity, parenthood and build strong healthy relationships. Through this partnership, men are empowered to be positive role models and active participants in their children's lives, ultimately creating stronger, more resilient families and communities.

"In addition to the curriculum and mentoring sessions, M.A.N.C.A.V.E. & Dad Together offer workshops, social events, and community resources to help fathers connect with their families and support overall well-being. Our goal is to create a supportive and inclusive community where fathers can learn from each other, share their experiences, and grow as men, husbands and fathers. 'I now see that failure has no authority over my life, and my struggles are now lessons that allow room for growth.'—Program Participant.

"If you are a father looking for support, guidance, and a community of like-minded individuals, we invite you to join M.A.N.C.A.V.E. & Dad Together. Together, we can navigate the challenges of fatherhood and celebrate the joys of parenting. Visit our website at azmancave.org or contact us for more information on how to get involved by texting "fatherhood" to 602-932-6633."

Part I: The Male Mental Health Crisis

Chapter 1: We Must Invest in Rescuing Our Sons

Kullman, Sean. "U.S. School Shooting Deaths, Injuries, and Incidents by Year from 2000 to 2023." *Wikipedia*. August 2024. https://en.wikipedia.org/wiki/List_of_school_shootings_in_the_United_States_(2000%E2%80%93present). Graph created by Sean Kullman from source. It should be noted that a particular incident in a particular year may have a high number of fatalities and/or injuries even if there were fewer incidents than other years, and one incident in any given year often explains the rise and fall of the number-of-deaths line.

Wright, Tim. *Searching for Tom Sawyer*. Bloomington, WestBow Press, 2013.

Bruenig, Elizabeth. "The latest schoolhouse slaughter shows we have been defeated." *The Spokesman Review*, February 16, 2018. https://www.spokesman.com/stories/2018/feb/16/elizabeth-bruenig-the-latest-schoolhouse-slaughter/.

"Male and Female Suicide Deaths." *Centers for Disease Control and Prevention, National Center for Health Statistics. National Vital Statistics System, Provisional Mortality on CDC WONDER Online Database*. Data are from the final Multiple Cause of Death Files, 2018-2022, and from provisional data for years 2023-2024, as compiled from data provided by the 57 vital statistics jurisdictions through the Vital Statistics Cooperative Program. Accessed at http://wonder.cdc.gov/mcd-icd10-provisional.html on Aug 24, 2024 2:45:31 PM (https://wonder.cdc.gov/controller/saved/D176/D403F743).

"Homicide Deaths by Race and Sex of those 25 and Under." Centers for Disease Control and Prevention, National Center for Health Statistics. National Vital Statistics System, Provisional Mortality on CDC WONDER Online Database. Data are from the final Multiple Cause of Death Files, 2018-2022, and from provisional data for years 2023-2024, as compiled from data provided by the 57 vital statistics jurisdictions through the Vital Statistics Cooperative Program. Accessed at http://wonder.cdc.gov/mcd-icd10-provisional.html on Aug 24, 2024 2:58:42 PM. (https://wonder.cdc.gov/controller/saved/D176/D403F744).

OECD – PISA data can be accessed via https://www.oecd.org/en/about/programmes/pisa.html and by exploring the oecd.org site. Particularly instructive is to go back over the last few decades and watch the evolution of the loss of males over that time span.

The *WHO* study and Global Disease Reports are very instructive and can be accessed via various sites and links. One to start with is https://www.who.int/data.

Fortin, Nicole M., et al. "Leaving Boys Behind: Gender Disparities in High Academic Achievement." *Journal of Human Resources*, Vol. 50, Summer, 2015. "Using data from the 'Monitoring the Future' surveys, this paper shows that from the 1980s to the 2000s, the mode of girls' high school GPA distribution has shifted from "B" to "A," essentially "leaving boys behind" as the mode of boys' GPA distribution stayed at "B." In a reweighted Oaxaca-Blinder decomposition of achievement at each GPA level, we find that changes to gender differences in post-secondary expectations occur as early as the eighth grade. Decomposition of achievement at each GPA level, we find that changes to gender differences in post-secondary expectations occur as early as the eighth grade.

Miller, Clair Cain. "A Disadvantaged Start in Life Harms Boys More Than Girls." *The New York Times*, October 22, 2016.

Shah, Neil. "U.S. Sees Rise in Unmarried Parents" *The Wall Street Journal*, March 10, 2015.

D'Agostino, Ryan. "The Drugging of the American Boy." *Esquire*, March, 2014.

In her fascinating book, Unbroken Brain, Maia Szalavitz points out that it is mainly men and boys who go to prison for addiction. What I have called "gender profiling" allows for this practice, though much of the practice in the criminal justice system is unconscious, not malicious.

Kerr, B.A. and Multon, K.D. "The Development of Gender Identity, Gender Roles, and Gender Relations in Gifted Students." *Journal of Counseling and Development*, April 2015, Vol 3: 163-191.

"Gender Differences in the careers of academic scientists and engineers." *National Science Foundation*, July 30, 2003. https://www.nsf.gov/publications/pub_summ.jsp?ods_key=nsf03322.

Healy, Melissa. "U.S. Tops in Mass Shootings." *Los Angeles Times*, August 26, 2015.

Skidmore Sell, Sarah. "Women Top CFO Pay Chart." *Associated Press*, December 19, 2015.

Superville, Denisa R. "Locked-Up Youths See Grim Prospects in Many States." *Education Week*. December 9, 2015.

Zakaria, Fareed. "America's Self-Destructive Whites." *The Washington Post*, January 1, 2016.

MacDonald, Heather. "The Myths of Black Lives Matter." *The Wall Street Journal*, February 12, 2016. MacDonald displays one of the ways that "headlines" distort reality. In "The Myths of Black Lives Matter," the implication of the headline (no doubt created by Journal staff to incite readers) is that MacDonald does not think black lives matter. Her article clearly speaks to the needs of blacks and all groups. Within the article, too, are statistics of interest, that might get lost in all the extreme headlines on both sides of the Black Lives Matter debate. The *Washington Post*, she notes, has been collecting data on fatal police shootings because of "deficiencies in federal tallies."

She writes, "According to the *Post* database, in 2015 officers killed 662 whites and Hispanics and 258 blacks. (The overwhelming majority of all those police-shooting victims were attacking the officer, often with a gun). Using the 2014 homicide numbers as an approximation of 2015's, those 662 white and Hispanic victims of police shootings would make up 12% of all white and Hispanic homicide deaths. That is three times the proportion of black deaths that result from police shootings."

She compares this statistic with black-on-black homicide rates, which are 6,095 black homicide deaths. "Almost all of those black homicide victims had black killers."

The race issues here are much more nuanced than headlines allow. Black lives matter a great deal, but we have to be wary of casting white policemen into yet another masculine system that destroys vulnerable groups. And we have to be wary of missing the constantly high rates of white homicide and white male privation in our zeal to help other needy populations. The constant casting of males into villains and our blindness to what is going on with white males keeps the Dominant Gender Paradigm (subject of Chapter 2) going strong while millions of males and, thus, females, end up suffering.

Parker, Kathleen. "The White Guys' White Knight." *The Washington Post*, December 23, 2015. Parker powerfully seconds the importance of seeing that the boy crisis affects all demographics, including white boys and men. She writes, "Based on my research and observations in writing, 'Save the Males,' conservative white guys aren't so much trying to hold onto power and privilege as much as they're trying to find their footing in a culture they feel devalues and disrespects them. They're tired of hearing that they're the source of all problems. They're sick of being the single demographic about which one can say anything at all and suffer only the annoyance of deafening applause."

For more statistics and analysis on what is happening to American boys across the demographics please also see:

- Richard Reeves' *On Boys and Men*
- Warren Farrell and John Gray's *The Boy Crisis*
- Michael Gurian's *Saving Our Sons*
- Richard Whitmire's *Why Boys Fail.*
- Christina Hoff Sommers's *The War Against Boys.* (Also please see her short video clips, "The Factual Feminist," produced by the American Enterprise Institute, where she is a resident scholar)
- Warren Farrell's work, including *The Myth of Male Power* and his book, with John Gray, *The Boy Crisis*
- *Raising Cain* by Dan Kindlon and Michael Thompson (put into a powerful video for PBS of the same name)
- William Pollock's *Real Boys*
- Leonard Sax's *Boys Adrift*
- Susan Faludi's *Stiffed*

- Kay Hymowitz's *Manning Up*
- Kathleen Parker's *Save the Males*
- Ongoing writings of columnists such as Leonard Pitts, Donald Brooks, and Kathleen Parker.

These resources by experts and journalists are joined by books, articles, and blogs on boys' distress and needs that may get less notice, but are popping up on the Internet and in print nearly every day.

Case, Ann and Deaton, Angus. "Rising morbidity and mortality in midlife among white non-Hispanic Americans in the 21st century," *Proceedings of the National Academy of Sciences*, Vol. 112, November 2015, 15078-15083.

Dwight, Eva. "Understanding my sons: Science explains boys' brains and what moms can do to connect." *USA Today*, July 2, 2018, https://www.usatoday.com/story/life/allthemoms/2018/07/02/boys-girls-learn-differently/751912002/.

Gurian, Michael. "Our Boys Are in Violent Crisis: Our Nation Must Invest in Helping Boys Thrive." *Gurian Institute*, February 18, 2018, https://gurianinstitute.com/boys-violent-crisis-nation-must-invest-helping-boys-thrive/.

Stuart, Elizabeth. "How Anti-Poverty Programs Marginalize Fathers." *Atlantic*, 25 February 2014, https://www.theatlantic.com/politics/archive/2014/02/how-anti-poverty-programs-marginalize-fathers/283984/.

Moses, Joy and Boggess, Jacquelyn are quoted from Elizabeth Stuart, "How Anti-Poverty Programs Marginalize Fathers." *The Atlantic*, February 25, 2014.

Wright, Tim. *Searching for Tom Sawyer*. Phoenix, *TWM Press*, 2014: For much more about these powerful rite of passage programs please visit www.timwrightministries.org.

Chapter 2: Diseases of Despair Among Our Males

Kullman, Sean. "Overdose Deaths Per 100,000 Population by Sex and Age of 15–34 Year Olds from 2000 to 2022 in Five Year Age Groups." Centers for Disease Control and Prevention, National Center for Health Statistics. National Vital Statistics System, Provisional Mortality on CDC WONDER Online Database. Data are from the final Multiple Cause of Death Files, 2018-2022, and from provisional data for years 2023-2024, as compiled from data provided by the 57 vital statistics jurisdictions through the Vital Statistics Cooperative Program. Accessed at http://wonder.cdc.gov/mcd-icd10-provisional.html on Sep 11, 2024, 6:32:45 PM. To see direct source go to https://wonder.cdc.gov/controller/saved/D176/D405F877. Links can expire.

Kullman, Sean. "Suicide Deaths Per 100,000 Population by Sex and Age of 15–34 Year Olds from 2000 to 2022 in Five Year Age Groups." Centers for Disease Control and Prevention, National Center for Health Statistics. National Vital Statistics System, Provisional Mortality on CDC WONDER Online Database. Data are from the final Multiple Cause of Death Files, 2018-2022, and from provisional data for years 2023-2024, as compiled from data provided by the 57 vital statistics jurisdictions through the Vital Statistics Cooperative Program. Accessed at http://wonder.cdc.gov/mcd-icd10-provisional.html on Oct 30, 2024 2:08:11 AM. To see direct source go to https://

wonder.cdc.gov/controller/saved/D176/D405F878. Links can expire.

Spencer, Merianne R., et al. "Drug overdose deaths in the United States, 2002–2022." NCHS Data Brief, no 491. Hyattsville, MD: National Center for Health Statistics. 2024. DOI: https://dx.doi.org/10.15620/cdc:135849.

Garnett MF and Curtin SC. "Suicide mortality in the United States, 2001–2021." NCHS Data Brief, no 464. Hyattsville, MD: National Center for Health Statistics. 2023, DOI: https://dx.doi.org/10.15620/cdc:125705.

Kullman, Sean. "Overdose Deaths and Suicide Deaths Combined Per 100,000 Population by Sex and Age of 15–34 Year Olds from 2000 to 2022 in Five Year Age Groups." Center For Disease Control and Prevention Wonder Database. June, 2024.

"Male Breast Cancer: A Rare, Increasing Trend." Johns Hopkins Medicine, Accessed September 2024, https://www.hopkinsmedicine.org/health/conditions-and-diseases/breast-cancer/male-breast-cancer-a-rare-increasing-trend.

Kullman, Sean. "Average Overdose and Suicide Deaths Combined from 2000-2022 Per 100,000 People By Selected Age Groups and Years." *Center For Disease Control and Prevention Wonder Database.* June, 2024.

Ryali, Srikanth, et al. "Deep learning models reveal replicable, generalizable, and behaviorally relevant sex differences in human functional brain organization." *Proceedings of the National Academy of Sciences, PNAS.* 20 February 2024, https://www.pnas.org/doi/10.1073/pnas.2310012121.

Reeves, Richard. "Melinda French Gates invests in boys and men: a new era for gender equality." *Of Boys and Men*, May 28, 2024, https://ofboysandmen.substack.com/p/melinda-french-gates-invests-in-boys.

Chapter 3: Diagnosing and Treating Male-Type Depression

Albert, Paul R, PhD. "Why is depression more prevalent in women?" *Journal of Psychiatry and Neuroscience*, 2015 Jul; 40(4): 219–221.

Wright, Jennifer. "It's Time to Let Boys Be Girly." *Harpers*, March 3, 2018, https://www.harpersbazaar.com/culture/politics/a19046540/how-to-stop-toxic-masculinity-raise-boys-to-embrace-femininity.

"Young men discuss the pressures of masculinity: 'You can't show sadness." *Today*, March 25, 2018, https://www.today.com/video/how-do-we-help-today-s-boys-before-they-turn-to-gun-violence-1194547779598.

Vedantam, Shankar. "The Lonely American Man." NPR's Hidden Brain, March 19, 2018, https://pandora.app.link/fQBkJG8ZXJb.

Heilman, Brian, et al. "THE MAN BOX: A Study on Being a Young Man in the US, UK, and Mexico." *Equimundo*, 2017, https://www.equimundo.org/wp-content/uploads/2017/03/TheManBox-FullReport.pdf.

Kullman, Sean. "Percent of U.S. Opioid Deaths by Sex and Year 2018-2022." *Kaiser Family Foundation*, July 2, 2024, https://www.kff.org/other/state-indicator/opioid-overdose-deaths-by-sex/?dataView=1¤tTimeframe=0&sortModel=%7B

%22colId%22:%22Location%22,%22sort%22:%22asc%22%7D.

Deak, JoAnn. *Girls Will Be Girls*. Hyperion, New York, 2002.

Gurian, Michael. *How Do I Help Him?* Gurian Institute Press, 2011.

Halpern, D.F., et al. "The Science of Sex Differences in Science and Mathematics." *Psychological Science in the Public Interest*, Volume 8, No. 1, August 2007.

Ingalhalikar, M., et al. "Sex Differences in the Structural Connectome of the Human Brain." *Proceedings of the National Academy of Sciences*, 2014, Vol 111, 823-828.

Killgore, W., et al. "Sex-Specific Developmental Changes in Amygdala Responses to Affective Faces." *NeuroReport*, 2001, Vol. 12, 427-433.

Gummadavelli, A, et al. "Spatiotemporal and Frequency Signatures of Word Recognition in the Developing Brain." Brain Research, 2013, Vol. 1498, 20-32.

Albert, P.R. "Why is Depression More Prevalent in Women?" *The Journal of Psychiatry and Neuroscience*, 2015 Jul; 40(4): 219–221.

Leger, Kate A, et al. "Let It Go: Lingering Negative Affect in Response to Daily Stressors Is Associated with Physical Health Years Later." *Psychological Science*, January 2018: 1-8.

Wertz, J, et al. "Genetics and Crime: Integrating New Genomic Discoveries Into Psychological Research About Antisocial Behavior." *Psychological Science*, February 2018, 1-12.

Grandjean, P., et al. "Neurobehavioral Effects of Developmental Toxicity." *Lancet Neurology*, Vol. 13, 333- 338, March 2014.

Stervo, M., et al. "Frequent Video Game Playing in Young Males is Associated with Central Adiposity and High-Sugar, Low-Fiber Dietary Consumption." *Eating and Weight Disorders*, 2014, Vol. 19, 515-520.

Vandewater, E., et al. "Linking Obesity and Activity Level with Children's Television and Video Game Use." *Journal of Adolescence,* 2004, Vol. 27, 71-85.

Alexander, R. "How Hits on the Field Translate to Brain Damage." *Spokesman Review*, March 30, 2018.

Amen Clinics. www.amenclinics.com.

The Center, A Place of Hope. www.aplaceofhope.com.

Chapter 4: We Can't Save Lives If We Won't Admit the Problem
Kullman, Sean. "U.S. Suicide Deaths from 2018-2022 by Race and Sex." Centers for Disease Control and Prevention, National Center for Health Statistics. National Vital Statistics System, Provisional Mortality on CDC WONDER Online Database. Data are from the final Multiple Cause of Death Files, 2018-2022, and from provisional data for years 2023-2024, as compiled from data provided by the 57 vital statistics jurisdictions through the Vital Statistics Cooperative Program. Accessed at http://wonder.cdc.gov/mcd-icd10-provisional.html on Sep 11, 2024 7:30:13 PM. Direct link to non-Hispanic populations (https://wonder.cdc.gov/controller/saved/

D176/D356F737), Hispanic Populations (https://wonder.cdc.gov/controller/saved/D176/D356F738).

Stone, Deborah, et al. "Suicides Among American Indian or Alaska Native Persons." — *National Violent Death Reporting System, United States, 2015–2020."* *MMWR Morb Mortal Wkly Rep 2022;71:1161–1168.* DOI: http://dx.doi.org/10.15585/mmwr.mm7137a1.

Kullman, Sean. "Deaths of American Indian/Alaska Native from 2015-2020 by Age and Sex Per 100,000 Persons." Centers for Disease Control and Prevention, National Center for Health Statistics. National Vital Statistics System, Mortality 1999-2020 on CDC WONDER Online Database, released in 2021. Data are from the Multiple Cause of Death Files, 1999-2020, as compiled from data provided by the 57 vital statistics jurisdictions through the Vital Statistics Cooperative Program. Accessed at http://wonder.cdc.gov/mcd-icd10.html on Oct 30, 2024, 2:44:27 AM. Direct link to source. (https://wonder.cdc.gov/controller/saved/D77/D412F454).

Kullman, Sean. "U.S. Male Deaths of Despair by Year 2018-2022." Center for Disease Control and Prevention Wonder Database, June 2024, https://wonder.cdc.gov/.

Kullman, Sean. "Alcohol Induced Causes of Death by Race and Sex 2018-2022." Single Race Not Hispanic (https://wonder.cdc.gov/controller/saved/D176/D358F709), Hispanic (https://wonder.cdc.gov/controller/saved/D176/D358F711), Centers for Disease Control and Prevention, National Center for Health Statistics. National Vital Statistics System, Provisional Mortality on CDC WONDER Online Database. Data are from the final Multiple Cause of Death Files, 2018-2022, and from provisional data for years 2023-2024, as compiled from data provided by the 57 vital statistics jurisdictions through the Vital Statistics Cooperative Program. Accessed at http://wonder.cdc.gov/mcd-icd10-provisional.html on Sep 11, 2024 7:39:10 PM.

Kullman, Sean. "Unintentional Overdose Deaths by Race and Sex 2018-2022." Single Race Not Hispanic (https://wonder.cdc.gov/controller/saved/D176/D399F461), Hispanic (https://wonder.cdc.gov/controller/saved/D176/D399F460), Centers for Disease Control and Prevention, National Center for Health Statistics. National Vital Statistics System, Provisional Mortality on CDC WONDER Online Database. Data are from the final Multiple Cause of Death Files, 2018-2022, and from provisional data for years 2023-2024, as compiled from data provided by the 57 vital statistics jurisdictions through the Vital Statistics Cooperative Program. Accessed at http://wonder.cdc.gov/mcd-icd10-provisional.html on Sep 11, 2024, 7:49:47 PM.

Kullman, Sean. "Suicide Deaths by Race and Sex 2018-2022." Single Race Not Hispanic (https://wonder.cdc.gov/controller/saved/D176/D356F737), Hispanic (https://wonder.cdc.gov/controller/saved/D176/D356F738), Centers for Disease Control and Prevention, National Center for Health Statistics. National Vital Statistics System, Provisional Mortality on CDC WONDER Online Database. Data are from the final Multiple Cause of Death Files, 2018-2022, and from provisional data for years 2023-2024, as compiled from data provided by the 57 vital statistics jurisdictions through the Vital Statistics Cooperative Program. Accessed at http://wonder.cdc.gov/mcd-icd10-provisional.html on Sep 11, 2024 7:51:19 PM.

"Mortality Rates and Causes of Death Among People Experiencing Homelessness in Los Angeles County: 2014-2021." *County of Los Angeles Public Health*, May 2023, http://publichealth.lacounty.gov/chie/reports/Homeless_Mortality_Report_2023.pdf.

Jackson, Sarah S., PhD, MPH et al. "Analysis of Mortality Among Transgender and Gender Diverse Adults in England." *Journal of the American Medical Association.* January 30, 2023.

Kullman, Sean. "Table for Addressing Number of Deaths of Despair by Race and Sex."

Kullman, Sean. "Table for Addressing Number of Deaths of Despair by Sex and Gender of Transgender People."

Kullman, Sean. "Table for Addressing Number of Deaths of Despair by Sex and Gender of Transgender People by Race, Sex, and Gender."

Kullman, Sean. "U.S. Drug Overdose Deaths from 2018-2022 by Race and Sex." Center for Disease Control and Prevention Wonder Database, https://wonder.cdc.gov/.

Kullman, Sean. "Deaths of the Respiratory System of Infants by Sex." Centers for Disease Control and Prevention, National Center for Health Statistics. National Vital Statistics System, Mortality 2018-2022 on CDC WONDER Online Database, released in 2024. Data are from the Multiple Cause of Death Files, 2018-2022, as compiled from data provided by the 57 vital statistics jurisdictions through the Vital Statistics Cooperative Program. Accessed at http://wonder.cdc.gov/mcd-icd10-expanded.html on Oct 30, 2024 2:53:32 AM. Select for direct link. (https://wonder.cdc.gov/controller/saved/D157/D398F803).

Kullman, Sean. "All Causes of Infant Deaths." Centers for Disease Control and Prevention, National Center for Health Statistics. National Vital Statistics System, Mortality 2018-2022 on CDC WONDER Online Database, released in 2024. Data are from the Multiple Cause of Death Files, 2018-2022, as compiled from data provided by the 57 vital statistics jurisdictions through the Vital Statistics Cooperative Program. Accessed at http://wonder.cdc.gov/mcd-icd10-expanded.html on Oct 30, 2024 2:55:11 AM. Select for direct link (https://wonder.cdc.gov/controller/saved/D157/D398F809).

Kullman, Sean. "All Causes of Death of Children 1-4 Years of Age by Sex." Centers for Disease Control and Prevention, National Center for Health Statistics. National Vital Statistics System, Mortality 2018-2022 on CDC WONDER Online Database, released in 2024. Data are from the Multiple Cause of Death Files, 2018-2022, as compiled from data provided by the 57 vital statistics jurisdictions through the Vital Statistics Cooperative Program. Accessed at http://wonder.cdc.gov/mcd-icd10-expanded.html on Oct 30, 2024 2:58:11 AM. (https://wonder.cdc.gov/controller/saved/D157/D412F456).

Chapter 5: What Was the American Psychological Association Thinking?
Gurian, Michael. "Blaming Masculinity Will Only Make the Male Crisis Worse." *The Federalist*, January 14, 2019, https://thefederalist.com/2019/01/14/blaming-masculinity-will-make-male-crisis-worse/.

"APA GUIDELINES for Psychological Practice with Boys and Men." *American Psychological Association*, August 2018, https://www.apa.org/about/policy/boys-men-practice-guidelines.pdf.

Gurian, Michael. "The Storm in My Mother's Eyes." *Michael Gurian Substack*, 2023-2024, https://michaelgurian.substack.com.

Chapter 6: False Allegations, Suicide, Opioid Deaths, and the Self-Medication of Boys

Mellen, Greg. "Long Beach Unified wins judgment against accuser in false rape case against Brian Banks." *Press-Telegram*, September 1, 2017, https://www.presstelegram.com/2013/04/11/long-beach-school-district-suing-accuser-of-brian-banks/?noamp=mobile.

Pidd, Helen. "Barrow men falsely accused of raping Eleanor Williams tell court they tried to kill themselves." *Guardian*, March 13, 2023, https://www.theguardian.com/uk-news/2023/mar/13/barrow-men-falsely-accused-of-tell-court-they-tried-to-kill-themselves.

Kamogelo, Moichela. "No charges against schoolgirl who 'joked' about rape." *IOL*, November 24, 2022, https://www.iol.co.za/news/education/no-charges-against-school-girl-who-joked-about-rape-60390e42-1933-4bb0-8de5-94999c6fd18b.

McCallister, Doreen. "'Rolling Stone' Settles Defamation Case with Former U.Va. Associate Dean." *NPR*, April 12, 2017, https://www.npr.org/sections/thetwo-way/2017/04/12/523527227/rolling-stone-settles-defamation-case-with-former-u-va-associate-dean#:~:text=Lawyers%20for%20Rolling%20Stone%20and,alleged%20gang%20rape%20on%20campus.

"Beneath the Statistics: The Structural and Systemic Causes of Our Wrongful Conviction Problem." *Georgia Innocence Project*, Accessed October 2024, https://www.georgiainnocenceproject.org/general/beneath-the-statistics-the-structural-and-systemic-causes-of-our-wrongful-conviction-problem/.

"Courtney B. Vance on the Importance of Mental Health." *MSNBC's Morning Joe*, December 15, 2023, https://www.msnbc.com/morning-joe/watch/courtney-b-vance-on-the-importance-of-mental-wellness-200299589707.

Vasquez, Ingrid. "Parents of '9-1-1: Lone Star' Actor Tyler Sanders Hope His Story 'Might Save Others' After His Death." *People*, December 30, 2022, https://people.com/tv/parents-of-9-1-1-lone-star-actor-tyler-sanders-speak-out-about-his-death-never-thought-this-could-happen-to-us/.

Reyes, Emily and Ellis, Rebecca. "Fentanyl deaths in L.A. County soared 1,280% between 2016 and 2021, report finds." *Los Angeles Times*, 29 November 2022, https://www.latimes.com/california/story/2022-11-29/fentanyl-deaths-in-l-a-county-soared-1-280-between-2016-and-2021-report-finds.

Kaiser Family Foundation analysis of *Centers for Disease Control and Prevention (CDC)*, National Center for Health Statistics. Multiple Cause of Death 1999-2022 on CDC WONDER Online Database. Data are from the Multiple Cause of Death

Files, 1999-2022, as compiled from data provided by the 57 vital statistics jurisdictions through the Vital Statistics Cooperative Program. Accessed at http://wonder.cdc.gov/mcd-icd10.html on May 7, 2024. https://www.kff.org/other/state-indicator/opioid-overdose-deaths-by-sex/?currentTimeframe=0&sortModel=%7B%22colId%22:%22Location%22,%22sort%22:%22asc%22%7D.

Centers for Disease Control and Prevention, National Center for Health Statistics. National Vital Statistics System, Provisional Mortality on CDC WONDER Online Database. Data are from the final Multiple Cause of Death Files, 2018-2022, and from provisional data for years 2023-2024, as compiled from data provided by the 57 vital statistics jurisdictions through the Vital Statistics Cooperative Program. Accessed at http://wonder.cdc.gov/mcd-icd10-provisional.html on Sep 13, 2024 12:07:36 PM (https://wonder.cdc.gov/controller/saved/D176/D406F079).

Han, B. et al. "Intentional drug overdose deaths in the United States." *The American Journal of Psychiatry*, DOI: 10.1176/appi.ajp.2021.21060604 (2022).

Kullman, Sean. Graph indicating the percent increase or decrease in overdose deaths from previous year, number of deaths per year, and number of deaths/100,000 per year." Centers for Disease Control and Prevention Wonder Database, June 2024, https://wonder.cdc.gov/.

Kullman, Sean. "U.S. Overdose Deaths by Year from 2000 to 2022." Center for Disease Control and Prevention, June 2024, https://wonder.cdc.gov/.

Chapter 7: How Can We Stop Male Violence If We Avoid "Male"?

Kullman, Sean. "Mortality of 15-19 Year Olds Males and Females per 100,000 population (Not Including Overdose, Suicide and Homicide Deaths)." Compiled using data from the Centers for Disease Control and Prevention, May 2, 2024, https://wonder.cdc.gov/.

Kullman, Sean. "Mortality of 20-24 Year Olds Males and Females per 100,000 population (Not Including Overdose, Suicide and Homicide Deaths)." Compiled using data from the Centers for Disease Control and Prevention, May 2, 2024. https://wonder.cdc.gov/.

Rosenstock, Summer. et al. "Sex differences in neonatal mortality in Sarlahi, Nepal: the role of biology and environment." *JM. J Epidemiol Community Health*, 2013 Dec 1;67(12):986-91. doi: 10.1136/jech-2013-202646. Epub 2013 Jul 19. PMID: 23873992.

Handelsman, David J. et al. "Circulating Testosterone as the Hormonal Basis of Sex Differences in Athletic Performance." *Endocrine Reviews*, Volume 39, Issue 5, October 2018, Pages 803–829, https://doi.org/10.1210/er.2018-00020.

Travison TG. et al. "A population-level decline in serum testosterone levels in American men." J *Clin Endocrinol Metab*, 2007 Jan;92(1):196-202. doi: 10.1210/jc.2006-1375. Epub 2006 Oct 24. PMID: 17062768.

Diamond, Jed. *The Irritable Male Syndrome*. Rodale, 2007.

Mohit, Khera. "Patients with testosterone deficit syndrome and depression." *Arch*

Esp Urol, 2013 Sep;66(7):729-36. PMID: 24047633.

Part II: Boys, Sexual Dimorphism, and the Culture of the Exception

Chapter 8: Why I Do Not Generally Use "Cisgender"

Straub, John J., et al. "Risk of Suicide and Self-Harm Following Gender-Affirmation Surgery." *Cureus* vol. 16,4 e57472. 2 Apr. 2024, doi:10.7759/cureus.57472.

Kuiri-Hänninen Tanja, et al. "Postnatal Testicular Activity in Healthy Boys and Boys With Cryptorchidism." *Front Endocrinol* (Lausanne), 2019; 10: 489. Published online 2019 Jul 23.

"Gay." *UCLA Williams Institute School of Law*, December 2023, https://williamsinstitute.law.ucla.edu/wp-content/uploads/LGBT-Adult-US-Pop-Dec-2023.pdf.

"How Many Adults and Youth Identify as Transgender in the United States?" *UCLA Williams Institute School of Law, December 2023*, https://williamsinstitute.law.ucla.edu/wp-content/uploads/LGBT-Adult-US-Pop- Dec-2023.pdf.

Brizendine, Louann. *The Female Brain*. Three Rivers Press, New York, 2007.

Brizendine, Louann.. *The Male Brain*. Harmony, New York, 2011.

Moalem, Sharon. *Better Half*. Farrar, Strauss, and Giroux, New York, 2021.

Woolley, CS. "His and Hers: Sex Differences in the Brain." *Cerebrum*. 2021 Jan 1;2021:cer-02-21. PMID: 34650671; PMCID: PMC8493822.

Moalem, Sharon. *How Sex Works*. Harper Collins, New York, 2010.

Soh, Debra. *The End of Gender*. Threshold Editions, New York, 2020.

Moir, Anne, and Jessel, David. *Brain Sex*. Delta Books, New York, 1992.

Straub, John J., et al. "Risk of Suicide and Self-Harm Following Gender-Affirmation Surgery." *Cureus*, 2024 Apr; 16(4): e57472. Published online 2024 Apr 2. doi: 10.7759/cureus.57472.

Schooley, Matt and Burton, Paul. "Massachusetts high school field hockey team forfeits game to avoid male opponent." *WBZ News,* September 10, 2024, https://www.cbsnews.com/boston/news/massachusetts-high-school-field-hockey-male-player/.

Levenson, Eric. "Swimmer Lia Thomas becomes first transgender athlete to win an NCAA D-I title." *CNN Sports,* March 17, 2022, https://www.cnn.com/2022/03/17/sport/lia-thomas-ncaa-swimming/index.html.

Eckert, Jared and Collins, Lucy. "Abuse of Women in Sports Under the Guise of Trans Rights Deserves a #MeToo Moment." *Heritage Foundation*, February 24, 2021, https://www.heritage.org/gender/commentary/abuse-women-sports-under-the-guise-trans-rights-deserves-metoo-moment.

"Italian boxer 'never felt punch like this' as she quit Olympic bout against athlete who failed 'gender test'." *The Standard,* August 1, 2024, https://www.standard.co.uk/news/world/italian-boxer-olympics-imane-khelif-angela-carini-quits-seconds-b1174213.html.

Roley, Amanda. "Controversy arises after transgender East Valley student wins state track championship." *KREM 2,* May 29, 2024, https://www.krem.com/article/news/local/east-valley-transgender-teen-wins-state-track-controversey/293-2120ce14-825c-46a6-b52e-2f57dedbac55.

Chapter 9: When a Student Is Suspended for Using the "Wrong" Pronoun

"Livermore Valley Joint Unified School District Official Notice of Suspension." Livermore Valley Joint Unified School District, November 9, 2023.

Kullman, Sean. "Percent of Livermore Valley Joint Unified Students who Scores Proficient/Advanced in English/Language Arts by Grade and Sex from 2014-2023." *California Department of Education Data Quest,* March 2024, https://dq.cde.ca.gov/dataquest/.

Kullman, Sean. "Percent of Males and Female Reading Above Standard in Livermore Valley Joint Unified School District from 2014-2023." *California Department of Education Data Quest,* March 2024, https://dq.cde.ca.gov/dataquest/.

Kullman, Sean. "Table 2 Percent of Males and Female Reading Above Standard in California from 2014-2019." *California Department of Education Data Quest,* March 2024, https://dq.cde.ca.gov/dataquest/.

Chapter 10: Not Breast-Feeding but Chest-Feeding?

Legato, Marian, M.D. *Eve's Rib: The New Science of Gender-Specific Medicine.* Harmony Books, New York. 2002.

Brizendine, Louann, M.D. *The Male Brain: A Breakthrough Understanding of How Men and Boys Think.* Harmony Books, New York, 2010.

Brizendine, Louann, M.D. *The Female Brain.* Harmony Books, New York, 2006.

Page, David C, M.D. "The Meaning of Sex: Genes and Gender Lecture One—Deciphering the Language of Sex." https://www.biointeractive.org/sites/default/files/Sex%2520Determination%2520Lecture%25201%2520Transcript.pdf.

Haier, Richard J, et al. "The neuroanatomy of general intelligence: sex matters." *NeuroImage,* 2005; 25 (1): 320 DOI: 10.1016/j.neuroimage.2004.11.019.

"Males and females differ in specific brain structures." *University of Cambridge.* https://www.cam.ac.uk/research/news/males-and-females-differ-in-specific-brain-structures.

Amen, Daniel G., M.D. *Unleash the Power of the Female Brain.* Harmony, NY. 2013.

Amen, Daniel G., M.D. "7 Differences Between Male and Female Brains." *Amen Clinics,* September 22, 2021, https://www.amenclinics.com/blog/7-differences-between-male-and-female-brains/.

Kimura, Doreen. *Sex and Cognition.* Bradford Book, 2000.

Geary, David C., Ph.D. *Male, Female: The Evolution of Sex Difference.* American Psychological Association, Washington D.C. 2021.

Pinker, Steven. "The Genetics of IQ," *The Wall Street Journal,* January 2, 2016.

Petersen, Andrea. "Training the Brain to Cope with Depression," *Wall Street Journal,* January 19, 2016.

Akst, Daniel. "Delay That's in Our DNA," *The Wall Street Journal,* April 12, 2014.

Dockser Marcus, Amy. "The Hard New Family Talk: Our Genes." *The Wall Street Journal,* September 28, 2015.

Dockser Marcus, Amy. "How One Family Faced Difficult Decisions About DNA Sequencing." *The Wall Street Journal,* September 28, 2015, https://www.wsj.com/articles/how-one-family-faced-difficult-decisions-about-dna-sequencing-1443406974.

Blair, C., et al. "Maternal and Child Contributions to Cortisol Response to Emotional Arousal in Young Children from Low-Income Rural Communities." *Developmental Psychology,* Vol. 44, 1095-1109.

Allen, Mark S. and Laborde, Sylvain. "The Role of Personality in Sport and Physical Activity." *Current Directions in Psychological Science,* 2014, Vol. 23(6) 460-465.

Madsen, Sue Lani. "State's New Gender-Restroom Rule." *The Spokesman Review,* January 16, 2016, quoting Williams' University of UCLA School of Law study, "0.3 percent of population are transgender."

See original study at: Gates, G.J., "How Many People Are Lesbian, Gay, Bisexual, and Transgender?" Retrieved from http://williamsinstitute.law.ucla.edu/qp-content/Gates.

Olson, Kristina R., et al. "Gender Cognition in Transgender Children." *Psychological Science,* 2015, Vol. 26 467-474.

A website and organization, Stop the Harm, https://stoptheharmdatabase.com/about/ has developed a database compiling medical insurance claims related to gender-affirming care for minors aged 17.5 and younger across all 50 states. The database doesn't include patients who aren't insured or anyone insured by Kaiser, a major provider on the West Coast, which does not make its data public, so these numbers might be low. "In the U.S., between 2019 and 2023, at least: 13,944 minors were given "gender-affirming" puberty blockers, hormones, and surgeries, 5,747 underwent gender-affirming facial, breast, and genital surgeries, 8,579 were prescribed cross-sex hormones and puberty blockers."

The whole March/April 2016 issue of *Psychotherapy Networker* is devoted to "The Mystery of Gender."

Healy, Melissa. "Study Links Autism, Anti-Depressants in Pregnancy." *The Los Angeles Times,* December 15, 2015.

Sbarra, David A, et al. "Divorce and Health: Beyond Individual Differences." *Current Directions in Psychological Science,* 2015, Vol 24, 109- 113.

Goossens, Luc, et al. "The Genetics of Loneliness: Linking Evolutionary Theory to

Genome-Wide Genetics, Epigenetics, and Social Science." *Perspectives on Psychological Science*, 2015, Vol. 10(2) 213-226.

Meyers, Laurie. "The Toll of Childhood Trauma." *Counseling Today*, July 2014, 29-36.

Antti, Latvala, et al. "Paternal Antisocial Behavior and Sons' Cognitive Ability: A Population-Based Quasiexperimental Study." *Psychological Science,* 2015, Vol. 26(1) 78-88.

Swan, Shanna. "Parents Needn't Wait for Legislation to Shield Kids from Toxins in Products." *San Francisco Chronicle,* January 9, 2006.

In a tiny two paragraph story off the wires, the headline reads, "Artificial Ingredient Sliced." The story is about Pizza Hut ending the use of artificial ingredients over the next year in its U.S. restaurants. Pizza Hut executives have studied the science and agree that BHA and BHT must be cut from meat to protect customers, as must artificial preservatives from cheese. This is the kind of responsible citizenship that should make front-page news, in my humble opinion. The epigenetics issues that preservatives, artificial ingredients, red dye, artificial sweeteners, and even simple things like aluminum can cause our children should be front page news whenever possible.

To learn more about male/female brain difference, please see *Boys and Girls Learn Differently, The Minds of Boys, The Wonder of Girls*, and the books written by all of the scientists I mentioned, e.g. Louann Brizendine and Daniel Amen. I have created a further resource, a list appearing on the website www.michaelgurian.com/Research that includes approximately 1,000 primary and secondary sources in gender neuroscience such as the study I mentioned: Diane Halpern, et al., including Camilla Benbow and Ruben Gur, "The Science of Sex Differences in Science and Mathematics." *Psychological Science in the Public Interest,* Vol 8, No. 1, August 2007.

Sex differences in the brain (what we now popularly call "gender differences") appear at all ages, including in earliest childhood and latest life-stages. For early childhood to late adolescent differences see especially: Yu, Vickie., et al. "Age-Related Sex Differences in Language Lateralization: A Magnetoencephalography Study in Children." *Developmental Psychology*, 2014, Vol.50, 2276-2284.

Ingalhalikar, Madhura, et al. "Sex Differences in the Structural Connectome of the Human Brain." *Proceedings of the National Academy of Sciences,* 2014, Vol 111, 823-828.

Killgore, William, et al. "Sex-Specific Developmental Changes in Amygdala Responses to Affective Faces." *NeuroReport,* 2001, Vol. 12, 427- 433.

Gummadavelli, Abhijeet, et al. "Spatiotemporal and Frequency Signatures of Word Recognition in the Developing Brain." *Brain Research,* 2013, Vol. 1498, 20-32.

Sacher, Julia, et al. "Sexual Dimorphism in the Human Brain." *Magnetic Resonance Imaging*, 2013, Vol 31, 366-375.

Dizik, Alina. "The Secret Subtext of Menus." *The Wall Street Journal,* March 25, 2015.

Winslow, Ron. "Genes May Explain Why Cancer Varies by Gender," *The Wall*

Street Journal, May 17, 2016.

Bartz, Jennifer A. "Oxytocin and the Pharmacological Dissection of Affiliation." *Current Directions in Psychological Science,* 2016, Vol. 25, 104- 110.

Shors, Tracey J. and Miesegaes, George. "Testosterone in Utero and at Birth Dictates How Stressful Experience Will Affect Learning in Adulthood." *Proceedings of the National Academy of Sciences 99,* no. 21 (October 15, 2002): 13955–60.

Shors, Tracey J. "Stress and Sex Effects on Associative Learning: For Better or for Worse." *Neuroscientist* 4, no. 5 (September 1998): 353–64.

Wade, Nicolas "Peeking into Pandora's Box." *The Wall Street Journal,* May 14-15, 2016. Wade explores themes in the new book by Siddhartha Mukherjee, *The Gene,* (Scribner, 2016). He makes a point that is perhaps common sense but also can get lost as we try to understand what is "sex" and what is "gender" from a biological viewpoint. While we can discuss "gender" as happening on a spectrum, as male/ female brains do happen on a spectrum, these brains are still male and female. So, while gender can feel fluid, when we come right down to living our lives and doing our daily tasks of surviving and thriving, sex (neurobiology) is far more powerful in us than some of the present debate allows for as we talk about gender fluidity.

Everyone who has had children has peeked into this truth; parents see the genes in their own family lab. Few if any parents of boys and girls cannot tell, within five years of the child's birth, that there are sex-different brains in those bodies. Even the parents of a transgender child see male/female brains in a way that science observes as "exceptions prove the rule."

So, the rule here should not be to force a transgender child to develop in a gender group that does not fit his/her internal map for gender; rather, the rule is that only .3 percent of children fit this profile, which puts more than 99 percent of children in a mind/body sync regarding gender, though the spectrum of that gender includes more than 7.3 billion kinds of boys/girls.

In a 2008 study published in the Journal of Personality and Social Psychology, a group of international researchers compared data on sex/gender and personality across 55 nations and confirmed that, throughout the world, women tend to be more empathically nurturing, risk averse, and emotionally expressive in words, while men are usually more competitive, risk taking, and emotionally flat in comparison (men feel fewer feelings and express fewer of those feelings in words).

These differences were obvious in all cultures, but highest in frequency between men and women in the more prosperous, egalitarian, and educated societies such as the US. According to the authors, "Higher levels of human development—including long and healthy life, equal access to knowledge and education, and economic wealth—were the main nation-level predictors of sex difference variation across cultures."

The idea, then, that male/female difference disappears in an economic democracy is patently false. The more males and females have the freedom to "be who they are," the more they evidence sex and gender differences. While their social roles become more parallel, their sex/gender differences—which affect their ability to learn well, grow well, survive and thrive—are robust and must be taken into account in all social theories or we will lose huge portions of both males and females to distress.

If you would like even more in depth understanding of the male brain as applied directly to parenting not covered in this book, I hope you will read:

- *The Wonder of Boys* (for understanding, parenting, and mentoring boys in general, especially if you are raising a boy under ten years old, including assistance with discipline and other parenting issues);
- *A Fine Young Man* (for understanding, parenting, and mentoring boys between ten and twenty, including assistance with rites of passage, media use, mentoring, and father-son/mother-son issues);
- *Nurture the Nature* (for nurturing core personality development of each child from birth to 25, with childhood and emerging adulthood divided into seven stages matching brain development);
- *Raising Boys by Design* (specifically connecting the science of the male brain with Christian parenting and Biblical wisdom, written in collaboration with Dr. Gregory Jantz, an evangelical Christian psychologist);
- *The Good Son* (which reveals male brain development from birth to adulthood in two year developmental increments); I want to thank all of my colleagues, collaborators, and colleagues in nature-based theory, including co-authors from both ends of the political spectrum, who prove that gender neuroscience and the sex-based theory developed from it can build bridges between us.
- Sax, Leonard. *Boys Adrift*
- Sax, Leonard. *Why Gender Matters.*
- Amen, Daniel. *Healing ADD*, New York, Berkeley, 2013. I highly recommend Dr. Amen's approach to ADD, which not only uses brain scans to aid in diagnosis and treatment, but also divides ADD into various types so that parents and professionals can fully understand the exact kind of ADD/ ADHD a particular child is experiencing. Like genome testing, the use of brain scans to aid in correct treatment can be very helpful.

Chapter 11: I Am A Boy, Hear Me Roar

Kullman, Sean. "Percent of 3rd to 5th Grade Students Proficient in English Language Arts by Race and Sex from 2014-2022." *Office of Superintendent of Public Education* (Washington State). A public information request was received from OSPE in January 2022.

Kullman, Sean. "Percent of 6th to 8th Grade Students Proficient in English Language Arts by Race and Sex from 2014-2022." *Office of Superintendent of Public Education* (Washington State). A public information request was received from OSPE in January 2022.

"Stanford Medicine study identifies distinct brain organization patterns in women and men." *Stanford Medicine News Center*, February 20, 2024. https://med.stanford.edu/news/all-news/2024/02/men-women-brain-organization-patterns.html.

U.S. Department of Education, National Center for Education Statistics, Earned Degrees Conferred, 1869-70 through 1964-65; Higher Education General Information Survey (HEGIS), "Degrees and Other Formal Awards Conferred" surveys, 1965-66 through 1985-86; Integrated Postsecondary Education Data System (IPEDS), "Completions Survey" (IPEDS-C:87-99); IPEDS Fall 2000 through Fall 2017, Completions component; and Degrees Conferred Projection Model, 1980-81 through 2028-29. (This table was prepared March 2019).

"Reference Tables." *National Center for Education Statistics*, Accessed September 2024, https://nces.ed.gov/programs/coe/current_tables.

Carnevale, Anthony P., et al. "The College Payoff." *The Georgetown University Center on Education and the Workforce*, 2009, https://www2.ed.gov/policy/highered/reg/hearulemaking/2011/collegepayoff.pdf.

National Center for Education Statistics. (2024). Annual Earnings by Educational Attainment. Condition of Education. U.S. Department of Education, Institute of Education Sciences. Retrieved [June 2024], from https://nces.ed.gov/programs/coe/indicator/cba.

Part III: The Big Three Politics That Keep Us From Helping Boys

Chapter 12: The Danger of Feminaphobia

Hoff Sommers, Christina. *Freedom Feminism: Its Surprising History and Why It Matters Today*, June 10, 2013.

Kullman, Sean. "America's Reading and Math Gaps." *In His Words*, December 29, 2023, https://open.substack.com/pub/gibm/p/americas-reading-and-math-gaps?r=7v0pb&utm_campaign=post&utm_medium=web.

Krupnick, Max J. "The Male-Female Longevity Gap Widens: Men's lower life expectancy fueled by COVID-19, overdoses." *Harvard Magazine: Health and Medicine*, November 13, 2023, https://www.harvardmagazine.com/2023/11/harvard-gender-gap.

Arias, Elizabeth Ph.D., et al. "Provisional life expectancy, by age, race and Hispanic origin, and sex: United States, 2021." *National Center for Health Statistics, National Vital Statistics System, Mortality*, August 2021, https://www.cdc.gov/nchs/data/vsrr/vsrr023.pdf.

Real, Terrence. *I Don't Want to Talk About It*. Scribner, NY, 1998.

"The Gender Gap in Mental Health." *News Medical*, January 21, 2022, https://www.news-medical.net/health/The-Gender-Gap-in-Mental-Health.aspx.

Eaton, Nicholas R., et al. "An Invariant Dimensional Liability Model of Gender Differences in Mental Disorder Prevalence: Evidence from a National Sample." *J Abnorm Psychol*, 2012 Feb;121(1):282-8. doi: 10.1037/a0024780.

U.S. Department of Education, National Center for Education Statistics, Parent and

Family Involvement in Education Survey of the National Household Education Surveys Program (PFI-NHES:2003, 2007, and 2012). (This table was prepared September 2014.) https://nces.ed.gov/programs/digest/d16/tables/dt16_225.80.asp.

Edwards, Sarah and Ramirez, Adam, J.D. "Disparity In Victims Of Violent Crime By Gender (2024)." *Consumer Shield,* June 27, 2024, https://www.consumershield.com/articles/victims-of-violent-crime-by-gender.

Federal Bureau of Investigation: Crime Data Explore. https://cde.ucr.cjis.gov/LATEST/webapp/#/pages/explorer/crime/crime-trend. Crime statistics pulled from the Crime Data Explorer database.

Carson, Ann E., PhD. "U.S. Department of Justice: Office of Justice Programs." *Bureau of Justice Statistics,* December 2022, https://bjs.ojp.gov/sites/g/files/xyckuh236/files/media/document/p21st.pdf.

Conversation between Michael Gurian and Marion Hill in August 2024.

Chapter 13: The Silent Killer, Males Not Written Into National, State, or Local Budgets

"Budget of the U.S. Government." *Office of Management and Budget*, Fiscal Year 2025, https://www.whitehouse.gov/wp-content/uploads/2024/03/budget_fy2025.pdf.

Labots, Geert et al. "Gender differences in clinical registration trials: is there a real problem?." *British journal of clinical pharmacology* vol. 84,4 (2018): 700-707. doi:10.1111/bcp.13497 "United Nations Office on Drug and Crime, World Drug Report 2023." *United Nations,* 2023. https://www.unodc.org/res/WDR-2023/WDR23_Exsum_fin_DP.pdf.

Kullman, Sean. "Percent of Unintentional Overdose Deaths by Sex and Year 2018-2023." *Centers for Disease Control and Prevention,* June 2024. https://wonder.cdc.gov/. Data source used to collect data and create tables and graphs. *Centers for Disease Control and Prevention*, National Center for Health Statistics. National Vital Statistics System, Provisional Mortality on CDC WONDER Online Database. Data are from the final Multiple Cause of Death Files, 2018-2021, and from provisional data for years 2022-2024, as compiled from data provided by the 57 vital statistics jurisdictions through the Vital Statistics Cooperative Program. Accessed at http://wonder.cdc.gov/mcd-icd10-provisional.html on May 19, 2024 11:47:12 PM. Centers for Disease Control and Prevention, National Center for Health Statistics. National Vital Statistics System, Provisional Mortality on CDC WONDER Online Database. Data are from the final Multiple Cause of Death Files, 2018-2021, and from provisional data for years 2022-2024, as compiled from data provided by the 57 vital statistics jurisdictions through the Vital Statistics Cooperative Program. Accessed at http://wonder.cdc.gov/mcd-icd10-provisional.html on May 19, 2024 11:47:48 PM.

Kullman, Sean. "Male Drug Overdose Deaths Cut Across All Racial Groups." *Centers for Disease Control and Prevention*, June 2024, https://wonder.cdc.gov/. Data sourced used to collect data and create tables and graphs.

Kullman, Sean. "Percent of Suicide Deaths by Year." *Centers for Disease Control and Prevention*. June 2024, https://wonder.cdc.gov/. Data source used to collect data and create tables and graphs.

Kullman, Sean. "Male Suicide Deaths Cut Across All Racial Groups." *Centers for Disease Control and Prevention*. June 2024, https://wonder.cdc.gov/. Data source used to collect data and create tables and graphs.

Kullman, Sean. "Global Initiative for Boys and Men State Reports on the Status of Boys and Men." *Global Initiative for Boys and Men*. Retrieved: June 2024, https://www.gibm.us/state-reports.

Kullman, Sean. "Education in Black and White." *In His Words*, August 11, 2022, https://gibm.substack.com/p/education-in-black-and-white.

Budgets of the United States Government from 1936-2025. "Issued by the Office of Management and Budget (OMB), the Budget of the United States Government is a collection of documents that contains the budget message of the President, information about the President's budget proposals for a given fiscal year, and other budgetary publications that have been issued throughout the fiscal year. Other related and supporting budget publications are included, which may vary from year to year." https://www.govinfo.gov/app/collection/BUDGET.

Chapter 14: When America Embraced Wonder Woman and Forgot G.I. Joe

"History: An Overview 1920-2021." *Women's Bureau: U.S. Department of Labor*, https://www.dol.gov/agencies/wb/about/history.

Ms. Vol 1, No. 1. Smithsonian National Museum of History. https://www.si.edu/object/ms-vol-1-no-1%3Anmah_1803345.

"Life Expectancy in the U.S., 1900-1998." *University of California Berkeley*. https://u.demog.berkeley.edu/~andrew/1918/figure2.html.

National Center for Educational Statistics. Table 303.70. Total undergraduate fall enrollment in degree-granting postsecondary institutions, by attendance status, sex of student, and control and level of institution: Selected years, 1970 through 2030, https://nces.ed.gov/programs/digest/d21/tables/dt21_303.70.asp.

Kullman, Sean. "Undergraduate enrollment in degree-granting post secondary institutions by sex 1970-2020." *National Center for Educational Statistics*, June 2024, https://nces.ed.gov/programs/digest/d21/tables/dt21_303.70.asp. Data sourced used to collect data and create tables and graphs.

Olson, Keith W. "The G. I. Bill and Higher Education: Success and Surprise." *American Quarterly*, vol. 25, no. 5, Johns Hopkins University Press, 1973, pp. 596–610, https://doi.org/10.2307/2711698.

Kullman, Sean. "Conferred Associate, Bachelor, Master, and Doctoral Degrees in U.S. by Sex in 50 Year Increments." *National Center for Educational Statistics*.

https://nces.ed.gov/programs/digest/2020menu_tables.asp.

https://nces.ed.gov/programs/digest/d18/tables/dt18_318.10.asp.

https://nces.ed.gov/fastfacts/display.asp?id=72.

"Understanding and Eliminating Expulsion in Early Childhood Programs." *U.S.*

Department of Health and Human Services: Head Start Early Childhood Learning and Knowledge Center, https://eclkc.ohs.acf.hhs.gov/publication/understanding-eliminating-expulsion-early-childhood-programs#:~:text=Preschool%2Daged%20boys%20are%20four,be%20expelled%20as%20girls%20are.

Gurian, Michael. "Gurian Institute Success Stories." *Gurian Institute,* June 2024, https://gurianinstitute.com/success/.

Hill, Marion and Gurian, Michael spoke in August 2024.

Kullman, Sean. "Percent of Children Living in Single Parent Homes by Race/Ethnicity 2021." *Kids Count Data Center, Annie E. Casey Foundation,* https://datacenter.aecf.org/data/customreports/1/107.

Kullman, Sean. "Number of Children Living in Single Parent Homes by Race/Ethnicity 2021." *Kids Count Data Center, Annie E. Casey Foundation,* https://datacenter.aecf.org/data/customreports/1/107.

"Fatal Force." *Washington Post.* https://www.washingtonpost.com/graphics/investigations/police-shootings-database/. This database is ongoing and reports each fatal force police shooting in the U.S.

Kullman, Sean. "Number and Percent of Police Shooting Deaths by Race and Sex from 2015 to April 2021." *Washington Post,* Accessed June 2021, https://www.washingtonpost.com/graphics/investigations/police-shootings-database/.

Metro Staff. "Man facing 22 charges killed in police pursuit in Marion County." *Metro News: The Voice of West Virginia,* August 9, 2017, https://wvmetronews.com/2017/08/09/man-facing-22-charges-killed-in-police-pursuit-in-marion-county/.

Chapter 15: Digging Deeper Into Our Spiritual Sickness Regarding Males

Blake, William. "The Poison Tree." *Blake's Poetry and Design,* Ed. Johnson, Mary Lynn and Grant, John, W.W. Norton and Company, 1979.

Clinton, Hillary. "First Ladies' Conference on Domestic Violence in San Salvador, El Salvador." November 17, 1998. https://clintonwhitehouse3.archives.gov/WH/EOP/First_Lady/html/generalspeeches/1998/19981117.html.

"Homicide and Organized Crime in Latin America and the Caribbean." *United Nations Office on Drugs and Crime Global Study on Homicide 2023,* https://www.unodc.org/documents/data-and-analysis/gsh/2023/GSH_2023_LAC_web.pdf.

Muggah, Robert, and John de Boer. "Consequences, Causes and Costs of Insecurity in Latin America and the Caribbean." *Security Sector Reform and Citizen Security: Experiences from Urban Latin America in Global Perspective,* vol. 18, Ubiquity Press, 2019, pp. 9–14, JSTOR, http://www.jstor.org/stable/j.ctv11cvx6v.11.

Barry, John. "An invisible hero for invisible victims: interview with domestic violence pioneer, Erin Pizzey." *The Centre for Male Psychology,* Accessed May 17, 2024, https://www.centreformalepsychology.com/male-psychology-magazine-listings/an-invisible-hero-for-invisible-victims-an-interview-with-domestic-violence-pioneer-erin-pizzey.

"Erin Pizzey: The creation and hijack of the women's refuge movement" *Hear the Truth: The ONRECORD Podcast*, Accessed May 17, 2024. https://www.youtube.com/watch?v=oOqjLeSLa68.

Moreau de Lyon, Alexander. "Erin Pizzey: The Story of the Feminist Who Was Threatened for Acknowledging Male Victims." *Medium*, July 20, 2023, https://medium.com/@alexandermoreaudelyon/erin-pizzey-the-story-of-the-feminist-who-was-threatened-for-acknowledging-male-victims-a5a810964857.

"Child Maltreatment 2018." U.S. Department of Health & Human Services Administration for Children and Families Administration on Children, Youth, and Families Children's Bureau, https://www.acf.hhs.gov/sites/default/files/documents/cb/cm2018.pdf.

Angst, Maggie. "New data shows grim tally for S.F.'s worst year for overdose deaths. These groups were hit hardest." *San Francisco Chronicle*, January 17, 2024, https://www.sfchronicle.com/sf/article/sf-drug-crisis-overdose-record-broke-fentanyl-18611325.php.

Sewell, David. "Report on 2023 Accidental Overdose Deaths." *Office of the Chief Medical Examiner*, San Francisco, January 17, 2024, https://www.sf.gov/sites/default/files/2024-01/2024%2001_OCME%20Overdose%20Report.pdf.

Kullman, Sean. "Table 1. CA Suicide Deaths from 2018-2022 by Race and Sex." Center for Disease Control and Prevention Wonder Database, June 2024, https://wonder.cdc.gov/.

Kullman, Sean. "Table 2. CA Overdose Deaths from 2018-2022 by Race and Sex." Center for Disease Control and Prevention Wonder Database, June 2024, https://wonder.cdc.gov/.

Chapter 16: The Death of 17-Year-Old Jack and the Story That Followed

Kullman, Sean. "Percent of Suicide Deaths of 15-19 and 20-24 Year-Olds by Sex in U.S. 2018-2022." Center for Disease Control and Prevention Wonder Database, June 2024, https://wonder.cdc.gov/.

Weiser, Benjamin and Tully, Tracey. "After Student's Suicide, an Elite School Says It Fell 'Tragically Short.'" *New York Times*, May 1, 2023 (updated).

Keane, Isabel. "NJ boarding school student Jack Reid's parents reveal last conversation before suicide." *New York Post*, May 2, 2023 (updated).

Gordon, James. "Top $76,000-a-year New Jersey boarding school admits 'more should have been done' to stop bullying of boy, 17, who took his own life after being falsely accused of rape for a year by cruel peers." *Daily Mail*, May 1, 2023 (updated).

Kullman, Sean. "Suicide Deaths Per 100,000 Males 15-19 & 20-24 Compared to Female Age Groups." Center for Disease Control and Prevention Wonder Database, June 2024. https://wonder.cdc.gov/.

Kullman, Sean. "How false allegations led to the deaths of 17-year-old-boys from different continents." *InHisWords.us*, May 5, 2023, https://gibm.substack.com/p/how-false-allegations-lead-to-the?utm_source=publication-search.

Solomon, Andrew. "Has Social Media Fuelled a Teen-Suicide Crisis?" *New Yorker Magazine*, September 30, 2024, https://www.newyorker.com/magazine/2024/10/07/social-media-mental-health-suicide-crisis-teens?utm_source=substack&utm_medium=email.

Reeves, Richard. "Willful ignorance of the male suicide crisis." *Of Boys and Men*, October 10, 2024, https://ofboysandmen.substack.com/p/willful-ignorance-of-the-male-suicide?utm_source=post-email-title&publication_id=789530&post_id=150061687&utm_campaign=email-post-title&isFreemail=true&r=kokrp&triedRedirect=true&utm_medium=email.

Hinshaw, Drew. "The 10,000 Kidnapped Boys of Boko Haram." *Wall Street Journal*, August 12, 2016, https://www.wsj.com/articles/the-kidnapped-boys-of-boko-haram-1471013062.

Rempfer, Kyle. "DoD IG: US troops were told to ignore child sex abuse by Afghan forces." *Military Times*, November 17, 2017, https://www.militarytimes.com/news/your-army/2017/11/17/dod-ig-us-troops-were-told-to-ignore-child-sex-abuse-by-afghan-forces/.

Boghani, Priyanka. "Why Afghanistan's Children Are Used as Spies and Suicide Bombers." *PBS: Frontline*, November 17, 2015, https://www.pbs.org/wgbh/frontline/article/why-afghanistans-children-are-used-as-spies-and-suicide-bombers/.

Chapter 17: Does the Child Have Brain Sex Dysphoria or Gender Dysphoria?

Rafael Loch Batista, et al. "Psychosexual Aspects, Effects of Prenatal Androgen Exposure, and Gender Change in 46,XY Disorders of Sex Development." *National Library of Medicine*, April 1, 2019, https://pubmed.ncbi.nlm.nih.gov/30388241/.

Wheelock et al. "Sex differences in functional connectivity during fetal brain development." *Developmental Cognitive Neuroscience*, Vol. 36. April 2019, https://www.sciencedirect.com/science/article/pii/S1878929318301245.

Russo, Francine. "Is There Something Unique about the Transgender Brain?" *Scientific American*, January 1, 2016, https://www.scientificamerican.com/.

"Understanding Gender Identity." *Cleveland Clinic*, March 29, 2022, https://health.clevelandclinic.org/what-is-gender-identity.

Ristori, Jiska, et al. "Brain Sex Differences Related to Gender Identity Development: Genes or Hormones?" *National Library of Medicine*, March 19, 2020. https://www.ncbi.nlm.nih.gov/pmc/articles/PMC7139786.

Votinov, Mikhail, et al. "Brain structure changes associated with sexual orientation." *Scientific Reports*, March 3, 2021, https://www.nature.com/articles/s41598-021-84496-z.

Littman, Lisa. "Parent reports of adolescents and young adults perceived to show signs of a rapid onset of gender dysphoria." *PLOS ONE*, 19 March 19, 2019, https://journals.plos.org/plosone/article?id=10.1371/journal.pone.0202330.

"Gay." *UCLA Williams Institute School of Law*, December 2023, https://williamsinstitute.law.ucla.edu/wp-content/uploads/LGBT-Adult-US-Pop-Dec-2023.

pdf.

"How Many Adults and Youth Identify as Transgender in the United States?." *UCLA Williams Institute School of Law*, December 2023, https://williamsinstitute.law. ucla.edu/wp-content/uploads/LGBT-Adult-US-Pop- Dec-2023.pdf

Robinson, Terry and Kolb, Bryan. "Structural Plasticity Associated with Exposure to Drugs of Abuse." *Neuropharmacology*, 2004, 47:33-46.

Carlezon, William, et al. "Understanding the Neurobiological Consequences of Early Exposure to Psychotropic Drugs." *Neuropharmacology*, 2004, Vol. 47, 47-60.

Gramage, Esther, et al. "Periadolescent amphetamine treatment causes transient cognitive disruptions and long-term changes in hippocampal LTP depending on the endogenous expression of pleiotrophin." *Addiction biology* vol. 18,1 (2013): 19-29. doi:10.1111/j.1369-1600.2011.00362.x.

Robinson, T E, and Kolb B. "Persistent structural modifications in nucleus accumbens and prefrontal cortex neurons produced by previous experience with amphetamine." *The Journal of neuroscience*: the official journal of the Society for Neuroscience vol. 17,21 (1997): 8491-7. doi:10.1523/ JNEUROSCI.17-21-08491.1997.

Pardey, Margery C., et al. "Long-term effects of chronic oral Ritalin administration on cognitive and neural development in adolescent wistar kyoto rats." *Brain sciences* vol. 2,3 375-404. 12 Sep. 2012, doi:10.3390/brainsci2030375.

Shrier, Abigail. "When Your Daughter Defies Biology." *Wall Street Journal*, January 6, 2019, https://www.wsj.com/articles/when-your-daughter-defies-biology-11546804848.

Shrier, Abigail. "Top Trans Doctors Blow the Whistle on 'Sloppy' Care." *The Free Press*, October 4, 2021, https://www.thefp.com/p/top-trans-doctors-blow-the-whistle.

Gurian, Michael. "At What Age Should a Child Be Confirmed as Transgender?." *Gurian Institute*, November 12, 2018, https://gurianinstitute.com/at-what-age-should-a-child-be-confirmed-as-transgender/.

Cass, Hilary, Dr. "The Cass Review: Independent Review into Gender Identity Services for Children and Young People, Final Report." April 2024, file:///Users/ seankullman/Downloads/CassReview_Final.pdf.

Armstrong, Kim. "Rain Before Rainbows: The Science of Transgender Flourishing." *Association for Psychological Science*, August 30, 2021, https://www. psychologicalscience.org/observer/transgender-flourishing.

Part IV: The Seven Point Plan to Rescue Our Boys

Chapter 18: Raise Our Boys to Thrive in the Family System

Time Staff. "Happy 80th Birthday Gloria Steinem: 8 of Her Funniest Quips." *Time,* March 25, 2014, https://time.com/36046/gloria-steinem-8-funny-quotes-80-birthday/.

Chapter 19: Provide Seven Nurturing Elements to Boys in Trouble

"Percentage of students suspended and expelled from public elementary and secondary schools, by sex, race/ethnicity, and state: 2013-14." *National Center for Educational Statistics*, Accessed December 5, 2021, https://www.courts.mo.gov/file.jsp?id=59716.

Kullman, Sean. "Male Percent of Suspensions, Juvenile Detentions, and Prison Population in Select States." *Global Initiative for Boys and Men.* https://www.gibm.us/state-reports. Data compiled from multiple state reports.

"Percentage of students suspended and expelled from public elementary and secondary schools, by sex, race/ethnicity, and state: 2013-14." *National Center for Educational Statistics*, Accessed December 5, 2021, https://nces.ed.gov/programs/digest/d19/tables/dt19_233.40.asp.

"2019 Profile of the Institutional and Supervised Offender Population." *Missouri Department of Corrections*, Accessed December 3, 2021, https://doc.mo.gov/sites/doc/files/media/pdf/2020/03/Offender_Profile_2019_0.pdf.

"Missouri Juvenile & Family Division Annual Report." *Supreme Court of Missouri Office of State Courts Administration*, Accessed, December 5, 2021, https://www.courts.mo.gov/file.jsp?id=59716.

"Percentage of students suspended and expelled from public elementary and secondary schools, by sex, race/ethnicity, and state: 2013-14." *National Center for Educational Statistics*. Accessed December 5, 2021, https://nces.ed.gov/programs/digest/d19/tables/dt19_233.40.asp.

"2020-2021 Discipline by Gender." *Colorado Department of Education*, Accessed October 21, 2021, https://www.cde.state.co.us/cdereval/disciplinebygender2020-2021sy.

"Crime & Justice in Colorado / 2009-2019." *Colorado Department of Public Safety*, Accessed October 26, 2021, https://cdpsdocs.state.co.us/ors/Docs/Reports/2020_CJ09-19.pdf.

"Colorado Division of Criminal Justice Adult and Juvenile Correctional Populations Forecasts." *Colorado Department of Public Safety*, Accessed October 26, 2021, https://cdpsdocs.state.co.us/ors/data/PPP/2021-PPP.pdf.

"Suspension Rate." *Data Quest: California Department of Education*, Accessed April 2021, https://dq.cde.ca.gov/dataquest/dqCensus/DisSuspRate.aspx?cds=00&agglevel=State&year=2015-16&initrow=Eth&ro=y.

"Offender Data Points." *California Department of Corrections and Rehabilitation*, Accessed July 2021, https://www.cdcr.ca.gov/research/wp-content/uploads/sites/174/2020/01/201812_DataPoints.pdf.

"2019 Spring Population Projections." *California Department of Corrections and Rehabilitation*, Accessed July 2021, https://www.cdcr.ca.gov/research/wp-content/uploads/sites/174/2021/03/Spring-2019-Population-Projections.pdf.

"National Youth Gang Survey Analysis: Demographic Age of Gang Members." *U.S. Department of Justice: Office of Justice Programs*, Accessed June 2021, https://

nationalgangcenter.ojp.gov/survey-analysis/demographics#anchorage.

"National Youth Gang Survey Analysis: Demographic Gender of Gang Members." *U.S. Department of Justice: Office of Justice Programs*, Accessed June 2021, https:// nationalgangcenter.ojp.gov/survey-analysis/demographics#anchorgender.

"National Youth Gang Survey Analysis: Demographic Age of Gang Members by Area Type." *U.S. Department of Justice: Office of Justice Programs,* Accessed June 2021, https:// nationalgangcenter.ojp.gov/survey-analysis.

Chapter 20: Train All Schools in Boy-Friendly Practices

"The Gurian Institute Center for Educational Excellence at Crespi." June 24, 2024, https://www.crespi.org/crespi-news/?id=7273/the-gurian-institute-center-for-educational-excellence-at-crespi.

Chapter 21: Complete Your Own Classroom Citizen Science

Gurian, Michael. "Roosevelt Middle School Reading Score before and after Gurian Success Model on Criterion-Referenced Test." *Gurian Institute,* 2005, https:// gurianinstitute.com/success/.

Gurian, Michael. "Percent Increase in Reading and Math at Chattanooga Preparatory School using Gurian Success Model." *Gurian Institute,* 2018, https:// gurianinstitute.com/success/.

Kullman, Sean. "Overall Assessment Table for Teachers Prior to Teaching." American Institute for Responsible Research, 2024.

Kullman, Sean. "In Class Assessment Table for Teachers." American Institute for Responsible Research, 2024.

Kullman, Sean. "Math Scores (Proficient/Advanced) for the Class of 2024 over time from 3rd to 11th grade in LVJUSD, OAKUSD, and CA Schools each Year by Grade and Sex." California Department of Education, June 2024, https://caaspp-elpac. ets.org/caaspp/Default. Prepared by the American Institute for Responsible Research.

Chapter 22: Compel School Boards to Include Sex Differences in Annual Reports

Pleasanton Unified School Board Meeting. March 25, 2021.

Kullman, Sean: "GIBM Webinar: PUSD —The Boy Gender Gap in Education." *Global Initiative for Boys and Men.* June 19, 2021, https://www.youtube.com/watch?v=-ppC3s7eCTM&t=2s.

Kullman, Sean. "Analysis of Pleasanton Unified School District (PUSD) Suspension Data from 2016-2020." Data received by the *Global Initiative for Boys and Men* after a freedom of information request to PUSD and received in May 2021.

Kullman, Sean. "Compiled California Suspension Data by Race and Sex from 2016-2020." *Global Initiative for Boys and Men,* June 2021. https://dq.cde.ca.gov/ dataquest/.

Chapter 23: Decrease the Male Gender Gap in College Education

"Education pays, 2022." Career Outlook, U.S. Bureau of Labor Statistics, May 2023, https://www.bls.gov/careeroutlook/2023/data-on-display/education-pays.htm.

"Education pays, 2021." Career Outlook, U.S. Bureau of Labor Statistics, May 2022, https://www.bls.gov/careeroutlook/2022/data-on-display/education-pays.htm.

Torpey, Elka. "Education pays, 2020." Career Outlook, U.S. Bureau of Labor Statistics, June 2021. https://www.bls.gov/careeroutlook/2021/data-on-display/education-pays.htm.

"Learn more, earn more: Education leads to higher wages, lower unemployment." Career Outlook, U.S. Bureau of Labor Statistics, May 2020, https://www.bls.gov/careeroutlook/2020/data-on-display/education-pays.htm.

Kullman, Sean. "Education in Black and White." *InHisWords.us*, August 11, 2022, https://gibm.substack.com/p/education-in-black-and-white?utm_source=publication-search.

"Women in Apprenticeship and Nontraditional Occupations." Women's Bureau: An agency within the U.S. Department of Labor, https://www.dol.gov/agencies/wb/grants/wanto.

"Trends in Pell Grant Receipt and the Characteristics of Pell Grant Recipients: Selected Years, 2003–04 to 2015–16." *U.S.* Department of Education, September 2019, https://nces.ed.gov/pubs2019/2019487.pdf.

"University of California Accountability Report 2023." University of California Regents, Accessed July 2024, https://accountability.universityofcalifornia.edu/2023/chapters/chapter-1.html#a1.1.1.

Kullman, Sean. "Ivy League Colleges and Selective Diversity." *InHisWords.us*, Accessed May 24, 2024, https://gibm.substack.com/p/ivy-league-colleges-and-selective.

"Learn more, earn more: Education leads to higher wages, lower unemployment." Career Outlook, U.S. Bureau of Labor Statistics, May 2020. https://www.bls.gov/careeroutlook/2020/data-on-display/education-pays.htm

Chapter 24: Build and Support Community Programs That Help Boys Thrive

Martin, Ian, Ed.D., et al. "Orchestrating a School Counseling and Community Collaboration: From Boys to Men." *University of San Diego: School of Leadership and Education Science,* https://boystomen.org/wp-content/uploads/2019/12/CaseStudy1.pdf.

Bibliography

Amen, Daniel. (2013). *Unleashing the Power of the Female Brain*. Bantam.

______. (2010). *Change Your Brain, Change Your Life*. Bantam.

______. (2006). *Healing A.D.D.* Bantam.

______. (2005). *Sex on the Brain*. Bantam.

Arnot, Robert (2001). *The Biology of Success*. Little Brown & Company.

Banks, Brian with Dagostino, Mark. (2019). *What Set Me Free*. Astria Paperback.

Baron-Cohen, Simon. (2003). *The Essential Difference*. Basic Books.

Bear, Mark; Connors, Barry; Paradiso, Michael. (1996). *Neuroscience*. Williams and Wilkins.

Benbow, Camilla and Lubinski, David. (1997). *Intellectual Talent*. Johns Hopkins University Press.

Blum, Deborah. (1998). *Sex On the Brain*. Penguin Books.

Borba, Michelle. (2016). *Unselfie*. Touchstone.

Brizendine, Louann. (2007). *The Female Brain*. Three Rivers Press.

______ (2011). *The Male Brain*. Harmony.

______ (2022). *The Upgrade*.

Brott, Armin. (2010). *The Expectant Father*. Abbeville Press.

______ (2009). *The Military Father*. Abbeville Press.

Browne, Rollo and Fletcher, Richard. (1994). *Boys in Schools*. Finch Publishing.

Bly, Robert. (1996). *The Sibling Society*. Addison-Wesley Publishing.

Carbone, June and Cahn, Naomi. (2014). *Marriage Markets*. Oxford University Press.

Carr-Morse, Robin. (1998). *Ghosts from the Nursery*. Atlantic Monthly Press.

Carr, Nicholas. (2010). *The Shallows*. W.W. Norton and Company.

Cooper, Joel and Weaver, Kimberlee. (2003). *Gender and Computers*. Lawrence Erlbaum.

Cumbo, Paul. (2025). *A Path to Manhood*. North Country Books.

Cumbo, Paul. (2020). *Wilderness Therapy*. One Lane Bridge Books.

Deak, JoAnn. (2003). *Girls Will Be Girls*. Hyperion.

Dent, Maggie (2021). *From Boys to Men*. McMillan Australia.

Diamond, Jed. (2005). *The Irritable Male Syndrome*. Rodale.

Duffy, James. (2023). Rescuing *Our Sons*. Mango Press.

Ells, Kimberly. (2020). *The Invincible Family*. Regnery Gateway.

Ellington, Joanna. (2015). *Slippery When Wet*. JDK Publications.

Faludi, Susan. (2000). *Stiffed*. Harper Perennial.

Farrell, Warren. (2000) *The Myth of Male Power*. Berkeley.

__________ (2024) *Role Mate to Soul Mate*. BenBella Books.

Farrell, Warren and Gray, John. (2018). *The Boy Crisis*. BenBella Books.

Flinders, Carol. (2002). *The Values of Belonging*. Harper.

Friedan, Betty. (1963). *The Feminine Mystique*. Norton.

__________ (1981/1998). *The Second Stage*. Harvard University.

Fogarty, Robin. (1997). *Brain Compatible Classrooms*. Skylight Professional Development.

Garbarino, James. (1999). *Lost Boys*. The Free Press.

Gilligan, Carol. (1998). *In A Different Voice*. Harvard University Press.

Gilmore, David. (1990). *Manhood in the Making*. Yale University Press.

Golden, T. R. (2000). *Swallowed by a Snake*. GH Publishing, LLC.

Goleman, Daniel. (1995). *Emotional Intelligence*. Bantam.

Greene, Vermelle. (2023). Please *Teach Me Like a Boy!* Xulon Books.

Gurian, J.P. & J. (1983). *The Dependency Tendency*. Rowman and Littlefield.

Gurian, Michael. (2017). *Saving Our Sons*. Gurian Institute.

__________ (2011). *How Do I Help Him?* Gurian Institute.

__________ (2006). *The Wonder of Boys*. Tarcher-Putnam.

__________ (2002). *The Wonder of Girls*. Pocket Books.

__________ (1998). *A Fine Young Man*. Tarcher-Putnam.

Gurian, Michael, with Kathy Stevens. (2005). *The Minds of Boys*. Jossey-Bass.

Gurian, Michael., et.al. (2011). *Boys and Girls Learn Differently!* Jossey-Bass.

Hari, Johann. (2022). *Stolen Focus*. Random House.

Harris, Judith R. (1998). *The Nurture Assumption*. Free Press.

Haidt, Jonathan. (2024). *The Anxious Generation*. Penguin.

Hallowell, Edward and Ratey, John. (1994). *Driven to Distraction*. Touchstone.

Hawley, Josh. (2023). *Manhood*. Regnery Publishing.

Haltzman, Scott. (2007). *The Secrets of Happy Families*. Jossey-Bass.

Hymowitz, Kay. (2012). *Manning Up*. Basic Books.

Jantz, Gregory; Gurian, Michael; MacMurray, Ann. (2013). *Raising Boys by Design*. Waterbrook/Multnomah.

Jantz, Gregory; Wall, Keith. (2021). *The Anxiety Reset*. Tyndale Refresh.

Jensen, Eric. (1995, 200 Rev.). *Brain-Based Learning*. The Brain Store.

Jessel, David and Moir, Anne. (1989). *Brain Sex*. Dell.

Johnson, Steven. (2004). *Mind Wide Open*. Scribner.

Jung, Carl, edited by Claire Dougla. (1997). *Visions*. Princeton University Press. Princeton.

Kandel Eric; Schwartz, James; Jessell, Thomas. (1995). *Essentials of Neural Science and*

Behavior. Appleton & Lange.

Karges-Bone, Linda. (1998). *More Than Pink & Blue.* Teaching and Learning Company.

Kearney, Melissa. (2023). *The Two Parent Privilege.* University of Chicago Press. Chicago.

Kipnis, Aaron. (1999). Angry *Young Men.* Jossey-Bass.

Kiselica, Mark; Englar-Carson, Matt; Horne, Arthur M. (Editors). (2007). *Counseling Troubled Boys.* Routledge Publishers.

Kindlon, Dan and Thompson, Michael. (2000). *Raising Cain.* Ballantine.

Krall, Brian. (2023). *Misandry Exposed.* Independently Published.

Kundtz, David. (2004). *Nothing's Wrong.* Conari Press.

Ladner, Joyce. (2003). *Launching Our Black Children for Success.* Jossey-Bass/John Wiley.

Levine, Mel. (2002). *A Mind at a Time.* Simon & Schuster.

Lukianoff, Greg and Haidt, Jonathan (2018) *The Coddling of the American Mind.* Penguin Press.

Lukianoff, Greg and Schlott, Rikki. (2023). *The Canceling of the American Mind.* Simon and Schuster.

MacDonald, Heather. (2020). *The Diversity Delusion.* St. Martin Press.

McElroy, Wendy. (2016). *Rape Culture Hysteria.* CreateSpace.

McGann, Patricia. (2024). *Steadfast Parenting.* Rowman & Littlefield.

Moalem, Sharon. (2021). *Better Half.* Farrar, Strauss, and Giroux.

_________(2010). *How Sex Works.* Harper Collins.

Moir, Anne and Bill. (1999). *Why Men Don't Iron.* Citadel.

Moir, Anne and Jessel, David. (1990). *Brain Sex.* Laurel.

Murphy, Shane. (1999). *The Cheers and the Tears.* Jossey-Bass/John Wiley.

Nathanson, Paul and Young, Katherine. (2006). *Spreading Misandry.* McGill-Queen's University Press.

Newell, Walter R. (2000). *What is a Man?* Regan Books.

Nylund, David. (2000). *Treating Huckleberry Finn.* Jossey-Bass/John Wiley.

Paglia, Camille. (1991). *Sexual Personae.* Vintage.

Parker, Kathleen. (2010). *Save The Males.* Random House.

Payne, Ruby. (2000). *A Framework for Understanding Poverty.* AhaProcess, Inc.

Pinker, Steven. (2003). *The Blank Slate.* Penguin.

Pollack, William. (1998). *Real Boys.* Henry Holt.

Ratey, John and Eric Hagerman. (2008). *Spark.* Little Brown.

Ravitch, Diane. (2003). *The Language Police.* Alfred A. Knopf.

Real, Terrence. (1997). *I Don't Want to Talk About It.* Fireside.

Reeves, Richard. (2022). *Of Boys and Men.* Brookings Institute Press.

Rhoads, Steven E. (2004). *Taking Sex Differences Seriously*. Encounter Books.

Rosiak, Luke. (2022). *Race to the Bottom*. HarperCollins Publishers.

Rosin, Hanna. (2013). *The End of Men*. Riverhead.

Salomone, Rosemary C. (2003). *Same, Different, Equal*. Yale University Press.

Sandberg, Sheryl. (2013). *Lean In*. Knopf.

Sax, Leonard. (2005). *Why Gender Matters*. Doubleday.

______________ (2009, updated 2016). *Boys Adrift*. Basic Books.

Shackleton, David. (2015). *The Hand That Rocks the World.* T2Now.

Shaffer, David Williamson. (2006). *How Computer Games Help Children Learn*. Palgrave Macmillan.

Siegel, Daniel J. (1999). *The Developing Mind*. Guilford Press.

Slocumb, Paul. (2004). *Boys In Crisis*. Aha Process, Inc.

Smith, Michael W. and Wilhelm, Jeffrey D. (2002). *Reading Don't Fix No Chevys*. Heinemann.

Soh, Debra. (2020). *The End of Gender*. Threshold Editions.

Sommers, Christina Hoff. (2000). *The War on Boys*. Touchstone.

Sommers, Christina Hoff. (2013). *Freedom Feminism*. AEI Press.

Sousa, David. A. (2001). *How the Brain Learns*. Corwin Press.

Sowell, Thomas. (2023). *Social Justice Fallacies*. Basic Books.

______________ (2011). *Economic Facts and Fallacies, 2nd Edition*. Basic Books.

Sprenger, Marilee (2002). *Becoming A "Wiz" at Brain-Based Teaching*. Corwin Press.

Stephenson, Bret. (2004). *Slaying the Dragon*. www.adolescent med.com.

Stein, David. (1999). *Ritalin Is Not The Answer*. Jossey-Bass.

Sutton, Mark. (2024). *How Democrats can Win Back Men*.

Sykes, Bryan. (2003). *Adam's Curse*. W.W. Norton & Company.

Szalavitz, Maia. (2016). *Unbroken Brain*. St. Martin's Press.

Tannen, Deborah. (1991). *You Just Don't Understand*. William Morrow.

Taylor, Shelley E. (2002). *The Tending Instinct*. Times Books.

Thompson, Michael. (2009). *It's a Boy!* Ballantine.

Tobin, James. (2023). *Triple Divide*. Pale Horse Books.

Twenge, Jean M. (2017). *iGen*. Atria Books.

Verhaagen, David A. (2010). *Therapy with Young Men*. Routledge.

Watson, William, SJ. (2012). *Sacred Story*. Sacred Story Press.

Walsh, William. (2014). *Nutrient Power*. Skyhorse Publishing.

Wexler, David. (2009). *Men in Therapy*. Norton.

Whitmire, Richard. (2010). *Why Boys Fail*. AMACOM.

Wilson, E.O. (2015). *The Meaning of Human Existence*. Liveright.

__________ (1999). *Consilience*. Vintage: New York.

Wiseman, Rosalind. (2014). *Masterminds and Wingmen*. Harmony.

Wolfe, Patricia. (2001). *Brain Matters*. Assoc. for Supervision and Curriculum Development.

Woody, Jane DiVita. (2002). *How Can We Talk About That?* Jossey-Bass.

Wright, Tim. (2014). *Searching for Tom Sawyer*. TWM Publishers.

__________ (2024). *The Toby Baxter Series*. TWM Publishers.

Zeff, Ted. (2010). *The Strong Sensitive Boy*. Prana Publishing.

Appendix

Here is a short blog from me (Michael) you can distribute without having to get my own or my publisher's permission as long as you credit the blog, "By Michael Gurian."

If I Were a Parent of a Boy…

By Michael Gurian, Author of *Saving Our Sons* and co-author of *Boys, A Rescue Plan* (www.michaelgurian.com)

In working with her family therapy clients for more than thirty years, my wife, Gail, said, "If I were a parent of a boy, I would really be worried." She was referring to her fear for the social, economic, emotional, and spiritual lives of America's boys.

As we raised our daughters, we asked our girls what they thought of the gender landscape around them. Gabrielle (16 in 2006) came home from high school and said, "We had a discussion in social studies about boys and girls—everyone was talking like girls had it hard, but boys had it easy. They were in denial." Davita, 19, came home from college for the holidays in 2011 and reported a discussion with her college friends. "I'm really glad I'm a girl not a boy. The boys aren't sure what to do, the girls are doing everything."

These discussions were anecdotal, of course. Both girls and boys, and women and men, can experience suffering in our world. Girls don't have it easy. Women don't have it easy.

But it is also true that boys and men are in substantial trouble today. They increasingly fill our principal's offices, ADD/ADHD assessment clinics, and homeless and unemployed populations. Boys and men are more likely to be victims of violence than girls and women, commit suicide at four times the rate of females, suffer emotional disturbance, behavioral and other brain-related disorders in higher numbers than females. They are suspended or expelled from school in much higher numbers than girls, receive two thirds of the Ds and Fs in schools, lag behind girls in standardized test scores throughout the nation. They abuse substances and alcohol at higher rates than girls and are incarcerated at exponentially higher rates (for more data in all these areas, please see *Boys, A Rescue Plan, 2025*).

Especially telling is this: the majority of government and philanthropic funding for gender-friendly programming goes to programs and innovations to help girls and women. The existence of this funding is to be celebrated, but the disconnect between the reality males face and the social justice attention males get needs to be examined by each of us. We are in denial about our males.

I believe this denial will continue (and we will ultimately rue and mourn the dangerous, socially debilitating consequences) unless we change our academic, media, government, and philanthropic programming to include a new truth: just as the traditionalist paradigm regarding girls and women needed to be deconstructed and replaced by the feminist paradigm in the last century, *the now dominant gender paradigm of males and females needs to be deconstructed and replaced if we are to meet the needs of both sexes and all genders.*

Why change it? Because it posits that females are victims of a privileged masculine society that systematically and universally oppresses them, but this isn't true in the developed world anymore. While individual girls and women can be dominated and demeaned by individual boys and men (and vice versa), we do not live in a culture that systematically teaches girls and women that they are second-class citizens and boys and men that they are superior.

While some areas of life are still populated by more males (mechanical engineering, senior leadership at some corporations and some areas of government), other areas of life and work are female dominant (management, health care, education, mental health professions). The original feminist paradigm posited systemic male dominance in our culture, but male dominance exists in small pockets of the culture while female dominance exists in others.

Can our culture open its mind to our new reality? To do so, we will need to make a distinction between gender issues in the developed world and the developing world. In many countries in the developing world, systemic and brutal patriarchy does prevail, and utilizing the second wave feminist model of male dominance/female victimization is essential for encouraging social justice. My own parents served in the State Department and helped build schools for girls in Afghanistan against impossible odds. In that world, systemic degradation of females was and still is prevalent.

But in the developed world, we can't keep operating out of a gender lens that blinds us to reality. If we do continue to remain blind, we will continue to avoid fulfilling our most human of imperatives: to take care of our children. If we do not fix what ails our sons—if we do not love them in the ways they need to be loved—we will create an increasingly dangerous society for girls and women, too. No parent of either sex or any gender wants that.

—Copyright Michael Gurian 2025

Here is a model of a blog you could write after starting it with your own stories of your own sons.

"I've discovered that, for many well-meaning academics, celebrities, and journalists, the painful state of boyhood in America can be summed up in looking at the discomfort our boys can experience when they are put down or called names. I agree that we must help boys feel feelings and express emotions in healthy ways. I agree that we must protect boys, especially our most sensitive and vulnerable boys, from hurt feelings. If a boy or girl is in danger, we must get right in there and protect that child immediately.

However, as a parent of sons, I also think we're oversimplifying things. We've created a huge industry around bullying but spend almost no time realizing all the subtle things our boys and girls are doing as they try to grow up, become adults, and develop real resilience to face a very tough existence.

Personally, as a parent of sons, I believe advocacy for boys now requires that we reshape the debate toward major priorities, not just hurt feelings and the ability to talk about repressed emotions. If a child is in trauma, getting at the repressed feelings is crucial, but we can't let that model completely overshadow the subtleties of growing our boys into good men. Feelings are good, they're fine, they're important, but they are not at the top of the list for most males in the way that they may be for lots of females. Every mom of adolescent sons knows this. Most of our social critics and commentators, though, seem to avoid this truth.

I know in writing about this this way I'll be called insensitive, as if I want to pull back on protecting boys and girls from bullying or hyper-masculinity, or as if I'm some throwback to male dominance and the patriarchy and all that, but let me say, just the opposite is true. I'm a good mom and I'm not insensitive—rather, I'm very sensitive to what children need. Boys need character development, purpose-development, fathering, mothering, positive workplaces, shared custody of children, a safe home and hearth. These are the themes we need to talk about to save our sons from continuing to disappear into prisons, basements, and unemployment."

You might get flack for this kind of blog (and please do change the language to fit your voice), but you will also help our culture see a healthier future for our boys and young men.

About the Authors

Michael Gurian is a marriage and family counselor in his thirty-fourth year of private practice (michaelgurian.com) and the *New York Times* bestselling author of thirty-six books. The Gurian Institute, which he cofounded in 1996, conducts research internationally, launches pilot programs, and trains professionals (gurianinstitute. com).

Michael has been called "the people's philosopher" for his ability to bring together people's ordinary lives and scientific ideas. Gurian provides keynotes, training, and consulting to conferences, community organizations, schools, governmental agencies, corporations, medical personnel, and faith communities.

Gurian previously taught at Gonzaga University, Eastern Washington University, and Ankara University. His more recent academic speaking engagements include Harvard University, Johns Hopkins University, Stanford University, Morehouse College, the University of Colorado, the University of Missouri–Kansas City, and UCLA. His multicultural philosophy reflects the diverse cultures (European, Asian, Middle Eastern, and American) in which he has lived, worked, and studied.

Michael's work has been featured multiple times in nearly all the major media, including the *New York Times, the Washington Post, USA Today, Newsweek, Time, Psychology Today, AARP Magazine, People, Reader's Digest, the Wall Street Journal, Forbes Magazine, Parenting, Good Housekeeping, Family Therapy Magazine, Redbook,* and many others. Gurian has also made multiple appearances on *Today, Good Morning America, CNN, PBS, National Public Radio,* and many others.

Gurian lives in Spokane, Washington. His wife, Gail, a family therapist in private practice, was the love of his life for forty years. She passed away from pancreatic cancer in 2023. Their daughters, Gabrielle and Davita, have since given birth to blessed grandchildren, Lev Micah Guen-Murray and Effy Gail Herrington.

Sean Kullman has taught middle school, high school, and college English at different points of his teaching career. He left teaching in 2014 to pursue writing, research, and advocacy on behalf of boys, and to become involved in helping youth groups. His leadership in athletic programs has improved sports for boys and girls in his community, dramatically increasing the participation of girls in youth basketball and forwarding the careers of coaches into the high school ranks. Some of the players in his youth program have played or are playing at the collegiate level.

Sean has become the go-to person for actualizing data on male development. His research and presentations have helped policymakers, writers, researchers, media, educators, parents, other non-profits, and advocates to understand the challenges boys face and the steps needed for our boys to thrive. His writings have appeared in major media such as the *New York Times, Kansas City Star,* and are regularly featured on his InHisWords substack.

Sean has appeared on television and radio and spoken at conferences and universities, most recently at the University of New Mexico. Sean has personally facilitated several town halls to explore boys' issues and travels throughout the country to bring this important information to the public.

Sean has also started The American Institute for Responsible Research (airr.pro) to help parents, policymakers, educators, media, and other groups gather reliable data on education, physical and mental health, the court systems, fatherhood, family and relationships, careers, and the male narrative in the public discourse.

About The Gurian Institute

THE GURIAN INSTITUTE (GI), founded in 1996, provides professional development, training services, and pilot programs in sexgender and diversity. The Institute's work is science-based, research-driven, and practice-oriented. GI's staff, trainers, and coaches work with parents, mental health professionals, teachers, school districts, law enforcement, corporations, the legal system, medical professionals, and others who serve boys and girls, and women and men.

The Gurian Institute team of certified trainers is committed to not only training professionals and parents but also to helping ensure that agencies, schools, corporations, organizations, and individual practitioners can be self-sufficient in their ability to provide ongoing assets to their communities. For more information or to bring the GI staff to your school, organization or community, please visit www.gurianinstitute.com.

Helping Boys Thrive® Initiatives

The Helping Boys Thrive® Initiative generally begins as a Helping Boys Thrive Summit® then can become an ongoing community-wide collaboration. It requires a small team of dynamic individuals—both in the private and public sectors—to take on the responsibility of putting on a Helping Boys Thrive Summit®. The Gurian Institute provides all materials needed to put on a successful Summit and partners with local resources to facilitate initiatives. To learn more or bring a Summit to your community, please visit www. helpingboysthrive.org then contact GI staff at info@gurianinstitute.com.

The Gurian Foundation

The Gurian Foundation was co-founded by Michael and Gail Gurian. It is a 501c3 corporation. Please go to www.gurianfoundation.org to learn more. If you feel so moved, please donate toward Summits, Initiatives, and community work in your area through the Foundation. Donations and some grant funds are eligible for tax deduction. To reach the Foundation directly, please contact Michael Gurian at michaelgurian@comcast.net.

The Global Initiative for Boys and Men

The Global Initiative for Boys and Men (GIBM) supports boys, men, and families through research and advocacy. GIBM is a 501(c)(3) under the U.S. Tax Code. Incorporated in Friday Harbor, Washington, it operates out of Pleasanton, California, where Sean lives.

GIBM's professional staff works closely with leading researchers, community groups, public and private institutions, nonprofits, and policymakers to support boys and men and the women who love them.

Motivated by leading research over the past 40 years, GIBM provides the essential research and data to inform policymakers, educators, parents, media, and government at all levels to collectively improve male outcomes in verifiable and measurable ways.

To learn more, please visit gibm.us.

The American Institute for Responsible Research

Sean Kullman started the American Institute for Responsible (airr.pro) in 2023 to help organizations, parents, policymakers, and others collect and present data for a variety of purposes. AIRR only collects and presents data that is verifiable and reliable. AIRR has the ability to help your group or organization by conducting your research with and for you. For help with your projects and citizen science, contact Sean at seank@airr.pro.

Index

A

abandonment xxii, xxiii, xxiv, 12, 17, 76, 128, 130, 131, 141, 142, 144, 153, 154, 162, 164, 179, 216
   abandoned boys 11
   abandonment of healthy male development 12, 128, 144
   abandonment of male xxiii
   abandonment of natural male development xxii
abuse xvi, xxi, 9, 28, 36, 50, 51, 58, 150, 175, 176, 177, 178, 232, 235, 283, 304, 315, 316, 327
   physically abused 30, 176
   sexual abuse xxi, 9, 51
   substance abuse 9, 36, 50, 58, 150
ADD see: Attention Deficit / Attention Deficit Hyperactivity Disorder
ADHD see: Attention Deficit / Attention Deficit Hyperactivity Disorder
adverse childhood experience 177
      ACE 177, 178
Alaska Native 35, 36, 258
alcohol 13, 28, 30, 32, 37, 39, 40
Altinay, Murat 208
Amen Clinics 32, 34
Amen, Daniel 33, 50, 118
American Association of University Women 58
American Indian 35, 36, 258
American Institute for Boys and Men 19, 20, 44, 185
American Medical Association 8, 41, 111
      AMA 111, 113, 114, 192
American Psychological Association x, 47, 49, 50, 51, 53
      APA 50, 51, 52, 139
      APA Guidelines 50, 52
amygdala see: brain
Angst, Maggie see: *San Francisco Chronicle*
annual reports xi, 255, 257, 259, 261, 263
APA see: American Psychological Association
APA Guidelines see: American Psychological Association

Arendt, Hannah 71
artificial intelligence 127
athletics 87, 97, 229, 249
Attention Deficit / Attention Deficit Hyperactivity Disorder
    ADD 6, 65, 68, 77, 84, 99, 115, 117, 120, 129, 158, 179, 195, 198, 218, 220
    ADHD 6, 48, 68, 101, 198, 199

B

Banks, Brian 55, 56
    What Set Me Free 56
Beerman, Bob 208
Biden, Jill 149
Biden, Joe 143
Biel, Jessica 242
Big Three x, xv, xviii, xxiii, xxiv, 4, 7, 8, 9, 10, 12, 13, 17, 18, 19, 20, 38, 44, 46, 49,
    56, 62, 66, 67, 76, 77, 79, 83, 87, 90, 110, 111, 112, 114, 129, 133, 135, 137,
    138, 139, 140, 141, 145, 155, 158, 162, 163, 164, 167, 170, 179, 184, 187, 194,
    197, 198, 200, 203, 215, 226, 261, 275, 310, 335
binary 81, 89, 111, 192, 193, 194
biochemistry 81, 120, 204
black males 44, 58, 61, 164, 167, 168, 257
    black males and suicide 61
boy-friendly xi, xviii, xxi, xxii, 11, 103, 106, 111, 129, 215, 216, 229, 234, 239, 240,
    241, 242, 243, 244, 245, 246, 248, 249, 251, 252, 253, 263
brain xi, xiii, xvii, xviii, xxi, xxii, xxiii, xxiv, xxv, 8, 9, 17, 18, 19, 20, 23, 24, 25, 26,
    27, 29, 31, 32, 33, 38, 41, 46, 48, 49, 50, 51, 53, 66, 68, 69, 70, 71, 73, 75, 76,
    78, 79, 80, 81, 82, 83, 84, 85, 86, 89, 98, 100, 101, 102, 103, 106, 109, 114,
    115, 116, 117, 118, 119, 120, 121, 126, 127, 128, 130, 131, 132, 139, 140, 158,
    165, 166, 167, 191, 192, 193, 194, 195, 196, 197, 198, 199, 200, 201, 202, 203,
    204, 205, 206, 207, 208, 209, 211, 219, 220, 222, 224, 230, 234, 235, 237, 240,
    241, 246, 248
    amygdala 25, 114
    brain scan technology 50
    brain sex differences ix, xiii, 18, 19, 25, 26, 38, 50, 75, 79, 81, 100, 106, 127 (see
        sex: sex difference)
    brain sex dysphoria xi, 41, 191, 192, 193, 194, 195, 196, 197, 199, 200, 201,
        203, 205, 207, 208, 209, 211
    cortex 25, 103, 119
    female brain xvii, 9, 18, 19, 20, 26, 38, 49, 50, 69, 70, 73, 76, 79, 80, 81, 83,
        100, 115, 116, 117, 120, 121, 126, 127, 128, 139, 140, 165, 198, 199, 200,

202, 204, 207, 208, 240, 241
  fetal brains 78, 194
  hard-wiring 76, 90, 198, 199, 201
  male brain xxii, xxiv, xxv, 8, 9, 17, 19, 20, 24, 26, 27, 31, 46, 48, 49, 50, 51, 53, 66, 68, 71, 73, 75, 76, 80, 81, 98, 102, 106, 115, 116, 119, 120, 126, 127, 128, 130, 140, 158, 165, 166, 167, 198, 199, 200, 207, 220, 230, 234, 235, 237, 240, 241
  prefrontal cortices 26
  soft-wiring 86, 90, 91
  trans brain 82, 84, 208
brain scan technology see: brain
brain sex differences see: brain
brain sex dysphoria see: brain
#BringBackOurBoys 187
#BringBackOurGirls 187
Brizendine, Louann 73, 81, 116
budgets x, 149, 150, 151, 153, 154, 155, 163, 189

C

California Department of Education 93, 98, 164, 256
Cass Review 199
Center, A Place of Hope 8, 34
Centers for Disease Control and Prevention 6, 36, 150, 177
  CDC 36, 150, 177, 178, 181
Child Maltreatment Report 176
chromosomes xxiii, 65, 81, 88, 89, 116, 220
  XX xxiii, xxiv, 65, 80, 88, 89, 199
  XY xxiii, 65, 80, 88, 89, 194, 199
cisgender x, 76, 77, 79, 80, 81, 82, 83, 85, 86, 87, 89, 91, 111, 115, 196, 197
citizen science xi, xxii, xxv, 41, 44, 70, 71, 99, 115, 146, 170, 186, 202, 247, 248, 249, 251, 253
civil rights 90, 112, 138
Clery Act 57
Clinton, Bill 142
Clinton, Hillary 142, 143, 149
coed schools see: education
college degrees see: education
college education see: education
Cook, Philip W. 174
cortex see: Brain

covert depression see: Depression

Crittenden, Danielle 145

culture of the exception x, xxiv, 73, 76, 90, 91, 93, 95, 109, 110, 111, 112, 113, 114, 115, 117, 119, 121, 123, 203, 226

D

dad deprivation xxi, 166, 235
    fatherlessness 144, 167

Daily Mail 184

Daniel Amen 33, 50, 118

data conflation trap 35, 38
    DCT 35, 36, 40, 41, 43

deaths of despair 16, 17, 19, 36, 39, 40, 41, 44, 46, 52

Department of Health and Human Services 150, 176

Department of Labor 149, 160

depression x, xxi, 4, 6, 7, 8, 9, 10, 11, 13, 16, 20, 21, 22, 23, 24, 25, 26, 27, 28, 29, 31, 32, 33, 34, 36, 38, 40, 46, 47, 48, 50, 52, 58, 59, 61, 62, 63, 65, 68, 69, 70, 82, 85, 90, 117, 139, 183, 189, 192, 193, 194, 196, 198, 199, 202, 203, 205, 207, 208, 209, 210, 211
    covert depression 22, 25, 65, 139
    female-type depression 27
    male-type depression x, 8, 10, 20, 21, 23, 24, 25, 26, 27, 29, 31, 33, 34, 36, 46, 48, 59, 139, 183, 210
    overt depression 16, 22, 23, 63, 139

DGP see: dominant gender paradigm

Diagnostic and Statistical Manual for Mental Disorders 193
    DSM 193, 195, 197, 200, 201, 207, 208

diseases of despair x, 13, 15, 17, 19, 20, 39, 40, 46

disposable male 187

domestic violence 140, 174, 175

dominant gender paradigm 24, 27, 46, 51, 57, 135, 138, 183
    DGP 24, 34, 52, 57, 76, 138, 144, 157, 162, 175, 183, 227

dopamine 13, 31, 114, 141

DSM see: Diagnostic and Statistical Manual for Mental Disorders

Dwight, Eva 205

E

education vi, xi, xv, xix, 6, 7, 49, 50, 66, 70, 75, 89, 93, 94, 95, 97, 98, 101, 102, 106, 110, 111, 115, 119, 122, 125, 126, 127, 128, 140, 149, 154, 159, 160, 164, 167, 201, 202, 216, 218, 223, 231, 234, 235, 236, 239, 240, 244, 245, 246, 251, 252,

256, 258, 259, 262, 265, 267

coed schools 86

college xi, xv, xxiii, xxv, 6, 15, 21, 30, 35, 47, 55, 56, 57, 58, 63, 77, 88, 93, 109, 125, 128, 129, 132, 137, 140, 145, 147, 149, 157, 158, 159, 160, 161, 162, 169, 173, 178, 183, 191, 216, 223, 232, 235, 241, 255, 256, 259, 261, 262, 265, 266, 267

college degrees 160, 161

college education XI, 265, 267

elementary education 102, 204, 232, 235

K-12 education. 159, 231, 239, 258, 259, 261, 262, 283, 289

school boards xi, 115, 137, 144, 239, 247, 255, 257, 258, 259, 261, 262, 263, 264

single sex schools 86, 127

ELA see: English Language Arts

elementary education see: education

English Language Arts 100, 101, 103, 239

ELA 101, 104, 107, 239, 242

F

false allegations x, 55, 56, 57, 58, 59, 61, 62, 183, 184, 185

Farrell, Warren xiv, xxi, 1, 14, 143, 145, 187

fatherlessness see: dad deprivation

female brain see: brain

female-type depression see: depression

feminaphobia x, 135, 137, 139, 141, 142, 143, 144, 145, 147, 150, 153, 155, 157, 158, 162, 177, 263

fentanyl 40, 43, 58, 59

fetal brains see: Brain

Floyd, George 167

freedom feminism 144, 145

Fryer, Roland 167

G

gang 3, 56, 67, 219, 232, 234, 235

Geary, David 120

gender xi, xiii, xv, xvi, xviii, xix, xxii, xxiv, xxv, 4, 7, 8, 10, 14, 18, 20, 24, 27, 36, 41, 46, 47, 51, 57, 63, 66, 67, 70, 71, 75, 76, 77, 78, 79, 80, 81, 82, 83, 84, 85, 86, 87, 89, 90, 91, 94, 98, 100, 101, 106, 109, 110, 111, 112, 113, 114, 115, 116, 117, 121, 122, 123, 126, 129, 135, 137, 138, 141, 143, 145, 154, 157, 159, 162, 164, 165, 170, 183, 191, 192, 193, 194, 195, 196, 197, 198, 199, 200, 201, 202,

203, 204, 205, 206, 207, 208, 209, 210, 211, 212, 227, 230, 239, 248, 254, 258, 261, 262, 265

    gender affirming care 84, 85, 197, 212

    gender dysphoria xi, 41, 78, 79, 82, 83, 84, 85, 90, 117, 164, 191, 192, 193, 194, 195, 196, 197, 198, 199, 201, 202, 203, 204, 205, 206, 207, 209, 210, 211

    gender fluidity xiii, xxiv, 83, 114, 117, 202, 203, 204, 206, 211, 212

    gender identity 78, 85, 86, 111, 196, 198, 199, 203, 207

    gender nonconforming 41, 76, 77, 82, 84, 85, 86, 87, 110, 117, 121, 193, 195, 196, 202, 203, 204, 208, 210, 254, 261

gender gap 7, 101, 106, 273

    achievement gap 122, 140, 248,

    behavior gap 106

    discipline gap 254

    gaps xi, xxiii, 5, 6, 16, 22, 63, 104, 105, 165, 256, 258, 259

Georgia Innocence Project 58

GI Bill 161

Global Initiative for Boys and Men vii, xi, xiii, xv, xxii, 19, 44, 153, 178, 231, 256

Gore, Deborah 210

Gray, John xxi, 1, 77

Gur, Ruben and Rachel 50, 120

Gurian Institute vi, viii, xi, xiii, xv, xxii, 6, 19, 120, 121, 127, 165, 194, 205, 239

gynandromorphy 79

H

hard-wiring see: brain

Harris, Kamala 144

heterosexual 24, 83, 89, 117, 201

Hill, Marion xvii, 165, 166

Hispanic 232, 257, 266

homosexuality 79, 82, 117, 201

Hunt, Sam 153

I

identity politics 174

immersion reading see: reading

incarceration 5, 58

    jail 56, 232

    juvenile detention 232

    prison 55, 56, 122, 147, 232, 234

income quartile 266, 273

J

jail see: incarceration
Jantz, Gregory vi, 8, 223
Journal of the American Medical Association 41
juvenile detention see: incarceration

K

Kimura, Doreen 119

L

Lawrenceville School 183
Legato, Marianne J. 116
LGB 79, 82, 83, 89, 196, 198, 201, 202, 203, 205
LGBTQIA xiii, xxiv, 79, 82, 83, 90, 91, 114, 121, 137, 138, 154, 164, 195, 196, 197, 203, 206, 207, 211
Livermore Valley Joint Unified School District 100, 253
loneliness xxi, 16, 52, 62, 63
Louann Brizendine 73, 81, 116

M

MacDonald, Heather 57
male brain see: brain
male fragility x, 63, 64, 65, 66, 67, 68, 69, 70, 71, 218
male mental health x, xxi, 1, 3, 5, 7, 9, 11, 13, 15, 17, 19, 20, 46, 52, 62, 66, 68, 70, 139, 170, 215
male violence 5, 7, 8, 10, 13, 14, 24, 66, 69, 70
male-type depression see: depression
marriage xiii, 66, 117, 162, 176, 223
masculine norms xv, xvi, xviii, xxiii, xxiv, 17, 20, 31, 34, 135, 155, 157, 234, 235
masculine norms theory xvi, xviii, 20, 135, 155, 157
masculinity vii, xiv, xvi, xvii, xviii, xix, xxi, xxii, xxiii, xxiv, 4, 7, 10, 11, 12, 13, 19, 23, 24, 27, 31, 46, 50, 51, 52, 56, 57, 62, 64, 67, 71, 76, 129, 135, 137, 138, 141, 145, 158, 161, 162, 164, 170, 175, 179, 180, 181, 184, 188, 215, 226, 228, 261, 263, 265
mass shootings see: shootings
maternity 87
math xvii, 6, 100, 140, 239, 244, 249, 252, 253, 262, 263
media viii, xv, xvi, xix, xxiii, 3, 7, 10, 17, 19, 22, 28, 30, 33, 46, 55, 56, 57, 58, 62, 70, 76, 77, 80, 84, 85, 91, 109, 111, 112, 113, 114, 115, 122, 129, 135, 137,

138, 141, 145, 149, 154, 157, 161, 163, 173, 176, 177, 181, 183, 184, 185, 186, 187, 189, 191, 192, 200, 203, 204, 205, 210, 215, 219, 224, 225, 226, 227, 229, 245, 264, 265
Media Politics 184
misandry 174, 175, 176, 177, 179, 180, 181
Moalem, Shäron 81
Mortenson, Thomas xix
mother xiii, 21, 55, 56, 69, 81, 85, 87, 93, 96, 109, 125, 130, 131, 168, 176, 177, 178, 217, 223, 228
Ms Magazine 159
My Brothers Keeper 154

N

National Center for Educational Statistics 128, 160
National Institute of Health 59
Native American 61
nature-based theory xvii, xviii
"New data shows grim tally" see: *San Francisco Chronicle*
New York Post 184
New York Times vii, 184, 185, 186, 189
New Yorker 186
non-binary 111, 192
nurture the nature vi, xviii

O

Oakland Unified School District 253
Obama, Barack 143
Obama, Michelle 187
Opioid x, 25, 37, 55, 57, 59, 61, 149
oppressor-oppressed 139, 141, 143, 144, 145, 149, 158
overdose xxi, 16, 17, 19, 20, 21, 35, 39, 40, 43, 44, 58, 59, 61, 62, 65, 66, 144, 150, 155, 164, 169, 179, 180, 189
overt depression see: depression
oxytocin 120, 121, 220

P

Page, David C. 80, 116
Pappas, Stephanie 51
paternity 87
Perry, Mark xix

Pidd, Helen 56
PISA 6, 7
Pizzey, Erin 174, 175
Pleasanton Unified School District 256
PNAS 18
police shootings see: shootings
prefrontal 26
prefrontal cortices see: brain
Press-Telegram 56
pressure of the exception 110, 113, 204
prison see: incarceration
pronoun x, 86, 87, 88, 93, 94, 95, 97, 99, 101, 103, 105, 107
puberty blockers 82, 199, 209, 210, 211

R

race 5, 30, 35, 36, 38, 40, 43, 44, 46, 52, 58, 61, 100, 122, 140, 153, 162, 163, 164, 165, 166, 167, 168, 169, 171, 179, 189, 216, 218, 256, 258, 259, 260, 261, 262, 264, 266
race and sex 40, 44, 46, 100, 163, 164, 169, 171, 256, 260, 266
Ramos, Bill 153
Rapid Onset Gender Dysphoria 204
ROGD 204, 205, 206
reading xxv, 17, 23, 29, 44, 46, 94, 100, 102, 103, 104, 105, 107, 125, 128, 139, 143, 169, 174, 189, 240, 241, 247, 248, 249, 251, 252, 262, 263
immersion reading 247, 248
Reeves, Richard xxi, 19, 44, 128, 185
Reid, Jack 183
ROGD see: Rapid Onset Gender Dysphoria

S

San Francisco Chronicle 179, 189
Angst, Maggie 179
"New data shows grim tally" 179
Sartre, Jean Paul 198
Sax, Leonard xxi, 50
school boards see: education
school shootings see: shootings
self-medication x, 13, 55, 57, 58, 59, 61
self-medicating 8, 30, 61, 62
serotonin 31

sex xi, xiii, xv, xviii, xix, xxi, xxiv, xxv, 18, 19, 34, 35, 36, 40, 41, 44, 46, 57, 58, 65, 66, 69, 75, 76, 77, 78, 79, 80, 81, 82, 83, 85, 86, 87, 88, 89, 90, 91, 94, 95, 98, 100, 106, 107, 109, 110, 111, 112, 113, 114, 115, 116, 121, 122, 123, 127, 128, 129, 130, 140, 147, 158, 159, 163, 164, 165, 166, 167, 169, 171, 184, 189, 191, 192, 193, 194, 195, 196, 197, 198, 199, 200, 201, 202, 203, 204, 205, 207, 208, 209, 211, 212, 216, 224, 226, 230, 249, 252, 255, 256, 257, 258, 259, 260, 261, 262, 263, 264, 266

    sex difference iii, xi, 18, 34, 46, 66, 75, 76, 81, 91, 100, 106, 107, 111, 113, 122, 127, 128, 158, 167, 194, 252, 255, 257, 258, 259, 261, 262, 263, 264, 268, 298

    sexgender 41, 114, 115, 116, 117, 120, 121, 122, 123, 126, 127, 129, 135, 137, 138, 142, 143, 146, 153, 159, 162, 195, 198, 200, 211, 216, 226, 239

    sexual dimorphism x, 19, 26, 34, 66, 73, 76, 79, 80, 82, 83, 85, 86, 89, 91, 100, 103, 110, 111, 112, 114, 115, 116, 117, 122, 126, 127, 191, 192, 194, 195, 198, 215

sex difference see: sex

sex education see: education

sex vs. gender 112

sexgender see: sex

sexual dimorphism see: sex

shootings

    mass shootings 3, 7

    police shootings 167, 169

    school shootings 3, 66

Shors, Tracey 50

Shrier, Abigail 204

single parent 224, 252, 254

single sex schools see: education

social contagion 196, 204, 205, 206, 212

social media xxiii, 22, 28, 30, 33, 46, 56, 62, 70, 76, 111, 113, 114, 115, 122, 129, 145, 163, 183, 186, 191, 192, 200, 203, 204, 205, 210, 215, 219, 225, 227, 229, 245, 264

social norm 112, 113

social norms theory 24

soft-wiring see: brain

Soh, Debra 81

Solomon, Andrew 186

Sommers, Christina Hoff xxi, 145, 255, 265

special education see: education

sports xv, 78, 87, 88, 91, 101, 131, 159, 219, 229, 232, 249 suicide x, xiii, xvi, xxi, 3, 5, 15, 16, 17, 19, 20, 21, 24, 32, 35, 36, 37, 38, 39, 40, 41, 50, 52, 55, 56, 57, 58, 59, 61, 62, 63, 65, 84, 139, 150, 154, 155, 164, 169, 183, 184, 185, 186, 187, 189, 203

surgery 82, 84, 88, 194, 195, 197, 199, 201, 208, 209, 210

suspension 21, 93, 94, 96, 97, 98, 99, 100, 107, 165, 256, 258

    suspensions 98, 100, 102, 118, 140, 165, 248, 256, 257, 258

T

Taylor, Shelley 120, 121

testosterone 28, 65, 66, 68, 69, 70, 75, 83, 88, 120, 121, 166, 200, 207, 220

The Atlantic 12

The Guardian 56

Three Family System xi, 215, 217, 218, 219, 221, 223, 225, 226, 227, 228, 229

    Three Family Structure 233

trades 162, 216, 231

trans brain see: brain

Trump, Donald xv, 71, 95, 142, 143, 144, 258

U

University of California 73, 81, 120, 202

University of Virginia 58

unsafe environment 93, 97, 98, 99, 100

V

Vance, Courtney B. 61

W

Wall Street Journal 187, 204, 208

Washington Initiative for Boys and Men 19

Washington Post 4, 167, 169, 175

Washington State Commission on Boys and Men 153

    Representative Mary Dye (R) and Senator John Lovick (D) of Washington formed bipartisan support for this bill along with 12 other bipartisan legislators. To see those who endorsed, go to https://waboysandmen.org/endorsements/

What Set Me Free see: Banks, Brian

white males 5, 7, 43, 164, 167, 168, 179, 180, 266

Windle, Michael 178

Witelson, Sandra 50

Wolf, Naomi 145

Wonder of Parenting Podcast xv, 8, 109, 222

Woolley, Catherine 81
Wright, Tim 14
WWII 159, 161

X

XX see: chromosomes
XY see: chromosomes

Z

zero-tolerance 97, 98, 265